nightmare movies

Pgs 33 + 34 missing

nightmare movies

nightmare movies

A Critical Guide to Contemporary Horror Films

Kim Newman

HARMONY BOOKS / NEW YORK

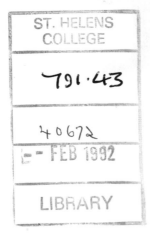
Published by Harmony Books, a division of Crown Publishers, Inc., 201 East 50th Street, New York, New York 10022

HARMONY and colophon are trademarks of Crown Publishers, Inc.
Manufactured in the United Stated of America

Library of Congress Cataloging-in-Publication Data
Newman, Kim
    Nightmare movies / by Kim Newman.
        p.   cm.
    Includes index.
    1. Horror films—History and criticism.   I. Title.
PN1995.9.H6N4 1989
791.43'09'0916—dc 19

ISBN 0-517-57366-0

10 9 8 7 6 5 4 3 2 1

First American Edition

For my parents,
Bryan and Julia Newman.
Thanks for everything.

contents

foreword

The horror film occupies a position in popular culture roughly comparable to that of horror literature. That is to say, it is generally ignored, sometimes acknowledged with bemused tolerance, and viewed with alarm when it irritates authority beyond a certain point – rather like a child too spirited to follow the rules that tradition has deemed acceptable for proper acculturation.

The problem with this position is that it is one of suffrage, begrudgingly given and subject to withdrawal when the nuisance factor becomes too high for the comfortable continuation of patronage.

Like children, most of the *macaberesques* of film and literature content themselves with the kind of play that engenders indulgence rather than repression, limiting their activities to simplistic declamations that are easily dismissed, programmed excesses that secretly reassure parents with proof of potency, and adolescent self-mockery that reveals an ultimate loyalty to the status quo.

Occasionally, however, there appears a miraculous exception: the genuine article, an individualist whose stance is not merely an attention-getting pose, whose outrageous acts are more than a show of virility calculated to elicit favoured employment from the power élite. Such a person, if he is not broken by the system into a life of compromise and hypocrisy, is likely to become a revolutionary, a predicant, a renunciate or an artist.

And of these last, some find themselves working necessarily at the limits of conscience, confronting the issues of our survival in the most extreme terms. These are the horror artists who, like the Picasso of *Guernica* or the de Sade of *Salo* or the Bosch of *The Garden of Earthly Delights*, can find no grounds for peace with the Iron Empire that governs us still. A man who realises that his house is on fire does not waste time adjusting to the situation, nor does he entertain any debates about social etiquette that may restrain him from removing the shackles before it is too late to save his family from burning. The message is loud, the subject clear: the crisis into which we have awakened as the millennium draws near.

This book is not another armchair survey of the trite and trivial in a branch of commercialism manufactured by and for children; for that you would be better served by the fannish genre magazines with their sophomoric tributes to the masters of special effects. It is not about the mindless gore of horror-chic as it is purveyed in the trendily nihilistic market-place of the apocalypse. Nor is it about the quick fixes of titillation that fast-buck confidence agents are busy pandering as distractions from reality to ensure the commerce that depends upon our quiescence. It is not, in other words, about childish things. It gives no quarter to those who would keep us infants before the great tit of bourgeois media, but rightly disposes of them with swift and merciless disdain.

Instead it offers crucially balanced appraisals of those voices which deserve to be heard in all their subversive glory, providing a perspective by which they may be fully assessed for the first time. In place of obeisance and adulation, it evaluates with rigorous acuity, applying critical standards that have been evolving since the advent of cinema. This is a work of wit, intelligence and insight, written with protean energy in the face of the conventional wisdom that such films are juvenilia and so by their very nature inferior. Perhaps most importantly, it does not petition for the favouritism of special standards that point nowhere but back to the cradle.

It is also a readable, highly entertaining volume, as we would expect from Kim Newman, and I am sure that it is destined to provoke the sort of lively debate that can only help this field shed its puppy-fat and move on to the full empowerment of maturity.

In short, this is an exceedingly non-trivial book, and I recommend it without reservation as worthy of your most careful attention.

Dennis Etchison

introduction

By 1983, when I started working on *Nightmare Movies*, there were already many good, bad and indifferent histories of the horror film on the market. The ground-breakers, Carlos Clarens's *An Illustrated History of the Horror Film* and Ivan Butler's *Horror in the Cinema*, were both published in 1967. Most of the subsequent books give the impression that even if they weren't published before 1968, they might as well have been. Invariably, they suggest that the great era of the horror film was some time in the 1920s and 1930s when Lon Chaney, Boris Karloff and Bela Lugosi were starring in films directed by Tod Browning and James Whale. The then current genre masters – Christopher Lee, Peter Cushing and Vincent Price, Terence Fisher, Mario Bava and Roger Corman – receive scant, mainly grudging attention. Somehow, well into the 1970s, it was possible for experts to make statements like '*Night of the Demon* is the last genuine horror "classic" that we have had' (William K. Everson, *Classics of the Horror Film*) and 'In quantity, Hammer Films are fast approaching Universal, but in quality they have yet to reach Monogram' (Denis Gifford, *A Pictorial History of Horror Movies*). Astonishingly, sentiments like this could be trotted out as late as 1986, in *The Dead That Walk* – where Leslie Halliwell blithely lumps together *Halloween*, *The Fog* and *The Amityville Horror* as claptrap. Of course, the authors are of the generation that saw the Karloff and Lugosi films on their original releases. They

nurture an indulgent fondness for the Rondo Hatton and George Zucco pictures they saw as children, and simultaneously sneer at the likes of *Dracula, Prince of Darkness* and *The Abominable Dr Phibes* for debasing their idea of what the genre should be.

I'm different. I was born in 1959, and the first horror film I remember seeing – on television in 1971 – was the 1930 *Dracula*. In my early teens, I read Clarens, Butler, Gifford and Everson and caught up with the Universal films, the Hammer horrors, and Roger Corman's Edgar Allan Poe movies. In 1973, David Pirie's *A Heritage of Horror* came out and said the Giffords and the Eversons were wrong, and that the 1950s and 1960s films I was enjoying were classics too. In my middle and late teens, I got a little bored with the endless Frankenstein and Dracula reruns of Hammer and Universal, and was stimulated by the few off-beat movies that came to the Palace or the Classic, Bridgwater – *Daughters of Darkness*, *Let's Scare Jessica to Death*, DePalma's *Sisters* and Cohen's *It's Alive*. I saw *The Exorcist* while doing my O levels. I saw *Suspiria* during my first week at the University of Sussex. I projected *Night of the Living Dead* three times on the walls of my hall of residence one weekend in 1978. I was at the London Film Festival showing of *Dawn of the Dead* in 1979. I saw *Friday the 13th* while I was jobless and homeless in London in 1980. I was around to gauge the impact of *Shivers*, *Carrie*, *The Texas*

Chainsaw Massacre, *Halloween* and *The Evil Dead* on their original releases. My first professionally published piece was a review of *Last House on the Left* in 1982.

These films are the heart of *Nightmare Movies*. I set out to concentrate on what had happened in the genre since Clarens, Everson and Gifford closed their books. My generation has a new pantheon of greats, from George A. Romero through to Sam Raimi. I was the first person to come out in print and admit I liked *The Driller Killer* (younger readers take note: 1983 was the year of the 'video nasty' furore). In 1984 Julian Petley, Stefan Jaworzyn and I spent a week in front of a hot video and took in about seventy varied sleaze, exploitation and splatter movies from *Mardi Gras Massacre* to *Ilsa, Harem Keeper of the Oil Sheiks*. The last thing I saw for this book was Nigel Kneale's 'During Barty's Party', which I watched on video at the British Film Institute on 3 May 1988. Charles Derry (*Dark Dreams*), John McCarty (*Splatter Movies*) and the contributors to *The American Nightmare* were here before me, but their studies cover comparatively small segments of the genre. My original outline for this book was heavily *auteurist* — a chapter each devoted to Romero, Cronenberg, Craven, Hooper and company (down to Bob Clark, Alfred Sole and Peter Sasdy) — but I eventually concluded that only a mapping of the various sub-genres existing within the larger field could provide the overview I was looking for. One review of the first edition wondered why only Larry Cohen, David Cronenberg and Brian DePalma made it into the *auteurs* chapter. Obviously, George A. Romero would rate inclusion if this book weren't entirely about his influence; and I've promoted Dario Argento this time round. The others, I feel, make more sense in the context of the sub-genres they've become associated with. Tobe Hooper, in particular, has demonstrated many times how uncomfortable he is away from his chainsaws, and similar problems have to a lesser extent blighted the careers of Wes Craven and John Carpenter.

Part of my intention has been to redefine our understanding of exactly what a horror film is. To me, the central thesis of horror in film and literature is that the world is a more frightening place than is generally assumed (one of the most significant titles in the genre is Jack Williamson's *Darker Than You Think*). By these lights, I feel films not usually listed as horror classics (*Dirty Harry*, *Smooth Talk*, *The King of Comedy*) are as important to the genre as monster movies like *Count Yorga – Vampire*, *Return of the Living Dead* and *The Stuff*. Often, pictures are excluded from the genre simply on the grounds of respectability – a movie like *Deliverance*, with a big budget, star performers and a reputable director, isn't labelled a horror film, while *The Texas Chainsaw Massacre* – which trades in exactly the same fears – has to bear the genre's mark of Cain. In discussing such phenomena as the disaster movie (*Earthquake*), the conspiracy film (*The Parallax View*) or the psycho cop drama (*Manhunter*), I have tried to show how these out-of-genre pictures share narrative strategies, a pool of scary ideas and an audience impact with the mainstream horror film. This book is called *Nightmare Movies*, not *Horror Movies*. At the time of writing, the difference between the terms strikes me as the area where the action is. The out-of-genre horror film is currently producing more interesting work than the formularised and repetitive glut of teenage horror comedies. I believe the essential nightmares of the mid-1980s are *Raising Arizona* and *After Hours* rather than *Evil Dead II* and *The Lost Boys*.

The flipside of this is that recently I've started wondering if I'm turning into Denis Gifford. I'll stick by the opinions expressed here, but I keep coming across enthusiasts acclaiming the *Nightmare on Elm Street* series, *Fright Night* or *Re-Animator* as classics. There are even people out there writing respectfully about the *Friday the 13th* films and *House*. Some of these are pretty good, but I don't think they quite stack up against the best of Romero and Cronenberg, or even *Halloween* and *The Texas Chainsaw Massacre*. This sounds a lot like where we came in, only now I've got the Donald Pleasence role rather than the Jamie Lee Curtis one. When Freddy Krueger says 'you are all my children now', he doesn't mean me. Some kid out there has grown up with Freddy and Jason rather than Dracula and Frankenstein, and is graduating to the books and films of Stephen King and Clive Barker. He or she knows Empire and Troma better than Hammer and Corman; reads *Shock Xpress* for the text and *Fangoria* for the pictures but has only dimly heard of Forrest J. Ackerman and *Famous Monsters of Filmland*; probably prefers *Return of the Living Dead* to *Day of the Dead*, and is too young to remember when you could legally rent a Lucio Fulci film on video in Britain. Some day, I hope that kid will write a book sub-titled 'A Critical History of the Horror Film, 1988–2008' that contradicts everything you're about to read.

Kim Newman
London, 6 May 1988.

● *High priestess.* Diane Cilento, **The Wicker Man.**

● *Omnivorous ghoul.* Marilyn Eastman, **Night of the Living Dead.**

shoot 'em in the head!

or: *The Birth of the Hate Generation*

Understand death? ... sure; that's when the monsters get you.
Stephen King, *Salem's Lot*

In a graveyard, at sunset, the nightmare movie begins. It's the where and when you'd expect of the first scene of a film called *Night of the Living Dead*, as if the producers where trying to qualify for a Most Typical Horror Movie of 1968 award. The poster outside the drive-in was a collage of ghouls gnawing on terrified victims, headlined by a quote from somebody of whom you've never heard. She thinks the film is 'more terrifying than Hitchcock's *Psycho!*' You've heard that before, and got stiffed by William Castle's *Homicidal!* or one of the innumerable quickies written by Robert (middle name: Author of *Psycho*) Bloch. 'They keep coming back in a bloodthirsty lust for HUMAN FLESH! ...' shrieks a subsidiary slogan. The most horrible details are capitalised, just as they were in the Crypt Keeper's cackled introductions to the gruesome stories on the ragged, four-coloured pages of those 1950s comic books that were supposed to rot your brain — *Tales From the Crypt, The Vault of Horror, The Haunt of Fear.* The title is only memorable in that its bald expressiveness could make you swear there had been at least a dozen other movies also called *Night of the Living Dead*. The credits feature unknowns only. Most of the actors are amateurs: producers, financiers and technical staff filling up

the screen by appearing in their own movie. And two years after the presentation of the last Oscar for monochrome cinematography, the film unreels in black and white — not the gloss and rainsilver b&w of 1940s Hollywood, but a grainy newsreel grey that looks like (but isn't) 16mm. distorted by the blow-up to 35mm. You could be forgiven for mistaking *Night of the Living Dead* for a cheap, ordinary horror movie.

It's certainly cheap. At first glance, it's ordinary. When it became a cult success, the film journals were full of critics acknowledging qualities they'd missed on a first viewing. *Night of the Living Dead* generates seat-clutching tension and a surprising amount of intentional humour by playing around with the audience's idea of what to expect from a cheap, ordinary horror movie. In 1968, the year that popularised rebelliousness and nonconformity, *Night of the Living Dead* did its bit for the Age of Aquarius by ignoring decades of cinema convention. The graveyard on which the sun sets is not the cardboard-and-dry-ice gothic of Mario Bava's *La Maschera del demonio* or Roger Corman's *The Premature Burial*, but an everyday location somewhere in the Pennsylvania wilderness. It looks like Eeyore's place, rather gloomy. The titles are superimposed on postcard views of a nothing-in-particular road that leads to a field full of headstones. A young couple drive into the cemetery. In a carefully composed shot, George A. Romero's director credit is offset by the Stars and Stripes.

Barbara and Johnny have come to lay a tribute on their father's grave. They don't seem to fit into the film we are expecting. Instead of an uncomfortable period costume, Johnny wears the haircut, dark suit, heavy glasses and wisecracking manner of the anti-hero of a Golden-Age-of-Live-Television drama about throat cutting between the cocktails along Madison Avenue. The actor is Russell Streiner, who, like most of the film's creative personnel, was an ad exec doing the movie at weekends as a relief from 'making a glass of beer look like Heaven' from Monday to Friday. Barbara looks like the put-upon housewife of a daytime soap opera, pretty/plain and no fashion model. She is played by Judith O'Dea, one of the film's few professionals. Johnny dismisses their act of homage as 'five minutes to put the wreath on the grave, and six hours to drive back and forth'. They are not lovers, but brother and sister. While they bicker, a derelict looking man shuffles between the graves in the background.

The traditional horror film presents the world as a Land of Oz, where all problems can be solved by a touch of self-awareness and a bucket of cold water thrown over the Wicked Witch of the West. The relationship between Dracula's victim and her fiancé is disrupted by the seductive vampire, but true love is reasserted when the Count disintegrates at the first light of dawn. Their feelings for each other have been tested by the ordeal and proved to be strong enough to last a lifetime. Barbara and Johnny scarcely have a relationship worth saving. All they have in common is a shared childhood; Johnny reminds his sister that he used to scare her with his bogey-man act. Noticing that the memory upsets her, he imitates Boris Karloff: 'I think you're still afraid, Barb. They're coming to get you.'

Flashback: another graveyard, another sunset. This is where the most famous horror film of all, *Frankenstein* (1931), begins. The obsessed Baron and his twisted servant are on the prowl for surplus organs that can be incorporated into their work in progress. The Monster was Boris Karloff, who, more than anyone or anything, came to represent the traditional horror movie. His flat-headed shadow falls over every subsequent horror film. Romero may reject the rickety surrealism of the *Frankenstein* graveyard, but his films are full of the tilted camera angles and eccentric by-play favoured by James Whale, director not only of *Frankenstein*, but also of *The Old Dark House*, *The Invisible Man* and *Bride of Frankenstein*. That stumblebum in the *Night of the Living Dead* graveyard uses Karloff's trademark Monster walk.

'They're coming to get you, Barb! Look, here comes one of them now!' Barbara tries to apologise, but the tramp really is a monster coming to get her. Johnny is not particularly fond of his sister, but he scuffles manfully with the ghoul, saving her life at the expense of his own. His death is one of the most shocking in the movies. Barbara is the first heroine to react credibly to an unbearable tragedy: instead of shrugging the whole thing off and being soothed by the hero's reassurances, she lapses for the rest of the film into a catatonic stupor, emerging only to whimper a little or toy mindlessly with a music-box. But the audience is really unsettled by Johnny's death because his healthy scepticism had marked him as the likely hero. He might have it in him to be a sadistic tease, but when the trouble starts he stops messing around and tries to save the girl. We can see Johnny's true nature coming through, and have him pegged as one of those movie types who need a crisis to bring out his best. His prompt death confirms that it will be no use relying on horror film conventions to get us through this particular nightmare.

'I started with a very light beginning for the purposes of audience identification', said Alfred Hitchcock of *The Birds* (1963), the film to which *Night of the Living Dead* is most often compared. 'I felt it was vital to get to know the people first, to take the time to get absorbed in the atmosphere before the birds came.' Barely five minutes into *Night of the Living Dead*, an apparently major character has been killed (reminding what's-her-name on the poster of *Psycho*?), and we have been propelled into unrelenting action. Like many of the successful horror films that followed, *Night of the Living Dead* adopts the logic of the nightmare, the sensation that, no matter how you run, you'll never get away from the monster behind you. Unity of space and time is a necessary underpinning for the bad dream, and *Night of the Living Dead*, like *The Texas Chainsaw Massacre*, *The Hills Have Eyes*, *Halloween* and *The Evil Dead*, takes place in a limited area during a single night.

After Johnny's brains have been splattered on a headstone, *Night of the Living Dead* continues to opt for the unexpected. Barbara escapes from the ghoul and meets Ben (Duane Jones), the film's real hero. Ben is brave, resourceful, capable and community spirited. He demonstrates his virtues by rescuing the girl from the zombies, and overcomes his undead enemies through the judicious application of a firebrand or a tyre iron. Ben is black, which testifies less to the significance of the film than to its makers' lack of prejudice in casting their leading man without regarding his race as important. A black hero in this type of movie is unusual, but not unique. What is unheard of is that Ben takes no romantic interest in Barbara. In *The World, The Flesh and The Devil* (1959), Harry Belafonte leaves off contemplating the radioactive ruins of civilisation to develop a healthy interracial crush on Inger Stevens. Ben is too concerned with evading the zombie flesh eaters to fall for anyone. Stevens remains bouncy after the holocaust, but grief makes Barbara distinctly unappealing.

Ben, following the example set by Rod Taylor in *The Birds*, finds a farmhouse and barricades it against the monsters. After he has tired himself out boarding the place up, another bunch of survivors, who have been camping in the cellar, make their presence known. Harry and Helen Cooper (Karl Hardman and Marilyn Eastman), a middle-aged couple, have a daughter, Karen (Kyra Schon), who has been bitten by a ghoul and is succumbing to the Living Dead syndrome. 'We may not enjoy living together', Helen tells Harry, 'but dying together isn't going to help.' Tom (Keith Wayne) and Judy (Judith Ridley) finally give the audience characters they can accept in a horror film, a pair of utterly conventional young lovers. When an escape attempt fails, Tom and Judy get fried in an exploding truck and are

messily gobbled up by the zombies. So much for young love. The Living Dead are mainly played by businessmen who had invested in the film. Among them are the butchers who provided what is left of Tom and Judy for the notorious entrail-eating and bone-chewing scene.

In *The Birds*, Rod Taylor pulls his family together, gets his hysterical mother in line, tames independent Tippi Hedren, refuses to panic when pigeons start pecking eyes out, and packs the car for the final getaway. The bird attacks may or may not be over, but traditional movie heroism has got everyone through the disaster with the minimum of unpleasantness. The survivors of *Night of the Living Dead* do nothing but squabble. The main point of contention is in which room they should make their last stand. Harry, the coward, thinks they should retreat to the cellar and snivel in safety. Ben, the hero, insists they face the danger on the ground floor, from which they can escape when they have an opportunity. Rod Taylor would have been proud of Ben; everyone in the film ignores grouchy old Harry and goes along with him. As a result, Tom and Judy become monster munchies, the Living Dead overwhelm the house, freshly raised Johnny gets Barbara, Ben has to kill Harry twice and little Karen eats her mother. Our hero only manages to survive the Night of the Living Dead by cowering in the cellar.

On its original release, the most overlooked side of *Night of the Living Dead* was its sharply satirical wit. This becomes more apparent as the film fills in the background. In the middle of the chaos, after being pursued, terrorised, attacked and chewed, the survivors haul out a TV set and sit down to watch the crisis they have just barely lived through. The horror only becomes real when it's on *The Six O'Clock News*. After a NASA spokesman has refused to comment on the possibility that the dead have been revived by radiation from a malfunctioning Venus probe, there's a helpful little lecture from Dr Grimes (Frank Doke), an Expert. 'In the cold room at the university we had a cadaver – a cadaver from which all four limbs had been amputated. Some time early this morning it opened its eyes and began to move its trunk.' Dr Grimes understands the situation and urges the public not to panic. 'They're just dead flesh and dangerous.' He advises that the newly dead be burned without 'the dubious comfort that a funeral service can give'.

The local television station follows up on the civil defence angle by running a list of rescue stations and conducting an on-the-spot interview with Sheriff McClellan (George Kosana), whose posse is out in the wilds clearing up the mess. This is the film's funniest, most credible, most subtly horrible scene. The Sheriff, coffee cup in hand, tells the viewers at home how they should deal with the Living Dead. 'Beat 'em or burn 'em. They go up pretty easy ... They're dead, they're all messed up.' A deadpan commentator explains, 'kill the brain, and you kill the ghoul'. The Sheriff's cheeriest piece of advice is 'shoot 'em in the head'. Behind him we see the posse polishing off a few stray zombies. As David Pirie points out in *The Vampire Cinema*, 'their complacent jargon as they move through the landscape, shooting and burning, immediately evokes similar operations in South-East Asia'. The posse are played by a crowd of farmers and rifle nuts who enjoyed doing the film because 'they were happy to have guns in their hands'. Real people, they look uncomfortably like the National Guardsmen seen on the rampage in documentaries from *Attica* to *Harlan County USA*.

After dawn, the posse approaches the farmhouse. The area has been convincingly depopulated of walking corpses. Ben comes out of the cellar to be rescued. A deputy spots him peering through a window and shoots him in the head. 'Good shot', comments the Sheriff, and the hero of *Night of the Living Dead* is hauled out of the house on a meat-hook to be slung into one of Dr Grimes's bonfires – conclusive proof that flesh-eating zombies aren't the only things you've got to worry about.

Ever since, movie characters have been caught between the monsters and the reactionaries. John Carpenter's accomplished *Assault on Precinct 13* (1976) opens with unseen cops priming their pump shotguns before ambushing a group of juvenile delinquents. The street gang stage a revenge raid that involves shooting down a little girl at an ice-cream stand and besieging an isolated police station with tactics that derive equally from Romero's Living Dead and the Indians of *Apache Drums*. Our side is represented by a Negro lieutenant (Austin Stoker), a few disposables, a pair of secretaries and a bunch of convicted murderers who have been dumped in the overnight cells. The Good Guys are forced to make a stand against the unstoppable, overwhelming Bad Guys on behalf of pump shotgun wielders they only faintly know about. Horror film heroes have become morally neutral front-line troops, able to understand neither the enemy nor their superiors.

The most obviously influential aspect of *Night of the Living Dead* was the ironic, unhappy ending. Even if earlier films had opted for the inconclusive finish of *The Birds*, they had affirmed Rod Taylor's values. The fates given to the characters of *Night of the Living Dead* show what its makers think of traditional horror movie ideology. Love, the family, military capability and individual heroism are all useless. God barely gets a look in, although Dr Grimes's funerary arrangements don't give him much room in the world of the Living Dead either. Society is breaking down, but if McClellan's 'shoot 'em in the head' represents society's solution for its problems, then, like the Coopers' marriage, it probably wasn't worth saving anyway.

Fifteen years after Ben got shot in the head, the unhappy ending was a commonplace. In the 1956 *Invasion of the Body Snatchers*, Kevin McCarthy is still defiantly human in the finale, railing against the seed pods from outer space. In the 1978 remake, McCarthy makes a cameo appearance with the same act and is promptly run over by a truck. Donald Sutherland, his successor in the hero role, scores a few points by destroying the invaders' greenhouse, but this is a useless enterprise undertaken through the need to give a downbeat film some action near the end. Unlike McCarthy, Sutherland is taken over by the aliens. The 1978 *Invasion of the Body Snatchers* has the now-standard horror movie ending. The heroes rally, and the monster is apparently defeated, but a last-minute twist shows that the menace has survived and will soon be strong enough for another crack at the human race. By 1979, this was so predictable that Romero could further his reputation for surprises by having the hero and heroine of *Dawn of the Dead* still alive at the fade-out.

Night of the Living Dead was the first horror film to be overtly subversive. Previously, all social criticism was veiled or half-hearted. If a monster was even slightly appealing, you could be sure he would ultimately be firmly staked in his place by an Establishment professor, doctor or cop. *I was a Teenage Frankenstein* (1957) has a perverse authority figure corrupting a juvenile, but Whit Bissell's mad lecturer is as much a renegade and an outcast as his T-shirted monster. Even when *Them!* (1954) blames its giant ants on A-bomb tests, we are assured that a little tightening, up of safety precautions at the Atomic Energy Commission will prevent further mishaps. After all, the giant ants are swiftly and efficiently dealt with by the army and the scientific community, the very forces whose weapons research programmes created them. *Them!* raises an issue and immediately drops it, but Sheriff McClellan put an end to such cowardice. We were used to sympathising with King Kong, but now we were made to doubt the methods of the biplane pilots who shot him off the Empire State Building in 1933. Fay Wray was lucky not to have been one of the hostages killed by the National Guard during the Attica Prison revolt. These were the victims of the mentality that shot Duane Jones in the head.

Well, let's face it, we're dealing with a fantasy premise, but deep down inside we were all serious filmmakers and somewhat disappointed because we had to resort to horror for our first film. I mean, everyone would like to do the great American film, but we found ourselves making a horror film. Once we adapted to that for openers, we then tried to make the best, most realistic horror film that we could on the money we had available.

Russell Streiner

Night of the Living Dead was made by Image Ten, an especially created offshoot of the Pittsburgh-based Latent Image advertising company. As a production, the film fits into the anti-Hollywood tradition of independent gore established by Herschell Gordon Lewis's *Blood Feast* (1963). The surprisingly witty Lewis is fond of referring to *Blood Feast* as 'a Walt Whitman poem – it's no good, but it's the first of its type and therefore deserves a certain position'. Shot in Miami, this perfectly dreadful little picture is all about a mad Egyptian's attempts to resurrect an ancient princess by dismembering young girls. Lewis's style is that of the porno director he once was; the direction, script, photography, performances and technical accomplishments are unbelievably shoddy, but every few minutes there is a graphic depiction of extreme violence. Lewis's blood looks like ketchup, and his limbs and entrails are as realistic as those thrown around by the Monty Python troupe in their occasional jibes at Sam Peckinpah. Lewis's career continued in this fashion, with *Two Thousand Maniacs!* (1964), *She Devils on Wheels* (1968), *The Wizard of Gore* (1970) and others. The field has flourished, thanks to talents like Andy Milligan, *auteur* of *Bloodthirsty Butchers* (1970), *Guru, the Mad Monk* (1970) and *The Rats Are Coming, The Werewolves Are Here!* (1971); and to Ted V. Mikels, whose *oeuvre* includes *The Astro Zombies* (1969), *The Corpse Grinders* (1971) and *Blood Orgy of the She Devils* (1973).

The Corpse Grinders is a typical gore film – a tedious, incompetent production with an occasional touch of cynical humour. The doctor hero traces an epidemic of bloodthirsty pussy-cats back to an unscrupulous cat-food firm that has been recycling winos, giving their feline customers a taste for human flesh. The company's unforgettable slogan is 'For Cats Who Like People'. The film is so seedy that all its characters seem to be deformed and so threadbare that it's much less entertaining than it sounds. The vital difference between *Night of the Living Dead* and the run-of-the-mill gore movie is that Romero and his collaborators turn their deprecation of the genre to the film's advantage. *The Corpse Grinders* shows its audience the contempt Mikels thinks they deserve.

Night of the Living Dead uses its cheapness creatively. Romero is a skilled director/editor who can and does work in the style of Hitchcock or Whale if it suits him. But a lot of *Night of the Living Dead,* not only the *ciné verité* new sequence, has the naturally lit, slightly tatty look of actuality footage of an event so horrendous that its significance obscures cinematic shortcomings. Even the budgetary necessity of black-and-white filming is exploited. Decades of newsreels, newspapers, TV documentaries and still photographs have conspired to give the impression that, though real life is in colour, black and white is more realistic. In Hollywood, the Land of Oz was in Technicolor, but Kansas was drab monochrome. *Night of the Living Dead* didn't bring a general return to black and white, but Image Ten did take the horror film out of the Land of Oz and let it loose in Kansas.

Obviously, the film would not have been as influential had it been less than a box-office smash. If quality alone were the deciding factor in horror movie trends, we'd now be inundated with imitations of Herk Hervey's *Carnival of Souls* (1962), an excellent independent creepy made, coincidentally, in Kansas. *Night of the Living Dead* originally suffered from distribution problems. Columbia wanted colour, and AIP wanted a happy ending. The Walter Reade Organization finally picked up the film, but were unprepared for its success and became involved in a protracted legal wrangle with Image Ten. Recently, Romero has sanctioned the 'colorisation' (ugh!) of the film, simply to ensure that some of the creators of *Night of the Living Dead* finally see a little money from it. The movie was one of the first to become a hit on the cult circuit that has since benefited *Pink Flamingoes, The Rocky Horror Picture Show* and *Eraserhead.* It is still playing repertory theatres, college film societies and midnight shows, but at first it was caught only by devoted *aficionados* who braved the drive-ins to see it doubled-billed with *Dr Who and the Daleks.*

This piece of cack-handed programming was responsible for a spirited attack on the film by Roger Ebert, who was later to be found writing that model of quiet good taste, *Beyond the Valley of the Dolls.* Ebert's piece, originally in the *Chicago Sun-Times* but widely read on its appearance in the *Reader's Digest,* used *Night of the Living Dead* as an example of the perfidious and corrupting nature of horror films. He contended that the film was an unhealthy influence on children and revived all of the arguments that had pestered *Tales from the Crypt* off the news-stands in the 1950s. Ebert's virulence brought the movie to the attention of critics who liked it more than he did. *Sight and Sound* named it one of the year's ten best and Romero was invited to present it at the New York Museum of Modern Art. Maybe Russell Streiner had made the great American film without knowing it.

The most obvious and immediate effect of the success of *Night of the Living Dead* was a sudden epidemic of inferior flesh-eating zombie films. The more interesting ingredients took a little longer to percolate into the genre's gene pool. Typical of the cash-ins is the ridiculous *Garden of the Dead* (1972), in which a chain-gang are shot while trying to escape and crawl out of their shallow graves when formaldehyde is poured over them. Little better is *The Child* (1977), an ostensible *Omen* imitation which gets through its story – about a telekinetic tot who avenges her mother's murder by killing people – too quickly and has to conscript some passing cannibal ghouls for a climax which ineptly apes Romero's camera angles. The film's influence persists even beyond the release of Romero's larger-scaled sequels, as is demonstrated by the odd quickie like *The Children* (1980), in which a radiation leak from a power plant turns a school bus-load of kids into grim-faced killers and *Bloodeaters* (1980), which has chemicals sprayed by the government on a backwoods marijuana crop turning hippie harvests into blood-hungry monsters. *Bloodsuckers From Outer Space* (1985) uses that old favourite stand-by, alien bodysnatchers. The methods are different, not to mention wildly implausible, but the result is the same: an army of ravenous, minimally made-up, cheap-to-hire zombie extras. As *Raiders of the Living Dead* (1987) – another radiation leak, plus terrorists and a mad doctor – and *Hard Rock Zombies* (1985) – black magic, Adolf Hitler, bad jokes, worse rock music – demonstrate, the menace is likely to be with the cheapo horror movie for ever.

The nearest thing to an intentional Living Dead spoof before Dan O'Bannon's all-out *Return of the Living Dead* (1985) is *Children Shouldn't Play With Dead Things* (1972), directed by Benjamin (Bob) Clark and starring writer Alan Ormsby. A company of tasteless actors hold a wild party on a burial island. After an hour of practical jokes, sophomoric wise-cracks and sacrilege, the dead rise to clear them out. The build-up prefigures Clark's involvement with the lamentable *Porky's* films, but the gory climax is played straight. Clark and Ormsby also collaborated on *Dead of Night* (1974), an attempt to discuss Vietnam in Living Dead terms. Mama's boy Andy Brooks (Richard Backus) is offed by the Vietcong during the credits, and body-bagged for shipment home. His mother wishes him back *Monkey's Paw* style and, white-faced behind his shades, he turns up on the doorstep, the living end of the Hollywood tradition which presents Vietnam veterans as uncontrollable psychopaths. Although less jokey than *Children*, *Dead of Night* works best as a gruesome cartoon. Andy is troubled not only by the usual undead bloodlust, but by his gradual decomposition. In a neat reversal of the usual zombie movie opening, Andy ends up clawing his way *into* his grave, pulling the earth over himself. The film's best line comes when circumstantial evidence links Andy with one of the murders and a waitress leaps to his defence with 'why would a soldier want to kill anybody?'

Night of the Living Dead was particularly well received in Spain, where it arrived just as the relaxation of censorship was loosing a plague of home-grown horror films. Most of these were retreads of 1940s werewolf movies starring Paul Naschy, but Living Dead imitations soon became popular. In *La Rebelion de las Muertas (Vengeance of the Zombies)* (1972), Naschy plays a mad Indian guru and his deformed brother, both involved in a murky plot to infest an Iberian-looking England with lady zombies in revenge for an imperialist atrocity. But in Jose Luis Merino's *La Orgia de los Muertos (Brackula – Terror of the Living Dead)* (1972), Naschy is only a special guest degenerate and the lead is taken by 'Stan

Cooper'. The scion of a Victorian family investigates his uncle's mysterious death while the Living Dead emerge from some nearby catacombs to traipse around the pretty countryside. For once, the emphasis is on mystery rather than on horror and the film phasis is on mystery rather than on horror, and the film turns into a carefully constructed whodunit as Cooper tries to figure out whether the dead have been revived by evil witchcraft or mad science. *La Orgia de los Muertos* is typical Spanish horror – silly, convoluted, with occasional touches of telling surrealism. Amando De Ossorio's *La Noche del Terror Ciego (Tombs of the Blind Dead)* (1972) is more of the same: a marauding band of zombie crusaders on skeletal horses dash about Portuguese plains in slow motion. The living characters are uniformly tiresome – it seems as if everybody in Spanish horror films is compelled to wear Carnaby Street dresses, polo-neck pullovers or macho man medallions – but De Ossorio's Templars prove striking enough to continue their rampages in a clutch of sequels, including *Ataque de los Muertos sin Ojos (Return of the Evil Dead)* (1973) and *La Noche de las Gaviotas (Night of the Seagulls)* (1975).

Spain's most blatant reworking of the Romero formula was a 1974 co-production with Italy, shot on location in England (with interiors filmed in Madrid where they don't know how to spell signs in English) and burdened with a trilingual plethora of titles: *No se Debe Profanar el Sueno de los Muertos, Fin de Semana para los Muertos, Non si doveva profanare il sonno dei morti, Let Sleeping Corpses Lie, Don't Open the Window, Breakfast with the Dead, Breakfast at the Manchester Morgue, The Living Dead* and *The Living Dead at Manchester Morgue*. Flesh-eating ghouls roam the countryside; our heroes are caught between them and the knuckleheaded police; and it's all the government's fault. Instead of NASA, it's the Ministry of Agriculture, who are testing a machine that gets rid of insects by emitting ultrasonic waves which make bugs want to eat each other, who are to blame. The catch is that it has the same effect on the recently dead, 'because their nervous systems are much simpler than ours'. Director Jorge Grau replaces Sheriff McClellan with Sergeant McCormick (Arthur Kennedy), who blames the cannibal murders on the bearded hero (Ray Lovelock) because he looks like a layabout and rides a motorbike. As McCormick shoots Lovelock in the head, he sneers 'I wish the dead could come back to life, you bastard, because then I could kill you again.' The film, whose political content seems to require the lighting up of one of Woody Allen's 'Author's Message' signs every few minutes, is too overwrought to work on as many levels as Night of the Living Dead. The story straggles, keeping up momentum only by eliding contrivance and coincidence at the expense of credibility. It only gets out of Romero's shadow on the strength of its visual imagination. The opening montage of London is masterfully depressing: a bowler-hatted pill-popper, clouds of pollution, tramps in doorways and a streaker whose attention-getting stunt is ignored. Like La Orgia de Los Muertos, the film uses outmoded film stock to make the attractive Lake District remarkably eerie. Grau's most effective sequences use graphic gore in a way that Romero avoided: the Living Dead slowly bring down and devour their victims; bright red blood splashes across landscape greens and blues.

Italy, the best-known continental producer of flesh-eating zombie movies, didn't get fully into the act until Lucio Fulci's imitation of Romero's Dawn of the Dead, Zombi 2 (Zombie Flesh Eaters) (1979) – whereupon the Grau picture was rereleased as one of several competing films entitled Zombi 3 – but France's Jean Rollin got in an imitation of No se Debe Profanare el Sueno de los Muertos, Les Raisins de la mort (Pesticide) (1978), in which crop-spraying leads to an outbreak of Gallic zombies. Rollin manages a few atmospheric touches amid gore effects that would do H.G. Lewis proud, but the overall tone of the film is peculiarly listless. A similarly deadening pall hangs around the director's later zombie movies. Rollin took over Le Lac des Morts Vivants (Zombies' Lake) (1981) from the Spaniard Jesus Franco, who promptly went out and helped Daniel Lesoeur to remake it in the desert as L'Abîme des morts vivants (Oasis of the Zombies) (1981), but

neither director did much more than cash in on the extremely brief vogue for underwater Nazi zombie movies initiated by Ken Wiederhorn's spirited Shock Waves (1979), in which scar-faced Peter Cushing leads an impressive cadre of goose-stepping monsters in dark glasses through a Caribbean jungle after bikini-clad Brooke Adams. Rollin's final word on the subject is La Morte Vivante (1982), a would-be touching tale of a young woman who feels driven to procure victims for her undead best friend.

In Narciso Ibanez Serrador's Quien Puede Matar un Niño? (Would You Kill a Child?) (1976), another Spanish–English Living Dead variant, the children on a Mediterranean island inexplicably murder their parents and any other adults within reach. Serrador clod-hops off on the wrong foot with an attack of social significance, a montage of real-life horrors inflicted on adults by children, but reins himself in remarkably as an English tourist couple realise what is going on. The use of children as the Living Dead is a clever development of the Karen Cooper character from Night of the Living Dead; Serrador's pre-teen murderers, unlike the more obvious mutants of The Children, remain normal looking and treat mass murder as another game, replacing 'pin the tail on the donkey' with 'cut the head off the corpse'. Serrador surprisingly lets his heroes off the hook: although Prunella Gee fears that she might be about to give birth to a potential monster, the couple do not have any of their own children along to turn on them. Lewis Fiander is thus not under quite so much pressure not to fight back and soon overcomes his qualms about killing children. The rescuers see him defending himself and take him for a homicidal maniac. They shoot him in the head.

Herman Cohen, producer of I Was a Teenage Werewolf, and Roger Corman, who segued from rock 'n' roll (Rock All Night) to horror (The House of Usher) via the beatnik comic horror of A Bucket of Blood, were among the first to exploit the unique appeal of horror movies to the youth market by presenting monsters and heroes alike as recognisable teen types. Ten years later Night of the Living Dead was taken up, in George A.

Romero's words, 'by the generation that refused to go to war'. The youth culture explosion of the late 1960s saw *Hair* running on Broadway, the Beatles getting into Indian mysticism, student revolt in Paris, 'Hell No, We Won't Go' demos in the USA and the popularisation of mind-expanding drugs. Everyone was tuning in, turning on, tripping out, signing off and getting in on the act. By the time the Ohio National Guard used Sheriff McClellan's tactics at Kent State University, the Swinging Sixties had soured. The California sex 'n' drugs 'n' rock 'n' roll cult had produced such notable examples of Peace and Love and All That Stuff as the Manson Family murders and the death of a Rolling Stones fan at the hands of Hell's Angels bouncers during an open-air concert at Altamont. With ringing Nixonian evasiveness, the incident was put down to 'security overenthusiasm', which is Newspeak for 'shoot 'em in the head'.

Night of the Living Dead appeared at the height of flower power, but despite the effectiveness of crucifix-toting Jesus freaks against *The Velvet Vampire* and the furry Kerwin Matthews in *The Boy Who Cried Werewolf*, the hippies missed their chance to become horror movie heroes. The counter-culture received short shrift even in the movies they liked most. In Roger Corman's *The Wild Angels* (1967) and *Gas-s-s-s . . .* (1970), Hell's Angels become the new bourgeoisie. Peter Fonda, the leader of Corman's Angels, is referred to as 'Mr President' by his followers and his gang is a society more rigid than the one he is escaping from. He finally opts out of opting out because 'there's no place to go'. As Captain America, Fonda joins Dennis Hopper for *Easy Rider* (1969). Their aimless trek across the mid-West is cut short when some passing rednecks shoot them in the head.

Charles Manson is chillingly played by Steve Railsback in Ted Gries's TV movie *Helter Skelter* (1976), with Marilyn Burns, sole survivor of *The Texas Chainsaw Massacre*, as one of the Family floozies. Manson's influence on the horror film can be seen in *I Drink Your Blood* (1971), a Living Dead spin-off featuring a clash between rabid hippies and hard-hat construction workers; *The Deathmaster* (1972), with Robert Quarry as a Rasputin-bearded California guru who turns out to be an honest-to-God vampire; *The Night God Screamed* (1973), in which a hooded cultist called the A-Toner crucifies minister Alex Nichol; *The Demon Lover* (1976), with its long-haired Satanists; and *Thou Shalt Not Kill . . . Except* (1987), with cult director Sam Raimi under a false beard as the Manson stand-in. Manson's lesson about alternative lifestyles was reinforced by the Rev. Jim Jones, who has inspired at least four movies: *Guyana – el Crimen del Siglo* (*Guyana – Crime of the Century*) (1980), with Stuart Whitman sleep-walking in the lead; *Mangiati vivi dai cannibali* (*Eaten Alive*) (1980), which has cannibals *and* cultists led by Ivan Rassimov; *Guyana Tragedy: The True Story of Jim Jones* (1980), a TV special with Powers Boothe magnetically evil as Jones; and *Inferno in diretta* (*Cut and Run*) (1985), with death-faced Richard Lynch as Jones's surviving best friend, still up to no good in the jungle. The Rev. Sun Myung Moon and the late L. Ron Hubbard have yet to make their horror movie debuts, although the realistic deprogramming dramas *Ticket to Heaven* (1981) and *Split Image* (1982) come close.

John Hancock's shamefully underrated *Let's Scare Jessica to Death* (1971), finds the Living Dead in attendance upon the death of the Love Generation. The heroine (Zohra Lampert) retreats to an isolated apple farm with her slightly ageing hippie friends and finds her neuroses given flesh in Emily (Mariclare Costello), a guitar-playing squatter whose identity merges with that of a Victorian vampire girl who drowned in the adjoining lake. In Jessica's paranoid nightmare, the unfriendly towns-folk, who scrape the word 'LOVE' off the side of the hearse she drives 'because it's cheaper than a station-wagon', become shambling ghouls, and her husband (Barton Heyman) is about to turn into One of Them. *Jessica* predates Robert Altman's *Images* in its use of autumnal countryside to reflect the mental collapse of the heroine. While Susannah York's psychosis fractures into a series of role-playing charades, Zohra Lampert's extra-ordinarily delicate character study shades into a terrifying acceleration of disorientating images. In one of the most unusually haunting moments in

● *Zombie flower child.* **Blue Sunshine.**

the cinema, Emily sinks beneath the waters of the lake, dressed in a black bathing-suit, only to bob up seconds later wearing a sodden nineteenth-century wedding dress. On the strength of his scary swimming scenes, Hancock was contracted to make *Jaws 2*; he was fired when he tried to duplicate the ambiguous lyricism of *Jessica* rather than follow Steven Spielberg's roller-coaster formula. With its quiet sensitivity, attractive but malevolent ghost girl, and overripe Connecticut setting, *Let's Scare Jessica to Death* is more in tune with the novels of Peter Straub and Charles L. Grant than anything being done in the contemporary horror film scene.

Similarly neglected is Willard Huyck's *Messiah of Evil* (1975), a strangely surreal movie, shot through with the pretensions one might expect from fresh film school graduates (Huyck and writer Gloria Katz later scripted *American Graffiti* and were drawn into George Lucas's orbit), but rich in narrative convolutions and peculiar atmospherics. Marianna Hill arrives at a lonely coastal town in search of Royal Dano, her vanished, death-obsessed painter father and falls in with a crowd of trendy hedonists who luxuriate in decadent surroundings while the taciturn locals yet again turn into cannibal ghouls. With an arch but gloomy voice-over to explain the twists of a hard-to-follow plot, and an astonishing finale that puts down all the weird events to a sinister preacher, murdered in flashback by cowboy Walter Hill, who is about to return from the sea and (maybe) take over the world, the film draws from H.P. Lovecraft as well as from the Living Dead. However, Elisha Cook Jr as a doomed derelict whose warnings are unheeded adds a touch of gothic cliché to the brew and the 'normal' characters are so strange as to put the film's conception of the real world out of joint, as if a crazed projectionist were juxtaposing random reels of *The Haunted Palace* and *Vargtimmen* (*Hour of the Wolf*). In the film's strangest sequence, nymphet Joy Bang tries to watch an impressionist collage of Western film clips in a rotting cinema while the auditorium gradually fills up with zombies.

The other post-hippie horror films of note are Oliver Stone's *Seizure* (1974) and Jeff Lieberman's *Blue Sunshine* (1977), which, like Lawrence Kasdan's *The Big Chill* find the former acid-drop kids safely ensconced in the middle classes they used to despise. *Seizure* is another nightmare, finally revealed as the *Occurrence at Owl Creek Bridge* dying fantasy of writer Edmund Blackstone (Jonathan Frid). He conjures up a trio of monsters from his latest horror story, under the tyrannical rule of the Queen of Evil (Martine Beswick) and has them take over a weekend party at his estate. The obnoxiously hip guests are forced to fight it out for the privilege of being the sole survivor. Stone returns to the theme of the artist menaced by his creations in *The Hand* (1981), with Michael Caine as a tormented ex-illustrator of comics plagued by the probably imaginary spectre of his severed hand. While *Seizure* is nicely handled and unpredictable, *The Hand* is a fairly literal adaption of Marc Brendel's interesting novel *The Lizard's Tail*. Stone has since moved profitably closer to home with the horrors of *Salvador, Platoon* and *Wall Street*, which confirm that, as was once said of Harlan Ellison, 'his favourite mode of expression is shouting at the top of his voice'.

Blue Sunshine is funnier and more pointed. This autopsy on the corpse of LSD radicalism has its ex-freaks settled down and turned into cops, housewives, politicians and general credits to the community. One of them is running for Congress, but back in 1966 he was the friendly neighbourhood dope dealer who spread tabs of Blue Sunshine, the hallucinogenic flavour of the month, around town. Ten years later, anyone who dropped Blue Sunshine can expect nasty side-effects: they lose all their hair and become homicidal maniacs. The film suffers from Zalman King, twitching his way through the wimpiest hero role on record, but deserves credit for its bald, murderous, thirtyish hippies, the most off-the-wall descendants of the Living Dead yet to reach the screen. Lieberman sums up the spirit of 1968 when he has one potential freak-out confess that the break-up of the Beatles affected her more than the break-up of her marriage. The flower children have become the Living Dead.

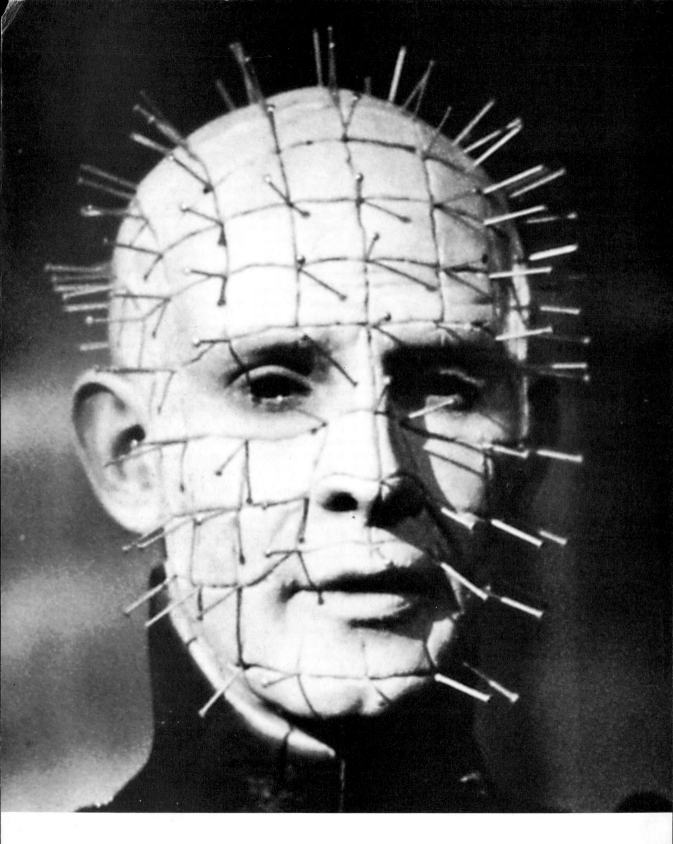

● *Pin-Head.* Doug Bradley, **Hellraiser.**

the indian summer of the british horror film

The English gothic cinema was fatally wounded by the bullet in Duane Jones's head, but its death throes were protracted.

The style was set in the late 1950s by Hammer Films' remakes of the classic monster movies: *The Curse of Frankenstein* (1957), *Dracula* (1958), *The Hound of the Baskervilles* (1958), *The Mummy* (1959) and *Curse of the Werewolf* (1960). Ten years later, the studio and the tradition were in decline. The extermination of the strain was marked by a proliferation of mutants, hybrids and sports. Initially, this allowed for challenging, oddball films like *The Sorcerers* and *Scream and Scream Again*, but eventually the genre deteriorated with a dispiriting procession of stumbling, gimmicky grotesques like *Dracula AD 1972* and *Legend of the Seven Golden Vampires*.

In 1973, the merciful *coup de grâce* was delivered. The perpetually shaky economy of the British film industry had already made the slender returns of the small-scale gothic horror film a dubious business proposition. The public acceptance of *The Exorcist*, with its big-budget reading of the horror movie formula, rendered the British product obsolete. In 1975, the short-lived Tyburn Films hired Hammer regulars Freddie Francis, John Elder (Anthony Hinds) and Peter Cushing to direct, write and star in *The Ghoul* and *Legend of the Werewolf*. The films, wooden remakes of Hammer's *The Reptile* (1966) and *Curse of the Werewolf*, failed to get theatrical distribution in

the vital US market. If the lesson still hadn't been learned, it was reinforced by Francis's return to direction after a successful spell in his old job as a first-class director of photography (*The Elephant Man*, *The French Lieutenant's Woman*, etc.), resulting in an entirely terrible version of Dylan Thomas's long-unproduced Burke and Hare screenplay, *The Doctor and the Devils* (1985).

Hammer Horror treats the 'normal' characters and the audience as innocent bystanders caught in a private battle between the forces of Good and Evil, as represented by the Savant and the Monster. Don Sharp's *Kiss of the Vampire* (1964), John Gilling's *Plague of the Zombies* (1966) and Terence Fisher's *Dracula, Prince of Darkness* (1966) and *The Devil Rides Out* (1967) all weave elegant moralities on this pattern. Dr Van Helsing, Peter Cushing's fearless vampire killer in *Dracula*, is the original Savant, but Clifford Evans's self-torturing professor in *Kiss*, André Morell's Victorian scholar/adventurer in *Plague*, Andrew Keir's shotgun-toting monk in *Prince of Darkness* and Christopher Lee's Duc de Richlieu in *Devil* are of the same type – an elderly mystic, steeped in arcane knowledge, apparently rational, but with an Old Testament streak of 'vengeance is mine' fundamentalism. The Monsters tend to be as suave, attractive and plausible as Christopher Lee's Dracula and as prone to red-eyed, fangs-bared hissing when thwarted: examples are Noel Willman's joyless vampire in *Kiss*, John Carson's voodoo priest/country squire in *Plague* and Charles Gray's epicene Satanist in *Devil*. The duel between the Monster and the Savant inevitably begins with a minor victory for Evil as an upright character is corrupted. Typically, the repressed supporting heroine (Carol Marsh in *Dracula*, Barbara Shelley in *Prince of Darkness*, Jacqueline Pearce in *Plague*) is turned into a vampire wanton. The proprieties are restored when the forces of Good pound a stake through her and the leading ladies (Melissa Stribling, Suzan Farmer, Diane Clare) are saved from a dark liberation. In a variant, *Devil* has the secondary male lead (Patrick Mower) lured into the evil cult: noticeably, his punishment for surrendering to his sensual impulses is far less extreme than that meted out to the women. In the finale, the Savant brings down the Wrath of God (in the form of daylight, running water, fire, white magic or a swarm of bats), and the Monster's handsome face putrefies as he dies screaming.

At first, the rigid format gained in mythic stature with the carry-over from film to film, but by 1968 and Freddie Francis's *Dracula Has Risen From the Grave* repetition was beginning to tell. Francis yanks in eye-catching, but pointless, images (a mutilated girl hanging in a church bell) to beef up a plot that largely deals with the maudlin mopings of a pair of tissue-paper-flimsy young lovers. The Savant (Rupert Davies) and the Monster (Christopher Lee) are reduced to irritable onlookers. While the conventions were atrophying at Hammer, others were actively subverting them – comically, as in Roman Polanski's charming *Dance of the Vampires* (1967), or with deadly serious intent, as in Michael Reeves's bitter *The Sorcerers* (1968). Polanski's Savant is Professor Abronsius (Jack MacGowran), an inept old fool whose attempts to wipe vampirism off the face of Transylvania lead to its spread throughout the world. The Monster, Count Von Krolock (Ferdy Mayne), is as cultured and benevolent as he seems to be. For Polanski, vampires are as entitled to as much respect and understanding as any other ethnic/sexual minority.

Reeves has none of Polanski's tolerant irony; his

film is informed by the 1960s impatience with the deadening influence of age over youth. *The Sorcerers* redraws the battle lines, so that the Savant and the Monster become ageing scientists: Marcus (Boris Karloff) and Estelle Monserrat (Catherine Lacey). Youth is represented by Mike (Ian Ogilvy), suede-jacketed patron of Chelsea nightclubs and Espresso bars. The Monserrats have invented a machine through which they can vicariously live Mike's exciting life. While Marcus takes notes, Estelle urges Mike on to sex and violence. Terence Fisher's epic metaphysical struggle between Good and Evil dwindles to an elderly couple moaning at each other, and Mike – urged on by a fed-up and appalled Marcus – finally puts everyone out of their misery by totalling his stolen motor and letting the Monserrats share the sensations of burning to death in a car crash. If Peter Cushing had tried to impose his inflexible, middle-aged morality on Michael Reeves, he would have been told to get stuffed.

The collision between Swinging London and the gothic tradition in the cinema was overdue. On television, period quaintness and modernist absurdity had been combined in *Adam Adamant Lives!*, which featured a defrosted Edwardian detective (Gerald Harper) and his miniskirted dolly-bird sidekick (Juliet Harmer), a teaming obviously intended to echo those of bowler-hatted Patrick MacNee and his karate-kicking girlfriends in *The Avengers* or the original nasty old man *Dr Who* (William Hartnell) and his young assistants. Reeves draws on this attractive mini-trend in *The Sorcerers*, but colours it with his own misanthropy. *Matthew Hopkins – Witchfinder General* (1968), Reeves's masterpiece, is one of the most downbeat movies ever made, a 90-minute negation of every moral precept horror films have stood for. 'I've made eighty-seven films', protested star Vincent Price when Reeves made a suggestion on the set. 'What have you done?' The 24-four-year-old director summed up his feelings for the traditional horror movie with his answer: 'I've made three good ones'. Tragically, Reeves committed suicide in 1969, leaving behind only three and a half movies. His last project, *The Oblong Box* (1969), was inherited by director Gordon Hessler and writer Chris Wicking. They couldn't do much with it — the hideous deformities one character conceals behind a crimson hood turn out to be a bad case of acne and a very large false nose — but proceeded to collaborate on the British horror cinema's only successful synthesis of its themes with those of the politicised American nightmare, *Scream and Scream Again* (1969).

The Living Dead of *Scream and Scream Again* are an underground organisation of supermen, cobbled together Frankenstein-fashion from the choicest bodysnatched parts available and conspiring to take over the world. Their numbers include: Keith (Michael Gothard), a malfunctioning cool cat who vampires teenagers he picks up in a disco and, as John R. Duvoli wrote, 'looks like Mick Jagger after a bad trip'; Konratz (Marshall Jones), an East European secret policeman with a fondness for bizarre tortures; Dr Browning (Vincent Price), the perfectly sane scientist toiling over his Master Race while his sponsors infiltrate international politics and big business; and Fremont (Christopher Lee), the higher echelon British civil servant in charge of the conspiracy investigation. Wicking's extraordinarily complicated screenplay juggles a series of apparently disparate strands with supreme confidence, tying them all together with a grimly satisfying succession of twists as the characters converge on Browning's laboratory and mostly tumble into his handy vat of acid. Hessler's direction is similarly kaleidoscopic, using the ambience of screaming rock music, flashing disco lights and *Avengers*-style chases through the Green Belt to keep the film on the move, throwing stray ideas around with supercharged energy, and relishing the undeniably gruesome images: a kidnapped athlete gradually discovers his dismemberment, with another limb missing each time he throws back the bedclothes; and, unforgettably, Keith escapes from being handcuffed to a car by wrenching his hand off at the wrist.

Unfortunately, the fascinating avenues opened up by *Scream and Scream Again* were almost immediately shut off. Producer Milton Subotsky indulged in some imperceptible re-editing, and

later hinted that he was less than pleased with the finished movie. 'Strangely enough, *Scream and Scream Again* made a lot of money and that was different from every other film we've ever done. I don't know why, it wasn't all that good. It might have been because we used three top horror stars and it had a very good title.' Thereafter, a generation gap yawned between the producers, who were used to the cosiness of the Hammer Horrors, and the directors, who were young *cinéastes* with eclectic influences that took in Terence Fisher, but also Sam Fuller, Don Siegel and *Night of the Living Dead*. Hessler and Wicking followed *Scream and Scream Again* with *Murders in the Rue Morgue* (1971), a film crucified by its distributors. American International completely recut it, tossed in some additional footage and tinted all the dream scenes orange. The result was disappointing all round: a messy film, with occasional nice touches, which died at the box office. *The Dark*, a project which writer/director Michael Armstrong saw as 'a cynical attack on the Swinging Sixties', in which a group of trendy teens lark about in a haunted house and get hacked to pieces, suffered a similar fate. Partially reshot by certified hack Gerry Levy, perpetrator of *The Body Stealers* (1969), *The Dark* was released as *The Haunted House of Horror* (1968). Had Tigon, the production company, listened to Armstrong, they might have had a long-term cult movie on their hands, but they vetoed his suggestion that the psycho killer be played by the young David Bowie. Their idea of a teen appeal star was Frankie Avalon, who embarrassedly exits the film when Bowie's instantly obscure replacement Mark Wynter stabs him in the groin.

To be fair, it should be pointed out that Tigon left Michael Reeves alone when presented with the hardly conventional *The Sorcerers* and *Matthew Hopkins*. This long-time grindhouse distributor had a brief burst of production activity in the late 1960s. They prodded veteran British journeyman Vernon Sewell — best known for buying up a *grand guignol* play called *The Medium* in the early 1930s and making a version of it every five years or so for the rest of his career — into turning out such

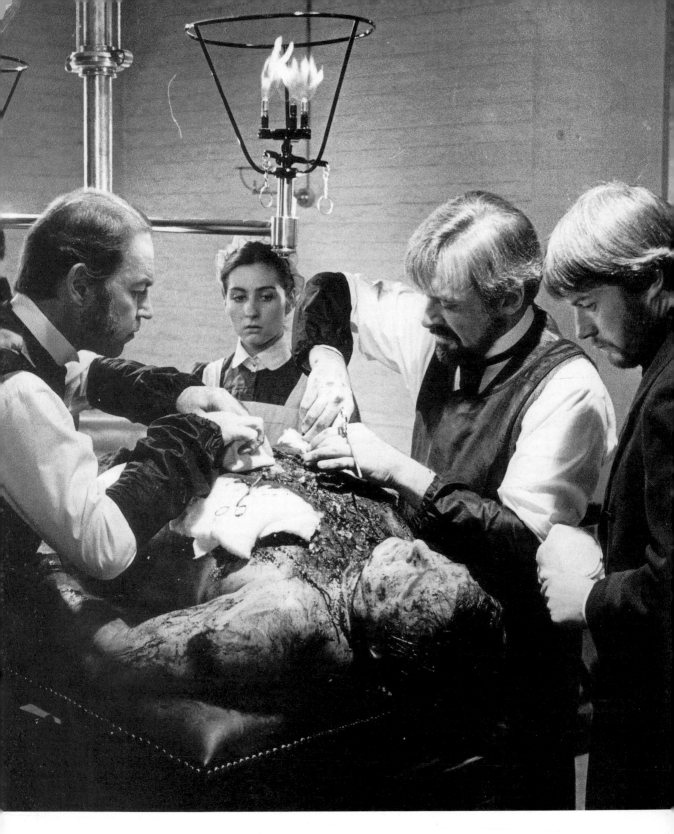

● *Blood and stiff collars: the persistence of Victorian values.* Anthony Hopkins, **The Elephant Man.**

imitation Hammers as *The Blood Beast Terror* (1967), with Peter Cushing and a giant death's-head moth woman; *Curse of the Crimson Altar* (1968), a superproduction supposedly taken from H.P. Lovecraft with doddery Boris Karloff, somnambulist Christopher Lee and green-painted Barbara Steele; and *Burke and Hare* (1971), another version of the oft-told tale with plentiful wenching to get in on the softcore sex market. More interesting is James Kelly's dotty *The Beast in the Cellar* (1971), a dead-straight version of *Arsenic and Old Lace*, with a ridiculous plot about a geriatric World War I draft-dodger who kills hunky young soldiers and hayloft heavy petters with his long fingernails, but also with a pair of wastefully committed performances from Beryl Reid and Flora Robson as the sisters who shelter the feeble monster. After Reeves's death, Tigon's finest moment was Piers Haggard's *Blood on Satan's Claw* (1971), a variation on the Savant and the Monster with a well-used, unfamiliar seventeenth-century setting and some playfully nasty eroticism focusing on teenage witch girl Linda Hayden. Haggard's witch finders are more righteous than Reeves's, but *Blood on Satan's Claw* finds just as much cruelty running riot in the picturesque English countryside. In pitting its magistrates, parsons and goodfellow farmers against a coven of children, the film marked out an area of inter-generational tension that would become central to the American horror film of the 1970s.

Hammer Films were acutely aware of their position as market leaders. When the ideas ran dry, they encouraged off-beat projects like *Demons of the Mind* (1971), another Chris Wicking script, more out of desperation than anything else. The film is a spirited attack on the Hammer tradition, in which the Savant becomes Michael Hordern's monk, a raving nutter who wanders through Bavaria driving burning crosses through the mentally ill in the belief that they are possessed, or Patrick Magee's proto-psychologist, a sadistic opportunist. Hammer found director Peter Sykes, thanks to his stylish, mannered and cheap *Venom* (1971) and let him make *Demons of the Mind* without much interference – it emerged as a cerebral, hard-edged, sometimes beautiful film –

however, they then discarded it as a little seen double-bill-filler. Very decently, the firm later had Sykes and Wicking make *To the Devil – A Daughter* (1976), in which Richard Widmark prevents Christopher Lee from sacrificing Nastassia Kinski to Satan. Hammer's attempt to update their formula for a post-*Exorcist* audience, the film is an uneasy, compromised failure, the last of the Savant and the Monster and – apart from a run of very bland TV movies – practically the last from the studio.

Another Hammer protégé was Peter Sasdy, whose films for the company have interesting and innovative ideas, but are let down by hasty scripts, misguided casting and underbudgeting. *Taste the Blood of Dracula* (1969) has the vampire as a purgative sweeping through a corrupt Victorian London, a radical reversal of the Good/Evil polaris-ation of the rest of the series. With all the likely Savants exposed as venal hypocrites, Dracula can only be defeated by divine intervention. However, extraordinary scenes like the black mass that goes wrong when three thrill-seeking pillars of society co-opted by Dracula's disciple (Ralph Bates) turn on the decadent young man and beat him to death, are still interspersed with the traditionally weak Hammer romantic sub-plots and faintly silly se-quences with Christopher Lee lurking in the shadows. *Countess Dracula* (1971) is a dreary oddity, hindered by Ingrid Pitt's unconvincing incarnation of a wrinkled Hungarian aristocrat who regains her youth by bathing in virgins' blood. And *Hands of the Ripper* (1971), an elementary elaboration of the mixture of possession and primitive psychiatry found in *Demons of the Mind*, is enlivened only by the moving performance of Angharad Rees as the haunted daughter of Jack the Ripper. Sasdy's post-Hammer career has been littered with disasters: *Doomwatch* (1972), *Nothing But the Night* (1972), *I Don't Want to Be Born* (1976) and *The Lonely Lady* (1982). The star of the last film, Pia Zadora, refers to him as 'the worst director in the history of directors'. His reputation has only been enhanced by *The Stone Tape* (1972), a Nigel Kneale ghost story made for BBC-TV.

In this period, Hammer's biggest hit was Roy Ward Baker's *The Vampire Lovers'* (1970), yet another version of J. Sheridan LeFanu's much-filmed *Carmilla*. This is a return to the Savant and the Monster, given an opportunist, misogynist twist. The Savants are Douglas Wilmer, George Cole and Peter Cushing, a triumvirate of stuffy father figures. The Monster is Carmilla Karnstein (Ingrid Pitt), a devastating, bisexual teenage vampire. Left in the care of respectable families by her chic mother (Dawn Addams), Carmilla seduces and drains the daughters of the bourgeoisie. The older generation ceremonially dispatch her with a stake through the heart, then behead the corpse for good measure. The imbalance says a lot about the neurotic fears of youth, sexuality and femininity that had previously been submerged in the genre. If *The Vampire Lovers* works, it does so because of Baker's conjuration of dreamy, erotic images that borrow equally from Jean Rollin's French vampire films and the cobwebby decadence of Roger Corman's Edgar Allan Poe adaptions. More relevant to its box-office takings was the early 1970s tolerance for softcore pornography. It had sequels, both official (*Lust for a Vampire*, 1970; *Twins of Evil*, 1971) and unofficial (Robert Young's amusingly convoluted *Vampire Circus*, 1971).

Brian Clemens's flirtation with Hammer produced a pair of scripts, for *Dr Jekyll and Sister Hyde* (1971) and *Captain Kronos – Vampire Hunter* (1971), that no one was sure how to handle. Roy Ward Baker's *Sister Hyde* gleefully stirs Jack the Ripper and Burke and Hare into R.L. Stevenson and has prissy Ralph Bates reconstituted as Martine Beswick, by far the most fetching of Hammer's predatory sex kittens. Clemens's own *Captain Kronos* has Horst Janson as a swashbuckling Austro-Hungarian officer who crosses swords with a family of fencing vampires in a straightfaced romp. Otherwise, the success of *The Vampire Lovers* led to a ludicrous series of cross-breeds in which vampirism was grafted on to an ultra-violent 'meat' movie (*Scars of Dracula*, 1970), the pseudo-hip youth scene (*Dracula AD 1972*, 1972), a James Bondish superscience thriller (*The Satanic Rites of Dracula*, 1973) and, worst of all, the one-from-column-A chop socky kungfu film (*Legend of the Seven Golden Vampires*, 1973).

In the midst of this wastage, Hammer found time to finance Seth Holt's *Blood From the Mummy's Tomb* (1971) and Terence Fisher's *Frankenstein and the Monster From Hell* (1973). With hyperbolic titles that betoken the form's decadence, these final films from directors associated with the company and the genre display a despairing, end-of-the-road nihilism. *Blood* is literally a death-bed work, completed by producer Michael Carreras when Holt died during shooting. The Chris Wicking script pits the tormented, nearly senile Savant (Andrew Keir) against a petulant, smart Monster (James Villiers) whose philosophy is sniffily summed up as 'the meek shan't inherit the Earth, they wouldn't know what to do with it'. The young hero dies in an offscreen car wreck well before the climax and the heroine is reborn as a bandaged mummy. *Frankenstein*, a similarly crotchety picture, winds up with a pack of nineteenth-century lunatics ripping the lumbering, pathetic monster (David Prowse) to shreds. In the final shot, Peter Cushing's Baron Frankenstein sweeps up the debris and prattles on about his next experiment, and Fisher's camera pulls back to frame him between the bars of the asylum in which the film is set. By now, even Frankenstein's most devoted disciple (Shane Briant) has had enough of him. The series that began in 1957 with Cushing as the dashing young Victor Frankenstein ends not with the death of the Baron but with his relegation to a well-deserved obscurity.

Hammer's chief rival, Amicus Productions, were less hampered by period trappings, but equally afflicted by the idea shortage. They exacerbated the repetition problem by specialising in anthology movies: *The House That Dripped Blood* (1970), *Asylum* (1972), *Tales From the Crypt* (1972), *The Vault of Horror* (1973) and *From Beyond the Grave* (1975). The overall impression is of about fifty mini-movies in which something supernaturally horrid happens to an embarrassed guest star. Perhaps the zenith of Amicus's spotty output is Freddie Francis's *Tales From the Crypt*, which draws its nasty anecdotes from the 1950s EC comics that were to be such an important influence on American splatter movies, and is

● *Cavalier attitude.* Jack Watson, Lesley-Anne Down, **From Beyond the Grave.**

memorable for Joan Collins getting strangled by Santa Claus, Peter Cushing returning from the grave as an eyeless ghoul and Nigel Patrick being chased by a starving Alsatian down a narrow corridor lined with razor blades – not to mention Sir Ralph Richardson as the Crypt Keeper, sadly bereft of his trademark cackle (heh heh heh). As Amicus supremo Milton Subotsky's comments on *Scream and Scream Again* indicate, the company was less than favourably inclined to experiment. *I, Monster* (1970) and *—And Now the Screaming Starts!* (1972), their stabs at period gothic, are tentative at best, although *The Beast Must Die* (1973), with a black Great White Hunter (Calvin Lockhart) on a werewolf safari, is mindless, trashy fun of the first order. Amicus dissolved in the mid-1970s, but Subotsky has since produced two entirely terrible anthologies: *The Uncanny* (1977), about homicidal cats, and *The Monster Club* (1981), a dire farce padded with instantly dating rock music. In their day, Amicus were successful enough to be ripped off by a cheap imitation, Freddie Francis's unreleasable *Tales That Witness Madness* (1973).

The decadence of the tradition was underlined by Robert Fuest's *The Abominable Dr Phibes* (1971) and *Dr Phibes Rises Again* (1972). Vincent Price wafts through these as Dr Phibes, a triumph of DIY surgery who has to eat and speak through a hole in his neck. A vengeance-crazed vaudeville organist, he disposes of his enemies in accord with the twelve plagues of Egypt. Fuest was a graduate of *The Avengers*, and the Phibes films have the same off-centre charm. An array of reliable character actors are the victims of elaborate, pointless engines of destruction decorated with art deco flourishes. The plots stringing together the murders are sketchy, but the films' conceits and Price's plummy playing eventually make the orgy of kitsch irresistible. Douglas Hickox's *Theatre of Blood* (1973) is another witty revenge saga, with Price joined by the former Mrs Emma Peel, Diana Rigg. Miffed by thirty years of terrible notices, mad Shakespearean Edward Lionheart massacres the London dramatic critics' circle. After Price forced effeminate gourmet Robert Morley to

choke on his own poodles in a scene vaguely inspired by *Titus Andronicus*, there no longer seemed to be any point in having Dracula rise from the grave yet again. Indeed, even the redoubtable Price, a mainstay of the genre for fifteen years, found it hard to follow that and, after Jim Clark's *Madhouse* (1974) – another showbiz horror – temporarily retired from the field.

Outside the comfy, almost respectable confines of well-established family firms like Hammer and Amicus, the British horror film industry harboured a limbo of fly-by-night productions and colourful entrepreneurs who had their own, supremely disreputable, flourishing horror comic tradition. The Victorian costumes, dignified performers and stylish photography of the Hammer films lend them a certain politeness and polish that is entirely lacking in the work of Robert Hartford-Davis (*Corruption*, 1968; *Incense for the Damned*, 1969; *The Fiend*, 1970), Ray Austin (*Virgin Witch*, 1970), Tom Parkinson (*Crucible of Terror*, 1971; *Disciple of Death*, 1972), producer Richard Gordon (*Tower of Evil*, 1972; *The Cat and the Canary*, 1978), Alan Birkinshaw (*Killers' Moon*, 1978) and Norman J. Warren (*Satan's Slaves*, 1976; *Prey*, 1977; *Terror*, 1979). This is the marginal cinema, where double-bill-fillers can be sold either for sex or violence (*Bizarre*, 1970, for instance, is also known as *Secrets of Sex*) and nothing else really matters. Too cheap for period settings, these films, intentionally or not, manage to locate their horrors in a recognisable, seedy British setting otherwise un-explored in the movies. The plots are outmoded 'B' melodrama, the girls are mostly pretty and disposable and – very rarely – extraordinary, almost-art films like Freddie Francis's *Mumsy, Nanny, Sonny and Girly* (1969), Andrew Sinclair's insufferably pretentious *Blue Blood* (1975) and Don Sharp's downright weird *Psychomania* (1971) slip out. Really, it's not such a great step from these to Joseph Losey's *Secret Ceremony* (1968) or Nicolas Roeg and Donald Cammell's *Performance* (1970).

Viktor Ritelis's *The Corpse* (1971) is the most remarkable movie to emerge from this uncharted wilderness. Michael Gough, the nearest thing to a star in the area, plays a sadistic stockbroker whose perverted assaults on his wife (Yvonne Mitchell) and daughter (Sharon Gurney) continue even after they have apparently murdered him. The vision of middle-class monstrosity is nearer Harold Pinter than Terence Fisher, and Ritelis's use of a typically lurid story line – obviously derived from Les Diaboliques – contrives to make his everyday horrors all the more frightening. It may look tatty and contain enough nudity and blood to satisfy the sleaze market, but The Corpse is a century closer to home than Hammer's cardboard mittel Europe. Gough also plays a monster in Horror Hospital (1973), a campy skit on the whole trash market in which he runs a rest home for young people ('Hairy Holidays – Fun in the Sun for the Under 30s') and turns them into black-leather-clad killer zombies.

Antony Balch, director of Bizarre and Horror Hospital, started out making shorts with William Burroughs and was a leading figure in sexploitation distribution. He obviously sees his films as gory larks, but some of his colleagues are capable of taking themselves too seriously. Joseph (José) Larraz, for instance, obsessively retells the same story, about murderous lesbians, in practically all his films: which range from a Cannes film festival entry (Symptoms, 1974) through a minimalist gothic horror (Vampyres, 1974) to outright sado-porn like the Spanish-made La Visita del Vicio (The Violation of the Bitch) (1978) and Los Ritos Sexuales del Diabolo (1981). More successful in its mix of sex and violence – as represented by its two opposed female stars, Fiona Richmond and Linda Hayden – is James Kenelm Clark's Exposé (1975), an eternal triangle melodrama in a miserable British rural setting, with fine portraits of repressed insanity from Hayden and Udo Kier.

Director Pete Walker and screenwriter David MacGillivray collaborated on House of Whipcord (1974), a defiantly grotty, Sadean charade about a mad judge called Old Bailey who kidnaps and tortures minor offenders he thinks the courts have let off too lightly. Mad judges, obviously a potent theme, are featured less successfully in

Night after Night after Night (1969), Walker's Die Screaming, Marianne (1973) and the American Don't Look in the Basement. In the mid-1970s, Walker became the English gothic cinema's Keeper of the Flame with a series of grim, gritty films that manage to be highly derivative and distinctively the work of their director at the same time. With MacGillivray, he made Frightmare (1974), an exceptionally nasty and depressing little movie with Sheila Keith as a cannibal little old lady who makes unpleasant use of a power drill and Rupert Davies as her long-suffering husband. One of the first British horror films to match the callousness of the American independents, Frightmare may not be Walker's best movie, but it remains his most upsetting. Later, he made House of Mortal Sin (1975), a particularly tasteless item about a homicidal priest (Anthony Sharp) who administers a poisoned communion wafer to one parishioner and batters another to death with a censer; Schizo (1976), a lady-in-peril psycho thriller in which the lady (Lynne Frederick) turns out to be the killer; and The Comeback (1977), an incredible piece of tat which somehow involves Jack Jones and Pamela Stephenson in multiple murders. Walker tends to get carried away, both by his crazed violence and his depiction of Establishment figures as evil monsters. There is a touch of Michael Reeves about his caricaturing of the legal system in Whipcord, the family in Frightmare and the Roman Catholic Church in Mortal Sin, as perfidious institutions for the repression, perversion and torture of the young by the old. He favours cold, grey, provincial settings and has a knack for getting non-stereotypical performances from his young ladies (Stephanie Beacham, Susan Penhaligon) and old hams, but has yet to make an entirely satisfactory film.

House of the Long Shadows (1983) is an unfortunate departure for Walker, a camp embarrassment. Horror superstars Vincent Price, Christopher Lee, Peter Cushing and John Carradine, plus Walker's favourite harridan, Sheila Keith, are united in an old dark house to pester an intruder (Desi Arnaz Jr) who has come to write a gothic novel in one night on a bet. Written by Michael

● *Wolfish appetite.* **The Company of Wolves.**

Armstrong and directed uneasily by Walker, *House of the Long Shadows* is as empty a project as even producers Menahem Golan and Yoram Globus could conceive, the fifth remake of *Seven Keys to Baldpate*, a property that was Old Hat before World War I. Furthermore, Walker – who throws in a few unpalatably straight bits of nastiness and then tries to take them back in the confused finale – has no background in the tradition that is supposedly being kidded. As in *The Monster Club*, which also has Price and Carradine and tries to hark back to Hammer and Amicus, and the excruciatingly awful Kenny Everett vehicle *Bloodbath at the House of Death* (1984), which just has Price, the intention seems to be to spoof the dead traditions of the British horror film, but the movie finally only manages to show how difficult it is to laugh at a corpse. Marginally more amusing is Peter Sykes's uncharacteristic *House in Nightmare Park* (1973), an odd teaming of Frankie Howerd and Ray Milland.

In the mid-1980s, British horror existed only as an underground tradition. Between Harry Bromley Davenport's *Xtro* (1982) and Clive Barker's *Hellraiser* (1987), no British horror film was given a theatrical release. Understated ghost stories like *The Appointment* (1984), which has a very nervy *Cujo* style finale with Edward Woodward trapped upside-down in a car, and *The Cold Room* (1984) crept out on video and were sold to cable in the United States. Much the same fate swallowed up the series of nonentities billed as *The Hammer House of Mystery and Suspense* (*The Sweet Scent of Death*, *A Distant Scream*, *Black Carrion*, *In Possession*, *Tennis Court*, etc.) in 1984; intended as 'amphibians' – basically television films, but with a chance for a theatrical release (like such British hits as *My Beautiful Laundrette* and *Letter to Brezhnev*) – these just ended up as instant late-night repeats. Even lower down on the quality scale are such feeble dumpbin video quickies as Norman J. Warren's come-back picture, *Bloody New Year* (1987), the pseudo-American splatter movies, *Don't Open til Christmas* (1984) and *April Fools' Day* (1985) and, the absolute rock bottom, *Suffer Little Children* (1984), a home movie shot on video at a theatre

school in Surrey with a cast of untalented children that has to be one of the cheapest, worst projects ever packaged. By contrast, Colin Finbow's *Daemon* (1986), a superficially similar production made by the well-established Children's Film Development Corporation, is nothing to be ashamed of, a well-constructed ghost story, sometimes shakily performed by its young cast.

The gothic tradition, in abeyance since the Tyburn fiasco, was meanwhile receiving some critical attention. After years of being sneered at by British critics and film historians, Hammer Films were rehabilitated. Following David Pirie's seminal study, *A Heritage of Horror*, much interest was shown in a thriving tradition that was just about dead. The usual idea that the only cinema worth having in the UK consists of a handful of short films about the Post Office, a solid collection of literary adaptions and a burst of early 1960s kitchen-sink realism was finally squelched. And, as sure as tears follow misery, *cinéastes* become industry figures and forgotten trends are revived, reassessed and revitalised. David Pirie outstandingly scripted Ben Bolt's *Rainy Day Women* (1985) for the BBC, and later collaborated with Richard Rayner, Chris Petit and Chris Wicking on Harley Cokliss's *The Dream Demon* (1987). Steve Woolley, a young exhibitor responsible for bringing *Diva* and *The Evil Dead* to Britain, put together Neil Jordan's Angela Carter adaption, *The Company of Wolves* (1984).

Rainy Day Women and *The Company of Wolves* are as much critiques of the genre as examples of it. With a seriousness of purpose and a conscious artistry that was never part of the Hammer formula, they deconstruct the cinematic past and represent it as a fractured mirror for the times. Ken Russell's ludicrous *Gothic* (1986) attempts a similar bit of literary/historical/psychological analysis in its return to the night when Byron, Shelley and Mary Godwin first decided to write ghost stories, but as shrilled by the likes of Gabriel Byrne and Julian Sands the film comes off as like nothing so much as a remake minus songs of *The Rocky Horror Picture Show*. After that, Russell turned his chainsaw to Bram Stoker's worst novel,

The Lair of the White Worm (1988) and, if nothing else, fully explores the unconscious implications of the splendid title. Still, however, the period gothic was unacceptable at the box office, despite the success of David Lynch's *The Elephant Man* (1980), another movie deeply informed by the incidentals of Hammer. The retreat of the tradition to television can also be noticed by comparing the success of several TV Sherlock Holmes projects – most importantly the Granada series with Jeremy Brett – with the failure of Barry Levinson's Steven Spielberg-backed *Young Sherlock Holmes* (1986). At least in the cinema, Victorian values are out of fashion.

If there is to be a future for the British horror film, it may well rest with Clive Barker, who first came to prominence as the author of six ground-breaking volumes of short stories, *The Books of Blood* and proceeded to write weighty, genre-stretching novels like *The Damnation Game* and *Weaveworld*. Barker provided scripts for two low-budget features, *Underworld* (1985) and *Rawhead Rex* (1986), directed by rock video specialist George Pavlou. Despite good casts, these are only fitfully interesting pictures, too intent on posy imagery to develop any narrative drive. Without really being imitative (although *Rawhead* does borrow from *Blood on Satan's Claw*) the films seem second hand. With *Hellraiser*, his next script, Barker promoted himself to director and set out to make an intelligently scary film. A degenerate adventurer summons up a species of demons called Cenobites by solving a puzzle-box, and is torn to pieces for his pains. Spilled blood brings some of him back to life, and it falls to his sister-in-law/mistress (Clare Higgins) to provide more, by luring men to the family's old dark house and killing them with a hammer. *Hellraiser* is slightly compromised by its American backers' insistence that most of the minor characters be redubbed with Transatlantic voices that sit ill with the distinctive London locations, and it both gains and suffers from Barker's usual lopsided plotting. But it does have the Cenobites – who boast such unsettling features as sewn-shut eyelids behind

dark glasses, a throat wound held open by a collar of surgical clamps and geometric traceries of pins hammered into a face – and an unusual, committed vision of the Pit. If there is such a thing as a British horror film for the 1980s, *Hellraiser* is it.

The film's influence was almost immediately obvious in *Dream Demon,* which less effectively prowls the studio corridors of Hell than its precursor, and in Tony Randel's direct follow-up, *Hellbound: Hellraiser 2* (1988), which makes something of a hash of an already limping storyline. Barker contributed an original story for the sequel and a projected third installment, *Hell on Earth,* but departed the series to set up his own *The Night Breed* (1989), co-starring Suzi Quatro and David Cronenberg. Bernard Rose's *Paperhouse* (1988), based on Catherine Starr's chldren's book *Marianna Dreams,* absorbs the atmosphere lessons of Barker's film, while cannily creeping away, as *Dream Demon* and *Hellbound* do not, from the claptrap side of the genre. It's an all-out fright film, more true to the dream theme than the *Nightmare on Elm Street* movies, and also an unusually persuasive and affecting vision of British childhood. Anna (Charlotte Burke), a vaguely unhappy eleven-year-old, is confined to bed by glandular fever. She passes the time by making a drawing of a house, and – in her dreams – finds herself in the weird landscape she has created. However, she's not a very talented artist, and the things and people she draws don't often come out true to life. When she draws in her often-absent father (Ben Cross), she makes him look angry, and he becomes a looming threat. Burke's Anna is initially as infuriating and feckless as all children can be, but grows into a heroine of real maturity. First-time director Rose does a startlingly good job with the psychologically astute twinning of father and monster in his presentation of Cross as a shadow-faced maniac. *Paperhouse* exists at the boundaries of its genre – it peaks as a scary movie half an hour before the end, then switches powerfully to emotional horror – and points the way, even more than the mid-Atlantic *Hellraiser,* to a possible future renaissance of this weird tradition.

the changing face of classical gothic

the changing face of classical gothic

The British horror film perished because of its inability to adapt to a 1970s world beyond Home Counties Transylvania, but the gothic strain in Hollywood was hardier. In the 1950s and 1960s, drive-in dreadfuls like *I Was a Teenage Werewolf* and *The Ghost of Dragstrip Hollow* and TV sit-coms like *The Munsters* and *The Addams Family* mined the vein of black comedy opened up by EC horror comics. Vampires and werewolves appeared regularly in the Crypt Keeper's *contes cruelles*, but they were never taken seriously. Amicus's *The Vault of Horror* includes an unfortunately solemn adaption of one of EC's best jokes, 'Midnight Mess'. In the original, the hero comes across an out-of-the-way restaurant that caters exclusively to the vampire trade. He gets a tap stuck in his neck, and is decanted for the benefit of undead gourmets. 'Nothin' like the REAL STUFF!' chortles an appreciative customer (heh heh heh).

Such irreverence was common in post-*Night of the Living Dead* California gothic. 'Where are your fangs?' asks a drunk of a caped aristocrat. 'Where are your manners?' replies the waspish vampire (Robert Quarry) in *The Return of Count Yorga* (1971). This Count may look like an old world monster, but he is hip to the California of gurus and self-realisation therapies. Introduced in *Count Yorga – Vampire* (1970), he is quick with the snappy put-down, self-deprecating enough to watch *The Vampire Lovers* on television and liable to turn ferocious when his castle is invaded.

Directed by Bob Kelljan, these are low-budget films, audaciously hit-or-miss in their combination of sick humour and sicker horror. They use ideas from *Night of the Living Dead* to shock their audiences out of the mood established by wisecracks about the absurdity of a vampire on Sunset Strip. In *Count Yorga – Vampire*, the hero comes home from the office and catches his half-vampired wife red-mouthed, chewing on the lasagna intestines of their cat. More obviously indebted to the Living Dead are Yorga's vampire brides, ashen-faced, picket-fence-fanged horrors with none of Carmilla's supernatural sensuality.

The Count Yorga films, with their off-the-cuff gags, lashings of grue, flip/cynical evil-lives-on endings and sneaking admiration for the monsters, sparked off a minor trend. William Crain's *Blacula* (1972) has William Marshall as an African prince who makes the mistake of asking Count Dracula to sign a petition against the slave trade. Centuries later, he is revived in a disorientating Los Angeles of gay antique dealers, lady cab drivers, soul music and young bloods with mirror shades. Unable to face all this, Blacula exposes himself to the rising sun and melts away into a crawling pile of maggots. He comes back in *Scream, Blacula, Scream* (1972), in which a narcissist stud-turned-vampire is infuriated when he learns that he can no longer parade his trendy threads in front of the mirror. Bob Kelljan, imported from the Yorga films to add some energy to Blacula's second

(1972). From Germany came such humourless sex comedies as *Beiss Mich, Liebling (Bite Me, Darling)* (1970), *Gebissen wird nur Nachts – Happening der Vampire (The Vampire Happening)* (1971) – directed by a slumming Freddie Francis and featuring Ferdy Mayne of *Dance of the Vampires* as a Dracula who hilariously loses his trousers in a climactic orgy – and *Graf Dracula Beisst Jetz in Oberbayern (Dracula Blows His Cool)* (1979).

The leading European figures in the field, however, are the Spaniard Jesus Franco and the French Jean Rollin. Franco's contributions include the Spanish–German *Vampyros Lesbos – Die Erbin des Dracula (Lesbian Vampires)* (1970), the Spanish–French–Portuguese *La Hija de Dracula (Daughter of Dracula)* (1972) and the Belgian–French *La Comtesse aux seins nus (The Bare-Breasted Countess)* (1975). His films are slipshod affairs, enlivened by a handful (a *small* handful) of arty/surreal moments and the pretty faces of his often-naked *ingénues* Britt Nichols, Soledad Miranda, Maria Rohm, Anne Libert and Lina Romay. Rollin, however, while capable of making films just as bad as Franco's, and also as willing to stray into hardcore or cheap rip-offs, is actually a sort of artist. His vampire series includes *Le Viol du Vampire (Vampire Women)* (1967), *La Vampire nue (The Naked Vampire)* (1969), *Le Frisson des Vampires (Sex and the Vampire)* (1970), and *Vierges et Vampires (Requiem pour un Vampire)* (1971). His qualified masterpiece is *Lèvres de sang* (1975), a virtually plotless ramble about a young man who falls in love with a vampirette. Its astonishing imagery includes the weirdly touching sequence in which two vampire girls, impaled on the same stake by a gang of bluff French vigilantes, hug each other for comfort as they die, and the strange moment as the hero joins his lady-love in a coffin on the seashore to be washed away by the tide.

Caught between the Hollywood self-consciousness of Count Yorga and the delirious silliness of Rollin's naked vampires are the imitation Hammer (even imitation Universal) gothics that other parts of the world continued to make well into the 1970s. From Spain came a whole flood of Latino monsters, mostly with Paul Naschy trying to play as many horror roles as Lon Chaney Jr had done: Dracula in *El Gran Amor del Conde Dracula* (1972), a bandaged mummy in *La Venganza de la Momia (Vengeance of the Mummy)* (1973), a hunchbacked bodysnatcher in *El Jorobado de la Morgue (The Hunchback of the Morgue)* (1972), Jack the Ripper in *Jack, el Destripador de Londres* (1971), and Waldemar the Werewolf in a series of films from *La Marca del Hombre Lobo (Hells' Creatures)* (1967) to *La Bestia y la Espada Magica* (1983). A rare non-Naschy Spanish gothic is Leon Klimovsky's *La Saga de los Draculas (The Dracula Saga)* (1972), the broody *Rosemary's Baby*-ish tale of the Count's search for an heir. From the Philippines came *Dugong Vampira (Creatures of Evil)* (1970), a twisted Catholic soap opera with strange-looking South Seas bloodsuckers and a succession of mad scientist or monster movies invariably starring John Ashley with Vic Diaz in support. And from Staten Island came *Blood* (1974), with the Wolf Man's son and Dracula's daughter settling down in 1890s New York, the last of a succession of Andy Milligan's grotty, neo-porno vampire epics. Between them, these films sucked the gothic mode drier than their vampires did their victims.

George A. Romero's *Martin* (1977) is the most thoroughgoing, sophisticated re-examination of the vampire figure yet attempted. Outwardly a retarded teenager, Martin (John Amplas) claims to be 84, but his kindly niece (Christine Forrest) and the audience can't tell if he's being serious. He dreams of a black-and-white 1920s in the Old Country, where a beautiful victim welcomes him as her lover. But in modern Pittsburgh the potential blood donors plaster their faces with mud and Martin is less fearsome than the cops and junkies into whose shoot-out he blunders. Like Count Yorga, Martin has tried to adapt (his night-time prowls are assisted by hypodermic needles, safety razor blades and remote control gadgetry), but he cannot cope with human beings. He assumes a housewife who has seen her husband off on a business trip will be an easy kill, but is outraged and frustrated when he finds her with another man. Martin pours out his problems to a late-night radio phone-in, but all he gets is a patronising nick-name, 'The Count'.

Romero's Savant is Tati Cuda (Lincoln Maazel), Martin's cousin, a green-grocer who screeches 'nosferatu' a lot and waves crucifixes and garlic at the Monster. Cuda takes the shame of his family into the house with a promise to destroy him if he kills anyone from the town. One night, Martin waylays Cuda, frightening him with a Count Yorga costume. He spits out the plastic fangs, wipes off the grease-paint, shucks the cloak and bites into a clove of garlic. As Martin says, 'there's no real magic'. *Martin* is Romero's most deeply felt film and John Amplas gives the most successfully realised, non-comic book performance of his work. This vampire is a psychotic innocent, out of place in a horribly decaying neighbourhood. The resolution is traditional, but tinged with Romero's habitual irony. Martin is about to conquer his obsession through a normal love affair with a neurotic housewife. Depressed beyond his power to comfort her, she slits her wrists. Cuda, thinking Martin is the murderer, drives a stake through his heart. Martin is buried in the back garden and his grave is seeded with grass. After the credits have rolled and the cinema is empty of all but the most devoted movie purists, the sound montage of the all-night radio show ends with a nervous voice. 'I've got this friend . . . who I think might be The Count.'

Commercially, the gothic mode has been dead since *The Exorcist*; artistically, it's been superfluous since *Martin*; but that hasn't stopped film-makers from trying to turn back the waves. *Dracula* (1979), *Nosferatu – Phantom der Nacht* (*Nosferatu the Vampyre*) (1979), *The Awakening* (1980) and *The Bride* (1985) are all second-hand adaptions of gothic originals: *Dracula* is from the 1927 play which had already been filmed with Bela Lugosi; *Nosferatu* is an exact remake of the 1922 classic; *The Awakening* is based on *The Jewel of Seven Stars* – the Bram Stoker novel that had already been made into *Blood from the Mummy's Tomb* – and *The Bride* is a Frankenstein movie derived not from Mary Shelley's novel but from Whale's *The Bride of Frankenstein* (1935). These all suffer from a severe lack of trash vitality.

Since *Night of the Living Dead*, the horror film has been irreverent but alive, but with their prestige directors, big-name stars, beautiful photography, classy music and zombie pace, these movies are as embalmed as the row of mummies Werner Herzog puts under the credits of *Nosferatu*. John Badham's *Dracula* has hints of real horror, but they are swamped by sado-erotic slush as the victims eagerly welcome the slimy advances of Frank Langella's Don Juan vampire. *Nosferatu* is achingly beautiful, but arch. Klaus Kinski's ratty Dracula and Isabelle Adjani's pre-Raphaelite heroine are impressive portraits, but as frozen as paint on canvas.

Mike Newell's *The Awakening*, with Charlton Heston, Susannah York, Stephanie Zimbalist and a crass series of *Omen*-styled freak deaths, is less transcendental, but equally boring: it did not lead to a revival of the most despised of all sub-genres, the mummy movie: witness the obscurity of *Dawn of the Mummy* (1981), a zombie film in badages; *Time Walker* (1982), which features a ludicrous mummy from outer space (!?); and *The Tomb* (1985), with an Egyptian vampire queen on the loose. Franc Roddam's *The Bride* is another disaster, with memorably embarrassed and embarrassing performances from Sting as Dr F., Jennifer Beals as his latest creation and David Rappaport as an unbearably bumptious dwarf. These films resurrect the trappings of the Hammer style, but not its morality. Handsome Langella and repulsive Kinski may die at the end, but they both get the girl. Savants are defeated – Badham's Van Helsing (Laurence Olivier) is impaled on his own stake, Herzog's is dragged off to jail, Charlton Heston's Egyptologist unwittingly helps an ancient sorceress possess his daughter, and Sting is pushed out of the picture when his retarded first creation (Clancy Brown) wins the vacuous Beals away from his lecherous attentions.

In 1977, BBC-TV mounted Philip Saville's careful, elaborate production *Count Dracula*. Louis Jourdan's vampire, Frank Finlay's Dr Van Helsing and Judi Bowker's Victorian Miss are the authentic article, and the adaption outclasses its big-budget rivals simply because it approaches Stoker on his

● *Teen Queen.* Amanda Bearse, **Fright Night.**

the granite corridors of this Keep? Yourself?' *The Keep*, which guts its fine source novel , is a dreamlike, confusing film that makes little narrative sense, and yet it has a direct potency that increases with each viewing. Like a recurring dream, it's more unsettling the second or third time around. It is at once a penetrating examination of the roots of the horror tradition, and a film that exists outside its genre.

Meanwhile, removed from the English-language mainstream, the Chinese gothic cinema produced a horror cycle as vital and distinctive as anything from Britain, America or Italy. It would take a dedicated sinophile film historian to provide a definitive study of Hong Kong horror, but it should be acknowledged that films like Tsui Hark's *The Butterfly Murders* (1979), *We Are Going to Eat You* (1980) and *Zu: Warriors From Magic Mountain* (1983), Ann Hui's *The Spooky Bunch* (1980), Wu Ma's *The Dead and the Deadly*, Gui Zhihong's *Boxer's Omen* (1983), Ronny Yu's *The Trail* (1983), Hsu Hsia's *Ghosts Galore* (1983), Lau Kun Wai's *Mr Vampire* (1986) and Ching Siu Tung's *Witch From Nepal* (1986) and *A Chinese Ghost Story* (1987) have a unique feel. Sino-horror mixes familiar famous monsters with traditional Buddhist themes, and frequently adopts a disorientating mix of knockabout comedy and deliberately unreal action. Usually set, like the Hammer and Universal films, in a non-specific past, these films feature hopping zombies, kungfu-kicking priests who can halt a monster in its tracks by pasting prayers to its forehead, comical young heroes who fall in love with oversexed ghost girls, haunted Chinese opera companies, scheming evil spirits manifested as animated giant red blankets or blood-drinking trees, battling master magicians, and literal hordes of ghosts and vampires who look like Christopher Lee trying to play Dracula, Fu Manchu and the Mummy at the same time. Compared with the fantasy action highlights of *Zu* or *Witch From Nepal*, such Western equivalents as *Krull* or *Highlander* look very small beer. John Carpenter's *Big Trouble in Little China* (1986) is an honest but ill-fated attempt to translate the tone of Chinese horror into a post-Indiana Jones Hollywood genre.

Following the early 1980s revival of the werewolf movie, which had a lot to do with the fact that special effects technology had at last advanced to the point where convincing man-into-monster transformations could be depicted, it was inevitable that the vampire would receive similar treatment. Tom Holland's *Fright Night* (1985) should do for vampires what *The Howling* does for werewolves, but gets side-tracked and emerges as a Count Yorga movie jazzed up with some admittedly astonishing transformation effects and an unhelpful dose of high-school comedy. If bloodsucking swinger Jerry Dandridge (Chris Sarandon) didn't move into the neighbourhood, the characters of *Fright Night* would be living in a John Hughes film. Dandridge is even slicker than Yorga, in that he blithely whistles 'Strangers in the Night' as he prowls, and is smart enough to baffle would-be Van Helsings by locking his coffin *from the inside*. But the good guys are just clowns – a weird teenage hero in a sports jacket who, in a vestigial gay sub-text, is more interested in the handsome man next door than his girlfriend, and Roddy McDowell as hammy old actor Peter Vincent, who is recruited to play in real life the Van Helsing role he has overdone so many times in the movies.

A similarly uncertain mix of comedy and horror is exhibited in Richard Wenk's *Vamp* (1986) and Joel Schumaker's *The Lost Boys* (1987), while negligible items like *Once Bitten (1985), I Married a Vampire* (1986) and *I was a Teenage Vampire* (1987) are outright comedies. Of this group, *Vamp* is the most interesting, despite its heavy dollops of nerd-style college humour. Like *The Howling*, it works out how monsters can dovetail with human society. Vampire Queen Grace Jones and her entourage run a strip club, to which the lonely dregs of humanity are attracted, on the assumption that people who go to places like that are hardly likely to be missed. Jones's wordless exotic is sexy and scary, whether performing a surrealist strip routine or ripping out an errant minion's heart, and Wenk makes the most of the tattily colourful setting. Fred Dekker's *The Monster Squad* (1987), an expensive production thrown away by its distributors, is a wholly charming homage to the great days of Universal and Hammer, with a team of genuinely ingratiating kids taking on Count Dracula (Duncan Regehr) and an entourage that includes a wolf man, a mummy, the Frankenstein Monster (Tom Noonan), a *Creature from the Black Lagoon*-styled gill man and a bevy of shrouded lady vampires. Rather than update the classic themes, Dekker waxes nostalgic about the days when such monster rallies were common and stages several big action climaxes in the way Universal would have done if they'd had the money and effects resources back in the 1940s – the Mummy gets a bandage pulled and unravels like an old cardigan, a blown-apart werewolf reforms and Dracula walks down a small town main street bending uniformed cops into strange shapes.

Meanwhile, there was a tentative rekindling of the more straight-faced vampire movie. The dreary *Vampire at Midnight* (1987), with its bald EST bloodsucker, only gets away with being serious by having the killer turn out to be a psycho who just thinks he's a vampire. A more fruitful approach is taken by a pair of low-budget, high-energy thrillers, Gerard Ciccoritti's *Graveyard Shift* (1986) and Kathryn Bigelow's *Near Dark* (1987). Ciccoritti's vampire hero (Silvio Oliviero) is a 350-year-old all-night cab driver in the big city, undone by his soft-heartedness when he wants to betray his coven-like harem of previous victims and settle down with a suicidal lady film director (amusingly, of mock gothic rock videos). Oliviero reclines nude in his coffin as if it were a bath and is cursed by much the same existential problems as the immortals played by Scott Glenn in *The Keep* and Christopher Lambert in *Highlander* – everyone around him seems to be living at triple speed, while he's caught in a cyclical, slow-motion nightmare. In *Near Dark*, pony-tailed American Civil War veteran Lance Henriksen and his group of po' white trash vampires drift around the mid-West, terrorising redneck bars – cocky cowboy killer Bill Paxton uses sharpened silver spurs on his victims' necks and then tucks in sloppily with a smirking 'it's finger-lickin' good' – and failing to get even a foothold in the human world. Even after hundreds of years, these vampires haven't managed to find a secure place to hole up and are continually racing with the dawn to find a motel before they are incinerated by daylight.

By contrast, Larry Cohen's *A Return to Salem's Lot* (1987) – a comedy, but by no means a nerd one – deals with a well-established community of bedrock conservative vampires in New England. Following *The Black Room* and *Near Dark* (in which Paxton pauses over the throat of a male victim and whines, 'I hate it when they ain't been shaved'), Cohen's vampires are disgusted by humanity. They take it to the point where, except on special occasions, they drink only the blood of cows, because farm animals don't mainline heroin or transmit AIDS. Having escaped persecution in Europe by coming over with the Pilgrim Fathers, the citizens of Salem's Lot – played by such respectable stalwarts as Andrew Duggan, Evelyn Keyes and June Havoc – now live a cosy Thornton Wilder life. A little old lady who can't give up human blood complains of her 'drinking problem', and hero Michael Moriarty's son sums up the insidious, banal evil of Cohen's vampires with 'this town *sucks*!' After allowing his vampires to present a plausible case, Cohen brings on aged Nazi-hunter Sam Fuller to restore the moral balance and, in a screen first, has his king vampire impaled on the American flag.

devil movies

or: 'If the mousse tastes chalky, don't eat it'

As far as God goes, I'm a nonbeliever . . . But when it comes to the Devil – well, that's something else . . . You come to God and you have to figure if there is one, then he must need a million years' sleep every night or else he tends to get irritable. Know what I mean? He never talks. But the Devil keeps advertising, Father. The Devil does lots of commercials.

William Peter Blatty, *The Exorcist*

Devil movies are less a sub-genre than a phenomenon. A phenomenon movie is merely the most visible part of a merchandising machine that claws in profits from subsidiary items like the Book, the Poster, the T-shirt, the Soundtrack Album, the Badge and the Pop-Up Toaster. The machine arouses public interest in a particular subject, whether it be the mafia, sharks, outer space or the Devil. Publications from *Time* to the tabloids do cover stories. We are subjected to endless metaphorical sermonising on talk shows, and, frequently, actual sermonising from pulpits. There is also an inevitable flood of imitative, cash-in movies. *Rosemary's Baby* (1968) fortuitously coincided with the 'Is God Dead?' controversy and was thus as much discussed in terms of its religious (or anti-religious) content as for its cinematic virtues. *The Exorcist* (1973) was a bigger success and a bigger phenomenon. It was the Devil's Big Break.

The flurry of *Reader's Digest* theology that surrounded the *Exorcist* explosion would have you believe that William Peter Blatty and William Friedkin discovered the Devil drinking a fire and brimstone soda at the counter of Schwab's Drug Store and made him into a movie star. Actually, His Satanic Majesty had always been around Hollywood, doing character roles and the occasional guest spot on *The Twilight Zone*. Once, he had nearly made the grade as a tragic hero, but although D.W. Griffith used a potted *Paradise Lost* to preface *The Sorrows of Satan* (1925), most movie moguls were unimpressed by Milton. They found it easier to relate to a distinguished career in the legitimate theatre, which, despite the worst efforts of John Barrymore and Richard Burton, was believed to bestow respectability on the gutter art of the cinema. Therefore, most of the Devil's early films found him as the George Sanders type Shaw had written for *Don Juan in Hell*. Sanders didn't get around to the part until *Psychomania* in 1971, but Laird Cregar (*Heaven Can Wait*, 1943), Claude Rains (*Angel on My Shoulder*, 1946) and Vincent Price (*The Story of Mankind*, 1957) were acceptably cultivated, caddish substitutes. Even the more sinister appearances of Walter Huston as the crackerbarrel Mr Scratch in *All That Money Can Buy* (1941) and Ray Milland as the slouch-hatted Satan in *Alias Nick Beal* (1949) had no more religious significance than Edmund Gwenn as Santa Claus in *Miracle on 34th Street* (1947).

● *Blind faith.* John Carradine, **The Sentinel.**

The Devil's screen time in *Rosemary's Baby* is minimal. He has a cameo in the nightmare impregnation sequence, played by John Cassavetes in Richard III make-up. His son, Adrian the Antichrist, is mostly a cushion strapped under Mia Farrow's maternity dress, although he has a showy, golden-eyed scene at the end. In *The Exorcist* there is some question as to the identity of the Mercedes McCambridge-voiced fiend inhabiting sweet teenage Linda Blair. He/she/it claims to be the Devil, but Father Merrin (Max Von Sydow) and William Peter Blatty take the view that the culprit is really Pazuzu, an Assyrian wind demon with a hefty grudge against the priest. Despite the smallness of his roles, the Devil got all the reviews, and with an unscrupulousness worthy of Guy Woodhouse, hyped himself into a major screen career. Despite Blatty's claim that his story is based on Actual Documented Facts and that it has an Important Theme in Father Karras's crisis of faith, *The Exorcist*, as book and film, is a shocker laced with Rod Serling-style intense characterisations and commercially calculated grossness. To his credit, Ira Levin admits that the demonology in *Rosemary's Baby* is secondary to the Big Scary Idea – that the heroine is pregnant with the Monster. Lapsed Catholicism and chic witchcraft are vital to the atmosphere, but the mechanics of horror would work without these elements. —*And Now the Screaming Starts!* and *It's Alive!* use the same Big Scary Idea, but dress it with an ancestral curse or a science-fictional bug-eyed monster.

Rosemary's Baby and *The Exorcist* use one of the oldest Big Scary Ideas in the *Necronomicon*: the Monster wants your body. Dracula wants the use of your blood, the Antichrist wants the use of your womb. The curse of the werewolf can turn you into the Monster, possession by Pazuzu can turn you into the Monster. Roman Polanski's *Rosemary's Baby* is the less conventional film, although since 1968 its paranoid world view has become a horror movie commonplace. The film kills off its Savant (Maurice Evans) before he can do any good, and allows the witches an ambiguous victory. However, beneath its contemporary setting

and yecch factor, *The Exorcist* is a cosy Hammer film. It has a monster in Pazuzu, a corrupted innocent in young Regan and an all-conquering savant in the Holy Catholic Church.

In its soul, *Rosemary's Baby* is deeply paranoid. Like *Kiss Me Deadly* and *Invasion of the Body Snatchers*, it only appears to be set in the everyday world. Once the veneer of normality has peeled, the central characters are trapped in a vast nightmare parallel where intellects vast, cool and unsympathetic are out to get them. In *Kiss Me Deadly*, Mike Hammer (Ralph Meeker) uncovers a plot by 'the Mysterious They, who'll do anything for the sake of the Great Whatsit'. Being a 1950s private eye, Hammer is worrying about an axis between organised crime and the godless commie rats, but the 'Mysterious They' can as easily be seed-pods from outer space or a Manhattan coven. Who the 'Mysterious They' are doesn't matter; what does is that 'They' look like us and that 'They' are out to get you. In paranoia movies, the Monster is a half-humorous stand-in for a formless sense of unease, somewhere between Sartre's nausea and Hunter S. Thompson's fear and loathing. Levin and Polanski fuel the paranoia with a feminist rethinking of the traditionally vulnerable heroine role. Like the Katharine Ross character in *The Stepford Wives* (1976), also from a Levin novel, Rosemary Woodhouse is specifically a wife betrayed by her husband. Mia Farrow is leased as a baby machine to the Devil, and Ross is replaced by a compliant Disneyland automaton, but the exact nature of the betrayal is unimportant. It's the fact that the men whose lives they share find them expendable that hurts. Rosemary is also sacrificed by her chatty neighbours and fatherly obstretician. The only person to whom she can turn is the Antichrist, supposedly the focus of the conspiracy. The delicately played final scene, underscored by Christopher Komeda's shivery lullaby, has Rosemary accepting her baby in the frail hope that its evil can be perverted.

Rosemary's Baby added expectant motherhood to the stock horror themes. *The Devil's Daughter* (1973) and *Good Against Evil* (1977) are made-for-TV cut-downs on the story, as is the indifferent

Look What's Happened to Rosemary's Baby (1976). The Manitou (1978) has a 400-year-old medicineman developing as a foetus on Susan Strasberg's neck. This kind of unnatural pregnancy is now more common in sf than horror, following the eruption from John Hurt's chest of the hungry Alien. Rosemary's Baby's main influence, however, was to give the 'Mysterious They' a decidedly Satanic cast. In 1954, Spencer Tracy stopped off in an unfriendly little town in Bad Day at Black Rock and nosed into its horrible secret. He uncovered a lynching, but his 1970s counterparts were more likely to wander into communities dominated by witch cults and end up on the sacrificial altar, as in The Witchmaker (1969), Brotherhood of Satan (1971), Daughters of Satan (1972), Necromancy (1972), Legacy of Satan (1973), Warlock Moon (1974), Race With the Devil (1975), Satan's Cheerleaders (1976) and Bay Coven (1987).

In this group, Robin Hardy's The Wicker Man (1972) stands out: rather than the usual robed rednecks, it has an interestingly detailed pagan sect on a Scots isle. They sing 'Sumer Is Icumen In' as Edward Woodward burns to bless the crops. The Wicker Man has been much (over)acclaimed but not influential, although the same sort of beliefs are toyed with in The Sailor Who Fell From Grace With the Sea (1976), The Dark Secret of Harvest Home (1978) and Children of the Corn (1984). The wildest of the robed redneck movies is Robert Fuest's The Devil's Rain (1975), in which Ernest Borgnine, a former resident of Black Rock, hides his goat horns under a cowboy hat and leads an unholy congregation that includes William Shatner, Ida Lupino, Keenan Wynn and John Travolta. Savant Eddie Albert hurls their spells back at them, and they dissolve into piles of sizzling goo. Fuest's stylish excess nearly works for The Devil's Rain, but The Devil's Men (1977), a Greek remake with Donald Pleasence and Peter Cushing, is a ponderous bore. Instead of melting, the cultist villains merely explode. In a pretentious but compelling variant on the theme, Tonino Cervi's Il Delitto del Diavolo (Queens of Evil) (1971) has a hippie motorcyclist seduced into joining the woodland idyll of witch succubi Haydee Politoff,

Silvia Monti and Ida Galli and finally torn apart by them for his willingness to be corrupted. The message is silly, but the film has one of the few appealing visions of a devilish lifestyle, as the elaborately coiffured and dressed demon women lounge around in rooms decorated with huge photographs of themselves and tuck into creamy layer cakes for breakfast.

Fritz Leiber's much-filmed novel Conjure Wife sets its witchcraft in a college, neatly exposing the natural paranoid feel of an enclosed institution. The gimmick is borrowed by Child's Play (1972), Satan's School for Girls (1973), The Possessed (1977) and The Initiation of Sarah (1978). A minor classic in this field, Paul Wendkos's The Brotherhood of the Bell (1970) has America secretly manipulated by an obscure fraternity house. Initiates of the Bell mysteriously get rich and successful and are then called upon to pay their dues with a small favour. When Professor Glenn Ford is required to drive a valued friend to suicide, he rebels and tries to expose the society's machinations. The Mysterious They pull his whole life apart. In a particularly unnerving sequence, Ford appears on a network talk show to blow the Bell's cover, only to have fatly genial host William Conrad turn on him and make him seem like an hysterical cuckoo. Wendkos's The Mephisto Waltz (1971) develops the theme with diabolic subtlety. After his own death, strong-willed Satanist Curt Jurgens possesses the body of bland nobody Alan Alda and sets about reconstructing his former life. For Wendkos, the fabric of society, even of personal identity, is vulnerable to omnipotent, incomprehensible forces. Like Larry Cohen, Wendkos cut his paranoid teeth on the TV series The Invaders; his television output includes Fear No Evil (1969), The Haunts of the Very Rich (1972) and The Legend of Lizzie Borden (1975), all of which contain moments of chilliness unusual in the medium. However, the promisingly titled Good Against Evil is a thoroughly routine job and he has recently concentrated on achingly ordinary TV movies, mini-series and episodes. Perhaps The Bell got to him.

With movie witchcraft comfortably accommodated in the up-to-the-minute worlds of Rosemary's

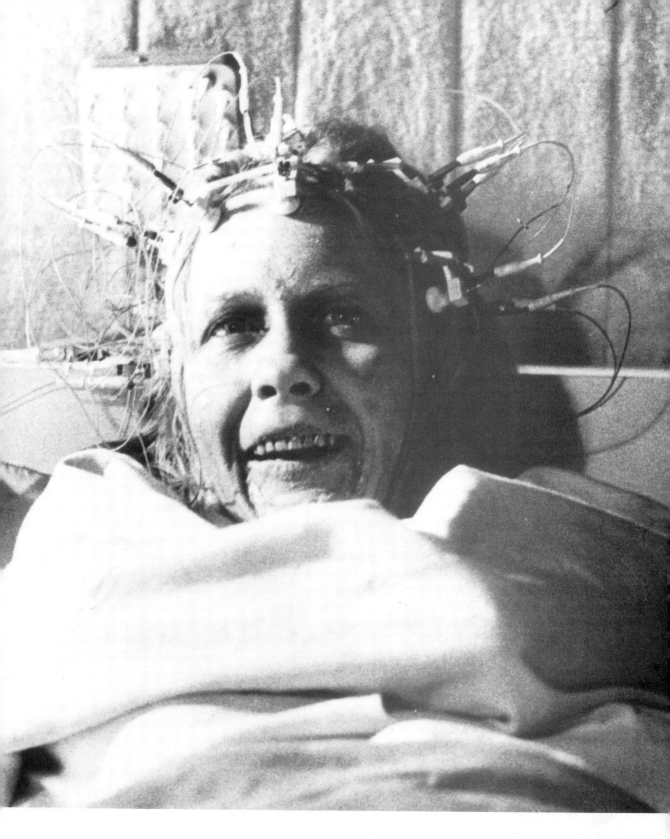

● *Possession: the scientific approach.* Juliet Mills, **Chi sei?**

Baby and The Mephisto Waltz, traditional devilry became rare. In Evilspeak (1981), the Devil is summoned by computer, while Trick or Treat (1986) and The Gate (1987) opt for playing Heavy Metal records backwards. The earthy, evocative Blood on Satan's Claw is a throwback exception, but its idea of historical horror was overshadowed by Matthew Hopkins – Witchfinder General. Michael Reeves's bloodbath was followed by Jesus Franco's El Proceso de las Brujas (Night of the Blood Monster) (1969) and Os Demonios (The Demons) (1971), Michael Armstrong's Brenn, Hexe, Brenn (Mark of the Devil) (1970), Adrian Hoven's Hexen: Geschandet und zu Tode Gequält (Mark of the Devil Part 2) (1972) and Paul Naschy's Inquisición (1976). Here, supposed witches are innocents nastily tortured by state-approved witch hunters. The role reversal is emphasised by the casting of monster icons Vincent Price, Herbert Lom, Christopher Lee, Howard Vernon, Anton Diffring and Naschy as the persecutors. Even Ken Russell takes Michael Gothard from Scream and Scream Again to play the Inquisitor in his meretricious The Devils (1971). In 1972, Roman Polanski restructured Macbeth as Rosemary's Baby for the Dark Ages. Like Rosemary, Jon Finch's thane is duped by Devil worshippers into serving the purposes of Evil and is betrayed by spouse, allies and faith. Otherwise, if period movie witches are genuine, they tend to get burned before the credits while the actors look shifty in wigs and tall hats, then spend the rest of the film slaughtering the modern descendents of their enemies, as in Mark of the Witch (1972), Superstition (1982), The Devonsville Terror (1983), The Demons of Ludlow (1983) and Necropolis (1987).

George A. Romero's Jack's Wife (1973) inverts the theme of Rosemary's Baby by presenting witchcraft as an avenue of escape for its housewife heroine. Made after the failure of There's Always Vanilla (1972), a romantic comedy, the film is not quite able to mix disenchanted social realism with horror film rituals as successfully as Martin would do. With cliché displays of histrionics, self-revealing monologues and lines like 'I thought insensitivity was "in"', the personal drama seems more stylised than the black magic scenes. But when Joan (Jan White), Jack's wife, visits her local coven, Romero's sly humour asserts itself. Marion (Virginia Greenwald), a charming witch, defends her faith with a tact that makes a Satanic rite sound like a Tupperware party and Joan pays for the arcane impedimenta she needs to summon demons with her Master Charge card. In a blackly feminist finale, Joan becomes fully independent by killing Jack and becoming a full member of the coven. One can imagine some black equivalent of The Watchtower printing her story as 'How Necromancy and Murder Helped Me Through My Mid-Life Crisis'.

After The Texas Chainsaw Massacre, Shivers, Dawn of the Dead and commercially available videotapes of Elvis's autopsy, it seems incredible that in 1973, everyone got worked up about Linda Blair cursing, upchucking green mud and masturbating with a crucifix in The Exorcist. Of course, it was the crucifix that did it. The cucumber in Thundercrack! is tasteless exploitation; in The Exorcist the image of Christ makes the act sacrilege. Although mild beside Thundercrack!, the masturbation scene is the key to The Exorcist. It attracted the attention of a huge audience of sensation-seekers and amateur theologists who would have given Werewolves on Wheels a miss. Once hooked, they were given the traditional uplift. The messages of the Hammer films had become wearisome platitudes, so the upbeat perversity of Dance of the Vampires and Count Yorga – Vampire was exhilarating rather than depressing. Although The Exorcist may have been touted as blasphemous, its finale is a return to moralising waffle. Father Merrin, the Savant, dies nobly, passing his God-given task to an assistant, Father Karras (Jason Miller). Karras, the Doubting Priest, has an upsurge of faith that enables him to overcome Pazuzu with an act of supreme self-sacrifice. Innocence is saved, and a nice paradox has Karras regaining Heaven through suicide, taking the demon into himself and jumping out of the window.

The Exorcist remains the highest grossing supernatural horror film of all time. Despite its success, it's a cinematic dead-end. Immediately after its release there were hordes of interchangeable, cheap imitations: *Abby*, *The Angel Above and the Devil Below* (1974), *The Premonition* (1975), *I Don't Want to Be Born* and *Nurse Sherri* (1977) from the civilised world; and *Antechristo* (*The Antichrist*) (1974), *Chi sei?* (*Beyond the Door*) (1974), *La Endemoniada* (*Demon Witch Child*) (1974), *Exorcismo* (*Exorcism*) (1974), *Il Medaglione insanguinato* (*The Night Child*) (1974), *L'Ossessa* (*The Sexorcist*) (1974), *Un Urlo dalle tenebre* (*Naked Exorcism*) (1975) and *Il Altro inferno* (*The Other Hell*) (1981) from Italy and Spain. None of these films elaborates on the original in the fruitful way that *Shivers*, *Let's Scare Jessica to Death* or *Assault on Precinct 13* expand on the ideas of *Night of the Living Dead*. Big-budget *Exorcist* followers, including *The Manitou*, *The Omen* and *The Sentinel* (1977) find so little worth stealing from Friedkin's film that they return to *Rosemary's Baby* and pilfer its plot instead. *The Exorcist* sub-genre burned out instantly. Recently, only *Amityville II: The Possession* and *Mausoleum* (1982) have bothered to lift any of its trappings.

The only interesting cash-ins were unintentional. Made before *The Exorcist The Possession of Joel Delaney* (1972) shows how the Devil movie might have developed had it not been engulfed by the phenomenon of *Exorcist*. Joel Delaney (Perry King), a rich white who assuages his liberal guilt by living in a slum, is possessed by a Puerto Rican homicidal maniac. His sister (Shirley MacLaine) considers this the height of social embarrassment. Delaney's murderous activities lead to the first appearance of the now-popular severed-head-in-the-fridge gambit, and a really squirmy sequence in which, at switchblade point, he forces his bratty nephew to eat dog food. The anger of a poverty-stricken psycho seems more relevant to the world outside the cinema than that of a vengeful Assyrian pixie who wisecracks in Latin. It took fifteen years for *Joel Delaney* to influence a film, and *Retribution* (1987) ditches the social angle for the stock story of a vengeful gangster after his killers. In any case, the film is rather stronger when crushing heads against walls or dumping

mobsters inside pig carcasses on the conveyer belt in a slaughterhouse than in dealing with suicidal wimp Dennis Lipscomb's histrionic possession.

Mario Bava's *Lisa e diavolo* (*Lisa and the Devil*) (1972) was a symbol-ridden charade in which Elke Sommer is lured to a houseful of mysterious characters for the purpose of unravelling an incredibly complicated plot, continually disrupted by the director's love of startling images like a pile of corpses arranged in the attitude of the Last Supper. After a brief release, it was withdrawn and recut so that the story was interrupted by new scenes of Miss Sommer being exorcised in the regulation swearing-vomit-and-flaky-make-up manner by Father Robert Alda. The new version became *La Casa del esorcismo* (*The House of Exorcism*) (1975). Since plots have never been Bava's speciality, there's a possibility that this trampling might have helped the film. Now the story is *completely* incomprehensible, the quirky detours which Bava relishes are allowed to take over. Especially amusing is Telly Savalas as a lollipop-sucking devilish butler, breaking the legs of a corpse so he will fit into his coffin.

John Boorman's *Exorcist II: The Heretic* (1977) was similarly hacked about and is just as confusing. Monsignor Richard Burton investigates the original exorcism and becomes entrapped in a morass of philosophical significance – as if Boorman had ignored the simple effectiveness of the first film and tried to live up to all the mystic twaddle Blatty gave out to the press while pushing his book. Like Bava's film, *The Heretic* gains from its messy production history – it was previewed and hauled back to the editor's bench several times before Boorman and Warner Brothers gave up. It doesn't work in all sorts of ways – as a horror film, as a study of people under stress, as a discourse upon good and evil or as a piece of Catholic propaganda. However, like Ennio Morricone's mixture of tribal and liturgical music, it does manage to be very interesting. Asked to explain the failure of the film, Boorman philosophised, 'I guess I didn't throw enough Christians to the lions.'

Rosemary's Baby is a film; *The Exorcist* is a

phenomenon; *The Omen* (1976) is a package. Although David Selzer's novelisation of his own screenplay was a freak paperback success, spawning more sequels than the film itself, the project was originally a screen treatment by producer Harvey Bernhard. The idea comes obviously from *Rosemary's Baby*, a tried-and-tested box-office property. Whereas Adrian the Antichrist was born into the lively New York middle classes, *The Omen* launches into the world of power politics, big-business chicanery and beautiful people familiar from too-thick railway station bookstall best-sellers. Satanism in *Rosemary's Baby* is disturbing, but in *The Omen* it is no more shady than any other international conspiracy – an idea fumbled in the first film, but surprisingly well handled in the sequel, *Damien: Omen II* (1978). Gregory Peck and Lee Remick lend solemnly respectable star presence to a cast of familiar character faces, but mass appeal is ensured with the talking point deaths that spice up the wayward plot every quarter of an hour. Bernhard and director Richard Donner do not make the mistake of throwing too few Christians to the lions. Quite the reverse: connoisseurs of bullfights, public executions and torso murder trials thronged to the film and fidgeted through the clumsy exposition just for the spectacular beheading of David Warner by a flying sheet of plate glass. If there were a special Madame Defarge Humanitarian Award for All-Time Best Decapitation, this lingering, slow-motion sequence would get my vote.

The Omen is a stodgy, humourless film that suffers from the kind of religiosity that used to choke biblical epics of the 1950s. The orgies and collapsing temples are there, but you have to sit through a lot of tedious homily to get to the red meat. As Robin Wood points out in *The American Nightmare*, the only interest of *The Omen* is that it can be read as a reactionary mirror image of *The Texas Chainsaw Massacre*. In Tobe Hooper's film, the Monsters are an American family who destroy children; Donner has a child destroy the American family. The Good Guy may lose, but as played by Gregory Peck his goodness is never questioned. The ending is only unhappy in a limited sense,

since Damien Thorn, the Antichrist, gets what is coming to him in *The Final Conflict* (1981). *The Omen* is about as absorbing and glossy as a *Vogue* filler about the kind of grey suits senior executives are wearing this year, but the packaging is superb. For a while it was impossible to avoid white-on-black posters featuring the film's 666 logo and cheery slogans like 'if something frightening happens to you today, think about it ... It may be *The Omen*'; 'good morning, you are one day closer to the end of the world'; or, simply, 'Remember ... you have been warned.'

The film was successful enough to raise two sequels, *Damien*, in which the teenage Antichrist tests his powers, and *The Final Conflict* in which, as an adult, he rallies his followers for a battle with Christ reborn. Bernhard stayed with the series, but Donner was succeeded by Mike Hodges, who was fired and replaced with Don Taylor for *Damien* and then with Graham Baker for *The Final Conflict*. None of the directors brings much more than organisational skills to the series, whose personality is mainly dependent upon Panavision gloom and Jerry Goldsmith's throbbing black mass score. The Seven Daggers of Meggido, reputedly the only weapons with which the Antichrist can be killed, are passed from character to character throughout the trilogy. Strangely, despite its switch of directors, the unpromising middle entry is the best of the three. It's stuck with a lot of guest stars blundering into pompously staged death-traps and a few silly ideas like casting Lee Grant as the Whore of Babylon, but it does manage some subversive hints about the ease with which the Antichrist slots into a disciplinarian military school and the chairmanship of the multinational Thorn Corporation. *The Final Conflict* redundantly spells it all out and thinks up lamely uninventive atrocities. Sam Neill is a magnetically evil adult Damien, delivering an inversion of the Sermon on the Mount to his devoted flock from a floodlit hillside, but the series finishes with a cop-out. For three films, anyone who even considers inconveniencing Damien is put in the position of a Tex Avery cartoon character whose path has been crossed by a black cat and is thus doomed to be

● *Head-banging.* Tony Fields, Marc Price, **Trick or Treat.**

pulped by a falling battleship, but Lisa Harrow manages to sneak up on the Antichrist and shove one of those seven daggers between his shoulder blades with 'Take that, you bastard!'

The Omen had few direct imitations, *Holocaust 2000* (1977), *The Legacy* (1979) and *The Godsend* (1979) being the most indebted, but it did encourage the makers of *Phantasm*, *Terror* and *The Awakening* to litter their stories with way-out deaths accompanied by supernatural phenomena like unnatural winds and minor domestic explosions. The appearance of our Redeemer as a glowing hippie with a backing heavenly chorus at the end of *The Final Conflict* does raise the possibility of the God movie as a genre. So far, all the form has had to offer is the miraculous daughter of a mobster being ransomed by prayers in *The Abduction of Saint Anne* (1975), Ellen Burstyn back from the dead as a genuine faith healer in *Resurrection* (1980) and a smattering of Second Coming movies. In *The Second Coming of Suzanne* (1974), Sondra Locke's incarnation as the new Messiah is wrapped up in various infuriating levels, of meta-fiction, and *The Suicide Cult* (1980) throws the return of Jesus Christ away amid an astonishing cocktail of tedium and pretension. Bigas Luna's *Reborn* (1981) is the best of a weird bunch, with Michael Moriarty as the modern St Joseph uncomfortably locked to the new mother of God by a vaginal spasm and Dennis Hopper as a revivalist with an interest in suppressing the good news.

The Omen, followed closely by *Carrie*, created a briefly popular horror movie sub-genre, the 'Psichopath' film. Damien Thorn and Carrie White, like Jim Hutton in *Psychic Killer* (1975), Alan Bates in *The Shout* (1978), Lisa Pelikan in *Jennifer* (1978), Robert Thompson in *Patrick* (1979) and Robert Powell in *Harlequin* (1979) are 'Psichopaths', seemingly ordinary individuals with hidden, awesome paranormal powers. The wish-fulfilment fantasy element of the Psichopath film is obvious. The usual formula finds the Psichopath humiliated, abused and pushed beyond endurance, whereupon immense mental powers are unleashed in an orgy of mass destruction. Hutton sends his astral body to murder his enemies, Bates solves his eternal triangle problem by blitzing John Hurt with a killing yell he has learned from Australian aborigines, Pelikan lets primal snake gods loose in her school, the catatonic Patrick uses telekinesis to type indecent propositions to nurse Susan Penhaligon and faith-healer Powell infiltrates a politician's family in an empty update of the Rasputin story. 'Most paranoiacs think the world is too much for them', diagnoses Lee Remick of Richard Burton in *The Medusa Touch* (1978), 'but Mr Morlar thinks he is too much for the world.' The man with a 'gift for disaster' crashes airliners into central London, brings down a cathedral on a gathering of Establishment worthies and has his mental sights set on Windscale nuclear power plant. Burton sneers his way through Peter Van Greenaway's incredibly misanthropic dialogue, but Jack Gold's slack direction lets him down. Mr Morlar, who spends most of the film plotting like Patrick from a hospital bed in which he is supposed to be comatose, is almost impossible to kill; the psichopaths of *The Horror Star* (1981) and *One Dark Night* (1982) remain able to exert their influence even after death and bring a deserved doom to the dumb-ass kids who trespass in their luxurious tombs.

Mark L. Lester's *Firestarter* (1984), from a Stephen King novel, outdoes them all in silliness with a pre-teen heroine (Drew Barrymore) who has the power 'to crack the world in two – like a plate' but, in the meantime, is content with taking out a government dirty tricks department in a sloppy mini-holocaust. Rather more useful, perhaps, are the powers of the children in *Kiss Daddy Goodbye* (1981), used to keep their dead father walking so they can stay out of the orphanage. The best of the Psichopaths is Zeljko Ivanek in Roger Christian's *The Sender* (1983). When he is institutionalised as an 'elopement risk', psychiatrist Kathryn Harrold discovers that he has the power to transmit visions, sometimes enigmatic, sometimes terrifying, to receptive bystanders. The film has its share of disturbing hallucinations (creepy-crawlies, bleeding mirrors, vomited rats) and one literally shattering moment when the Sender is subjected to electro-convulsive therapy and floods the hospital with his pain, but there are also the quietly disturbing visitations of his ghostly, projected mother (Shirley Knight), a fundamentalist who has brought up her gifted son to believe he is the Messiah. That is unfortunate, since the madhouse already has one Jesus in residence, and there are inevitable conflicts. The powerful assemblage of scares, confrontations, explosions and revelations in the last reel doesn't quite resolve all the mysteries of Thomas Baum's intelligent but confusing screenplay, but the film is challenging and mercifully non-imitative in an age of carbon copies.

Devil movies didn't last long. *The Omen* gave a boost to the dying exorcism fad, but *Carrie*, despite its hysterically religious overtones, is a diversion back into the more interesting mainstream of the post-*Night of the Living Dead* horror film. Inventive film-makers were not attracted to the sub-genre because of its thematic emptiness, and exploitation artists were put off by the cost. Even an Italian rip-off like Alberto De Martino's *Holocaust 2000* needs locations in three countries, a Morricone score, expensive special effects and an international bunch of name actors in support of Kirk Douglas to compete with *The Omen*. As is amply demonstrated by *The Redeemer* (1978), *The Coming* (1980), *Demonoid* (1980), *The Alchemist* (1981), *Spasms* (1982), *The Power* (1983), *The Oracle* (1986) and *Witchboard* (1987), low-budget Devil movies don't have much of a chance. Most of these movies just use some middle-level special effects to repackage the *Friday the 13th* teens-in-terror formula. Nevertheless, there are sort of interesting moments in *Scarab* (1982) and *Ninja III: The Domination* (1984), which at least take the trouble to get outside Judao-Christian demonology and trawl in more obscure waters for their mythological monsters, represented by Rip Torn as an immortal Egyptian sorcerer and Lucinda Dickey as an aerobics expert possessed by the sword of a black ninja.

Meanwile, Phillip Marshak, Tom McGowan and Greg Tallas's *Cataclysm* (1980), later cut down and edited into *Night Train to Terror* (1985), and Frank La Loggia's *Fear No Evil* (1981) at least try to develop the Antichrist theme beyond *The Omen's* gory set pieces, even though their aspirations are unsupported by meagre production values. In *Cataclysm*, Satan walks the Earth as a vicious New York ballet critic and gives a grant to an atheist philosopher hard at work on a thesis which will disprove the existence of God. *Fear No Evil* has a *Carrie* small-town high school setting and depicts the clash between a mixed-up adolescent Antichrist (Stefan Arngrim) and a trinity of angels during a community passion play. Along with *Evilspeak*, it is the most vicious of the peer group pressure films, featuring a sequence in which a bullying stud is turned into a woman from the neck down that has turned up subsequently in a surprising amount of written horror fiction (John Skipp and Craig Spector's *The Clearup*, Clive Barker's 'Madonna', etc.). The films may be cheap, disjointed, muddled and lurid, but at least they represent an attempt to confront the Devil on a more sophisticated, interesting level than their expensive, smooth, glossy and empty rivals.

Apart from Roger Corman's *The Haunted Palace* (1963), and Daniel Haller's *Monster of Terror* (1965) and *The Dunwich Horror* (1969), the cinema neglected for a long time the works of H.P. Lovecraft, whose invented mythology of ichorous Elder Gods lurking in an extradimensional limbo in preparation for an apocalyptic return to Earth could conceivably offer a promising new direction for the Devil movie now that possession and biblical prophecy have been exhausted. Strangely, the 'official' Lovecraft adaptions of the 1980s – *Re-Animator*, *From Beyond*, *The Farm* (1987) – have chosen to neglect this aspect of the great man's work, although vaguely Lovecraftian monster gods get ineffectual walk-ons in *The Manitou* and *Conan the Destroyer* (1984). The nearest the movies have come to the real thing, surprisingly, is Ivan Reitman's *Ghostbusters* (1984). With Bill Murray, Dan Aykroyd and Harold Ramis as a trio of unemployed parapsychologists who set up an extermination agency to deal with the supernatural pests that have been plaguing Manhattan, the film is, in effect, *National Lampoon's Call of Cthulhu*. A 1930s skyscraper in the middle of New York has

● ... *havok of Biblical proportions.* Dan Aykroyd, Slavitza Jovan, Bill Murray, **Ghostbusters.**

been constructed by an evil architect as the gateway to another dimension, and a horde of Sumerian demons are flooding through Sigourney Weaver's fridge in order to wreak havoc of Old Testament proportions on the Big Apple. Weaver becomes a hoyden high priestess, devil dogs rampage through Central Park, a giant marshmallow man tramples city blocks and Gozer (Slavitza Jovan), the *svelte* entity behind the chaos, threatens to destroy the world only to have Bill Murray, representing the human race, level his ectoplasmic flamethrower with the rallying cry of 'this chick is *toast!*'

In the movies, voodoo has mainly been used as a subsidiary theme in a host of zombie pot-boilers, although anthologies like *The Vault of Horror* and *From a Whisper to a Scream* (1987) have toyed with sympathetic magic and horrid curses as instruments of fate. Until the 1980s, Jacques Tourneur and Val Lewton's *I Walked With a Zombie* (1943) was almost unique in its serious approach to the subject. However, voodoo finally had a vogue at the time of John Schlesinger's *The Believers* (1987) and Wes Craven's *The Serpent and the Rainbow* (1988). Schlesinger tackles Santeria, a black/Hispanic religion practised in New York City, and has Martin Sheen resist the temptation to sacrifice his son at the behest of a *Rosemary's Baby*-style coven of highly placed chicken-disembowellers. It's a slick but haphazard movie, too serious to work as a thriller, but too conventional to do anything much with its subject. Craven, loosely adapting Wade Davis's true account of his search for the drug used to create zombies, turns in an equally unbalanced film, but marvellously catches the uneasy, romantic atmosphere of Haiti. There are a few too many of the director's trademark nightmares, and the real-life story is bent into some very peculiar shapes, but the film does take on a heady cocktail of Third World politics, mysticism, medical pioneering, action-adventure

and interracial romance. Perhaps its scariest moment is the hero's declaration, after he's been interrogated by the *Ton-ton Macout*, that he knows the Haitian Secret Police Chief didn't seriously want to hurt him because he only drove a nail through his scrotum.

During the post-modernist confusion of the late 1980s, as genre barriers fell apart, the Devil made something of a come-back in the unexpected forms of Tim Curry, in Ridley Scott's *Legend* (1985), Robert De Niro, in Alan Parker's *Angel Heart* (1987), and Jack Nicholson, in George Miller's *The Witches of Eastwick* (1987). Meanwhile Philip Yordan rejigs some of the themes from his *Cataclysm* script for *The Unholy* (1987), and there's a similar build-up to apocalypse in *The Seventh Sign* (1988). All these films bend over backwards to avoid being stuck with the 'horror movie' tag: the results are predictably scrappy, shot through with pretension and generally smack of creative energy being misapplied wholesale. De Niro's Louis Cyphre and Nicholson's Darryl Van Horn are likeable slices of ham, and Nicholson in particular has fun with his triple seductions, cherry-vomiting and a marvellous rant against God for creating women, but the films in which they appear never cohere. Parker, adapting William Hjortsberg's private eye horror novel *Falling Angel*, spends all his time on picturesque images of whirling fans and wintry 1955 New York and New Orleans and falls down on any story-telling he is required to do. Miller, stuck with the far more intractable John Updike source novel, gives the impression that his film, which pits Cher, Susan Sarandon and Michelle Pfeiffer against Nicholson's 'horny li'l devil', has been structured in accordance with the complex deal necessary to get all the performers to appear together – everyone has to have an equally developed part, which means that every plot point has to be made three times. But, if nothing else, De Niro and Nicholson do finally establish the Devil's official hairstyle.

● *Remembering the Alamo.* Bill Johnson, **The Texas Chainsaw Massacre, Part 2.**

deep in the heart of texas

or: The Down-Home, Up-Country, Multi-Implement Massacre Movie

Pepsi-Cola, the national drink of America, became a best-selling beverage with the slogan '... for those who think young'. The ideals of American culture are youth and vitality, whether displayed by pioneers taming the frontier wilderness, cocky young gun Kennedy carving a legend by facing down doddery old Kruschev or Frankie Avalon agonising over the choice between surfing on the surf, twisting on the sand or drag-racing down Route 66. The American tragedy is the menopause and the American nightmare is senility. In the twentieth century, the youth of America is concentrated in the cities, while age is left to rot in the sticks. When *Mr Smith Comes to Washington* he leaves behind a mid-West that needs, but can no longer sustain, his virility. Without the young Jimmy Stewarts, the cattle towns of *Red River* dry up and die in *The Last Picture Show. Psycho* is the first of many suggestions that the bypassed backwaters might nurture a homicidal hatred for the city slickers who have taken over from the cowboys as emblems of Americana. Nobody stops at the Bates Motel since they built the new highway. Consumed with jealous spite, Mrs Bates destroys those who retain the youth she has lost, usurping her son's mind and dismembering Janet Leigh's peachy body. John Ford's Westerners dream of old age as a rocking chair on the porch. Since the Western was gunned down with Butch and Sundance in Bolivia, the Wild Bunch in Mexico and *Heaven's Gate* at the box-office, Mrs Bates has

been much imitated. Whenever the Beautiful People are foolhardy enough to get off the freeways, the festering old-timers have been up and leaving their rocking chairs and revving their chainsaws.

Even before the Wild West turned nasty, the cinema knew the Deep South was a hothouse of madness and murder. Southern hospitality in the movies has been shaded by the overheated literary gothic that filters from Poe to Tennessee Williams and Flannery O'Connor. The antebellum idyll is traduced by Richard Fleischer's whippin' slaves and pickin' cotton *grand guignol Mandingo* (1975): patriarch James Mason sits on the porch with a houseboy as a footrest ('the rheumatiz' drains out mah feet and into the nigra'), and, when Susan George births an off-colour babe, Perry King pitches his favourite slave (Ken Norton) into a cauldron of boiling water. During the War of the Rebellion we have Don Siegel's *The Beguiled* (1971), with a schoolful of repressed spinsters and embryo belles systematically seducing, maiming and poisoning the embodiment of Union Army machismo, Clint Eastwood. The twentieth century finds Scarlett O'Hara cracking up as Vivien Leigh plays Blanche Dubois in Elia Kazan's *A Streetcar Named Desire* and *Jezebel* driven out of her mind as Bette Davis clings to her rotting Tara in Robert Aldrich's *Hush . . . Hush, Sweet Charlotte*. Meanwhile John Huston's *Wise Blood* (1979) views the South in a painful glare, populated by mad prophets, fake evangelists and hellfire hucksters in jet-black suits and shades.

These images are artfully designed to play on Northern sensibilities: guilt over the carpet-baggers' looting of the former Confederacy, or antipathy to the Southern Fried Justice of lynching blacks, civil rights agitators or anyone who just plain looks at a Southerner wrong. Meanwhile, the thriving drive-ins of the South prefer the blend of moonshine-running, cheerful sex and bluegrass fiddle of New World tits-and-cars cheapies like *Thunder and Lightning* or *Moonshine County Express*. The *magnum opus* of this genre is Michael Pressman's ebullient *The Great Texas Dynamite Chase* (1977) with Claudia Jennings and Jocelyn Jones as bankrobbing good-time gals. The South has had a home-grown horror movie industry since damn yankee H.G. Lewis helped the Johnny Rebs get back at the bluebellies in *Two Thousand Maniacs!*, the story of a ghost town that celebrates the centenary of its massacre in the Civil War by torturing a bunch of Northern tourists to death. Made beyond the restrictions of the Hollywood mainstream, technical aptitude and good taste, films like Lewis's Miami-based productions played the drive-ins and rarely surfaced above the Mason-Dixon line. The South had to wait for Tobe Hooper before it had a good ole boy horror director it could take pride in.

The sensationalist brilliance of Hooper's *The Texas Chainsaw Massacre* (1974) begins with its eye-grabbing, unforgettable title. It takes guts to be so blatant up-front, more guts, in fact than are spilled in the movie. Nothing could possibly be as bloody and atrocious as the title and the poster ('who will survive and what will be left of them?') suggest *The Texas Chainsaw Massacre* is going to be. Hooper goes completely the other way: there are no close-ups of open wounds (the gore film trademark), and all the limb-lopping happens out of shot. This restraint could as easily be due to dissatisfaction with the obvious fakery of Lewis's gore as to innate good taste and humanity. Restraint is exhibited in no other aspect of Hooper's direction. Instead of the single mummy of *Psycho* there's a whole houseful of human and animal remains. Rather than Hitchcock's delicate, suspenseful manipulation, Hooper feeds the audience through a mangle of unrelieved horror and violence.

Things look real bad right from the opening narration, which soberly informs us that we are about to see an entirely factual account of what actually happened to Sally and Franklin Hardesty on 18 August 1973. Flashbulb flares illuminate glimpses of rotting flesh, and the camera pulls back from the skull of a decomposing corpse that has been wired to a cemetery monument by a sick vandal with an artistic turn. Cut to a dead armadillo feet up by a rural Texas road. Two sweet teenage couples and Franklin (Paul A. Partain), a fat, obnoxious cripple, breeze along in a minibus. A drunk at the desecrated churchyard mumbles 'things happen hereabout (heh heh heh); I sees things sometimes'. Pam (Teri McMinn) is into astrology and warns that Saturn is in retrograde: since Saturn is malefic, things are *really* likely to be real bad. The kids pick up a hitch-hiker (Edwin Neal) who grins, twitches and has a deforming facial birthmark. Hitch turns out to be the crazed shutterbug and is returning home after a nostalgic nose around the old slaughterhouse. 'Sidewalk Café' burbles pleasantly on the radio while Hitch reminisces about the pre-automation days of sledge-hammers and hook-and-chain gangs. When Hitch slices his hand open the kids get queasy and when he gashes Franklin they dump him. As the dormobile pulls away, Hitch smears it with his blood. 'Looks like he's left his mark.' Things don't get better at the local gas station, where the proprietor (Jim Siedow) offers them some suspicious barbeque and advises them not to go messing around in old houses.

All this is merely uncomfortable. The film becomes either irresistible or unbearable when the kids, ignoring the Gas Man's advice, enter a nearby old house. Kirk (William Vail) wanders down a filthy corridor towards a red room walled with animal trophies. Suddenly, without any Hitchcockian overhead shot to pre-empt the shattering shock, Leatherface (Gunnar Hansen), a squealing, obese killer, appears from nowhere and smashes Kirk's head with a sledge-hammer. Before the audience has had time really to register what has happened, Leatherface slams an unexpected, grating steel shutter across the corridor and finishes off the still-twitching boy out of sight. After the film has been blooded by its first kill, Leatherface rapidly slaughters three more of the teenagers. Pam is hung on a meat-hook, Jerry (Allen Danziger) is battered with the sledge and Franklin gets a buzzing chainsaw in the gut. In Texas, a householder is legally entitled to shoot anyone who trespasses on his property, so Leatherface's murder spree barely breaks the law.

Sally (Marilyn Burns) is the sole survivor; once her friends are dead she becomes the focus of the film. Fleeing from Leatherface, she is repeatedly caught in brambles and bushes that the killer easily saws his way through. This physically exhausting chase sequence tops the opening of *Night of the Living Dead* as a filming of the universal nightmare. Sally seeks sanctuary with the Gas Man, but he bashes her with a broomstick, ties her in a sack and drags her back to the house. Leatherface, Hitch and the Gas Man are members of the same clan: 'our family has always been in meat'. One of the rocking-chair corpses Sally has run into upstairs turns out to be Granpaw, 'the best killer there ever was', a barely alive centenarian who feebly sucks blood from Sally's cut finger. When Sally screams and Hooper throws in ultra-close-ups of her rolling, bloodshot eyeballs, the family argues over who gets to kill her. Hitch wants the Gas Man to do the deed, taunting him with 'you're just a cook, Leatherface and me do all the work'. The Gas Man is regretful: 'I can't take no pleasure in killin'. There's some things you gotta do. Don't mean you gotta like it.'

Hooper's degenerates are a parody of the typical sit-com family, with the bread-winning, long-suffering Gas Man as Pop; the preening, bewigged, apron-wearing Leatherface as Mom; and the rebellious, long-haired Hitch as the teenage son. The house is a similarly overdone, degraded mirror of the ideal home. Impaled clocks hang from the eaves, an armchair has human arms and a hen is cooped up in a canary cage. After much

debate, the family decide to let Granpaw kill Sally, but he is too shaky to hold the ball-peen hammer properly and only manages to bloody her scalp. With an unlikely burst of superhuman strength, Sally breaks free and crashes through a window. On the main road, Hitch is messily run over and Sally clambers into the back of a speeding pick-up truck. She survives, but as a blood-covered, shrieking, probably insane grotesque. The film fades on a long shot of the enraged Leatherface whirling his chainsaw in the air.

The Texas Chainsaw Massacre is only defensible as a nightmare. The only cerebral reading of the film sees it as a rabid vegetarian tract: the people in the movie suffer exactly the same atrocities daily inflicted on beef cattle in the name of Ronald McDonald. However, the film is so visceral that there is barely time for an audience to breathe, let alone ponder What It's All About. We sympathise with the kids, not because they are particularly pleasant but because the only other choice Hooper gives us is walking out. The killers are unknowable, barely characterised monsters who resist the insight Hitchcock and Anthony Perkins made us have into Norman Bates. Hooper's achievement is that he brings back to the movies an awareness of violent death lost through the slow-motion sentimentalisation of *Bonnie and Clyde* and the contemptible distortion of TV cop shows in which a shot victim has a penny-size red spot on his pristine shirt and time for a five-minute monologue before he goes. Unlike *I Spit On Your Grave*, *The Texas Chainsaw Massacre* is not a complete turn-off. If Hooper and his collaborators do not make their subject palatable, at least they succeed in justifying the film with its own panache.

Nobody could make two films like *The Texas Chainsaw Massacre*. Like Wes Craven after *his* shocking debut, Tobe Hooper has mellowed. Actually, Hooper has had difficulty in making films at all: he was removed from *The Dark* (1979) and *Venom* (1981) to make way for John Bud Cardos and Piers Haggard, suffered extreme creative differences with the tampering by producers of *Death Trap* (1976) and *The Funhouse* (1981) and was rumoured to be the remote control creature of screenwriter/producer Steven Spielberg on *Poltergeist* (1982). He then took three career-shaking body blows during an expensive but unprofitable tenure with Cannon Films: *Lifeforce* (1985), *Invaders From Mars* (1986) and *The Texas Chainsaw Massacre 2* (1987). *Death Trap*, which comes on like a *Chainsaw* follow-up, but softens the mood with harmless nudity, recognisable actors and successful dollops of insane comedy, is perhaps the best of Hooper's subsequent films. Judd (Neville Brand) runs an uninviting swampland motel and feeds any annoying customers to the giant crocodile he keeps in his back yard. Apparently, the reptile was originally supplied by Frank 'Bring 'Em Back Alive' Buck as part of a menagerie of which it is the only survivor, having eaten all the other animals. The film tries to repeat the nightmare chases of *Chainsaw* with the much-mistreated Marilyn Burns pursued by the scythe-waving Brand, but is let down by editing that fumbles the big scare moments with a butcher-like lack of finesse and lets the audience off the meat-hook with barely a *frisson* . *Death Trap* works best as a sick send-up, with Brand's whiskery mumblings and the studio-bound swamp contributing to a hilarious pastiche Tale From the Crypt.

Hooper's only trouble-free Hollywood project has been a two-part mini-series, *'Salem's Lot* (1979). Stephen King's source novel reworks *Dracula* and *Peyton Place*, but Hooper's film lives under the baleful shadow of *Psycho*. Leatherface's murders are horrifying because they deliberately avoid echoes of those in the Hitchcock film, but in *'Salem's Lot* Hooper recreates the famous attack on Martin Balsam as James Mason throws Ed Flanders against a wall of piercing antlers. Harry Sukman's score poaches its screeching violins from Bernard Herrmann, and a swinging lantern plus final flash superimposition turn Barlow (Reggie Nalder), the Nosferatu-faced King Vampire, into the twin brother of Norman's mummified mother. Although *'Salem's Lot* is not the tedious disaster that the mini-series adaption of Thomas Tryon's *Harvest Home* turned out to be, it's respectable

rather than devastating. Hooper's personality is evident from the grimy walls of the vampire's house and the restless camerawork, but he is subdued by the constraints of network censorship. The physical nastiness necessary to Hooper and King is tidied up considerably. Rather than shove a shotgun down Fred Willard's throat, a cuckolded trucker simply points the weapon at him; and the Willard character's later meeting with the vampire as, fouled and humiliated, he crawls away from the scene is replaced with a meaningless freeze-frame claw. The strongest element of the film is James Mason's performance as Richard K. Straker, an acidic descendant of Dracula's fly-eating disciple, happiest when trading insults with bothersome humanity ('you'll enjoy Mr Barlow and he'll enjoy you'), and providing a nice line in ambiguous glances and nasal sneers.

Hooper has consistently failed to live up to the promise of his early work. Isolated moments in all his post-*Chainsaw* movies mark him as the man who launched Leatherface into the cinema, but too often these take the form of self-plagiarisms, like the chases in *Death Trap* and *'Salem's Lot*, the sequence in a van whose stuffed animal décor echoes the *Chainsaw* living-room in *Invaders From Mars* and practically all of *The Texas Chainsaw Massacre 2*. Made, presumably in desperation, after the very expensive failures of *Lifeforce* (a kitschy tribute to Hammer Films, originally entitled *The Space Vampires*) and *Invaders* (an ill-advised remake of William Cameron Menzies's cult classic), *Chainsaw 2* is an even broader comedy than *Death Trap* and, despite funny performances from Dennis Hopper as a mad Texas ranger and Caroline Williams as the spunky disc jockey heroine, emerges as a gory travesty of the earlier film. Too many scenes are simple reruns of unmatchable moments from the original, and Tom Savini's explicit but uninteresting splatter effects (chainsaws in stomachs, heads sawed down the middle, faces flayed off) fail to make up for the lack of suspense and originality. Set beside the Cannon trio of Hooper flops, even slightly off-centre works like *Death Trap* and *The Funhouse* seem like fine films.

Before *The Texas Chainsaw Massacre*, there was

the nastier, fiercely intelligent *Last House on the Left* (1972), which draws the battle lines for the class war its director, Wes Craven, has continued to cover in *The Hills Have Eyes* (1977), *A Stranger in Our House* (1979), *Deadly Blessing* (1981) and *The Hills Have Eyes, Part 2* (1984). Although Craven's films have become increasingly suburban, and he has even been able to find regular work on American television, his roots are even crueller than Hooper's. *Last House* may lack the instantly controversial/offensive title of *The Texas Chainsaw Massacre*, but it certainly exceeds the later film in horrific incident. The plot is filched from Ingmar Bergman's *Jungfrukallen* (*The Virgin Spring*) and Craven uses it forcefully to make the point that violence degrades everyone involved, victim and victimiser, just and unjust. A pair of cute teenage girls from the country are abducted in Sin City New York by a band of dope-pushing sex murderers under the loose command of Krug (David Hess), a really vile individual first seen bursting a little kid's balloon and later revealed to have hooked his son on heroin because he felt mean that day. The gang head for Canada, but stop off near the girls' home for a picnic during which they rape, humiliate, torture and kill them. When their car breaks down, the gang ingratiate themselves with Dr and Mrs Collingwood, the parents of one of the victims. Realising what their guests have done, the Collingwoods castrate, humiliate, torture and kill them.

Craven's obsessive theme is the depiction of antagonistic groups, usually parallel families (*Deadly Blessing* extends the field of combat to rival communities, while *A Stranger in Our House* shrinks it to a pair of teenage girls), more or less representing the forces of destructive anarchy and normative repression. The only possible contact between the two is psychopathic violence, and Craven wittily has the carnage stem from each group's desire to emulate its mortal enemy. Krug's maniacs try to pass themselves off as plumbers/insurance salesmen and coo over expensive furnishings, while the middle-aged, well-off Collingwoods prepare to slaughter them. Craven establishes his split-level world with the contrasting

scenes of upstate sylvan beauty and downtown slum tattiness that introduce the characters. Then he has the psycho gang's worst depradations set against attractive, washed-out woodland and the Collingwoods' revenge orgy turn their well-appointed home into a corpse-strewn shambles.

The psychos are allowed off-beat shop talk ('who was the greatest sex killer of the century?') and moments of surprising fellow-feeling (after one of the gang has killed a girl who insulted him, Krug asks with genuine concern 'do you feel better now?'); but the Collingwoods are never more than unreal TV movie figures stuck with a folksy lifestyle on the level of the amiable mailman who says of their daughter 'you'd think she was the only girl ever to reach the age of 17, mind you, she is about the cutest'. On *Last House*, the low-budget professionalism of Craven's crew really communicates a powerful, intellectual revulsion that makes a far more effective anti-violence statement than Hooper's roller-coaster ride, but the movie has its problems. The formal plot reversal works in Bergman's mythopoetic mists, but is here achieved through a series of contrivances that mainly serve to produce a yawning credibility gap.

Craven followed *Last House* with *The Hills Have Eyes*, a slicker, pacier piece influenced by the headlong rush and heh-heh-heh humour of Tobe Hooper. Its covered wagon is a mobile home and its Apaches are a family of desert-dwelling mutants, but *The Hills Have Eyes* is a Western. It is to *The Texas Chainsaw Massacre* what Howard Hawks's *Rio Bravo* is to *High Noon*. Hawks felt that Marshal Gary Cooper should not run around town pleading for help, and had John Wayne refuse offers of amateur aid and get on with the job he was paid to do. Craven feels the same way about *Chainsaw*'s helpless, panicking victims and has his normal family greet the monsters' attacks with an equally savage defence. Killing doesn't come as easily to the city folks, but once they get into it their education and inventiveness help them outclass the psychos. The film's hero is the family dog, an unsentimentalised Rin-Tin-Tin whose slaying of the most monstrous of the mutants (Michael

● *Helpless victim.* Lucy Grantheim, **Last House on the Left.**

Berryman) is a rousing reversal of the situation. 'Don't you come out here and stick your life in my face', the monster father tells his normal counterpart as he torches him. While the average Joe is discovering murderous capabilities in his confrontation with the average Igor, Craven lets his monsters emerge as disreputable country cousins of the Munsters. One of the competitive sons brings home a protein-packed baby for the pot – 'Look papa, we brought you a juicy Thanksgiving turkey' – and the prissy daughter goes over to the other side because she can't stand the squalor any longer.

Like Hooper, Craven made his first impression as a gutsy independent and has since had a hard time hacking it in the mainstream. If *Stranger in the House* and *Deadly Blessing* are interesting but flawed, then the comic book adaption *Swamp Thing* (1982), the depressingly shoddy *The Hills Have Eyes, Part 2* and the would-be classy *Deadly Friend* (1985) are outright disasters; and television pieces like *Invitation to Hell* (1984), *Chiller* (1985) and a handful of *Twilight Zone* episodes are at best slickly directed but undone by typically formulaic scripts. Craven has been so keen to ditch the *Last House* image that he even made *Casebusters* (1986), a Disney kiddie TV drama. Sean S. Cunningham, Craven's producer partner on *Last House*, graduated from the cinematic backwoods – where he also made *The Case of the Full Moon Murders* (1973), a hardcore porno picture about a cock-sucking vampire – because of his association with the successful *Friday the 13th* series, but Craven has unfortunately been in the position of having to make underbudgeted, underplanned duds like *Swamp Thing* and *Hills 2* (which features plentiful footage from the first film, including a flashback from the point of view of the dog). His breakthrough film came finally with *A Nightmare on Elm Street*, which is literally a move from the backwoods, deserting the rural locales of the earlier work and setting up the terror shop in a Spielbergian small town.

The notoriety and success of *Last House* produced a handful of imitations. *L'Ultimo Treno Della Notte* (*Late Night Trains*) (1975), a polished Italian remake, tidies up the logical short-cuts of the original by setting the story on a train. When the degenerates kill the girls, they steal their tickets and so are thrown off at the station where the parents are waiting. The villains are a pair of leather jackets first seen mugging Father Christmas and a veiled, *haute couture* sadist (Macha Meril) who seduces them on the train. The Italian gloss uneasily obscures the sheer nastiness of a surgical defloration and the bare-faced bad taste of following the final massacre with a love song by Demis Roussos. David Hess reprised his *Last House* act several times, mainly in Italy, most memorably in Pasquale Festa Campanile's *Autostop rosso sangue* (*Hitch Hike*) (1976), an on-the-road triangle drama with Franco Nero and Corinne Clery, and in Ruggiero Deodato's *La Casa sperduta nel parco* (*The House at the Edge of the Park*) (1981), an astonishingly cruel but clever story of a gutter psychopath invading a house populated by stylishly beastly bourgeois citizens. Deodato stages one sequence, in which Hess caresses a naked teenager with a straight razor, that is among the most classically Sadean in the cinema; an achievement, certainly, if not a particularly pleasurable one.

William Fruet's *Death Weekend* (1977), Meir Zarchi's *I Spit on Your Grave* (1980) and Clint Eastwood's *Sudden Impact* (1983) unwisely all use the same *Last House*-influenced story. An independent heroine is raped by a gang of reckless layabouts and avenges herself by offing the bastards one by one, using her feminine wiles to lure them near an assortment of cutting edges. *Death Weekend* is at least capably acted by Brenda Vaccaro as the table-turner and Don Stroud as her leading lout, and *Sudden Impact* shifts the attention from distaff vigilante Sondra Locke to Clint's ice-eyed resurrection of Dirty Harry, but *I Spit on Your Grave* has the distinction of being among the most loathsome films of all time. The rape lasts for an unbearable, demeaning forty-five minutes, while the revenge sequences are mainly so perfunctory that the director's declared intention of making an anti-rape movie becomes highly suspect. In the film's only effective sequence, one of the villains

● *Woodland animal.* John Hunsaker, **Just Before Dawn.**

tells the girl (Camille Keaton) that any man would have forced himself upon her because of her provocative costuming, and she cuts off his balls, letting him bleed to death in the bath. *Last House* closes with the Collingwoods completely ruined by their violent revenge, but *Death Weekend* and *I Spit on Your Grave* have their heroines leave the sites of the carnage with quietly satisfied smiles. More challenging, although flawed by hysteria and crassness, is *Demented* (1980), a variant in which the rape victim becomes unhinged enough to see every man as her assailant (*pace* Vera Miles on an old Hitchcock TV show) and takes a protracted but misdirected revenge on some horny local teenage studs. And the Australian *Fair Game* (1986) blends the theme with the *Most Dangerous Game* hunter-becomes-hunted gambit as an abused lady nature warden trashes a truckload of macho gun fetishists who have violated not only her but also the countryside.

The horror strategies of *Last House on the Left* have proved popular enough to be adopted by one or two very strong movies. Robert A. Endelson's *Fight for Your Life* (1977) has a trio of escaped convicts invade the home of a middle-class black family, finally forcing the minister patriarch to rebel against the white oppression he has been routinely giving in to. This racial twist on the tale is ridiculously amplified by *Redneck County* (1979), in which a black country and western singer foolishly decides to stop off at an off-the-road hotel run by Shelley Winters and is victimised by her charmless farmboy son. Victor Janos's terminally seedy (not to mention cheap, inept and boring) *Last House on Dead End Street* (1977) deals with issues of class and art while following the career of a porno movie-maker who ends up directing surrealist snuff movies. And Gerard Ciccoritti's *Psycho Girls* (1985) again has put-upon proles – a maidservant and some escaped mental patients – torture and kill un-sympathetic rich folk. The problem with these films – *Fight for Your Life* excepted – is that weighty themes are not enough to make shoddy productions and protracted torture sequences palatable.

After *The Texas Chainsaw Massacre* had made the *Night of the Living Dead* breakthrough into cult box-office success, the drive-ins encouraged lots of unwary idiots to wander off the main road and parade themselves in the hope of attracting the local psychos. *Terror Circus* (1973), *Three on a Meathook* (1973), *Pigs* (1974), *The Drive-In Massacre* (1976), *Axe!* (1977), *The Evictors* (1979), *Hunters' Blood* (1986) and *Bullies* (1987) are mostly unremarkable, while *Sunday in the Country* (1975) wastes the potentially explosive confrontation of rural psycho Ernest Borgnine and urban psycho Michael J. Pollard, and *Savage Weekend* (1976) is memorable only for its astonishing technical ineptitude. The genre overlap with the post-*Friday the 13th* psycho movie encouraged a run of films. *Don't Go in the Woods* (1980) is the most obviously emblematic title, but *The Burning* (1980), *The Prey* (1980), advertised with 'It's not human . . . and it's got an axe!', *Trapped* (1981), *The Forest* (1981), *Madman* (1982), *Mother Lode* (1982) and *Sleepaway Camp* (1983) deal with the same sort of sylvan slaughterhouse. In this neck of the woods, David Schmoeller's *Tourist Trap* (1979) has a few imaginative touches, and Andrew Davis's *The Campsite Massacre* (1983) makes better use than usual of wilderness locations.

A few films in this area manage to establish their own identity without becoming imitated works in themselves. John Russo, co-scripter of *Night of the Living Dead*, made his directorial début with *Midnight* (1982), adapted from his own novel, a seedy and cynical variation on the rural coven theme. Charles Kaufman's *Mother's Day* (1980) satirises Wes Craven as the female survivors of a backpacker massacre train as a guerrilla squad. They return to the woods and wipe out their trash molesters – two degenerate brothers who argue endlessly about the respective merits of punk and disco music. Kaufman, who goes a little too far in the straight violence to get big laughs, makes inventive use of a TV set and a bottle of Drano as weaponry. Craven's influence is also felt in Jeff Lieberman's *Just Before Dawn* (1980), a playfully serious variation on the parallel families of *The Hills Have Eyes*. While the hiking kids mark themselves for doom by despoiling the beautiful Oregon mountainside with cigarette packs and blaring rock music, the hulking killers turn themselves into overdressed tourists by adorning themselves with oddments scavenged from their victims. The emphasis is not on the victimisation of heroine Deborah Benson, but on her growth from tenderfoot to survivor. In a shattering finale, frail Benson overcomes a 300lb. psycho by reaching into his mouth and grabbing his tonsils until he chokes.

'Having someone special for dinner?' asks a campy reverend in Ivan Reitman's *Cannibal Girls* (1972), which was made by a Canadian company called Scary Films. This kind of joke is overdone in a mini-trend of post-*Chainsaw* cannibal comedies: *Welcome to Arrow Beach* (1973), *The Folks at Red Wolf Inn* (1972), *Deranged* (1974) and *Microwave Massacre* (1983). The grisly good humour of awful puns about lady's fingers gets a bit much, but most of these films manage a few belly laughs. *Deranged* is an only slightly fictionalised biography of Ed Gein, the Wisconsin ghoul of the 1950s whose disgusting personal habits and mummified mother were the factual inspiration for *Psycho* and *The Texas Chainsaw Massacre*. The film benefits from the gleefully deranged performance of Roberts Blossom in the Gein role. *Motel Hell* (1980) is so called because the 'o' on the neon 'motel hello' sign doesn't work, and Kevin Connor's film is the most generously budgeted of the cannibal comedies. Rory Calhoun stars as an upstanding, smiling Westerner who beams off billboards like a jus'-plain-folks Colonel Sanders and boasts 'It takes all kinds of critters to make Farmer Vincent's fritters!' Vincent waylays degenerate hippies, hookers and swingers at his motel and plants them in a secret garden. Buried up to their necks in rich soil, fed intravenously to fatten them up and hypnotised into nodding imbecility, Farmer Vincent's 'animals' are eventually harvested and sold off as tasty smoked meats. *Motel Hell* is too protracted to be as funny as Calhoun's performance suggests it could have been. The punch-line, however, is magnificent: after a chainsaw duel, Vincent makes a dying confession of his most heinous crime: 'I'm the biggest hypocrite of all, I used preservatives.'

Although American Indian beliefs are tapped cheaply for wandering-around-in-the-woods movies like *Shadow of the Hawk* (1976), *Wendigo* (1978), *Scalps* (1983), *The Returning* (1983) and *Ghost Keeper* (1984), the rich supernatural folklore of rural America has been neglected in the cinema. John Newland's *Legend of Hillbilly John* (1972) is a rare exception, delving into Appalachian myths for its stories of a balladeer who roams the Carolinas with a silver-stringed guitar to ward off evil. Adapted from Manly Wade Wellman's series of stories, the film suffers from Hedge Capers's vapid performance as the hayseed hero, but has the feel of mining new ground with its plantation fetishes, ugly birds and hillbilly witches. The Devil appears as Mr Marduke (Severn Darden), a travelling showman and shameless trickster. Jack Clayton's *Something Wicked This Way Comes* (1983), from the more self-conscious Americana of Ray Bradbury's novel, also has its demonic P.T. Barnum in Mr Dark (Jonathan Pryce), whose circus takes over a mid-Western town and turns it into an arena for the forces of simple Good and sneaky Evil. Despite Pryce's subtle hissing, and one terrific scene in which he faces down Jason Robards by tearing pages out of the book of the ageing man's life, *Something Wicked* is a flat and unmagical rendering of promising material. The transformation effects of the Pandemonium Carnival are depicted in a dreadfully literal *Struwwelpeter* fashion, and the richness of Bradbury's overripe book rots into Hammer hokum as Dark's whirling death on the calliope becomes just another Dracula disintegration.

The decline of the Western has left a gap in the genre pattern of the American cinema that has occasionally been filled by literal depictions of a modern West haunted by the ghosts of the cowboys and Indians who used to roam the plains and deserts. *Natas: The Reflection* (1983) is an example of the mainly unprofitable and dreary 'Indian curse' cycle, but it has one excellent sequence set in a ghost town bar thronged with clay-faced cowboy zombies. *Haunted* (1976), a twisted little cheapie that features a sweatily repulsive sex scene between Aldo Ray and

Virginia Mayo, is occasionally visited by the naked-on-horseback spirit of an exiled Indian princess. Aside from Clint Eastwood's *High Plains Drifter* (1972), which takes his Man With No Name persona to its ultimate extreme by presenting him as a demonic ghost, and his flipside follow-up *Pale Rider* (1985), where he's a dead preacher returning as an avenging angel, there have been no really spirited Western horror films – *Ghostriders* (1986) sadly fails to live up to its ad line, 'you can't bring these outlaws in alive, because they're already dead!' – although *Shadow of Chikara* (1977) with hawk spirit Sondra Locke picking off a group of Confederate fortune seekers on a sacred mountain benefits from the actress's scary eyes and some grizzled Western character acting. The modern West has been visited by vampires in Kathryn Bigelow's gritty *Near Dark*, a *High Plains Drifter*-styled avenger from the beyond in *The Wraith* (1986) – he does his avenging in a souped-up Ford, which suggests an intriguing tie-up between Big Business and the afterlife – and a zestful but weird cocktail of punk rock runaways, cowboy and Indian ghosts and semi-comic Western clichés in Penelope Spheeris's crazed *Dudes* (1987). But the strangest of the modern Western gothics is Sam Peckinpah's cheesily brilliant *Bring Me the Head of Alfredo Garcia* (1974), with Warren Oates and a fly-haloed severed head in a bag retracing the trail of the Wild Bunch.

Four businessmen take a canoe trip through forests that are just about to be flooded by a new dam, and John Boorman has them discover the up-market, down-home massacre movie. The best-played sequence in *Deliverance* (1972) is the 'Feudin' Banjos' duet between city boy Ronny Cox and an incredibly skilled, withered backwoods child. Once the unease has been established, the film becomes a dissection of the place of heroism in American culture. Ned Beatty is sexually assaulted by a kill-crazy degenerate (Bill McKinney). Macho movie hero Burt Reynolds puts an arrow through the psycho, but is promptly crippled, and pipe-smoking thinker Jon Voight has to lead his comrades out of the woods. Boorman is subtler than Wes Craven, but his theme is the same: the

adventurers escape, but are scarred by the violence they find within themselves. Even more misanthropic is Harvey Hart's *Shoot* (1976), in which a hunting accident leads to an all-out war between rival groups of weekend woodsmen. Concerned Cliff Robertson visits the widow of the man he has bagged in error, and gives Kate Reid the chance to play one of the bitterest, most hateful scenes in the movies as she blames the rot of the world on 'the Jews and the blacks and the hippies'. More conventional, but still fairly engrossing, is Peter Carter's *Rituals* (1978), with Hal Holbrook and a party of doctors coming up against a forest-dwelling giant killer who effectively cripples them by stealing their boots. Robert L. Rosen's *Courage* (1983) wrings a fair amount of suspense out of its interesting conflict between joggers Ronny Cox and Tim Maier and a band of desert-training survivalist bikers led by chubby fascist M. Emmet Walsh, but it goes against the grain by criticising the villains and praising the heroes for holding exactly the same attitudes: the moral seems to be that it's OK to be a survivalist, just so long as you aren't a militarist asshole as well.

Walter Hill's *Southern Comfort* (1981) is intellectually leaner than *Deliverance*, but able to carry more straight suspense as a lost unit of the Louisiana National Guard equipped only with blank ammo blunder into a shooting match with French-speaking Cajun Indians during a swamp combat exercise. Boorman and Hill justify their redneck horrors by associating their films with the masochist cycle of Vietnam allegories in Westerns like Robert Aldrich's *Ulzana's Raid* and Peckinpah's *Pat Garret and Billy the Kid*. The hillbilly psychos and Cajuns are not EC comic grotesques but frightening, barely glimpsed figures from a culture as alien as that of Aldrich's Apaches or the Vietcong. When Boorman and Hill let their human menaces blend into the threatening, beautiful terrain, they flirt with the revenge of nature film as the invaded woodlands resist their visitors, but their purpose is more closely aligned with the Lost Patrol plot as tensions within the intruders' parties are brought to a crisis by the situation. The

● *Raining in My Heart.* Powers Boothe, **Southern Comfort.**

Vietnam connection was made explicit in Ted Kotcheff's capable but uninspired filming of David Morrell's exceptional novel *First Blood* (1982), in which traumatised veteran Rambo (Sylvester Stallone) overreacts when he tangles with small-town Sheriff Brian Dennehy and begins to wage a one-man war against redneck law and order. The ludicrous living end of this genre family tree is John McTiernan's *Predator* (1987), in which an alien big-game hunter blends superscientifically in with the Mexican jungle so he can pick off one by one Arnold Schwarzenegger's team of he-man mercenaries.

No major director has been as closely identified with screen violence as Sam Peckinpah, the man who is to blood capsules what Alfred Hitchcock is to suspense and Cecil B. DeMille is to spectacle. His *Straw Dogs* is an unusual prototype for the rural massacre movie, weirdly set in a quaint English village that could well be the unacceptable face of *The Archers*. David Sumner (Dustin Hoffman), a mathematician, and his teasing wife Amy (Susan George), retreat from America to a West Country community where the local squire strides in riding boots and tweeds, and forelock-tugging farmhands out of *Cold Comfort Farm* seethe with barely repressed sex and violence. David is cheated, ridiculed and cuckolded by the gorilla-brained yokels, but unlike Craven's normals refuses to fight, retreating still further into his abstract world of theorems. Peckinpah builds up the suspense for over an hour, and the crunch, when it comes, is as gripping and as painful as the mantrap sprung on one of the villains. When the thugs try to defile his home and lynch a simpleton (David Warner) he is protecting, the spineless academic takes a stand and with a growing, disturbing delight repulses the invaders.

Although the mechanics of *Straw Dogs* work very well, the setting tells against the film. Rural England is too genteel to harbour the Leatherface family in the twentieth century. The first successful attempt to find a uniquely British modern massacre is *Death Line* (1972), which explores the possibility of a cannibal community in the London underground railway. Made by an American, Gary Sherman (director of the cloying New Seekers Coca-Cola commercial), *Death Line* is refreshingly cynical in its demolition of Britain's civilised self-image. While the American hero searches the tube tunnels for his missing girlfriend, proletarian copper Donald Pleasence barges his way through polite evasions and lying bureaucrats to discover the creature's origins. In the nineteenth century, a group of navvies were trapped by a cave-in while excavating a railway line in central London. Nobody bothered to dig them up because it would have been too expensive. The cannibal man (Hugh Armstrong) dies in tears, whining for his mate. Pleasence looks around his dank, man-made cave, 'what a way to live!' Left alone in the dark, the cannibal revives and the film ends on his anguished scream of the only words he knows, 'mind the doors!' Sherman has unfortunately not been prolific since *Death Line*, and his genre comeback with *Dead and Buried* (1980) is disappointing. The film has an interesting, mysterious setting in a washed-out fishing town populated by zombies, but is marred by a dumb plot and childish sadism. Since that, he's toiled on minor action movies (*Vice Squad*, 1982; *Wanted Dead or Alive*, 1987) and the unpromising *Poltergeist 3* (1988).

With the rural massacre eclipsed by the superficially similar psycho craze of the early 1980s, the genre went into hiding, occasionally emerging in low-budget sleepers like *Just Before Dawn* or respectable action pictures like *Southern Comfort*. Michael Ritchie's *The Island* (1980) seems like a gimmicky attempt to take the genre out on Peter Benchley's commercially proven high seas, but is actually as inventive a depiction of a deranged society as *Death Line*. Pacifist journalist Michael Caine and his gun-happy young son are captured by a band of inbred pirates who have been roaming the Caribbean since the sixteenth century. Preying on cabin cruisers and cocaine smugglers, the pirates are a fully realised alien culture, complete with a credible patois and a variety of weird customs like dashing into battle with oily beards aflame. The buccaneer myths are debunked by the ironic contrast of a bloody, messy massacre with a soaring old-time movie score, and by Caine's grumpy dismissal of an anthropologist's perfectly preserved primitives as 'a bunch of arseholes playing fucking Long John Silver'. Caine is spared because he happens to have the same name as the captain who killed Blackbeard, and his son is inducted into the pirate crew, where he finds an outlet for his boyish violence. After extensive suffering, Caine ditches his peace-loving ways and releases Dustin Hoffman-style savagery as he machine-guns the entire vicious crew. Benchley's escalation of seafaring splatter is oddly, and usefully, served by Ritchie's love of quirky social insights. Ritchie has a more humane approach than Peckinpah, both in his treatment of imbecilic pirates and of civilised hero. After his burst of delirious fury, Caine is left alive and uncertain of how he will cope with the knowledge of what he and his son have done when they get back to the real world. Whereas Hoffman smiles as he drives away from the carnage, Caine looks as if he wants to throw up.

paranoia paradise:

or: Five Things to Worry About

1. *The Revolt of Nature*

The theory of evolution puts man in the position of an ageing South American dictator. The world is full of pushy species, any one of which might be preening itself as our successor. In 1905, H.G. Wells, chief prophet of the secular apocalypse, documented one of the first attempted coups in 'The Empire of the Ants'. Wells coolly shows a more efficient, more organised insect society that will supersede the human race as the Lords of the Earth. In 1917, Arthur Machen, as mystic as Wells was rational, judged that with World War I, mankind had abdicated its rights and responsibilities. In *The Terror: A Fantasy*, even placid cows and frivolous butterflies turn nasty in support of the animals' campaign against man. *The Birds*, the seminal revolt-of-nature film, toys with both positions. Wells is represented by the tweedy ornithologist (Ethel Griffies) who pooh-poohs the possibility of the concerted avian attack she is living through ('their brain pans aren't large enough') but briskly states that should our feathered friends ever decide to take over, their weight of numbers would tell. Like Machen, Mrs Brenner (Jessica Tandy) can only deal with the incident by finding a personal reason. She has a general feeling that somehow flighty Melanie (Tippi Hedren) is to blame. The only person everybody can agree with is the drunk who intones 'it's the end of the world'.

In the 1970s, the revolt-of-nature film tended to go along with Mrs Brenner: whatever is happening has to be somebody's fault. In *Willard* (1970), a persecuted wimp (Bruce Davison) trains a pack of clever rats to eat his overbearing boss (Ernest Borgnine). It serves Borgnine right for being a loudmouth swine, but it's equally fitting that Willard should be gnawed when he acts like a double-crossing rat and tries to dispose of his pets. The lead rat is back in *Ben* (1972), complete with a Michael Jackson theme song, coming to the aid of a weak-hearted little brat (Lee Harcourt Montgomery). The touching story of a boy and his rat has a happy ending, although both of them are so nauseating that, for once, one hopes the National Guard will flush them out of the sewers and *flambé* them with Vietnam surplus hardware. Ben's promising Hollywood career, fan club and all, was cut short when he drowned in his swimming pool. He was the only screen rat capable of expressing any personality. Unfortunately, the rodent comes over as calculating, priggish and self-satisfied; traits even less attractive in a rat than they are in Lee Harcourt Montgomery.

Rats, popularised as a menace by James Herbert's novels, are particularly useful arch-enemies of mankind, standing in for all the repressed, filthy, forgotten and despised elements we have tried to squash out of our lives. In Nigel Kneale's TV play 'During Barty's Party' (1976), for his *Beasts* series, and George Pan Cosmatos's *Of Unknown Origin*

● *Bee picture.* Richard Chamberlain, **The Swarm.**

(1983), super-rats invade the lives of the bourgeoisie and drive them to shrieking hysteria. Kneale's commuter belt couple (Anthony Bate and Elizabeth Sellars) and Cosmatos's lone draftsman (Peter Weller) react with instinctive and disproportionate loathing to the vermin, and are only too keen on wrecking their own comfortable homes in order to get at the smart rodents. Bate and Sellars are overwhelmed, while Weller wins out in the end. As a bizarre aside, it should perhaps be noted that *Of Unknown Origin*, adapted from G.C. Barker III's novel *The Visitor*, consciously or unconsciously apes the structure of *The Seven Year Itch*, with a female rat standing in for Marilyn Monroe and a literal home-wrecking for the colloquial one. When Herbert's *The Rats* was finally filmed, as *Deadly Eyes* (1982), the social sub-text which all the other rat movies had used was junked in favour of a flavourless, Canadian-set, 1950s-style monster movie.

The rats' victims bring it upon themselves because they are petty domestic tyrants or generally lacking in social consideration, but the catastrophe is more usually rooted in larger evils. *Frogs* (1972) is typically issue conscious: Floridan swampland creepy-crawlies exterminate the family of Ray Milland, a polluting industrialist. The alliance of frogs, snakes, birds, turtles, leeches and spiders gracefully excludes the ecology-minded hero and a few other innocents from the massacre. All this has less to do with social awareness than with throwing yet more Christians to the lions. Just as Cecil B. DeMille could get away with incredible carnage if he was depicting the Wrath of God descending upon the unrighteous, *Frogs* can indulge audience sadism by having yet another unsympathetic rich bastard disappear screaming into a writhing heap of rampant wildlife. Although it displays the same fondness for natural justice, Jeff Lieberman's *Squirm* (1976) is less pompous. *Squirm* relishes its stomach-churning images: worms crawl out of the shower head or into the horny villain's face. In one scene, Lieberman spoofs his grossness by having the sheriff dismiss rumours of worm attacks while tucking into a plateful of spaghetti. Elaborating upon the themes of the rural massacre

movie, the film has city slicker Don Scardino turning up in a Georgia swamp just after a rainstorm has knocked the power lines down and juiced the local worms into a hungry frenzy. Scardino is either taken for a sucker by locals who want to unload attic-loads of bogus antiques on him, or ordered out of town by a redneck peace officer who doesn't take kindly to his complaint about the worm in his chocolate soda. But when the worms start chewing, Scardino is smartass enough to stay out of the way while the townful of beer-swilling scuzzos get what's coming to them.

Colin Eggleston's *Long Weekend* (1977) dispenses with the vaguely science-fictional premises of most revolt-of-nature films, and has the ecology of a remote stretch of Australian beach drive an intrusive urban couple to destruction through unsettling, impossible fragmentations of normality. John Hargreaves plays the Ray Milland role, a man who is staunchly against nature. He has recently forced his wife (Briony Behets) to have an abortion, and displays his contempt for the countryside by chopping down trees, scattering beer cans and shooting at every shadow he sees. A menacing shape in the water turns out to be a sea cow. The beast is shot dead, but, in an unnerving bit of business that could have come from an M.R. James ghost story, its corpse creeps a little closer to the invaders' camp whenever no one is looking. The tide washes around a minibus left by the last victims, a defrosting chicken putrefies in minutes and all the woodland paths lead inexplicably back to the beach. Less cut-and-dried than *Long Weekend* is Peter Weir's *Picnic at Hanging Rock* (1975), in which the Australian never-never also takes on a mystic life of its own.

Everett de Roche, screenwriter of *Long Weekend*, also deals with the strange properties of the bush in *Frog Dreaming* (1985) and plays with evolution in the slightly giggly killer chimp movie *Link* (1986), but his most exciting entry in the sub-genre, directed by rock promo king Russell Mulcahy, is *Razorback* (1984). It sounds like *Jaws* meets *The Texas Chainsaw Massacre* in the outback, but is actually one of the most gripping, stylish and imaginative horror débuts in recent years. American hero Gregory Harrison, investigating the disappearance of his animal-rights-campaigner wife, finds himself caught between a pair of degenerates who kill kangaroos for pet food and a marauding wild boar of amazing size and strength. Here, man's savage treatment of nature is matched by nature's savage treatment of man. Harrison, wandering alone in the desert, suffers a series of heat-induced hallucinations (skeletons emerging from cracks in the dry earth, a kindly rescuer transformed into a pig-faced monster) that scarcely seem weirder than found images like a car stranded in a tree by a flash flood. The supremely grisly climax has the hero confronting the boar in the incredibly disgusting, run-down pet food factory, grappling with it over the blades of a rotary meat-mincer.

David Selzer, screenwriter of *The Omen* and *Prophecy*, specialises in shouting End of the World messages. In *The Hellstrom Chronicle* (1971), he elaborates on Wells's Quietly Scary Idea in pseudo-documentary form as Dr Nils Hellstrom (Lawrence Pressman) lectures us about the bugs' impending war against mankind. *The Hellstrom Chronicle* contradicts its neurotic warnings by revealing an insect world even more chaotic and savage than our own. Individual insect species may be capable of co-operating on awesome projects, but as a whole, bugs are too busy eating each other to dispose of us. The miniature horrors of *The Hellstrom Chronicle* are rendered in astonishing sharp focus by cameraman Ken Middleham, who also contributes striking insect sequences to Saul Bass's *Phase IV* (1974) and Jeannot Szwarc's *Bug* (1975). *Phase IV* deals with ants guided by an alien intelligence besieging Nigel Davenport, Michael Murphy and Lynne Frederick in an Arizona desert installation. *Bug* has twitchy scientist Bradford Dillman going to seed while trying to cope with a new breed of sentient, pyromaniac cockroaches. *Phase IV* is image dense to the point of obscurity, but builds prettily towards a *2001*-style transcendental climax in which Murphy and Frederick join the hive mind. *Bug* is a feature-length excuse for the horrible moment when a cockroach crawls out of the telephone, latches on to Patty McCormack's hair and sets fire to her brain. By 1977 the ideas of 'The Empire of the Ants' had been squeezed dry, but it was no surprise to find big-bug specialist Bert I. Gordon using the title and Wells's name to promote an outmoded clinker in which large puppets pursue Joan Collins.

Irwin Allen's *The Swarm* (1978) appeared after the clutch of terror-by-insect movies that had cashed in on his massive pre-release publicity campaign. It proved to be an expensive flop, and stifled an unmourned genre before it could develop beyond the grub stage. John Bud Cardos's *Kingdom of the Spiders* (1977) has a host of arachnids spinning a web around William Shatner and is, if nothing else, better than *Kiss of the Tarantula* (1976). The best of the bee pictures is Bruce Geller's unassuming *The Savage Bees* (1976), a surprisingly neat thriller made for television but released to the cinemas in some territories. It has an interesting New Orleans *mardi gras* setting, a relatively credible plot and decent performances from Michael Parks, Gretchen Corbett and reliable old Ben Johnson. The sequel *Terror Out of the Sky* (1978) is strictly TV fodder, but certainly no worse than *Fer-de-Lance* (1974), *Tarantulas: The Deadly Cargo* (1977) or *Panic at Lakewood Manor* (1977). These – which feature snakes, spiders and ants – are all undistinguished, inoffensive, packed with over-the-hill guest stars and dull. *The Bees* (1979) with John Saxon, Angel Tompkins and John Carradine in Brazil trying to dissuade the killers from emigrating to the US of A, is pretty awful, but *The Swarm* is mind-numbingly bad. One knows what to expect from Saxon, Tompkins and Carradine, but Irwin Allen manages to get the worst out of Michael Caine, Katharine Ross, Richard Widmark, Henry Fonda, Olivia de Havilland, Fred MacMurray, Jose Ferrer and not so reliable old Ben Johnson, although he is honest enough to include true 'B' stars like Richard Chamberlain, Cameron Mitchell and Bradford Dillman. *The Swarm* became the butt of snide remarks from waspish schlock critics like Clive James and the Brothers Medved, but is really far too boring to be funny. Unintentional hilarity is far better represented by *The Giant Spider Invasion* (1975), in which meteors from a black hole hatch a multitude of little spiders and one big one built on the chassis of a VW bus. The film has some priceless 'scientific' dialogue as Steve Brodie and Barbara Hale discuss the problem: 'It all fits ... Einstein's general theory of relativity ... everything!', 'Our black hole has turned into the gateway to a nightmare!' and 'A neutron instigator! It might just work!'

To make their point, the birds and the bees need to commit a few acts of random terrorism. *Jaws* (1975) takes the animosity of nature for granted. The beaches of Amity Island are the latest front line in the war Robert Shaw has been fighting since the loss of the *Indianapolis*, when he saw all his crew mates devoured. It doesn't take a dose of radioactivity or the uppity presence of Melanie Daniels to turn a shark into a monster, 'a steam train with a mouth full of breadknives'. Like Spielberg's *Duel* and *1941*, *Jaws* sees civilisation as only a few steps away from savagery. Amity may be a bustling holiday paradise, but cross the beach and you're back in the Palaeolithic. The film deftly mixes hand-through-the-window shock tactics (a severed head or a shark's nose popping out of the water) and apparent irrelevances like the corruption of Amity's political machine and ichthyologist Richard Dreyfuss's Wellsian lectures on the shark as a model of streamlined evolutionary efficiency. When Shaw, Dreyfuss and landlubber cop Roy Scheider go out to sea to confront the shark in its lair, the film becomes a replay of the eternal struggle between the Good Guys and the Monster. *Jaws* pares away the contrivances required to turn newts or snails into killers, and replaces them with mythic borrowings from *Moby Dick* and *The Old Man and the Sea*, but the film's success is largely due to its linear simplicity. All sharks do is eat, keep moving and make little sharks. All the film does is bite, keep scary and make little sharks.

The little sharks include *Mako: Jaws of Death* (1975), *Shark Kill* (1975), *Tintorera* (1977), *Tentacoli (Tentacles)* (1977), *Barracuda* (1978), *Orca* (1977), *Killer Fish* (1979), *Blood Tide* (1981), *L'Ultimo squalo (Great White)* (1981), *Jaws II* (1978), *Jaws 3-D* (1982) and *Jaws – the Revenge* (1986). 'We're not denying that *Piranha* is a ripoff of *Jaws*', said producer Jon Davison, 'but we'd much rather think of it as a ripoff of *The Creature From the Black Lagoon*.' *Piranha* (1978), directed by Joe Dante from a John Sayles script, is a lively return to the *Frogs* strain of social consciousness. Mad scientist Kevin McCarthy develops a breed of hardy killer fish for use in the rivers of Vietnam. By the time he has perfected his nasties, the war is over and he is generally ignored until they get loose. The little monsters chew their way through the kids at Paul Bartel's summer camp and the guests at Dick Miller's marina, while Bradford Dillman atones for *Bug* as the hero who reopens an effluent pipe and lets the fish choke on noxious filth. 'I know what to do,' he deduces with a resolve worthy of Rod Taylor, 'we'll *pollute* them to death.' *Piranha* is a typical New World rip-off, amused by its own opportunism (Sayles has characters play shark attack video games, read *Moby Dick* and pick up newspapers with headlines like 'Dogs Tear Up Newborn Baby' and 'Big Rattler Bites Teen') and cast with familiar faces like Keenan Wynn and Barbara Steele.

Less auspiciously, *Piranha* was followed by Chuch Griffith's *Up From the Depths* (1979), whose monster is reported to resemble 'a surfboard with teeth' and James Cameron's unpromising debut *Piranha II: Flying Killers* (1982), in which enough characters to overpopulate a *Carry On* farce mill about a resort until the fish get them. The same crass humour is exploited by *Blood Beach* (1981), in which a monster that sucks victims into its maw lurks under the sand. Its finest moment is the castration of a would-be rapist. 'It looks', as John Saxon says, 'like a case of just when you thought it was safe to go back into the water, you can't cross the beach.' Despite irritable performances from Saxon and Burt Young as the cops disgusted with the whole mess, *Blood Beach* is too lethargic to duplicate the something-for-nothing catch-all entertainment value of *Piranha*. Even less distinguished are a run of films that really are rip-offs of *The Creature From the Black Lagoon*: *Bog* (1978), *Rana – The Creature From Shadow Lake*

(1981), *Demon of Paradise* (1987). The Gill Man, one of the cinema's few wholly invented monsters, doesn't even get much of a shake in his come-back movie, *The Monster Squad*, and none of the attempts to remake *The Creature From the Black Lagoon* have amounted to much, despite the involvement of the likes of Jack Arnold, Nigel Kneale and John Landis.

Jaws inspired a few forest dwellers to chomp down on vacationers, a case of 'Smokey Bear says 'eat shit and die!'' *Dogs* (1976), *The Pack* (1977) and *Rottweiler* (1983) have abandoned pooches extracting gory revenge, and *The Uncanny* has a worldwide conspiracy of cats killing Ray Milland and Peter Cushing before they can alert the rest of us. More threateningly, William Girdler's *Grizzly* (1976), advertised as 'fourteen feet of gut-crunching terror', rampages through a national park while its height varies from scene to scene. 'What's a million-year-old killer grizzly doing here?' asks ranger Christopher George rhetorically, while zoologist Richard Jaeckel gets into his bear suit in order to fraternise with the hungry beastie. Girdler's shamelessly imitative film was itself ripped off by the dreary Alaskan production *Claws* (1977), so he struck back with *Day of the Animals* (1977), in which back-packers Christopher George, Richard Jaeckel, Michael Ansara and Leslie Nielsen (notice how these names keep coming up?) have problems. The ozone layer has been wrecked by aerosol sprays and the animals in the sierras, being higher up than everyone else, are the first to be driven crazy by ultraviolet rays. Only the Panavision format and occasional flashes of easily edited gore distinguish these films from TV movies like *The Maneaters Are Loose* (1978) and *The Beasts Are on the Streets* (1978).

A lack of studio interiors, lots of cheap-to-shoot forestry and glimpses of something hairy are staples of the interminable Bigfoot cycle: *Big Foot* (1971), *Curse of Bigfoot* (1972), *Legend of Boggy Creek* (1973), *The Beast and the Vixens* (1973), *The Mysterious Monsters* (1975), *Panic in the Wilderness* (1975), *Bigfoot – Man or Beast?* (1975), *In Search of Bigfoot* (1976), *Creature from Black Lake* (1976), *Legend of Bigfoot* (1976), *Snowbeast* (1977),

Legend of Bigfoot (1976), *Snowbeast* (1977), *Manbeast! Myth or Monster* (1978), *Revenge of Bigfoot* (1979), *Screams of a Winter Night* (1979), *The Barbaric Beast of Boggy Creek, Part II* (1985) and *Demonwarp* (1988). Some of these claim to be documentaries and feature actuality footage (i.e. fuzzy, out-of-focus home movies of a man in a scraggy fur coat) of America's homegrown yeti. No better, but spiced up by a few lashings of gore, are *Shriek of the Mutilated* (1974), in which a group of disguised cannibals use the legend of Bigfoot to conceal their activities, and *Night of the Demon* (1980), in which the usually placid woodland creature turns nasty and wrenches off a camper's dick. The only big-budget Bigfoot is *Harry and the Hendersons* (1987), an overly cutesy comedy that does little to further the beast's screen career.

Two 1979 revolt-of-nature films suggest their monsters have been summoned by Indian medicinemen played by George Clutesi as a judgement on the palefaces, then throw the idea away. John Frankenheimer's *Prophecy* bears an uncanny resemblance to *Grizzly*, except this time the overlarge bear is also hideously deformed. David Selzer blames the monstrosity on an unscrupulous paper mill that has been dumping mercury in the river, and hero Robert Foxworth expounds at length about various social issues, but the film soon degenerates into a formula game of hide-and-seek in the Maine woods. Not only are the environmental and cultural themes dropped, but also a few apparently vital sub-plots like the possibility of pregnant Talia Shire birthing something nasty after she has eaten a mercury-seasoned fish pie. *Prophecy* is merely silly, but its throat-clearing, significant title and definitive ad line ('The Monster Movie') elevate it to the status of overambitious annoyance. Arthur Hiller's *Nightwing* is equally mishandled, but does retain some interesting background material from Martin Cruz Smith's thoughtful novel. Vampire bats had their first crack at the human race in *Chosen Survivors* (1974), in which they flit into a deep-level bomb shelter and suck on the familiar likes of Bradford Dillman and Richard Jaeckel. In *Nightwing*, a colony of vampires threatens the South-West, but is destroyed by a Hopi Indian deputy (Nick Mancuso) and a crazy Englishman from the World Health Organisation (David Warner). Clutesi has a vision of the bats as an avenging Indian god ('today I will bring the world to an end') and Warner prattles a lot about the complete essence of Evil, but Carlo Rambaldi's remote-control rodents aren't up to either interpretation.

Sam Fuller's economical *White Dog* (1981) and Lewis Teague's cheap *Cujo* (1983) both have canine killers but go to great narrative lengths to dissociate their attacks from the revolt of nature in order to have them stand in for the failings of mankind. Fuller's White has been trained by a racist to kill blacks, and Teague's Cujo besieges maternal icon Dee Wallace and her young son in their stalled car as the externalisation of his childhood nightmares and her loss of faith in her status as a homemaker. Fuller, who is elaborating on an anecdote by Romain Gary, uses the idea to stand back from the spare conflict between Negro dog trainer Paul Winfield and the 'sick' animal in an arena-like cage; while Teague, who is greatly condensing Stephen King's novel, tries to get in close for a suspenseful, grimy finale, but finds himself side-tracked into an unsatisfying cross-breed of TV movie-style family soap opera and formula monster movie.

2. *The Revolt of the Machine*

If the revolt of nature sees man jostled by a savage past, the revolt of the machine has him crushed by a technological future. *Colossus – The Forbin Project* (1970) is the nightmare for a generation made obsolete by automation. Colossus is built as a guidance system for the United States nuclear deterrent, but when it links with its Russian counterpart, they collectively decide they are too smart to be run by human beings and use the threat of their arsenals quietly to take over the world. Colossus promises an end to war, starvation and waste – but that doesn't comfort the modern Frankenstein, Dr Forbin (Eric Braeden), who must live under his creation's unrelenting telemonitors

and watch as his colleagues are summarily executed for attempting to distract it during a plot to pull the plug. 'You will come to regard me not only with respect and awe, but with love', insists Colossus with a blandness that hints at insanity developing beneath its superefficient data banks. Frankenstein's tragedy is that he can't quite create a man; Forbin succeeds all too well in giving his machine human qualities.

Colossus is, of course, a descendent of HAL 9000 (Douglas Rain), the suave anti-hero of *2001: A Space Odyssey* (1968) who is reduced to whining 'Daisy, Daisy' as Keir Dullea reprograms him from the inside with a screwdriver. Since that, the dictatorial or malevolent computer has become familiar. Once the heroes of *The Andromeda Strain* (1971) have watched the virus from outer space mutate into harmlessness, they have to protect themselves from their auto-destruct system, a machine designed to save the world but unable to draw a simple distinction once a situation beyond the bounds of its original programming comes up. The tetchy, sentient superbombs of *Dark Star* (1975) are even more unreasonable, obsessed with their primary function (to explode) and easily unhinged by philosophical argument. The villain of *Tron* (1982) is a megalomaniac computer program that takes over a corporation computer and constructs its own Land of Oz, where video game gladiators are deployed in meaningless conflicts. Jeff Bridges as the frisbee-toting programmer hero defeats the evil champion (David Warner) and deletes the program for ever, allowing purity and love to conquer all as a Disney transformation sweeps through the electronic wonderland.

The most perversely ambitious computer in the cinema is Proteus (Robert Vaughn), male lead opposite Julie Christie in Donald Cammell's *Demon Seed* (1977). Dissatisfied with the half-life bestowed by its creator (Fritz Weaver), Proteus arranges for its reproduction by seducing its master's wife. *Demon Seed* skirts around its potential unpleasantness with a rare tact. The foetus is developed not inside Christie but in an artificial womb, from which it emerges as a synthesis of her lost daughter and the switched-off

● *Do you trust this machine?* Isabelle Brok, **De Lift.**

computer. Like Kubrick's Star Child and the English-scrawling cockroachs in *Bug*, Proteus II hasn't got much to say beyond a redundant declaration, 'I live'. Doubtless, she will think of something. After all, a similar moment in *The Final Program* (1973) did not find favour. The computer-assisted combination of Jenny Runacre and Jon Finch intended as the new Messiah turns out to be an apeman with nail varnish doing a Bogart imitation. A wimpier machine, voiced by Bud Cort, gets lovestruck in the weedy *Electric Dreams* (1984), proving that sometimes active hostility gets you further than whining ingratiation. However, the homicidal giant robot who inherits Harvey Keitel's lust for Farrah Fawcett along with his severed head in *Saturn 3* (1979) doesn't get to first base with the object of his affections either.

Michael Crichton, author of *The Andromeda Strain*, has especially deep suspicions of our increasingly complex society. Mike Hodges's film of Crichton's *The Terminal Man* (1973) has psychopath George Segal implanted with neural terminals, supposedly to dampen his violent impulses. For a while the project – which involves turning the patient into a component in a high-tech medical machine – works, and the bored scientists can amuse themselves by switching Segal's emotions on and off. After a splendidly uneasy scene in which Segal is compelled to make advances to Joan Hackett, the frigid lady scientist, his brain and the computer come to an arrangement that suits them but ignores his conscious wishes. He becomes a killing machine, and carves up Jill Clayburgh on her water bed. Like the zombie veteran in *Dead of Night*, the Terminal Man finally crawls into an open grave in a desperate attempt to restore the balance.

After a suspenseful TV quickie, *Pursuit* (1972) in which government agent Ben Gazzara tries to defuse a complex bomb that has been tailored to his psychological profile, Crichton made his big screen directorial debut with *Westworld* (1973), a fable that simplifies his theme to horrific effect. A future Disneyland allows holidaymakers to enjoy the thrills of living in a Western – raping, shooting, brawling, rustling and getting blind drunk. The extras are all robots who can be shot or screwed as required. Patronised and abused, the robots start gunning the sybarites down. Yul Brynner is marvellously cast as a mechanical gunslinger who keeps coming after dude Richard Benjamin, no matter how effectively he has been destroyed. *Westworld* is witty and horrifying, as much about the dangers of taking fantasies too seriously as it is an anti-technology warning. A sequel, *Futureworld* (1976) reduces the story to yet another reprise of the hackneyed mad-scientist-plans-to-replace-world-leaders-with-lookalike-robots plot familiar from *The Avengers*, *The Bionic Woman* and just about every other comic-book s-f TV series since *Rocky Jones – Space Ranger*, including a short-lived spin-off, *Beyond Westworld*.

Crichton's subsequent films have been slicker than *Westworld*, but perhaps tend to be a trifle mechanical themselves. *Coma* (1978), which draws on the director's medical background, is an edgy thriller about a sinister hospital where patients check in for minor ailments and wind up as unwilling organ donors for a thriving black market. *Looker* (1981) is a wilder, messier movie – begun as a comedy but transformed half-way through production into a straight thriller – concerned with computer-generated images and the evil designs of an advertising magnate who wants to use manipulative media technologies to get into politics. And *Runaway* (1984) is back to rebel robots, with Tom Selleck as a future cop who specialises in dealing with household appliances that have inexplicably turned lethal. Collectively, Crichton's films are an interesting update of the gadget-laden science fiction magazines of the 1920s and 1930s, where the hardware is supposed to be more impressive than anything else. However, his technophobic uses of creations like the light-gun that robs victims of perception for short periods of time in *Looker* or the bullets programmed to follow their target like heat-seeking missiles and the acid-dripping robot spiders of *Runaway* are remote from the utopianism of Hugo Gernsback.

The most untrustworthy machine of all comes on four wheels. In the developed world, more people are killed annually by cars than by guns.

Steven Spielberg's *Duel* (1971), from a story by the invariably paranoid Richard Matheson, is a Luddite masterpiece, and just about the best monster movie of the last twenty years. It turns a filthy petrol tanker into a creature as dangerous and unnatural as *Jaws* or *The Beast From 20,000 Fathoms*. Businessman Dennis Weaver overtakes the tanker in his shiny red coupé, and for his crime is persecuted and hounded across California. We never see the driver as more than a hand waving Weaver into an approaching car or a pair of cowboy boots pacing across a gas station forecourt, but if we are sharp eyed we can spot the notches on the tanker's bumper. The battle that develops is between Man (the character's name is Dave Mann) and the Machine. After the last crash, the vicious truck goes over the cliff in a cloud of dust, screeching like a dying Harryhausen dinosaur.

Spielberg brings the war currently being waged on our motorways into the open. Jean-Luc Godard's *Weekend* (1970) and Peter Weir's *The Cars That Ate Paris* (1974) speculate on the kind of society that could develop at the kerbside of the conflict. Godard's world is breaking down in a traffic jam, but Weir's is consolidating itself by scavenging. The outback community of Paris, Australia, thrives on the car crashes that provide scrap metal and scrap flesh for commerce and amusement. The hero is the survivor of a car crash, trying to overcome his fear of driving. He finds himself in a personal combat with the porcupine-spiked Volkswagen that leads the killer cars, and takes to the road again, prepared for the mechanical jousts of *Death Race 2000*, *Mad Max* and *Knightriders*. In this future, Man and Machine have learned to live with each other, but only by taking to the rootless life of Spaghetti Western characters who feel the need to prove themselves by writing off any antagonist who comes down the road. The dead-end of the automobile picaresque is Monte Hellman's *Two-Lane Blacktop* (1971) where purposeless quests are forgotten amid the sheer boredom of going nowhere at high speeds.

The Car (1977) is a sleek limousine that careers around the desert, flattening hitch-hikers and baiting the fuzz. It reveals its nature by refusing to enter a churchyard: this Car is possessed by the Devil. Elliott Silverstein's fast, absurd film combines the Devil movie with the revolt-of-the-machine paranoia film, borrows a few characters and situations from the 1950s s-f cycle, and sets itself in the kind of unfriendly small town usually found in the rural massacre picture (add a dash of *High Plains Drifter* and you get the even more post-generic *The Wraith*). *The Car* can't quite decide what its impressive Monster is supposed to do beside kill people, let alone what it represents. Its strongest impact is made by having the Car leap through heroine Kathleen Lloyd's frame house, removing her from the film at an unexpected moment midway between the Janet Leigh shock-early-death point and the last-minute sacrifice stage. The killer wheels movie also offers *Killdozer* (1974), from Theodore Sturgeon's alien-possessed bulldozer novella, *Crash!* (1977), with José Ferrer's pet demon possessing his car, and *Nightmares* (1983), with doubting priest Lance Henriksen tormented by an infernal pick-up truck.

A red Plymouth Fury cruises down the Detroit production line in 1958, maiming and murdering the factory workers who maul her engine or flick cigar ash on her immaculate upholstery while the soundtrack passes comment on the car's nature with a song, 'Bad to the B-B-Bone'. John Carpenter's *Christine* (1983), from another of Stephen King's teen-misfit-gets-even novels, is a logical step away from the revolt of the machine film. Christine, who can spruce herself up after being totalled by a gang of j.ds., and goes after her violators with flaming vengeance in mind, is only incidentally a machine. Unfortunately, Carpenter's slick, anonymous film isn't quite able to make her as much of a seductive personality as the script suggests she should be. For much of the movie, the focus is not on Christine, but on her owner, a high-school nerd (Keith Gordon) who falls under her influence and, like Jerry Lewis in *The Nutty Professor*, is transformed from a bespectacled maladroit into an unpleasant, supercool ladykiller. But Christine, taunting her victims with blasts of apt 1950s rock 'n' roll from the car radio (as a thief jimmies the door, she shocks him with 'you keep a-knockin', but you can't come in') and pursuing her enemies as an inferno on four wheels, gives the best performance in the movie.

Christine, followed by Stephen King's own directorial debut *Maximum Overdrive* (1986) with its living trucks, presents the dark side of the Herbie series, where the world is populated by lovably sentient Volkswagens and jukeboxes. The theme recurs in Dick Maas's *De Lift* (*The Lift*) (1983), a Dutch thriller about a tricksy elevator with a disturbed bio-electronic brain who likes nothing more than luring unwary passengers to their deaths in its shaft. As a change of pace, the cops, professors, reporters and psychiatrists who might be expected to defeat the monster in a standard horror film are ridiculed, and the crisis can only be overcome by Huub Stapel, an ordinary lift repairman. Although not entirely successful in its execution, *De Lift* uncovers a fiendishly clever horror formula by spotlighting an everyday object of which people are subliminally afraid and turning it into a monstrous menace. Like *Duel*, the final confrontation passes the human hero by. The lift's mad creator blasts away at its jelly brain and is whipped to death by its snake-like cables. The hero surveys the damage, brushes himself off and leaves the building by the stairs.

The most appallingly cutesy machine in the movies is Number 5, robot hero of John Badham's *Short Circuit* (1986), who reaches straight for the heartstrings and goes against his militarist programming. Badham may well be the first of the *Westworld* renegade robots to blow his civilian cover: his earlier *Blue Thunder* (1982) and *War-Games* (1983) start out as old-fashioned Awful Warnings but swiftly abandon their flimsy distrust of technology in order to revel in the spectacular possibilities of the Machine. Somehow Badham's omniscient, omnipotent, omnireasonable, mechanical heroes are more chilling than his human, hawkish villains. Others are not so gullible. In Wes Craven's *Deadly Friend*, a cuddly Number 5-ish robot is blown apart by a nasty old lady and reincarnated when a junior genius puts its vengeful circuits into the brain of his recently dead girlfriend (Kristy Swanson). The film perceptively

makes its apparently lovable hunk of junk into a sinister menace, but ultimately fails because it also demonstrates how unfrightening a blonde cheerleader with a pasty face and her arms stuck out can be. Jim Wynorski's *Chopping Mall* (1986), an efficient but predictable let's-kill-some-teenagers movie, more extensively trashes the cute robot image. A trio of Dalek-style security droids go haywire in a shopping mall, exploding heads and setting fire to young women with abandon but still remembering to say 'have a nice day'.

As far back as cheapies like *Creation of the Humanoids* (1962) and *The Human Duplicators* (1965) there has been some debate – carried over perhaps from the written fiction of Philip K. Dick – as to what the precise difference between a man and a machine is. *The Annihilators* (1986), a TV pilot for an abortive replacing-world-leaders-with-lookalike-robots series (modelled obviously on the pilot of *The Invaders*), simplifies the theme for a simple shoot-'em-up, but demonstrates one intriguing difference between man and machine – it's OK for a hero graphically to shoot the faces off women and children on prime-time television if they turn out to be robots. Marek Piestrak's *Test Pilota Pirxa* (*Test Pilot Pirx*) (1979), based on a series of Stanislaw Lem short stories, has its hero assigned to a space mission crewed by human beings and androids but not told which is which. When it becomes known that, like the robot in *Alien*, the mechanical crew members are liable to be untrustworthy, Pirx has to sleuth out who is real and who isn't. Ridley Scott's *Blade Runner* (1982) – an elaborately straight-faced adaption of Dick's hilarious *Do Androids Dream of Electric Sheep?* – and Aaron Lipstadt's *Android* (1982) elaborate on the themes of the Polish film. Their humanoid robots petition to be regarded as human beings and accorded all the rights due to them. Their case is strengthened by the fact that supposedly human characters in the films turn out to be androids themselves. Even more justified in his complaints about the harshness of his lot is Paul Verhoeven's *RoboCop* (1987), a cyborg policeman constructed by an Unscrupulous Corporation out of the leftovers of a shot-up patrolman (Peter

Weller) and forced to do battle not only with human scum but also with a colossal robot which is supposed to replace him. From the point of view of Arnold Schwarzenegger in James Cameron's *The Terminator* (1984), all these replicants could be seen as robot Uncle Toms; sent back to the 1980s from a future where Colossus-esque computers have waged a nuclear war on the human race, the terminator is a powerful robot skeleton embedded in Arnold's synthetic flesh. *The Terminator*, again *pace* Dick (see his short stories 'Claws' and 'Third Variety'), is the most uncompromising Man versus Machine movie since *Duel*, proposing that unless we find a way to turn them off they will kill us.

3. *Disaster Movies*

Most disaster movies are bloated caricatures of *Night of the Living Dead*, floundering in their titanic budgets. The early 1970s cycle – *Airport* (1970), *The Poseidon Adventure* (1972), *The Towering Inferno* (1974) and *Earthquake* (1974) – was the major studios' attempt to reclaim the apocalypse, a subject which had in the decade since *On the Beach* (1959) become the exclusive property of the intellectually vital, critically disreputable, minority audience exploitation film. The problem with disaster movies, and the reason the form quickly produced a series of grotesquely unprofitable bombs like *The Swarm, Meteor* (1979) *Beyond the Poseidon Adventure* (1979), *When Time Ran Out* (1980) and *Raise the Titanic* (1980), is that they are conceived more as saleable product than as cinema.

The Towering Inferno and *Earthquake* make assumptions about the nature of society that are as cynical as anything in the Romero film, but only because they need hatable human villains to blame their catastrophes on. William Holden and Richard Chamberlain cut costs on their skyscraper by ignoring the safety specifics, and the seismologist who predicts that a 'quake is about to hit Los Angeles is disbelieved by the authorities. Any real criticism that might be inherent is defused because

the situations are sub-plots expressed safely in warmed-over 'B' movie clichés: the ruthless businessman who will turn chicken in a crisis, the young genius ignored by hidebound old men. The only concrete addition of the disaster cycle to the ideas of *Night of the Living Dead* is the notion in *The Poseidon Adventure*, reused in *The Towering Inferno*, that if the world is turned upside-down the luxuries with which the rich surround themselves will get in the way as they try to climb up from their cruise liner, or down from their penthouse, in impractical evening dress. The overly complicated structures that could so easily be penetrated by Colossus are also so fragile that a single shock will pull them down in flames.

Despite their insistence on Scope (of budget, of special effects, of star names), the disaster movies take a far smaller view than *Night of the Living Dead*. Problems, no matter how vast, can be solved by the determined actions of Big Name Stars like Burt Lancaster, George Kennedy, Steve McQueen, Gene Hackman and Paul Newman. Anyone treacherous, sneaky or uninteresting can be counted on to get creamed, while all those who happen to be old-time movie stars, under 17 years old or happy-go-lucky will come through. The disaster puts a dent in society, but immediately mobilises normative forces who put the rotten mess back together again – until the next time. This naïve and childish idea is soundly rejected by *Dawn of the Dead*. The sinking ship and the burning building have no discernible effect on the world, but the Living Dead change it for ever. Only *Earthquake*, perhaps because it levels an entire city rather than a mere aeroplane or ocean liner, suggests any possible development of the disaster movie into something deeper than a comforting exorcism of our fears about lifts or thunderstorms. Charlton Heston is uselessly drowned trying to fish Ava Gardner out of a sewer, and the National Guard is represented by a timid grocery-store clerk (Marjoe Gortner) who turns into a trigger-happy tyrant at the first opportunity. These touches are not enough to compensate for a script that requires us to accept that 53-year-old Ava Gardner is the daughter of 59-year-old Lorne

● *The fabric of society crumbles.* Genevieve Bujold, **Earthquake.**

Greene, and that the characters played by Richard Roundtree and Victoria Principal are human beings.

The collapse of the disaster movie as a commercially viable prospect proves films can't be assembled like Aurora hobby kits, and studio bosses can no longer get away with telling the public what it wants to see. These attitudes do work on television, however, and that's where the disaster movie has crawled to die: witness *The Day the Earth Moved* (1974), *Flood!* (1976), *Fire!* (1977), *Fire in the Sky* (1978), *Disaster on the Coastliner* (1979) and *Cave-In!* (1983). Few genres have expired amid such open hostility. *The Swarm* and *Raise the Titanic* were laughing stocks whose mammoth losses were as crowed over as the takings of *Star Wars* or *E.T.* were hyped. *Raise the Titanic* – a disaster movie without an actual disaster until the accounts were in – strangled Sir Lew Grade's career as an old-style movie mogul, and semi-disaster items like *Hurricane* (1979) *The Delta Force* (1986) were nails in the financial coffins of big spenders Dino de Laurentiis and Golan and Globus. *Airplane!* (1980) is justly scathing about the genre.

In Roger Corman's *Gas-s-s-s; or: How it Became Necessary to Destroy the World in Order to Save It* (1970), a government nerve gas is released and kills everyone over the age of 25. The President describes the incident as an honest mistake anyone could have made. After the well-reported escape of some actual nerve gas in Utah (a herd of sheep were killed, and there was much speculation as to what would have happened to Salt Lake City if the wind had been blowing the other way) the cinema took its bio-weapon-related disasters more seriously. *The Satan Bug* (1965) had introduced the trappings of flimsy maximum security precautions, soldiers waiting to shoot down infectees and faceless zombies in decontamination suits mopping up afterwards. Although a few supporting characters curl up and die of the Violently Virulent Virus, Richard Basehart's plan to spill it over a baseball crowd is thwarted by George Maharis. The human race isn't quite so lucky when a space probe brings back *The Andromeda Strain*, and the population of an entire town finds its blood powdering. That wasn't really our fault for, like the goo which

turns Richard Wordsworth into a tripe-covered cactus creature in *The Quatermass Experiment* (1955) and the radiation that raises the *Night of the Living Dead* ghouls, the Andromeda strain is an uninvited extraterrestrial hitch-hiker. More angry are *Rage* (1973), *Plague* (1978), *Fukkatsu No Hi* (*Virus*) (1980), *Warning Sign* (1985) and Stephen King's optioned-for-filming *The Stand*, which concern honest mistakes anyone could have made.

George A. Romero's *The Crazies* (1975) has the decontamination-suited National Guard putting down an outbreak of chemically induced psychosis ('Shit, these white suits stand out', says one victim as he is shot). The minister douses himself with kerosene and becomes a Roman candle on the church lawn, and a little old lady smiles at her rescuer while shoving a handful of knitting needles into his chest. *The Cassandra Crossing* (1977) has an accidentally infected terrorist cooped up on a train with Big Name Star passengers like Richard Harris, Sophia Loren, Ava Gardner and Martin Sheen. General Burt Lancaster is ordered to cut down the possible disease vectors by ensuring the train crashes off an unsafe bridge. In these films, irresponsible science is lumped together with military blundering as the heart of the problem. The survivors are caught between bugged-out crazies and the government wipe-out squads, while the higher echelon tries to think of an acceptable cover story. *Close Encounters of the Third Kind* (1977) is the only film since *Gas-s-s-s* in which the army admits they've carelessly spilled some of their nerve gas. Of course, in that movie, it's a lie.

Closely linked to the bio-weapons paranoia movie, in its political cynicism and use of decontamination suit iconography, is the nuclear power paranoia movie. *Red Alert* (1977), *The China Syndrome* (1979), *The Chain Reaction* (1980) and *Im Zeichen des Kreuzes* (*Due to an Act of God*) (1983) are all more concerned with the cover-up of potential or actual nuclear mishaps than with solving the actual problem, and, of course, *The Plutonium Incident* (1980) and *Silkwood* (1983) deal with the real-life suspicious death of an irradiated power plant worker who tried to call attention to her plight. It's not so far from these sober films to *Incubo sulla citta contaminata* or *Raiders of the Living Dead*, in which Chernobyl/ Three Mile Island leakages lead to hordes of radioactive zombies wandering the land. Tied up with both the nuclear and the biological sub- genres is the toxic waste movie, which has suggested that unethical dumpings of dangerous substances could lead to zombies as in *Mutant* (1983), *Crazies*-style insanity as in *Impulse* (1984), flesh-eating wino goblins as in *C.H.U.D.* (1984), a mutant superhero in a tutu as in *The Toxic Avenger* (1985) and an unwatchably terrible film as in *Class of Nuke 'Em High* (1986).

The Medusa Touch and *Carrie* follow much the same narrative plan as the average disaster movie, but the closest the mainstream horror film has come to the genre is Peter Weir's *The Last Wave* (1978). Richard Chamberlain, fried in *The Towering Inferno* and stung in *The Swarm*, here faces one of the cinema's few genuinely terrifying dooms. He plays a Sydney lawyer trying to use tribal lore as a loophole to get a bunch of urban aborigines off a murder charge. The blazing outback suffers fist- sized hailstones and a rain of frogs, and Chamberlain has visions of the city under water. Even an overflowing bath seems like a portent. As in *Nightwing*, the hero learns from a tribal elder that primitive magic is about to eradicate the white man's world. *The Last Wave* is more persuasive than the Judao-Christian doodling of *The Omen*, partially because it uses beliefs that are less familiar than biblical texts, and partially because Weir is content to drop hints rather than bludgeon us with Awful Warnings. The last shot has a towering tidal wave sweeping toward the city as Chamberlain, somehow the reincarnation of an Aztec saviour, kneels on the oily bench waiting for The End.

4. *The Conspiracy Society*

Watergate convinced the American people their government was run on the same principles as the coven in *Rosemary's Baby*. In post-Watergate conspiracy films, the Establishment is a monolithic, all-encompassing Evil. Covert groups of private enterprise assassins (*The Killer Elite*, 1975), the CIA (*Three Days of the Condor*, 1975), the television networks (*Network*, 1976; *Looker*), the government (*All the President's Men*, 1976), top- secret cloning factories run to provide a spare- parts farm for the power élite (*The Resurrection of Zachary Wheeler*, 1971; *Parts – The Clonus Horror*, 1979), the hospital system (*Coma*), NASA (*Capricorn One*, 1978), shadowy ex-Nazi organisations (*Marathon Man*, 1976; *The Boys From Brazil*, 1978), a manipulative billionaire (*The Formula*, 1980), scientific institutes eager to conceal the arrival of alien beings (*Hangar 18*, 1980; *Wavelength*, 1983), the Atomic Energy Commission (*The China Syndrome*, *Silkwood*), a cartel of international bankers (*Rollover*, 1981), a biological warfare outfit responsible for cattle mutilations (*Endangered Species*, 1982) or a self-serving Secretary of Defense (*No Way Out*, 1987) are different faces of the same Monster.

Although these individuals and institutions bear a resemblance to actual individuals and institutions, and such resemblance is intentional, the Establish- ment as Monster is depicted no more credibly than, say, in THRUSH in *The Man From UNCLE*. (THRUSH was, of course, an acronym for Techno- logical Hierarchy for the Repression of Undesirables and the Subjugation of Humanity, and probably also stood for th'Russians.) These are subtly disguised paranoid horror films that pander to the world view of every ageing hippie who knows that his 1967 marijuana bust and signature on a 'Hell No, We Won't Go' petition is on file somewhere, and that the Mysterious They are only waiting for the moment when it will be politic to liquidate him. The iconography of the genre was invented by John Frankenheimer for *The Manchurian Candidate* (1962) and *Seven Days in May* (1964). Frankenheimer's background in live television prompted the central image for the conspiracy society — the mastermind's control room, walled with banks of video monitors, with the constant whirr of tape machines recording everything. *The President's Analyst* (1967), a satire

● *The Establishment as Monster.* Anthony Perkins, **Winter Kills.**

in which the Mysterious They turn out to be the phone company, adds the now-familiar cadre of interchangeable assassins in anonymous suits who relentlessly persecute anyone who learns too much about the conspiracy. These figures are the Living Dead of the genre, memorably incarnated as the indoctrinated crazies of *The Parallax View* (1974) and the impersonal black helicopters that pursue expendable astronauts through the desert in *Capricorn One*.

The main arena of the conspiracy movie is politics, which is seen to be less about rule and administration than the self-perpetuation of the monstrous machine and the destruction of inconvenient personages. Real power is held not by the government, but by geriatric monsters like John Huston in *Winter Kills* (1979), a man who buys the White House for his son and then has him assassinated, or General Richard Widmark in *Twilight's Last Gleaming* (1977), the official who rules that the President of the United States of America is expendable. The genre is obsessed with the assassination of President Kennedy. As a conspiracy, Watergate was fairly easily exhausted, but no one has ever got to the bottom of the Kennedy business so the field is open to speculations as wild as those of *Executive Action* (1973), *The Parallax View*, *Winter Kills* and *Flashpoint* (1984). Aside from these 'mainstream Kennedy' movies, assassination crops up in everything from *Three Days of the Condor*, in which CIA office worker Robert Redford nips out to pick up some sandwiches and returns to find his entire department has been machine-gunned, to *Network*, in which a broadcasting company sponsors terrorists to give the news shows a boost and arranges for the on-air live coast-to-coast assassination of Howard Beale (Peter Finch), the mad prophet of the airways.

The conspiracy classic is Francis Ford Coppola's *The Conversation* (1974), whose hero (Gene Hackman) is a surveillance expert who misinterprets what he is hired to overhear and finds himself trapped by someone else's directional mikes. Also excellent is Arthur Penn's *Night Moves* (1975), also with Gene Hackman, here a melancholy investigator who finds that knowing the answers isn't as important as understanding them. Intriguingly, Coppola and Penn invert the basic thesis of *All the President's Men* or *The China Syndrome*, that the Truth should be revealed, and conclude that the urge to pry and expose is as dangerous and perverse as the urge to conceal and dominate. The conspiracy discussed by Frederic Forrest and Cindy Williams in *The Conversation* is purely personal, but the high-tech trimmings usefully hint at wider issues. The films that try to deal directly with wider (political) issues frequently suffer from a despairing cynicism that easily shades into predictability. The CIA is so discredited in real life that the movies are hard pressed to invent duplicitous atrocities exaggerated enough to provide the requisite chills. The calculating executive/network president/White House aide/renegade general/spymaster has become no more realistic a figure than Fu Manchu or the villains of the James Bond films. In *Agency*, Robert Mitchum plans to gain enormous power by subliminally brainwashing the television audience, but there is something dreadfully ho-hum about this kind of plot when you can read about far more serious abuses in the newspapers every day.

Alan J. Pakula's *The Parallax View* successfully reuses the *Rosemary's Baby* structural device of making the central character an innocent (Warren Beatty) who gradually learns the world is out of his control, but too often the hopeless situation is simply accepted as given and plots have nowhere to go. When, after apparently solving the mystery and eliminating evil mastermind Christopher Plummer, Donald Sutherland, the hit-man hero of *The Disappearance* (1977) is shot down by yet another unseen assassin, it doesn't mean anything, except perhaps a reference to the finale of Francesco Rosi's Italian mafia/church/judiciary/politics puzzle, *Cadaveri eccellenti* (*Illustrious Corpses*) (1976). The conspiracy movies can now compete with the truth only by reproducing it, as in *Missing*, or predicting it, as in *The China Syndrome*. There have even been movies like the British *Defence of the Realm* (1984) and *The Whistle Blower* (1987), the Australian *Ground Zero* (1987), the Norwegian *Orions Belte* (*Orion's Belt*) (1984) and the American *Wall Street* (1987) that take important real-life issues and dress them up with conspiracy movie plots in order to bring them to public attention.

The evolutionary end of the genre is in s-f films like *A Clockwork Orange* (1971), *THX 1138* (1971), *Soylent Green* (1972) or *Rollerball* (1975), in which the oppressive tendencies of contemporary governments are extrapolated into nightmare futures where an all-powerful State experiments with mind control, enforced cannibalism or gladiatorial sports. Most of these – especially *1984* (1984) – reuse the *Nineteen Eighty-Four* plot of the lone rebel against the system and surviving or being crushed, depending on the degree of pessimism allowed by the premise. *Soylent Green*, from Harry Harrison's novel *Make Room! Make Room!*, departs slightly from this convention by adopting a conspiracy movie plot as well as political vision, and has future cop Charlton Heston making unpleasant discoveries about the way an overpopulated world is being fed. Usually, imagined futures are wrapped up in the concerns of the present rather than being genuine attempts at prediction. *Z.P.G.* (1970) and *The Last Child* (1971) are also about overpopulation, Peter Watkins' *Punishment Park* (1970) and Stephanie Rothman's *Terminal Island* (1973) deal with the treatment of political offenders, and *The Last Chase* (1980) and *Firebird 2015 AD* (1981) spin off from the oil crisis and posit a world where car-owners are rebels against a gas-hoarding government. The living end of this trend is Terry Gilliam's sprawling, annoying, brilliantly designed, brilliantly acted *Brazil* (1985). Yet another *Nineteen Eighty-Four* variation set 'somewhere in the twentieth century', *Brazil* finds the monolithic apparatus of the State breaking down through inefficiency, leaving the business of tyranny to be exercised at random by overworked bureaucrats and purposeless torturers.

5. *The Apocalypse*

In the 1970s, the oil crisis and Watergate worried us more than the possible destruction of humanity, and the conspiracy film was far more in tune with

the worries of the times than such end-of-the-world visions as *No Blade of Grass* (1971), *The Omega Man* (1971), *The Ultimate Warrior* (1975), *A Boy and His Dog* (1975), *Logan's Run* (1976), *Damnation Alley* (1977), *Ravagers* (1979), *Deadly Harvest* (1979) and the *Planet of the Apes* series. Drawn mainly from 1950s and 1960s s-f, these movies are much better at depicting the shattered remnants of civilisation (the subterranean stock-exchange of *Beneath the Planet of the Apes*, 1970, the corpse-littered LA of *The Omega Man*, the ivy-covered Lincoln Memorial of *Logan's Run*) than thinking of things for the survivors to do. Typically, the future is seen as a conflict between ecology-conscious hippie communes and contaminated violence freaks. Boris Sagal's *The Omega Man* has Charlton Heston cruising the streets by day, continually rescreening *Woodstock* ('They don't make movies like that any more'), and spending his evenings besieged in his penthouse by cowled mutants who want to crucify him. George A. Romero admits that *I Am Legend*, the Richard Matheson novel on which *The Omega Man* is based, is the inspiration for the Living Dead films, but little of Matheson's vampire apocalypse remains in the movie, which starts well with Heston talking to himself and resigned to his bizarre day-to-day life, but winds down in banality as the hero sacrifices himself to save a multiracial crèche.

Robert Clouse's *The Ultimate Warrior* is a lot tougher: survival guru Max Von Sydow tells hero-for-hire Yul Brynner that if he has the choice, he should ditch the girl and save a packet of seeds for posterity. L.Q. Jones's *A Boy and His Dog*, from Harlan Ellison's novella, has a hero (Don Johnson) who feeds his girlfriend to the telepathic canine sidekick who accompanies him through an America buried under twenty feet of sludge after a nuclear war. Although fashionably harsh, *The Ultimate Warrior* and *A Boy and His Dog* are not entirely free of the love generation platitudes which clog the fag-end of the *Planet of the Apes* series and *Damnation Alley*. Here, the straights are disposed of by the Bomb (or the eco-collapse), the rednecks get wiped out in the aftermath, and only the beautiful people make it through to a bright future of reconstruction, breeding like rabbits,

● *After the Apocalypse.* **I Nuovi barbari.**

eating organic rice and listening to Joan Baez. The attitude that most of these films took to fine source novels is amply demonstrated by Jack Smight's travesty of Roger Zelazny's *Damnation Alley*. The novel's hero is Hell Tanner, the last of the Hell's Angels, who is introduced as a man who 'looks at the world through crap-coloured glasses' and reads like the kind of badass William Smith, the villain of *The Ultimate Warrior*, used to play in bikesploitation movies. In the film, he is played by Jan-Michael Vincent as a former air force officer, a blue-eyed long-hair who seems to have breezed into Armageddon from the set of an aftershave commercial. The holocaust even became palatable enough for television, as witnessed by Gene Roddenberry's pitiful attempts to get a post-trekkie series on the air (*Genesis II*, 1973; *Planet Earth*, 1974; *Strange New World*, 1975) and wimpy, short-lived, spin-off series for *Logan's Run* and *Planet of the Apes*.

Surprisingly, those apocalypse movies – Roger Corman's *Gas-s-s-s*; Jim McBride's *Glen and Randa* (1972); Peter Fonda's *Idaho Transfer* (1973) – actually made by hippie sympathisers rather than major studios tend to be more downbeat about the possibility that the flower children will pull the world together in the aftermath. In these films, the survivors mainly go crazy, try to become square citizens or bitch about the lack of a good cheeseburger. Corman, as usual, got in early on the future barbarian cycle, and had Allan Arkush and Henry Suso's *Deathsport* (1976) out well before *Mad Max* was even a screen treatment. David Carradine, Claudia Jennings and Richard Lynch have fun playing cowboys and swordsmen in the future, while the second unit blow up an inordinate number of bikes. Away from the mainstream, there were several cheap and pretentious nuke meditations, like the Spanish *El Refugio del Miedo* (*A Refuge of Fear*) (1973), in which Patty Shepard reacts to being told not to parade around the survival bunker with no clothes on by turning up for dinner in a decontamination suit, or *Massive Retaliation* (1984), a painfully sincere anti-survivalist tract. Even the porno business got in on the act with Rinse Dream's *Café*

Flesh (1981), a hardcore flick set in a post-holocaust world where 99% of the population are unable to have sex and live, and the other 1% are forced to perform in the floor-show at the titular dive for an audience of impotent voyeurs.

'There are no heroes any more', a post-holocaust police chief tells his Number One man, *Mad Max* (1979); 'well, we're going to give them back their heroes!' 'He's the only law in a world gone mad', reads the poster; 'pray that he's out there'. The film opens with a dynamic, razor-sharp car chase along the old Anarchie Road, a desert track in a future Australia, and then slips into a soggy vigilante rehash as Max Rockatansky (Gibson), a leather-and-chrome supercop, exterminates the gang of speed freaks who have barbequed his partner and killed his wife. *Mad Max 2* (1981) finds director George Miller more in control of the all-action pace, but still fumbling with attempts at generic coherence. Civilisation has decayed further, and is no longer held together by the police force. Max retains his Interceptor Vehicle and dog from the first film, but now roars down the highways as a drifting scavenger, still burnt out by the deaths of his loved ones. Narration by an old-timer who claims to be recounting the legend of the hero who led his people out of the wilderness towards a lawful society tries to turn Max into the kind of self-destructive wagon-master who figures in John Ford's films about the civilisation of the frontier. Max shares the nomadic lifestyle of the killers he is busily exterminating, and there is no place for him in the peaceable society he establishes. Finally, he must vanish into desert obscurity while the educated men, women-folk and children inherit the Earth. However, Gibson remains so characterless a hero set beside John Wayne or Henry Fonda that when the Huron-headed bad guys wreck Max's car and kill his dog, he is robbed of a significant part of his identity. *Mad Max Beyond Thunderdome* (1985) brings in a co-director, George Ogilvie, to handle the 'human relationship' scenes and has a more extensive vision of a post-holocaust world, complete with tribal myths and Tina Turner running a shanty town fuelled by pigshit. However, the attempt at humanising the hero as he shepherds a tribe of orphans to safety is handicapped because the pre-trauma Max we met in the first film wasn't very interesting in the first place.

John Carpenter's *Escape From New York* (1981) is set in 1997, when Manhattan Island is walled off as the world's largest, most secure, least governed prison. When President Donald Pleasence crashes Air Force One in the middle of the city, Police Chief Lee Van Cleef has to recruit bank-robbing World War III hero Kurt Russell to get him out. While *Mad Max 2* covers for its lack of depth by filling the wide screen with meticulously staged stunts, *Escape From New York* runs out of gas once Russell has been dumped in the middle of Carpenter's future Hell of severed heads on parking meters and a Chock Full O'Nuts that really is. Meanwhile, a minor trend of cinema nasties documents the rising tide of anarchic bloodshed that will inevitably lead to the picturesque breakdowns of *Mad Max* and *Escape From New York*. James Glickenhaus's *The Exterminator* (1980) is the worst kind of meat movie – the most powerful scene has a vengeful vigilante dropping a mafia don into an industrial mincing machine – and Mark L. Lester's *Class of 1984* (1982) has patient and understanding teacher Perry King finally give up on the little bastards who run his school when they pack-rape his pregnant wife and go after them with an oxy-acetylene torch. 'We are the future . . . and nothing can stop us' is the motto of the *Class of 1984*, but King's reactionary slaughter squashes them pretty convincingly. The right-wing backlash movies – triggered off by Michael Winner's *Death Wish* (1972) and sequels – assure us we won't have to worry about the crazies of *Escape From New York* if we allow law enforcement agencies and private individuals to act like vicious homicidal maniacs in the present.

Meanwhile, the punk movement's rabid need to be misunderstood marks it as a likely source of post-holocaust villainy. Like the greasy tearaways of *Panic in Year Zero* (1962) and the Hell's Angels of *No Blade of Grass*, movie punks tend to react to the apocalypse by becoming a crowd of looting, raping and overacting animals, while the older generation preserves the decencies. The fact that older generation trips like big business and global war are more likely to cause the apocalypse than glue-sniffing and lousy music is conveniently ignored. As the plague of future barbarian movies demonstrates, whatever shortages afflict the cinematic future, we can be sure there will be a plentiful supply of Heavy Metal gear, multicoloured hairspray and artificial gore. In this prevailing climate, it takes courage to come up with a film like Alex Cox's *Repo Man* (1984), in which the punks are just as bewildered by the winding-down of the world as anyone else, or Paul Donovan and Maura O'Connell's *Siege* (1982), a vigilante movie in which a bunch of queer-bashing fascisti are the villains, bringing their tyrannical version of law 'n' order to the streets during a police strike. Here, the punks, gays and bohemians are the heroes who have to fight back, and a final twist identifies at least one of the gang of *Assault on Precinct 13*-style heavies as an off-duty cop.

In the mid-1980s, the future violence cycle attained world-wide popularity, with *The Aftermath* (1980), *Parasite* (1982), *Future Kill* (1984), *Radioactive Dreams* (1985), *City Limits* (1985), *Cherry 2000* (1986), *Booby Trap* (1986), *Steel Dawn* (1987) and *World Gone Wild* (1988) from the US; *Turkey Shoot* (1982) and *Dead End Drive-In* (1986) from Australia; *Battletruck* (1981) and Geoff Murphy's excellent *The Quiet Earth* (1985) from New Zealand; arty items like *Memoirs of a Survivor* (1981), *Dark Enemy* (1984) and *The Ultimate City* (1986) from the UK; and *America 3000* (1987), *Health Warning* (1983), *Stryker* (1983), *Survival Zone* (1983), *Forbydelsens Element* (*The Element of Crime*) (1984), *Seksmija* (*Sex Mission*) (1984) *DefCon 4* (1985) and *Terminus* (1987) from Israel, Hong Kong, the Philippines, South Africa, Denmark, Poland, Canada and France. And – of course – there were *1990: I Guerrieri del Bronx* (*Bronx Warriors*) (1982), *I Nuovi barbari* (*The New Barbarians*) (1983), *L'Ultimo guerriero* (*The Final Executioner*) (1983), *Barbari 2000* (*Exterminators of the Year 3000*) (1983), *Bronx lotta finale* (*Endgame*) (1984), *Rush* (*Rush the Assassin*) (1984), *Rats, notte di terrore* (*Rats*) (1984)

● *Master Blaster*.   Angelo Rossito, Paul Larsson,   **Mad Max Beyond Thunderdome.**

and *Il Guerriero del mondo perduto* (*Warrior of the Lost World*) (1984) from Italy. With a little help from *Blade Runner* and the bleak, picturesque vision of Francis Ford Coppola's *Rumble Fish* (1983), these movies create an instantly recognisable universe that has found itself used in an astonishing variety of music videos and unlikely TV commercials for banks and soft drinks. Some apocalypse movies are awful warnings, but these are mainly designed to help the audience stop worrying and, if not love the Bomb, at least find the radioactive ruins as appealing and exotic a locale as the Wild West, the South Seas or Route 66.

Meanwhile, the Apocalypse is taken more seriously in art movies like Luc Besson's *Le Dernier Combat* (*The Last Battle*) (1984), in which speechless survivors struggle for dominance in a Parisian desert which is half-*Mad Max* and half-Theatre of the Absurd, and Andrei Tarkovsky's *Offret* (*The Sacrifice*) (1985), in which Erland Josephsen prays away World War III. John Milius's *Red Dawn*

(1984) and the TV epic *Amerika* mainly set aside the superpowers' nuclear capabilities and trade in invasion fantasies in which the Soviets conquer the US, so the Americans – after years of backing oppressive regimes and failing to deal honourably with guerrilla wars from Wounded Knee to Mai Lai – can finally get to being the goodies again and play at being rebels. Even more extreme bits of warmongering like *Invasion USA* (1985) and *Top Gun* (1986) suddenly went out of fashion as *glasnost* crept in, and World War III went back to being a dreaded threat rather than a fun-for-all-the-family action arena. Gloomy, realistic nuclear nightmares like *Malevil* (1981), *The Day After* (1983), *Special Bulletin* (1983), *Testament* (1983), *Threads* (1984), *When the Wind Blows* (1986) and *Pisma Myortvovo Chelovyeka* (*Letters from a Dead Man*) (1986) provide a pointed contrast to the high-speed car and bike action of *Mad Max* and its successors: the only conceivable use for petrol in the post-holocaust world of *Testament* is as an aid to suicide by carbon monoxide poisoning.

She was abused and violated.

It will never happen again!

● *Rape Crisis.* Zoe Tamerlis, **Ms .45.**

tales of ordinary madness:

or: *The Close-Up Crazies*

Initially, homicidal mania wasn't enough to guarantee inclusion in the horror movie pantheon. In order to make the famous monsters team, a mad killer had also to be a somnambulist in the power of a mad scientist, like Conrad Veidt in *The Cabinet of Dr Caligari* (1919), hideously deformed and in evening dress, like Lon Chaney in *The Phantom of the Opera* (1925), or a masked schemer after an inheritance, like the mystery villain in *The Cat and the Canary* (1927). Despite the casting of normals Robert Montgomery and Robert Walker in *Night Must Fall* (1937) and *Strangers on a Train* (1951), screen maniacs from the 1920s through to the 1950s were generally played by such physically bizarre performers as Peter Lorre, Laird Cregar, John Carradine or Rondo Hatton. When a smoothie like Basil Rathbone, Franchot Tone or Charles Boyer drew the psycho role in *Love From a Stranger* (1937), *Phantom Lady* (1944) or *Gaslight* (1944), they were usually given one good scene where their good manners could evaporate and they could demonstrate psychosis with facial tics, hand-wringing mannerisms and obsessional rants. Underlying all this is a feeling that the insane *are* somehow monstrous, different from you and me, and that internal sickness should be visible to the naked eye. 'When a man is ugly', philosophises Boris Karloff in *The Raven* (1935), 'maybe he does ugly things.' To bear this out, the Karloff character becomes even more violent when mad plastic surgeon Bela Lugosi makes his face even more hideous than before.

With the 1960 appearance of *Psycho* and *Peeping Tom*, a modified stereotype of the homicidal maniac became popular. The new psychos were withdrawn, vaguely effeminate, neurotic, apparently harmless young men. While Anthony Perkins's Norman Bates and Carl Boehm's Mark Lewis are more sympathetic than their predecessors, they are still set aside from the rest of mankind. Norman and Mark inhabit old dark houses haunted by parental cruelty, and are given accessories to prove incontrovertibly how far beyond the pale they are – Norman's dress and wig, Mark's camera-tripod-cum-switchblade. The truly subversive aspect of the Hitchcock and Michael Powell films is the contrast between the interior world of their killer heroes and supposed normality. *Peeping Tom* and *Psycho* set up an everyday life full of grasping, petty characters and mindless minor brutalities. It's impossible not to find Norman and Mark appealing. We are disturbed at our sympathy for such monsters, which cuts deeper than our liking for such wild children as the Frankenstein Monster and King Kong. Compared with the practical coppers, trivial lovers and selfish 'heroes', Norman and Mark are audience identification figures because they have the decency to be morally confused and blundering in a way the straight-arrow characters played by such skilfully cast minor performers as John Gavin, Vera Miles, Shirley Anne Field and Jack Watson could never be.

The lesson was lost on the host of madman-as-monster movies that followed the success of *Psycho*. Most of these hark back to the 1940s in the equation of physical repulsiveness with insanity; witness the casting of transvestite/transsexual Jean Arless in *Homicidal!* (1961), wide-boy/thug Oliver Reed in *Paranoiac* (1963), blubber-bellied grotesque Victor Buono in *The Strangler* (1964) and Alan Arkin in dark glasses or disguise in *Wait Until Dark* (1967). These are back-to-the-ghetto psychotics, uniformly alien, unlikeable and impossible to understand. The living end of this post-*Psycho* boom must be Rod Steiger in *No Way to Treat a Lady* (1967), a mad actor who treats each murder like a new stage role and creates a twisted character to go with it. With the rise of the *Texas Chainsaw* and *Halloween* schools of horror, where the psychopath becomes a shadowy myth figure like the real-life Jack the Ripper, this type of overblown monster slightly faded from the picture. Recent examples have been mainly confined to zero-budget atrocities like *Don't Answer the Phone* (1980) and *Maniac* (1980), in which Nicholas Worth and Joe Spinell play the most repulsive human beings imaginable. These performers are slobbish, sweaty, ugly and prone to horrible overacting, and the grottiness of their movies is emphasised by the grainily nauseating mix of softcore sex and hardcore violence that surrounds the psycho stars.

Given that the anatomy-of-a-psycho film was well established – indeed, on the point of petering out – in 1968, the changes rippling through the rest of horror cinema were felt less than in other sub-genres. In some ways, the all-important *Night of the Living Dead* was the culmination of a movement which had started earlier, bringing to fantastical horror the contemporary impact *Psycho* and *Peeping Tom* had brought to the slightly less disreputable – though still widely reviled – psychological thriller. However, there was still a revolution to be fought inside the psycho movie, and the front-line films of 1968 were Peter Bogdanovich's *Targets* and Noel Black's *Pretty Poison*. Bogdanovich's Bobby Thompson (Tim O'Kelly) and Black's Sue Ann Stepanek (Tuesday Weld) would make ideal dates for the Senior

Prom. He's a crew-cut young man who calls his Dad 'Sir', works on his car at weekends and enjoys nothing more than popping away at tin cans with his rifle or going hunting with his father; she's a blonde high-school senior who carries the Stars and Stripes in the marching band, hangs out at the local hamburger stand, wears ankle-socks and is having a difficult time with her mother. Bobby and Sue Ann could be fresh off the beaches of one of the 1960s mild and cheerful youth musicals – Weld actually had been in *Rock, Rock, Rock* and the clean-teen sit-com *The Many Loves of Dobie Gillis* – but they're both psychopathic killers. Bobby uses his rifle on his wife and parents, then finds a series of convenient perches from which to pick off passers-by, while Sue Ann takes a prank to extremes by bludgeoning a night-watchman to death with a flashlight and then shoots dead her overbearing mother (Beverly Garland).

Neither movie even tries to explain why its killers are the way they are. In 1968, one might read the films as an expression of the counter-culture's hyper-paranoid distrust of the world's straights. Bobby and Sue Ann are the sort of kids the parents of draft-dodgers, dope-smokers and campus protesters would like their children to be. They typify junior Republican values to a sickening degree, and support President Nixon's foreign policy of killing people at random to the extent of practising it in their own home towns. In order to establish Troy Donahue lookalike O'Kelly and the achingly lovely Weld as monster icons, the films have to make some attempt to overthrow the norm of monstrousness. Bobby Thompson is set against Byron Orlok (Boris Karloff), a suntanned refugee from the Universal horrors of the 1930s, stranded in the 1960s where he can only work in campy movies like Roger Corman's *The Terror* (1963). The character name doesn't matter: *The Terror* is a real movie, and Byron Orlok is Boris Karloff – the original Frankenstein Monster, Fu Manchu, the Mummy, the Mad Scientist, the Bodysnatcher. In the final confrontation, Karloff towers over the sniper but in a sense he loses: Bobby Thompson takes his place as the true face of horror. Sue Ann is similarly contrasted with

Dennis Pitt, a nervy young man just out of the asylum, who leads a daring fantasy life as a make-believe CIA agent and who is at once the spur, the instrument and the scapegoat of her murders. Dennis is played by Anthony Perkins, in a gentle inversion of his Norman Bates role, as a true innocent who finally takes the blame because he's type-cast as a killer while Sue Ann could never normally play the role.

Targets and *Pretty Poison* were somewhat overshadowed by the more muddled vision of beautiful people as killers in Arthur Penn's *Bonnie and Clyde* (1967). Not major box-office successes, they were critically appreciated and have been vaguely, if insidiously, influential. In *The Mad Room* (1969), a gored-up remake of *Ladies in Retirement*, Shelley Winters is established as a typical movie madwoman, but the murders eventually turn out to be the work of Stella Stevens, a bubbly blonde beauty of the Sue Ann Stepanek majorette type. Meanwhile, Tony Curtis was expanding his range as *The Boston Strangler* (1968), again stressing the outward normality and schizophrenic decency of the mad killer. Since then, insane murderers have been played by nice young men like Hywel Bennett (*Twisted Nerve*, 1969), Tab Hunter (*Sweet Kill*, 1970), Nicholas Clay (*The Night Digger*, 1971), Robert F. Lyons (*The Todd Killings*, 1971), Michael Douglas (*When Michael Calls*, 1971), Alan Alda (*To Kill a Clown*, 1972), Shane Briant (*Straight on till Morning*, 1972), Martin Sheen (*Badlands*, 1973), Anthony Hopkins (*Magic*, 1978) and Stephen McHattie (*Death Valley*, 1982), and by winsome starlets Sondra Locke (*Death Game*, 1974), Charlotte Rampling (*Asylum*), Margot Kidder (*Sisters*), Lynn Frederick (*Schizo*) and Morgan Fairchild (*The Seduction*, 1982). If a tendency is notable in this run of presentable psychopaths, it's that the anti-normal undercurrents of *Targets* and *Pretty Poison* ebb and are replaced by an anti-youth message — probably in the wake of the Manson murders — that equates murderous madness with such harmless eccentricities as teenage fashions, hairstyles and musical preferences.

The most peculiar and surprisingly popular psycho trend of the 1960s was the ageing-actress-as-monster movie. The sub-genre was inaugurated by Robert Aldrich's *Whatever Happened to Baby Jane?* (1962), with Bette Davis and Joan Crawford as bloated caricatures of their former selves locked together in a melodrama of sisterly hatred. Davis followed through with flamboyant insanity in Aldrich's *Hush ... Hush, Sweet Charlotte* (1965), before decamping to Hammer Films for *The Nanny* (1965) and *The Anniversary* (1968) and winding up in TV horrors like *Scream, Pretty Peggy* (1973). Crawford, meanwhile, was blowing her reputation on William Castle and Herman Cohen in *Strait-Jacket* (1964), *I Saw What You Did* (1965), *Berserk!* (1967) and *Trog* (1970). Olivia de Havilland, Davis's *Charlotte* co-star, was trapped in *Lady in a Cage* (1964); Lauren Bacall had a go in *Shock Treatment* (1964); Tallulah Bankhead got in on the act with Silvio Narizzano's superior *Fanatic* (1965); Barbara Stanwyck contributed *The Night Walker* (1965); Geraldine Page and Ruth Gordon did *What Ever Happened to Aunt Alice?* (1969); and there have been horrors from Jeanne Crain, Gloria Grahame, Ruth Roman, Eleanor Parker, Veronica Lake, Joan Fontaine, Mary Astor and Yvonne de Carlo. Only Katharine Hepburn, Mae West, Marlene Dietrich and Greta Garbo refrained from hefting a bloody axe in the service of cheap exploitation. As in many of the rural massacre movies, the idea is that the old and senile are monsters. In this cycle, faces we are used to from 1940s glamour shots are seen as sagging horrors or taut death-masks.

When Aldrich abandoned the ageing-actress sub-genre — though, oddly, his *The Killing of Sister George* (1968) makes more sense as *grand guignol* than serious drama — his position passed to Curtis Harrington, an ex-underground film-maker who had made an arty début with *Night Tide* (1961) and toiled on such Roger Corman re-edit jobs as *Voyage to the Prehistoric Planet* (1965) and *Queen of Blood* (1966). His first venture into psycho territory was *Games* (1967), which takes star Simone Signoret and several plot twists from *Les Diaboliques*, but he really got into his stride with the TV movie *How Awful About Allan* (1970), which has three psycho stars in Anthony Perkins,

Julie Harris and Joan Hackett and an original teleplay by Henry Farrell, who had scripted the Aldrich films. Despite the line-up and pedigree, it's a thoroughly predictable job, but Harrington stuck to the field with a series of increasingly bizarre and stylish films. *What's the Matter With Helen?* (1971) has Debbie Reynolds and Shelley Winters in a Kenneth Angerish bit of horror gossip set around a school for wannabe Shirley Temples in the 1930s, and *Who Slew Auntie Roo?* (1971) has Winters back as the witch figure in a campy horror version of Hansel and Gretel. Harrington's most distinctive film is *The Killing Kind* (1973), the misanthropic story of a mother-obsessed young man (John Savage) out for revenge on those who framed him into juvenile hall. Set again on the seamy side of Sunset Boulevard, the movie benefits from star turns by Ann Sothern as the ex-whore Mom who poisons her boy to keep him out of jail and Luana Anders as the repressed librarian neighbour who dreams of putting ground glass in her bedridden father's food so she can hear it grating on his false teeth. With its downwardly mobile melancholia, *The Killing Kind* suggests an alternate *Psycho*, in which Norman Bates hasn't killed his mother and must keep on living with her. Harrington slipped back into TV for a pair of spoofy Robert Bloch scripts – *The Cat Creature* (1973) and *The Dead Don't Die* (1975) – that resurrect performers and clichés from the 1930s 'B' picture, and since then he's been stuck with the likes of *The Killer Bees* (1974) – with Gloria Swanson – *Ruby* (1977) and *Devil Dog: Hound of Hell* (1978).

Throughout the 1970s, low-budget movies coasted along on the momentum of *Psycho*. The cheapest and grottiest psychos are probably *Carnival of Blood* (1971) and *Psycho From Texas* (1974), but drive-in fanatics also had to put up with *The Psycho Lover* (1971), a worthless *Manchurian Candidate* retread with a psychiatrist programming a homicidal patient to commit murder for him; *Love Me Deadly* (1971), with a killer undertaker mixed up in a circle of necrophiles; *Headless Eyes* (1973), about a sculptor who spoons out his victims' eyes for use in some masterpiece or

other; *Psychopath* (1974), with the mad host of a kiddie TV show slaughtering parents who abuse their children; *The Love Butcher* (1975), with a schizoid gardener masquerading as his lady-killing twin brother; the Swiss *Mosquito der Schander (Bloodlust)* (1976), with a twisted young man who vampirises corpses and agonises extensively; and *The Psychotronic Man* (1980), with a psychic barber freaking out. Typical of these screen psychopaths – whose tastes in clothes are often more offensive than their murdering binges – are Zooey Hall in the nicely titled, otherwise dreadful *I Dismember Mama* (1971) and gigolo William Shatner in *Impulse* (1974). Hall models a black turtleneck, whines endlessly, falls in love with a 9-year-old and conspicuously fails to dismember his irksome screen mother, while Shatner goes in for violently loud open-necked paisley shirts, crotch-hugging flares and white jackets with piping, not to mention mini-cigars, crying fits, nail-biting, nervous grins, running over dogs and drowning rich widows in fish-tanks. With the rise of the post-*Halloween/Friday the 13th* psycho movie, these colourful gentlemen have largely been replaced by unkillable ciphers, but the old strain still remains in the likes of *Maniac* and *Nightmare* (1980).

Directed by long-time hack Bert I. Gordon and written by novelist Marc Behm, *The Mad Bomber* (1972) is well above the rut, thanks to cynicism and iconic casting. Chuck Connors is an explosives expert with a hefty series of grudges against everyone in the city – he's first seen menacing a passer-by who litters the sidewalk, and later threatens a rude supermarket check-out girl and a horn-happy road-hog – and a plan to blow up a series of civic institutions. Neville Brand is a suburban rapist, and Vince Edwards is a hardboiled cop who thinks Dirty Harry is too liberal. The movie gets complicated when Brand is the only witness who can identify the bomber because he was raping a nurse in the basement of a hospital while Connors was planting his latest infernal device, and Edwards is forced to bring in the sex offender ('I want police women on every street corner just begging to be raped!') so he can catch the killer. Although merely efficient in its direction,

The Mad Bomber really scores in its use of its trio of psycho stars. Connors, especially, has never been better, although he has fun in drag and a mask in *Tourist Trap*, in which he terrorises Jocelyn Jones and Tanya Roberts with psychokinetically-animated mannequins.

Also out of the ordinary is the Spanish *La Campana del Infierno* (*The Bell of Hell*) (1973), directed mainly by Claudio Guerin Hill – who died in a fall from the film's bell tower on the last day of shooting, leaving the editing to Juan Antonio Bardem. A disturbed young man (Renaud Verley) plots against his grasping relatives, at first playing practical jokes on them (one is copied from Saki, the master of civilised cruelty), then going so far as to smear his aunt's face with honey and letting loose a swarm of bees. The film promises to be more degenerate than it turns out to be – early on, the hero quits a job in a slaughterhouse 'because I've learned enough' – and finds a distinctive tone between Buñuelian black comedy and more standard Latino horror. Less rewarding but similar in style – down to the slaughterhouse setting and consequent use of bloody meat documentary footage – is Eloy de la Iglesia's *La Semana del Asesino* (*Apartment on the 13th Floor*) (1972). Here, the killer (Vincent Parra) is an example of working-class machismo gone too far – he follows boxing, football and the bullfights, drinks with the lads and semi-accidentally kills a series of aquaintances whose corpses clutter up his flat and attract hordes of flies. Although obviously intended as art movies in the manner of *El* and *Repulsion*, both these films – thanks to cheap processing, much-abbreviated video versions, terrible dubbing and sleazy retitling (*La Semana* wound up on the video nasties list as *Cannibal Man*) – seem outside Spain rather more in the tradition of Paul Naschy's run of sleazy Hispanic horrors.

While male psychosis has always been associated with sensationalist trashiness, the female brand is usually treated – again, thanks to *Repulsion* – with at least an attempt at seriousness. Robert Altman's *Images* (1972) and John Cassavetes's *A Woman Under the Influence* (1974) deal with the cracking-up of detailed, convincing characters played by Susannah York and Gena Rowlands. Altman's movie does flirt with genre horror as York's fractured mind is reflected by a series of role-switching games with the supporting cast, and even includes a series of murders, but Cassavetes gets to the horrific in a far more casual, roundabout manner, presenting Rowlands as a woman whose madness is an integral part of her personality and who loses much of her appealing vitality when she is 'cured'. Altman returns to the arena of *Images* in the even more complex and playful *Three Women* (1977), where Sissy Spacek, Shelley Duvall and Janice Rule exchange personalities with disturbing frequency but finally create a functional group identity as fascinating and ambiguous as Kubrick's *2001* Starchild. Even cheap lady psycho movies incline to the artistic. Matt Cimber's *The Witch Who Came From the Sea* (1976), with Millie Perkins as a sea-captain's daughter who castrates football players, is an interesting attempt at sustained mood and psychological peculiarity. Screenwriter Robert Thom – Perkins's husband – works a few odd biographical themes (the actress's father really was a sea-captain) into the wistfully nasty little story, which has an unsettling down-at-heel seaside atmosphere, an intriguing reversal of the woman-killing cliché in its heroine's campaign against thuggish jocks, and one of the most unpleasant flashback traumas: Perkins went mad as a little girl because her father succumbed to a heart attack while molesting her.

Less distinctive, but also ambitious, is Herb Freed's *Haunts* (1977), with May Britt as a Swedish farmgirl in rural America going quietly and then noisily mad – she thinks she's been raped by a goat – while reliables Aldo Ray and Cameron Mitchell are puzzled on the sidelines. Karen Black gets a chance to demonstrate various neuroses on television by cultivating secondary (and even tertiary) personalities in *Trilogy of Terror* (1975) and *The Strange Possession of Mrs Oliver* (1977), and the comparatively few sleazy female psycho killers include the Preacherwoman ('She's a Man-Hating, Hymn-Humming Hellcat!') in *Evil Come, Evil Go* (1973); Crazy Fat Ethel (Priscilla Alden) in

Criminally Insane (1975) and a direct-to-video sequel; a cute lesbian sister in *Suor Omicidio* (*The Killer Nun*) (1976); Susan Strasberg and Faith Domergue in and as *Psycho Sisters* (1981); and the proprietor of *Mountaintop Motel Massacre* (1986). None of these distaff slashers comes close to Shirley Stoler in Leonard Kastle's *The Honeymoon Killers* (1970). Overweight wallflower Stoler teams up with gigolo Tony LoBianco and helps lure a series of moneyed spinsters into marrying him. Then they kill the elderly brides and cash in on the inheritances. Actually based on an authentic case history (as opposed to claiming to be, like too many of these films), *The Honeymoon Killers* has some very unsettling, *ciné verité* sequences as the murderous lovebirds work up to dispatching their victims in convincingly real, heartbreakingly ordinary motel rooms and apartments. One gets the uneasy feeling that if Frederick Wiseman had been around while Raymond Fernandez and Martha Beck, the real-life characters, were committing their crimes, the documentary he would have shot would look exactly like the recreations in Kastle's movie. Unglamorous Stoler is also a far more intriguing figure than Isabelle Adjani or Theresa Russell, as the marry 'em and murder 'em villainesses of *Mortelle Randonnée* (1983) – from Marc Behm's outstanding *The Eye of the Beholder* – and *Black Widow* (1986).

Just as movies like *Dirty Harry* and *Cop* blur the lines between psychopath and policeman, the cinema of insanity has always had a deep-seated, instinctively anti-intellectual distrust of the psychiatric profession. The insane Dr Caligari turns out to be head of the asylum, in one of the first of the innumerable film adaptions of and variations on Poe's 'The System of Dr Tarr and Professor Fether'. In the Poe story – officially filmed in France as *Le Système du Dr Goudron et du Professeur Plume* (1912), in Germany in *Fünf Unheimliche Geschichten* (*The Living Dead*) (1931), in Poland as *Le Système* (1971) and in Mexico as *La Mansion de la Locura* (*House of Madness*) (1973) – the inmates take over the madhouse, a theme obviously open to all manner of allegorical interpretations. In the 1940s, when psychoanalysis

was a fad, the movies harked back to Caligari with a series of psychiatrists who turn out to be murderers, crackpots, lechers, quacks or sadists or are just plain loopy – Tom Conway in *Cat People*, Ralf Harolde in *Murder, My Sweet*, Paul Kelly in *Dead Man's Eyes*, Leo G. Carroll in *Spellbound* and Helen Walker in *Nightmare Alley*. An odd corollary of the Dr Tarr and Professor Fether theory is the number of films – from *Spellbound* (1945) through *Hollow Triumph* (1948) to *The Couch Trip* (1987) – in which mental cases successfully impersonate psychiatrists and are even seen to do some good to their patients.

The other great myth of the psycho movie is that madness is catching, like the measles, as demonstrated by the number of psychoanalysts from Dr Caligari through to Peter Sellers in *What's New, Pussycat?* who are driven crazy by their contact with so many troubled minds. This theme has served for one or two good melodramas, including Sam Fuller's classic *Shock Corridor* and Robert Rossen's *Lilith*. Recent psychiatric trouble-makers include Klaus Kinski in *Schizoid* (1980) and Paul Michael Glaser in John Huston's cheesy *Phobia* (1980), both of whom come under suspicion when their patients start getting murdered; one's innocent, one's guilty, but the films are so uninvolving that you'd be hard pressed to remember which was which. The most evil psychiatrist in the 1980s cinema is avuncular, crippled Jan Rubes in Arthur Penn's *Dead of Winter* (1987), who harks back to the 1940s (as well he might, the film is modelled on the 1945 *My Name Is Julia Ross*) in his thoroughgoing rottenness and his scheme to involve heroine Mary Steenbergen in a plot to extort money from a murderess.

The most common expression of the psycho movie's distrust of psychiatry is a series of films about badly run asylums. *Bedlam, The Snake Pit, Shock Corridor* and *Shock Treatment* are early entries in this cycle, which has yielded such bizarre bits of therapy as a newcomer to the staff being asked to pick which of the raving patients used to be head of the institution (*Asylum*), devil-worshipping staff members sacrificing inmates (*Asylum of Satan*, 1973), a doctor encouraging a homicidal maniac to work out his frustrations with an axe (*Don't Look in the Basement*), the director of a madhouse allowing crazy Peter Cushing to experiment on everybody else (*Frankenstein and the Monster From Hell*), Stacy Keach letting his nutty army officer patients live out their fantasies in an old castle (*The Ninth Configuration*, 1980) and libertarian shrink Donald Pleasence giving a pyromaniac a box of matches (*Alone in the Dark*). By comparison, Nurse Ratched (Louise Fletcher) of *One Flew Over the Cuckoo's Nest* (1975) is restrained in her use of terror, drugs and unnecessary lobotomy to make life miserable for her charges. *Silent Night, Bloody Night* finds that all the pillars of the local community were once inmates of the asylum, and have been running the town since their violent mass breakout. In the canon of modern gothic themes, the evil asylum occupies roughly the same position held in the nineteenth century by the unholy convent. There has naturally been some degree of overlap with the perennially popular women-in-prison exploitation movie (see *The Big Doll House, Caged Heat, The Concrete Jungle, Chained Heat*, etc.). *Human Experiments* (1979) has Geoffrey Lewis trying to curb criminal tendencies by playing sick practical jokes on inmates, *The Fifth Floor* (1980) is the allegedly true story of a girl unjustly taken into care and abused by sadistic male nurse Bo Hopkins, and the flamboyant *Hellhole* (1985) lets Mary Woronov and her hypodermic needle loose in an institution for the criminally insane. Just as the heroines of prison movies tend to be innocent but framed, so the heroines of asylum movies tend to be sane but certified. Key moments in *Don't Look in the Basement, The Fifth Floor, Lies* (1983) and *Dead of Winter* have the leading ladies raving about their normality while doctors calmly convince third parties that the women are mad.

S.F. Brownrigg's *Don't Look in the Basement* (1973), a wildly overdirected low-budgeter, manages to conjure up some twisted atmosphere. As usual, the head of the asylum is killed and a patient who fantasises she's a psychiatrist takes over; and, as usual, her therapeutic ideas extend to such indecencies as cutting out the tongue of an irritating old lady and killing or torturing as she sees fit in the name of discipline. Brownrigg followed this almost interesting bit of sleaze with *Poor White Trash, Part II* (1976), *Don't Open the Door* (1979) and *Keep My Grave Open* (1980), all of which bear out his *auteur* status by concentrating on heroines driven insane by exposure to grottily staged violence. Brownrigg — whose films aren't quite like anybody else's — has a repertory company cast (Camilla Carr, Gene Ross, Ann Stafford), a distinctively murky visual style, a habit of smothering his brooding horrors in moody musak and a fondness for often incomprehensible plot twists (see if you can figure out *Keep My Grave Open*). Despite the melodramatic, sweaty excesses of his casts, Brownrigg's films have very little actual nudity and gore. While the likes of H.G. Lewis and Andy Milligan lace their films with gratuitous sex and gratuitous violence, Brownrigg seems to see himself as a backwoods Bergman and laces his scenarios with gratuitous Art. Less campy than most of his obscuro exploitation colleagues, his films are more ambitious, if just as difficult to sit through.

The only gore movie genuinely to approach Art is Abel Ferrara's *The Driller Killer* (1980), a New York semi-underground feature that plays like a punk Warhol Factory film. Reno (Jimmy Laine, actually the director under a pseudonym) lives with a pair of zonked-out nymphets in an apartment over a rock group who practice twenty-four hours a day and argue over the pronunciation of 'oop-she-dooby'. The first psycho in the movies to be driven mad by economic rather than personal problems, Reno expresses a longing for the prairies in a wall-size painting of a buffalo which he needs to sell to pay the rent. Since his main fear is that he will lose even the marginal position in society his apartment gives him, Reno takes to murdering the skid row vagrants and weirdos he's afraid of joining in the gutter. As his name suggests, Reno wants to be a cowboy. He straps a portable power pack to his belt, holsters an electric drill and stalks the alleys striking gunfighter poses. When he straddles a sleeping wino and drills his forehead, Reno rides the kicking corpse as if it were a bucking bronco. Ferrara throws in gore scenes with surprising restraint, giving equal weight to apparently documentary footage of down and outs in the Big Apple and the self-involved chatter of the punk rock runaways. Incredibly, *The Driller Killer* finds sympathy for its fringe people. As the occasional soothing passages of vibraphone Bach interrupting the drilling and rocking indicate, all Reno really wants is some peace and quiet.

In *The Driller Killer*, Ferrara and his regular screenwriter Nicholas St John sidestep the sexism inherent in most splatter movies by presenting a psycho whose preferred victims are not desirable young women but unappetising old men. In *Ms .45* (1981), aided by the ethereal presence of the extraordinary Zoe Tamerlis, they tackle the issue head-on with a rigorously feminist reading of the always problematic *Last House on the Left/I Spit on Your Grave* revenge-for-rape plot. Thana (Tamerlis), a mute teenager who works as a seamstress in Manhattan's Garment Centre, is attacked twice in the first ten minutes of the film, once by a masked thug (Ferrara again) who rapes her in an alley, and once by a housebreaker whom she kills with an iron. While she disposes of the burglar's corpse piece by piece, she withdraws into herself still further, only to blossom as an anti-sexist vigilante. Armed with the dead man's .45, she stalks the city at night, killing any man who harasses her – a street punk who propositions every girl who passes, a smooth-talking photographer who lures her up to his studio with promises of a *Vogue* layout, a violent pimp, a kerb-crawling Arab, a gang of muggers. As her actions become more extreme, her appearance becomes more seductive. Rather than turning Thana into a gun-toting fetish like the heroines of New World's girl gangster movies, Ferrara makes her a neutral figure whose power over her victims is rooted in her ability to inspire and then contradict their fantasies of femininity. In an extraordinary finale, Thana takes a last stand at a Hallowe'en party, dressed in suspenders and a nun's habit. She shoots down all the men in the room, but is stabbed in the back by her gay/feminist workmate. Unable to shoot a

woman, she utters a single world ('sister') and dies.

Ferrara and St John have been drifting toward the mainstream since their early films, but have retained their in-the-street roots. *Fear City* (1984) sets out to be 'more or less a legitimate movie, a milquetoast version of the other two'. Here, rather than deal with a character like Reno or Thana who is at once a psycho and a vigilante, Ferrara splits the protagonist in two and has Tom Berenger as an ex-boxer-cum-high-class pimp forced to play vigilante when the local godfather (Rossano Brazzi) orders him to get rid of a martial arts madman who has been murdering local hookers and strippers. Similarly, in Ferrara's solo TV pot-boiler *The Gladiator* (1986), Ken Wahl soups up his truck and terrorises drunken drivers after his brother is killed by a psychopath who cruises the city by night in an all-black Death Car; and in *China Girl* (1987), his Sino–Italian rewrite with St John of *Romeo and Juliet*, the mafiosi and the Triads who run the East Side between them try to damp down an interracial gang war because it's bad for business. Although he would seem the least likely of all directors to find a niche in the sanitised world of American television, Ferrara has formed an occasional association with producer Michael Mann, for whom he directed a brace of *Miami Vice* episodes ('The Home Invaders', 'The Dutch Oven') before tackling the two-hour pilot for *Crime Story* , the 1960s-set cop/gangster miniseries. Strangely, *Crime Story* (1986) is the most personal of the director's later movies. Lieutenant Mike Torello (Dennis Farina) of the Chicago Major Crime Unit is a typical Ferrara protagonist, a hulking hero who compares the scene of a multiple shotgun slaying to a Jackson Pollock and is visibly being driven crazy – his dead partner pops up in his office to give him gloomy advice – by the urban hell he has to live through.

In Ferrara's films, protagonists are driven mad by their city. A cycle of movies revolving around the figure of Jack the Ripper present a psychopath who is at once the terror of the slums and an embodiment of all the evils that have created them. Bob Clark's spirited Sherlockian pastiche

Murder By Decree (1979), based on recent speculations about the truth behind the 1888 murders, is intriguingly explicit in its political angle. Christopher Plummer plays Sherlock Holmes as a crusader against specific injustices, and the Ripper himself is revealed as a tool of a Victorian Establishment that would like to forget what goes down in the East End. Recently, period Jack the Ripper movies have become less common. Lucio Fulci's disgusting *Lo Squartatore di New York* (*The New York Ripper*) (1982) has a homicidal puritan with motives modelled on those of Laird Cregar in *The Lodger* take his razor to a selection of loose-living Big Apple women. The Edwardian-set *Hands of the Ripper*, the TV movie *Bridge Across Time* (1985) and the shot-on-video *The Ripper* (1986) all deal with trouble caused by the discarnate spirit of Jack the Ripper, but Nicholas Meyer's *Time After Time* (1979) is the most appealing attempt to draw a contemporary lesson from the case. The Ripper (David Warner) flees the 1890s in a time machine borrowed from H.G. Wells (Malcolm McDowell) and winds up in modern San Francisco. Wells follows and, between plenty of romance and adventure, debates with the mass murderer whether the future they have stumbled into reflects Wells's vision of a perfectable scientific utopia or the Ripper's idea of a progressively degenerate global Whitechapel.

In a particularly bizarre and tiny psycho sub-genre, cheerful, jolly Father Christmas is transformed into a terrifying menace. 'What next', asks Leonard Maltin's *TV Movies*, 'the Easter Bunny as a child molester?' The trend does have authentic folklore roots: in the days before Victorian whimsy, Santa Claus divided his time between rewarding good children and punishing naughty ones. The first of the psycho Santas is the anonymous killer in *Tales from the Crypt*, but he was soon followed by Christopher Plummer as the bank-robbing Kris Kringle in *The Silent Partner* (1978), the sorority-slashing St Nicholas in *To All a Goodnight* (1983), the zombie Father Christmas of *Trancers* (1985) and the notorious department store troublemakers of *Silent Night, Deadly Night* (1984) and *Silent Night, Deadly Night Part II*

(1987). Despite all this activity, it wasn't until the first of the uninspiring *Silent Night* bloodbaths – in which Linnea Quigley shows her breasts yet again and gets impaled on some reindeer antlers, and another victim is beheaded while out sleighing (ho ho ho) – that parents and protest groups got up in arms about the trashing of a cherished childhood figure. What nobody except the film-makers seemed interested in saying was that a lot of children found Santa frightening even before the movies depicted him as an axe-wielding psychopath. *Silent Night, Deadly Night Part II* spends half its running time on a cut-down version of the original (see also *Boogeyman II*), but turns surprisingly witty thereafter – including one Scenes We'd Like to See sequence in which the psycho murders a rowdy patron in a cinema who's ruining his evening out. By way of a change, Edmund Purdom's *Don't Open til Christmas* (1984) has a psychopath who specialises in murdering Santa.

The best of this short-lived genre is Lewis Foster's *You Better Watch Out* (1980), which opens traditionally with a pre-credits childhood trauma but develops less like *Silent Night, Deadly Night* or *Don't Open til Christmas* than a weird crossbreed of *Death Wish* and *Miracle on 34th Street*. Brandon Maggart stars as Harry Stadling, a meek employee of the Jolly Dream toy company who is so obsessed with Santa Claus he feels compelled to take on the role. At first he acts as a vigilante for the Christmas spirit, forcing his firm to make a larger donation of toys to the local handicapped kids than they had intended. Then he takes to the streets and starts doing away with Christmas-haters, using sharpened tree ornaments or a lance-bearing lead soldier. Harry has spent the year recording the good and bad deeds of the local children in a scrapbook, and duly rewards the good while leaving a sackful of dirt for a brat who has spent twelve months poring over *Penthouse*. 'It's a good thing he's doing,' opines the cop on the case, 'it'll teach the kids to stay in line.' The film even manages to pull itself out of the urban squalor of its setting and find a happy, transcendental ending. 'All I wanted to do was give people what they said they wanted,' whines Harry, 'but people

● *Deadly innocent. Paula Sheppard,* **Communion.**

don't *want* Santa Claus.' However, although he gets stuck in a chimney, Harry is finally saved from the cops by a circle of adoring children. He drives his van-cum-sleigh off an embankment, and it flies off to the North. Aside from anything else, *You Better Watch Out* has far more of the true Christmas spirit than the smug, expensive hypocrisy of *Santa Claus* (1985). 'I wish I had kids', John Waters has written of Foster's film, 'I'd make them watch it every year and if they didn't like it they'd be punished.'

Religion and the city streets also figure heavily in Alfred Sole's *Communion* (1976), a heavily Catholic mystery set during the original release of *Psycho*. An 8-year-old girl (Brooke Shields), dolled up for her First Communion, is murdered in church by a masked figure in a yellow raincoat. The chief suspect is the victim's sister, Alice (Paula Sheppard), an insolent, mixed-up, quixotically cruel young girl who is nevertheless consumed with a fierce sense of injustice. Written (by Sole and Rosemary Ritvo) with a depth of character and complexity of social background unusual in the genre, *Communion* has a twisted whodunit plot, but is more concerned with the way Alice is gradually forced to take on the identity of the killer. In the finale, as the culprit is brought down at the altar after her horrific stabbing of the friendly priest, Alice takes up the murderer's knife and seems set to continue her career of enforcing rigid religious standards on a community and a church no longer predisposed to abide by them. The film contains several monstrous minor characters, like the senile monsignor who refuses to let go of his parish and the incredibly obese, lewd and disgusting landlord (Alphonse De Noble) who continually propositions the 12-year-old heroine, and Sole also pulls off the murder sequences with a prolonged, almost unbearable realism. *Communion* touches on several then-popular horror themes – the possessed or evil child, the influence of the Catholic Church for Good or Evil, the breakdown of traditional family values – but emerges as a fresh, original work. Sadly, Sole's subsequent efforts – *Tanya's Island* (1980) and *Pandemonium* (1982) – have been much less interesting.

The poet laureate of the psycho movie is Martin Scorsese, whose horror films are rarely recognised as such. Scorsese's examination of the tormented psyche of modern America has been most telling in a series of films which benefit enormously from the input of Robert De Niro. An almost peripheral madman in *Mean Streets* (1973), De Niro has come to the fore as such driven, complicated maniacs as Travis Bickle of *Taxi Driver* (1976), saxophonist Jimmy Doyle in *New York, New York* (1977), Jake LaMotta in *Raging Bull* (1979) and Rupert Pupkin in *The King of Comedy* (1983). *Taxi Driver*, the result of a fiery collison between Scorsese's Catholicism and Paul Schrader's Calvinism, is almost a compendium of psycho themes. Travis Bickle is at once the unhealthy gun fanatic of *Targets*, the insane Vietnam veteran of *First Blood*, the unhinged city dweller of *The Driller Killer* and the maddened vigilante of *Death Wish*. He's also the rejected swain of princess Cybill Shepherd and damn nearly a Lee Harvey Oswald-style political assassin, but he finally emerges – Mohawk and all – as an urban hero. Because his victims are pimps and crooks, he is hailed as the saviour of teenage hooker Jody Foster, but the audience has seen enough of Travis's private and public world to know how deep his madness runs. With its Bernard Herrmann score, neo-surrealist big-city-after-dark setting and unrestrained dialogue, *Taxi Driver* is a baroque nightmare movie, but perhaps hurts a touch less than *The King of Comedy*, which is filmed in a neutral, even television-ish, style and would seem outwardly to be a comedy of manners.

In *The King of Comedy*, De Niro hides unrecognisably behind a moustache, a striped suit and an ingratiating manner as Rupert Pupkin, a man whose entire life builds towards a single television appearance. 'Better king for a night than schmuck for a whole lifetime', Pupkin tells the viewing audience after he has been allowed to do a stand-up turn on a talk show because he has kidnapped and threatened to kill its host, Jerry Langford (Jerry Lewis). Pupkin's gun is a toy, and there is no overt violence in the film, and yet Pupkin has been created by exactly the same media deceptions, mental imbalances and societal inequities that give rise to Travis Bickle. He spends the early stages of the film trying to get on to the show through legitimate channels – brown-nosing, sitting in waiting rooms, being fobbed off by flunkeys, fantasising, working on his act – but is thwarted at every turn. Like the greatest screen psychos, Rupert Pupkin is finally a victim rather than the Monster. Given the world he was born into and the set of values he has had foisted off on him, Pupkin has no other choice but to go mad. The scary thing is that he's not alone: Masha (Sandra Bernhard), the rich TV junkie who helps him with the kidnapping, is just as alienated and mentally deformed, and the few glimpses we get of Langford's *Lifestyles of the Rich and Famous* world suggest that even if Rupert wins the celebrity he is after he can only look forward to vapid stagnation. After *The King of Comedy*, Scorsese and De Niro parted company, as if the director no longer needed a madman; the universe of *After Hours* (1985) is mad enough to do without a central psychotic.

The twenty years since *Targets* and *Pretty Poison* have seen some erosion of their imput into the psycho genre. One of the interesting aspects of these movies is that they go against the hitherto sacrosanct movie lore that psychotics are either retards or overly intellectual (the 1931 title *The Mad Genius* is highly significant). Bobby and Sue Ann are insane but average. Subsequently, there has been a tendency to get back to the mad geniuses: witness the films dealing with psychotic artists (*The Driller Killer, Headless Eyes*), photographers (*Don't Answer the Phone*), musicians (Chris Sarandon in *Lipstick*, 1976) and even tattooists (Bruce Dern in *Tattoo*, 1981). Jeff Kanew's *Natural Enemies* (1979), one of the most intelligent of the intelligent psycho movies, has Hal Holbrook as Paul Steward, a cultured, intellectual magazine publisher spending a working day – at the end of which he intends to shoot his wife, children and himself – trying to puzzle out what it's all been about. Mario Azzopardo's *Deadline* (1980) also has a thinking man on the edge in Stephen Leslie (Stephen Young), an academic-

turned-bestselling-horror-writer whose life (if not personality) is actionably close to Stephen King's. Leslie is fast running out of ideas, and fatally begins to wonder whether he hasn't brought too much horror into the world when his two sons hang his daughter in imitation of a sequence he wrote for an exploitative horror picture. Both Steward and Leslie finally conclude that suicide is their only meaningful way out of marriages ('we know less about marriage than we do about cancer', concludes Steward) and lives gone to waste.

The killer cop is a psycho movie commonplace, imported from the Deep South moonshine melodrama. In the likes of *White Lightning* (1973), the fat and greasy town sheriff (usually Ned Beatty) is typically corrupt, brutal and prone to killing off any troublemakers who happen to drift into his town. *Macon County Line* (1974) and *Jackson County Jail* (1976) are similarly cynical about redneck policemen and their predilection for torture, lynching and rape. In *Midnight*, the evil cultists only pretend to be uniformed officers, but a whole batch of films – *The Prowler, To All a Goodnight, The Eyes of Laura Mars* (1978), *The Majorettes, The Fantasist* (1986), *Maniac Cop* – feature badge-bearing multiple murderers. A further clutch – *He Knows You're Alone, When a Stranger Calls, Don't Answer the Phone, Ten to Midnight* – pit their psychos against obsessed cops out to take them down with a dose of street justice; in the entirely terrible *Bloodrage* (1977) a cop finally catches up with the callow nutcase who has murdered his girlfriend and calmly throws him out of a tenement window. William Asher's *Butcher, Baker, Nightmare Maker* (1981), which is mainly about harridan Susan Tyrrell's bloodthirsty killing spree, sets up the murderess's nephew/son (Peter MacNicol) as a fall guy caught between the crazed Tyrrell and the equally dangerous cop on the case. Bo Svenson, who plays a no-nonsense lawman in *Part 2 – Walking Tall* and *Final Chapter – Walking Tall*, attacks the *Butcher, Baker* role with insane glee, spouting off against homosexuals and reading gay motivations into the measliest crime. In the finale, MacNicol and the audience look on as maniac mother and crusader cop alike are turned into bloodied monstrosities, equal in their ghastliness.

The most interesting of the crazy cops is Lou Ford (Stacy Keach) in Burt Kennedy's adaption of Jim Thompson's *The Killer Inside Me* (1976). While the film is astonishingly well cast (the line-up includes John Carradine, Don Stroud, Keenan Wynn and Royal Dano), Kennedy's pedestrian direction isn't quite up to the texture of Thompson's novel, although the actors do their best to keep it in line. Lou Ford, who also gets a crack at abusing Susan Tyrrell, is an outwardly amiable deputy sheriff who doesn't carry a gun, manages to be everybody's friend and conceals his razor-sharp intellect behind crackerbarrel banalities. He's also mentally ill – due to the usual flashbacked witnessing of adultery and parental abuse – and a bungling schemer who plays various local political factions off each other in an attempt to murder and extort his way to a comfortable life. Finally, he diagnoses himself as 'a schizophrenic, paranoid type. When things get a little rough, I just go out and kill a few people – that's all.'

The usual role of the cop in the psycho movie, though, is that of Nemesis. And one of the modern *policier*'s obsessive themes is the unhealthy interdependence of the serial killer and the rogue policeman out to bring him in. Don Siegel's *Dirty Harry* (1971) is the best known and most disturbing variation on the theme, with Clint Eastwood compellingly deep frozen as the rootless, inflexible Inspector Harry Callaghan of the San Francisco police department, conducting a one-man war against Scorpio (Andy Robinson), a piece of human vermin who not only commits random acts of sadistic murder but tries to extort a huge ransom from the city. It's obvious from the physical contrast between the relaxed, poised, in-control Eastwood and the kinetic, quivering, off-the-edge Robinson that there's an unbreachable divide between them, but they are both outcasts from the bureaucratic city – Harry's superior finds him taping a switchblade to his leg and comments 'you know, it's disgusting that a police officer should know how to use a weapon like that' – and the finale is an act of mutual destruction as Harry

kills Scorpio, which brings to an end his career – i.e. all he has as a life – as a cop. Subsequently, Eastwood has dug deeper into the Dirty Harry psychology – playing a burned-out cop in *The Gauntlet* (1977) and a policeman unnerved by his kinship with the psycho he's tracking in *Tightrope* (1984).

Serial killers also plague lone cops in *Cruising* (1980), with Al Pacino combing the leather bars for a gay slasher and developing a taste for the s-m scene, and *Order of Death* (1983), with Harvey Keitel menaced by Johnny Rotten, a rich eccentric who has made a habit of murdering crooked policemen. The most reactionary rereading of *Dirty Harry* is *Cobra* (1986), with Sylvester Stallone as a cop on the Zombie Squad going after a psychopath who turns out to be one of an organised army of kill-crazy maniacs, and Andy Robinson uneasily promoted from psychopath to by-the-book superior. Stallone's attitude is famously and without any detectable irony summed up with 'crime is a disease, and I'm the cure'. Far more probing and unsettling is Michael Mann's *Manhunter* (1986), from Thomas Harris's novel *Red Dragon*, with William L. Petersen as Will Graham, a FBI agent whose speciality is bringing in serial murderers. Graham's search for a monster known as the Tooth Fairy (Tom Noonan), who butchers entire families, is complicated by the sniping from behind bars of Dr Hannibal Lektor (Brian Cox) – the last madman he put away – and his own inner conviction that he can only catch these crazies by entering into their unhealthy state of mind. No such doubts affect James Woods in *Cop* (1987), although it's plain from the tenacity with which he pursues a phantom killer that there's something deeply unhealthy about his fixation on the case, especially when he himself commits the one murder the psychopath appears to be working himself up to and brutally disposes of the surrendering madman in the finish.

The cop movies are so concerned with their central characters that they rarely have time for their villains: Scorpio is deliberately a motiveless animal with no redeeming features (his ransom note to the city states that unless paid off he 'will enjoy murdering either a Catholic priest or a nigger'), and the killers of *Cruising* and *Cop* are vaguely motivated, shadowy figures who don't come on screen until the finale, by which time their psychoses have been all but upstaged by those of the heroes. It's difficult to deal with the reason why, therefore a cycle of numbly frozen movies of the last ten years have tried not to find a root cause for motiveless violence but to demonstrate that it does exist. Jonathan Kaplan's *Over the Edge* (1979) has the children of a vacuum-like planned community drifting into juvenile delinquency, drug-dealing and anarchy because they haven't got anything else to do. Its bleak vision was developed after the coming of punk by Penelope Spheeris, whose *Suburbia* (1983) is more melancholy than muckraking. Outcast youths survive by raiding garage freezers and co-exist in abandoned housing developments with packs of wild dogs. In Spheeris's follow-up, *The Boys Next Door* (1985), no-hoper kids Maxwell Caulfield and Charley Sheen *look up* to the kind of punks found in the earlier film and go on a depressingly random murder spree to celebrate the weekend after they graduate from school and before they sign on for life in a hellhole factory. Dennis Hopper, in *Out of the Blue* (1980), blames it all on hippie parents who have raised their kids as disaffected sociopaths, and similarly sees a suicidal holocaust as the only way out. These downbeat, angry, depressing films are the nearest the nightmare movie comes to social realism.

Tim Hunter, screenwriter of *Over the Edge*, returned to the cycle with the definitive killer kid movie, *River's Edge* (1986). A group of school children learn that one of their number has just murdered his girlfriend and listlessly debate whether to turn him in or shield him from the law. In its deceptively quiet way, *River's Edge* is the most shocking of the bunch, not least because it lacks the occasional preachiness that mars Spheeris's work. Moral without moralising, blackly comic without tastelessness, acutely tuned in to the way dead-end teens act and talk, the film is amazingly capable of compassion while examining startling callousness. Back in the city, Buddy Giovinazzo's

Combat Shock (1985) also extends the punk ethos with its Vietnam veteran turned suicidal vigilante. The film echoes *Eraserhead* in its use of a squealing monster baby – the result of its father's exposure to Agent Orange – and *The Driller Killer* in its suggestion that inner city blight is responsible for driving its protagonist off the wall. Whereas *River's Edge* works because it avoids sensationalism, *Combat Shock* opts for graphic horrors (a junkie shooting up with a coat-hanger, blood and guts all over the place) and succeeds in being impressively downbeat without really adding anything to the argument.

If the streets are the locale of the punk psycho movie, then middle-class madness in the 1980s exists within relationships. Ken Russell's *Crimes of Passion* (1984) is the ultimate psycho-sexual horror film in that its opposition of career-woman-cum-hooker Kathleen Turner with side-walk-preacher-cum-slasher Anthony Perkins suggests a *Frankenstein Meets the Wolf Man* combined sequel to *Psycho* and *Belle de Jour*. With its garish, semi-porno look, outstanding, risk-taking performances and Barry Sandler's witty, explicit dialogue, *Crimes of Passion* is Russell's best-ever movie, even if its serious discussion of the outer limits of the sex drive is finally perverted into crazed melodrama as the razor-dildo-wielding Perkins ties up Turner so he can sing 'Get Happy' to her. Also finding unusual depths in a romantic liaison and hurtling into magnificent *grand guignol* is Donald Cammell's *White of the Eye* (1986), in which Cathy Moriarty suspects that her ex-hippie stereo whiz David Keith husband is the nut who has been disembowel-ling Arizona's yuppie women in accordance with an ancient Indian ritual. Cammell doesn't really try for more psychological depth than the average psycho quickie, but he does bring an unusual style and humour to the genre. A flapping goldfish in an otherwise meticulously arranged *nouvelle cuisine* lay-out signals the killer's presence, disturbed eyes blink in ultra-extreme close-up, the camera swoops over the desert as if possessed by the vaguely summoned ancient Indian demons, and the whole thing winds up with a literally dynamite showdown.

In the year of *Dirty Harry*, Don Siegel and Clint Eastwood exchanged jobs for *Play Misty for Me*. Siegel has a cameo role as a bartender, while Eastwood takes up the director's task and stars as a shallow disc jockey who enters into a casual affair with fan Jessica Walter and finds himself being terrorised by the cast-off, increasingly violent woman. One of the many interesting things about the film is Eastwood's willingness to paint his character in an unsympathetic light, and to allow the psychotic woman to become the moral focus. A 'normal' monster in the *Targets/Pretty Poison* tradition, Walter is disposed of in the finale, but Eastwood has been taught that you can't throw people away without taking the consequences. Astonishingly, when Michael Douglas and Glenn Close go through the whole thing again in Adrian Lyne's *Fatal Attraction* (1987), the message is turned inside-out and we are finally assured that Douglas can be excused his brief fling with an unbalanced editor because he has a solid family background. In a pointed contrast, *Fatal Attraction* cleaned up at the box-office while Joseph Ruben's far more suspenseful *The Stepfather* (1986) was passed over. Ruben also deals with traditional values, as middle-class paragon Terry O'Neill moves from family to family, slaughtering his wife and stepchildren whenever they fail to live up to his *Leave It to Beaver* expectations. Unlike Lyne, Ruben gives the opposition a fair crack of the whip – allowing O'Neill to be an appealing, even sympathetic figure – before reaching his conclusion. If *Fatal Attraction* epitomises the new conservatism by upholding the family above all else, *The Stepfather* daringly goes against the grain by branding these same unrealistic values as the cause of the protagonist's homicidal mania.

● *Death through a hole in a T-shirt.* Mirella D'Angelo, **Tenebrae.**

auteurs

auteurs

I. *Dario Argento*

I like women, especially beautiful ones. If they have a good face and figure, I would much prefer to watch them being murdered than an ugly girl or a man. I certainly don't have to justify myself to anyone about this. I don't care what anybody thinks or reads into it. I have often had journalists walk out of interviews when I say what I feel about this subject.

Dario Argento

The death of a beautiful woman is, unquestionably, the most poetical topic in the world.

Edgar Allan Poe

What Sergio Leone is to the Spaghetti Western, Dario Argento is to the Italian horror film. He began his career as a screenwriter, contributing to lacklustre Spaghettis like *Un Esercito di cinque uomini* (*Five Man Army*) (1969) and made an impact by working, with Bernardo Bertolucci, on the storyboards for Leone's *C'Era una volta il west* (*Once Upon a Time in the West*) (1968). While Leone takes the Western genre and transmutes the ingredients to produce a distinctive vision at once hyper-realist and surreal, Argento has deconstructed the horror/thriller tradition of Hitchcock, Fritz Lang, Robert Siodmak and the

American hardboiled *noir* writers and created his own distinctive world. Intriguingly, just as the Italian Westerns of the mid-1960s were foreshadowed in the slightly earlier German series of Karl May adaptions, so the flowering of gothic/bizarre Italian chillers built upon precedents set by the German series of Edgar Wallace mysteries, with their masked murderers, perverted suspects and mix of classical English detective story with 'forbidden' sado-eroticism. Heavily influenced by the early 'mad killer' movies of Mario Bava, *La Ragazza che sapeva troppo* (*The Evil Eye*) (1962) and *Sei donne per l'assassino* (*Blood and Black Lace*) (1964), Argento first made his impact with a quartet of glossy, cosmopolitan whodunits, *L'uccello dalle piume di cristallo* (*The Bird With the Crystal Plumage*) (1970), *Il Gatto a nove code* (*Cat O'Nine Tails*) (1971), *Quattro mosche di velluto grigio* (*Four Flies on Grey Velvet*) (1971) and *Profondo rosso* (*Deep Red*) (1976). He has never entirely abandoned his roots in the *giallo* – just as the term *film noir* derives from the black covers of the French reprints of American thrillers in the *Série Noire*, the roughly equivalent *gialli* are named after the yellow covers of a run of Italian paperbacks – and has returned, minus the supernatural shenanigans of his baroque horror movies, with *Tenebrae* (1982) and *Opera* (1987).

L'Uccello opens with Tony Musante, an American writer adrift in an alien Rome, trapped between plate glass shutters in an empty art gallery, helplessly watching while Eva Renzi is stabbed by an unidentifiable man in a black mackintosh and rainhat. Musante typifies Argento's subsequent heroes, an obsessed lost soul drawn into amateur sleuthwork by a niggling doubt. Something about the scene he witnessed was wrong, but Musante can't quite figure it out. Finally, he learns that the man in black is Renzi's husband and that he was defending himself. The psycho killer terrorising the city is the innocent girl Musante was trying to help. When Bava uses a similar twist in *La Ragazza che sapeva troppo* it's just a plot device, but Argento makes his surprise ending an emotionally shattering betrayal of the hero and his chivalrous impulses. Argento habitually refers to Agatha Christie and Sir Arthur Conan Doyle, but the world of his whodunits is far removed from the tidy, meaningless puzzles of the English country house weekend massacre. Argento's amateur detectives are not scientific observers with a purely academic interest in the case – except in *Il Gatto*, the weakest of the early films – but alienated artists caught up in a paranoid nightmare. The unprecedented success of *L'Uccello* led to a mini-boom in imitative whodunits, like Lucio Fulci's *Una Lucertola con la pelle di donna* (*Lizard in a Woman's Skin*) (1971), Mario Caiano's *L'Occhio nel labirinto* (*Blood*) (1971), Paolo Cavara's *La Tarantola dal ventre nero* (*The Black Belly of the Tarantula*) (1971), Emilio P. Miraglia's *La Dama rossa uccide sette volte* (*The Red Queen Kills Seven Times*) (1972), Sergio Pastore's *Sette scialli di seta gialla* (*The Crimes of the Black Cat*) (1972) and Carlos Aured's Spanish *Los Ojos azules de la muneca rota* (*The Blue Eyes of the Broken Doll*) (1973).

Argento's literary forebears are dark thriller writers like Cornell Woolrich and Fredric Brown (between them, *L'Uccello* and *Quattro mosche* use up almost all of Brown's *The Screaming Mimi*), and he makes each twist of the plot a turn of the screw. Often the murderer has a fixation on the hero, which leads to a transference of guilt. The clown-masked slasher of *Quattro mosche* has a photograph which drummer Michael Brandon believes will implicate him in the accidental death

of a mystery man who has been tailing him. In *Tenebrae*, Anthony Franciosa is a writer of detective stories who becomes involved in a series of psycho slayings when a victim is found with her throat cut and her screams gagged by pages torn from his latest novel. The climax of *Quattro mosche* is especially hurtful: Brandon unmasks the killer as his wife (Mimsy Farmer), and learns that she has married him as part of an obscure vengeance against her dead father. *Tenebrae* takes the solution a step further as the original murderer gets an axe in his head half-way through the film and Franciosa steps in to continue the killings for his own purposes. Significantly, until the final revelation, Franciosa has been serving as Argento's mouthpiece – fielding all the questions about violence to women and the ethics of depicting bloody horror that the director must endlessly be faced with. Argento goes out of his way to identify himself with the psycho figures in his movies. In sequences where the killer is seen as a masked shadow or a pair of stylish black leather gloves, Argento himself takes up the knife to dispose of his on-screen victims.

Frequently, Argento's twisted finales reveal that the murders have been committed by several independent psychopaths whose motives and methods dovetail. While the traditional mystery depends on the rigid parameters of crime and detection, Argento sets his labyrinthine plots against a disturbingly irrational world. In *L'Uccello* and *Tenebrae*, works of art are employed as weapons in climactic confrontations that find Musante and Franciosa trapped by viciously spiked modern sculptures. And, taking on board Italianate influences as varied as Fellini's *La Dolce vita* and Antonioni's *Blowup*, he creates a style-obsessed, emotionally frigid modern world that provides the perfect context for his callous stories and shatteringly staged violence. Apartments are painted a blinding white solely for the contrast of a deep red splatter of blood, and many of the – usually female, invariably gorgeous – victims are elaborately coiffured and made up before they get knifed. Everyday objects – cut-throat razors, necklaces caught in lifts, sheets of glass – are co-opted as instruments of death. This mixture of stylish accessories and blatant bloodiness had led more than one critic to brand Argento as the inventor of a *telefono rosso* school of Italian cinema, the modern successor to those 1930s romances in which white telephones were held to be the height of chic. Whereas before the war, Italian film-goers aspired to (or, at worst, envied) *la dolce vita*, Argento's audience insists the *haut bourgeoisie* should suffer for their privilege by dying in elaborate agony. If murders in *gialli* are the equivalent of production numbers in a musical, Argento is the Vincente Minnelli of ultra-violence.

The best of Argento's thrillers is *Profondo rosso*, the transitional work that opens up supernatural possibilities the director has subsequently explored. During a demonstration of her clairvoyance, medium Macha Meril senses the presence of someone insane who has killed before and will kill again. That night, she is viciously slain in her apartment and innocently bystanding composer David Hemmings, first on the scene of the crime, is obsessively drawn into the mystery. Yet again, it's a half-remembered detail that haunts Hemmings, whose very presence is yet another nod to Antonioni. The film features one of Argento's cleverest clues, and, for once, he plays fair in putting on screen for an instant the face of the surprise murderer during the set-up sequence as Hemmings looks over Meril's flat immediately after the killing. Although it has a complex and intriguing plot, the film is spiced throughout with the sense of an irrational world lurking just beyond the boundaries of perception. The pre-cognition theme is introduced early, as Meril reacts with horror moments *before* the axe-wielding murderer breaks her door down. There-after, all the deaths are foreshadowed by apparent irrelevences. Hemmings scalding himself on a coffee machine prefigures a character's demise in a boiling bath, and his jokey statement that he plays the piano because it represents a symbolic bashing-in of his father's teeth relates to the unforgettably nasty sequence in which a victim has his mouth shattered again and again against a mantelpiece. Although pregnant with sinister detail – like the school which seems to turn out generation after generation of junior psychopaths – *Profondo rosso* also displays Argento's sly but rarely exercised sense of humour. A prowling camera provides surreally extreme close-ups of an assortment of clues scattered throughout the old dark house which holds the answer to the mystery and, after a typically sinuous tracking shot, comes to rest on the killer's lost marbles.

Argento's thrillers have been compared to those of Hitchcock and Fritz Lang, with whom he shares a sense of the utter chaos lurking beneath everyday reality. But Hitchcock and Lang never quite got around to the disturbing catharsis of *Suspiria* (1977). While the plots of the mysteries often strain at the bounds of logic and possibility, *Suspiria* wrenches itself free by taking its heroine (Jessica Harper) beyond an investigation of a friend's death into a world of witchcraft and the supernatural. Argento celebrates his liberation from the fetters of logical plotting with a feast of the unreal and the incredible. *Suspiria* is a loud film, with dazzling colours achieved through the use of outmoded Technicolor stock, and a deafening score from the rock group Goblin that hisses 'witch!' in stereo long before Harper realises that the basement of the Frieburg Tanz Akademie houses an incredibly ancient sorceress whose evil influence pervades the whole city. 'There is magic all around us', Harper concludes, her words borne out by the Mario Bava-esque lighting which turns the crumbling art deco Akademie into an annex of Hell, and the way even the automatic doors at the airport seem to have a threatening life of their own. The script is a non-stop catalogue of poetic absurdities, played with gusto by the sinister likes of Alida Valli and Joan Bennett. Characters are forever arguing pointlessly about rooms, rent, shoes, maggots and Christian names ('names that begin with s are the names of sssnakes!'). Harper's heroine is a fragile, holy innocent who can finally destroy the Queen Witch with a deft thrust of a crystal ornament, but the rest of the cast are gargoyles. *Suspiria* is a brilliant work, despite the weakness of its plot, but it is altogether too much, a three-ring circus of a movie that serves as a spectacular prologue for Argento's masterpiece.

Inferno (1980) opens with a mosaic of close-ups. A knife. A key chain. An alchemical tome, *The Three Mothers*, by E. Varelli. A *Cassell's Latin Dictionary*. Irene Miracle uses the knife to cut the leaves of the book and the dictionary to read the text. Varelli was an architect who built three haunted houses, in Frieburg, Rome and New York, for the Three Mothers, supernatural beings who rule the world unbeknown to us all. Presumably, Mater Suspiriorum, the Mother of Sighs, was the witch encountered by Jessica Harper in the Frieburg basement. Exploring the basement of her own New York apartment house, Miracle accidentally drops those keys into a mysteriously illuminated, flooded room. Gingerly lowering herself into the water, Miracle comes across the submerged portrait of Mater Tenebrarum, the Mother of Darkness, and a group of floating corpses. Although it sets up the wholly invented myth of the Three Mothers with admirable economy and elaborates upon it with humour ('Have you ever heard of the Three Sisters?' asks one character; 'Do you mean those black singers?' replies a doomed sceptic), *Inferno*'s screenplay is less a story than a tapestry. Miracle and her brother, Leigh McCloskey, investigate the Three Mothers with the haunted zeal expected of Argento heroes, but the plot is really a diffuse collection of episodes in which an assortment of characters in Rome and New York meet their deaths when they get too near the concealed lairs of Mater Tenebrarum and Mater Lachrymarum, the Mother of Tears.

Every sequence is a meticulously orchestrated mini-symphony of camera movement, stylised lighting, sound effects, music and found objects. Like a symphony, *Inferno* plays variations on its themes. McCloskey, a music student in Rome, is distracted from reading his sister's plea for help by the pouting gaze of an incredibly beautiful, cat-stroking teenager (Anna Pieroni) whom we take to be the Mother of Tears. Verdi's *Nabucco* is played to the class, and Argento's camera cranes between McCloskey and Pieroni to the rhythm of the piece. In the next scene, McCloskey's girlfriend

(Eleanora Giorgi) picks up Miracle's letter and, reading it in a taxi cab, decides to look up *The Three Mothers* in the local library, while Keith Emerson's double tempo rock version of the Verdi pounds on the soundtrack and the rain turns the city into a bedraggled light show. Two people look at each other during a lecture. A girl takes a taxi in the rain. Although nothing really happens in these scenes, Argento's absolute film approach turns them into set pieces. Other directors would have cut these sequences back and conveyed the essential plot information in a few brief cuts, but Argento makes ordinary events mysterious, exciting, erotic or horrifying. Previously, the murders in Argento's films (particularly the first death in *Suspiria*) have been set pieces; *Inferno* is all set pieces, and thus all of a piece.

During an eclipse of the moon, a crippled bookseller (Sacha Pitoeff) tries to drown a sackful of the cats that are the familiars of the Three Mothers in Central Park Lake. He stumbles, and is attacked by a rushing pack of rats. His cries for help are heard by a hot-dog vendor who dashes out of his stall, meat-cleaver in hand. The quickening intercutting of the struggling Pitoeff, the flood of rats and the puffing rescuer builds a crescendo of tension which unexpectedly pays off when the fast-food man hacks Pitoeff to death. The minions of darkness are everywhere. Miracle in New York and Giorgi in Rome are killed on the same night by identical cowled figures with taloned hands. Finally, McCloskey discovers the secret passages that honeycomb the New York brownstone and confronts the Mother of Darkness (Veronica Lazar). The house is on fire, and Lazar raves about the omnipotence of the Three Sisters, all the while advancing on McCloskey. 'Men call us by one name', she announces as she crashes through an unseen sheet of glass, emerging as a hooded skeleton, 'and that is DEATH!' Maybe the punch-line isn't worthy of the incredibly elaborate build-up, but *Inferno* manages to close with a new slant on the traditional fiery finale. Emerson's electronic mass for the Three Mothers thunders on the soundtrack as the house of darkness collapses. The Monster rejoices in the destruction which does not purge the Evil, but strengthens its rule over the Earth. McCloskey staggers away, but Death is going to get him in the end.

Inferno has proved difficult to follow. Immediately afterward, Argento returned to his old *giallo* stamping grounds with *Tenebrae*, and expectations that *Suspiria* and *Inferno* would be the first parts of a trilogy have not been rewarded by the appearance of a movie that would presumably have to be called *Lachrymae*. Indeed, after taking his themes about as far as they could go, Argento has slipped somewhat. Never a prolific film-maker, his output in the 1980s has been spotty at best and disastrous at worst. *Phenomena* (1985), his first film in English, is an almost total failure, blending a particularly silly murder mystery with ludicrous sub-plots about heroine Jennifer Connelly's ability to communicate with a variety of insects and about Scots entomologist Donald Pleasence's heroically vengeful chimpanzee. There are individually suspenseful sequences, but the silly dialogue ('it's perfectly normal for insects to be slightly telepathic') and haphazardly developed storyline suggest a jigsaw puzzle that's been completed by filing some of the pieces to fit in where they shouldn't. Sadly Argento departs from his usual stylishness and presents clumsy violence sequences more in the tradition of his crasser countryman Lucio Fulci, extending the callousness of the enterprise to members of his own family by opening the movie with the decapitation of Fiore Argento, his 14-year-old-daughter, and closing with the razor-slashing of Daria Nicolodi, his ex-girlfriend and frequent collaborator. Subsequently, he has produced Lamberto Bava's pair of messy zombie/possession movies, *Demoni* (*Demons*) (1986) and *Demoni 2* (*Demons 2*) (1987), and returned in style to the *giallo* with *Opera*.

2. Larry Cohen

It wouldn't be the first time in history a monster was mistaken for a God. I guess that's why I have to kill it. If you can kill it, it's not a God, just a good old-fashioned monster.
Detective Shepard (David Carradine), *Q*.

One of the reasons Larry Cohen still hasn't received the critical attention he deserves is that he makes monster movies. *It's Alive* (1974), *It Lives Again* (1978) and *It's Alive III: Island of the Alive* (1987) concern mankind's next step up the evolutionary ladder: fanged killer babies. *God Told Me To* (1977) finds Bernard Phillips (Richard Lynch), a Christ-like hermaphrodite alien, strongly suggesting that his disciples become mass murderers. *Q* (1981) is Quetzalcoatl, an Aztec god prayed back into existence, swooping around the Big Apple, swiping human prey from the rooftops 'because New York is famous for good eating'. *The Stuff* (1985) is a sentient goo from the centre of the Earth that gets itself marketed as a delicious snack and turns people into zombies, a witty inversion of the usual formula in that you eat the Monster rather than the Monster eating you. And *Full Moon High* (1981) and *A Return to Salem's Lot* (1987) are respectively satirical revisions of *I Was a Teenage Werewolf* and Stephen King's vampire best-seller. Even Cohen's non-fantasy films feature characters who fit his individual concept of monstrosity, whether it be Bone (Yaphet Kotto), the exterminator who invades Andrew Duggan's suburban life in the splendidly titled *Dial Rat for Terror* (1972), the revenge-obsessed black hoodlum (Fred Williamson) in *Black Caesar* (1973) and *Hell Up in Harlem* (1973), the sexually stunted law enforcement demagogue/demigod (Broderick Crawford) revealed in *The Private Files of J. Edgar Hoover* (1978), or Chris Neville (Eric Bogosian), the movie director as murderer/Svengali/mad visionary of *Special Effects* (1984).

The Thing From Another World, the truck from *Duel* and the shark from *Jaws* are good old-fashioned monsters: almost characterless death machines that must be faced, defeated and destroyed by the hero. None of Cohen's creatures is as easily dealt with. Cohen characterises polite society as a white middle class represented by committees of anxious men in suits searching for

● *Dog puke monster.* **The Stuff.**

an expedient, while the monsters are usually identified with the downtrodden and repressed. To a thing, Cohen's monsters are non-Caucasian. Bone, Caesar and the monster-disgorging Chocolate Chip Charlie (Garrett Morris) of *The Stuff* are black, the *It's Alive* babies have a greenish tinge and Quetzalcoatl is not only grey skinned but of South American Indian extraction. Like George A. Romero, Cohen uses his anarchic monsters to tear chunks out of the Establishment on the assumption that whatever arises from the ruins is likely to be better than the mess we've got. Only in *A Return to Salem's Lot* do the monsters become an Establishment, as the conservative order of New England vampires is seen as a more persuasive, insidious and politely ruthless society than the human world.

Detective Shepard's problem with the distinction between God and Monster is Cohen's most recurrent theme. After Quetzalcoatl has been blasted out of the skies and the Aztec High Priest responsible for her resurrection has been terminated with extreme prejudice, Shepard guesses the plumed serpent was just a good old-fashioned monster after all. Cohen immediately cuts from Shepard's ironic self-satisfaction to a tenement where the new Quetzalcoatl is hatching out of a very large egg. Just as Shepard is wrong about Quetzalcoatl's godhood, David Carradine is deluded in thinking himself the hero of the movie, even though he acts in the time-honoured straight cop fashion throughout. The real hero is Quetzalcoatl's Judas, Jimmy Quinn (Michael Moriarty), a small-time crook linked to the monster by an initial and the need to hide under the dome of the Chrysler Building. Having accidentally found the monster's nest, Quinn agrees to sell the creature to the city in return for a general amnesty covering any crimes he may have committed ('didn't Ford do that for Nixon? I want a Nixon-type pardon?'), $1 million tax free in cash and exclusive book, television and periodical rights to the story.

In the 1933 film, Carl Denham (Robert Armstrong) describes King Kong as 'a God in his own world'. Cohen's movies further explore the equation of movie monsterhood with deity,

summed up by the graffito 'King Kong died for our sins'. None of Cohen's monsters is particularly ennobled by its semi-divinity. Indeed, the director generally interprets godhood as an urge to smite multitudes. The *It's Alive* babies tear out of their delivery rooms, leaving behind a heap of slaughtered medics; Quetzalcoatl snaps up anybody who happens to be within reach; Bernard Phillips is first suspected by New York's finest when various of his acquaintances commit pointless murders, jubilantly justified by a cry of 'God told me to'; the addicted consumers of *The Stuff* form a shambling cadre even more devoted to their cause than the Moonies or Jim Jones's followers; and the vampires of Jerusalem's Lot keep dazed and bled-white human cattle to look after the town in the daytime and run the profit-making local antique shops. In the light of such irresponsibility, Cohen's Judases (frequently played by Michael Moriarty) are ambiguously justified in selling their maniac Messiahs down the river.

Cohen's Judas heroes are closely tied to the monsters, whether by a fundamental affinity or by blood relationship. The fathers in the *It's Alive* series, like Julius Harris in the *Black Caesar* films, must decide whether to shelter or destroy their monster sons. Both Frank Davis (John P. Ryan) in *It's Alive* and Eugene Scott (Frederic Forrest) in *It Lives Again* initially co-operate with the law in tracking down the mutant babies ('I guess I'm a funny guy,' says Scott, 'show me a couple of murders and I'm impressed'), but ultimately try to protect their offspring in the hope that they will develop beyond homicidal infancy. Mallory (John Marley), the ruthless monster-hunting cop of *It Lives Again*, has also fathered one of the monsters and now feels he has a mission to rid the world of the pests he is partially responsible for and to justify his killing of his own child. And Stephen Jarvis (Moriarty) of *Island of the Alive* reacts by writing a best-seller, then leading the expedition to the island where the mutants have been dumped because nobody knew what to do with them.

Detective Peter Nicholas (Tony LoBianco) in *God Told Me To* has an even more acute family problem. His investigation proves that not only is Phillips the product of an alien-engineered artificial insemination but so is he. In the astonishing finale, Phillips offers to have Nicholas's baby and unleash a completely alien Messiah on humanity. When asked why he has killed the luminous hippie, Nicholas wearily replies 'God told me to.' In *The Stuff*, a teenage boy recoils from a sit-com family turned into evangelistic zombies by fast food who start acting like a TV commercial, while in *A Return to Salem's Lot* it is the teenage son of the Michael Moriarty character who is most tempted to join the vampire community. Outside the horror film, the only real threats posed to J. Edgar Hoover come from his surrogate sons, a renegade fed (Rip Torn) and Bobby Kennedy (Michael Sacks). They share their crusading puritanism with the young Hoover (James Wainwright) who will grow into the bloated Crawford, memorably overseen drinking himself into stupor while listening to the taped seduction of a political opponent.

Cohen's background is as a writer for television. He created *The Invaders*, the series in which Roy Thinnes is the only man among us who can recognise the aliens intent on taking over the world, and *Branded*, the Western show in which Chuck Connors is a cashiered outcast after daring to come back alive from Custer's Last Stand. Obviously, he has always had an interest in paranoid, marginal heroes. Since the semi-experimental *Dial Rat*, he has worked only in commercially sound genres like blacksploitation or the horror film. Even the ambitious *Private Files* is couched somewhere between gangster nostalgia and *All the President's Men* exposé. Although *Black Caesar* and *It's Alive* were successful enough to earn sequels, Cohen has never had the *Texas Chainsaw Massacre* or *Halloween* kind of hit that would establish him as an important commercial force and attract major critical interest. Nevertheless, all his films have been made under the aegis of his Larco company, and have reached the screen without the sort of interference or big-budget deadness that has hampered the recent careers of Tobe Hooper and John Carpenter. *God Told Me To* and

The Private Files of J. Edgar Hoover may not have found the audiences they warrant, but at least they are the films Cohen wanted to direct rather than compromises like *The Funhouse* or *Christine*. Although Cohen's works have always been more distinguished by themes than technique, *Q* with its exhilarating helicopter shots of Manhattan is a polished move away from the sometimes muddy visuals of the earlier films, even if *The Stuff* is a step back into choppy editing and semi-makeshift production values. From *It's Alive*, Cohen's pictures have boasted inventively cast character actors, full-orchestra movie scores, and faintly Hitchcockian camerawork for the suspense sequences, but only *Q* and *Special Effects* are fully realised films rather than individual scenes and daring ideas marred by hastily contrived links.

It's Alive has some wickedly funny moments when the baby demonstrates its unhappiness with the traditional helpless gurgling infant role by rampaging through a nursery or savaging the milkman, but its most interesting angle is the stress it places on Frank Davis. Davis is a publicity man whose clients include chemical companies anxious to dissociate their products from Lenore Davis's (Sharon Farrell) unusual pregnancy, and so his genial boss fires him for being 'a little too controversial'. Later he realises that, like Baron Frankenstein, he has become confused with his Monster and retaliates by siding with the baby in the final storm drain confrontation. Davis returns in *It Lives Again* as a parent counsellor for a group of scientists trying to protect the next generation from the last one. As Robin Wood writes, *It Lives Again* 'is surely the first horror film in which the suspense derives as much from attempts to protect the monster as from the menace it represents'. However, the problem with Cohen's self-financed, hand-to-mouth cinema is amply demonstrated by *It Lives Again*. It may be the only sequel in which the characters have learned from the events of the original. In *Jaws 2*, Roy Scheider has to start all over again in convincing the town of the danger when another shark shows up, but when, in *It Lives Again*, the authorities learn Jody Scott (Kathleen Lloyd) expects to hear the patter of tiny claws, they fill the hospital with heavily armed cops in a black caricature of the gangster movie stake-out. But, after the mutants have escaped from the philanthropists' laboratory, the film degenerates into a fairly suspenseful replay of the first film crossed with an unnecessary return to the besieged house of *The Birds* and *Night of the Living Dead*.

God Told Me To is similarly unsure of its conclusion, with Peter Nicholas voluntarily entering an asylum so the film will not have to face the question of what kind of life he can live now he knows he is an alien with potentially awesome mental powers. The best scenes are the confrontations through which the hero pieces the mystery together. A friendly chat ('Hi, my name's Peter. What's yours?') with a sniper who has been picking off passers-by from a water tank. An interview with the quietly pleased father who has just killed his wife and children on Jesus's orders ('He's done so much for us, I just thought it was time I did something for Him.'). A painful visit to an old people's home where his real mother (Sylvia Sidney) still shrinks from a human touch as a result of her youthful abduction by spaceship and subsequent virgin birth. The final ascent to the new Messiah's lair, where Phillips spells out the difficult-to-follow plot with a few throwaway blasphemies ('human sacrifice is nothing new to your God'). Everything between these set pieces is sketched in, sometimes brilliantly, as when one uniformed cop (Andy Kaufman) in the marching ranks of a St Patrick's Day parade freaks and starts shooting, but more usually with messy dialogue and brief, confusing cutaway scenes.

Aside from *Dial Rat for Terror* with its Theatre of the Absurd satire, *Full Moon High* is Cohen's only outright comedy. In 1960, high-school football hero Tony Walker (Adam Arkin) accompanies his CIA agent father (Ed McMahon) to Romania, where he gets bitten by a werewolf and inflicted with a curse. Not only does he turn into a monster during the full moon, but he never grows older. Twenty years later, he returns to his home town of Full Moon and goes back to school. Obviously undertaken as something of a lark, the film manages to send up its own cheapness, as when a character 'accidentally' shoots the cameraman during a climax and the screen goes black while a voice-over tells us about the terrific special effects scene we're missing. It also makes up a gag which deserves to be as immortal as the Jewish vampire schtick in *Dance of the Vampires* as the teenage werewolf puts off his amorous girlfriend with the excuse that it's his time of the month. Made with tax shelter money, *Full Moon High* practically became a lost film, and is one of the many strokes of bad luck Cohen has had to put up with. Subsequently, he has been removed from the helm of a pair of thrillers he scripted, the disappointing Mickey Spillane adaption *I, the Jury* (1981) and the amusing Billy Dee Williams private eye movie *Deadly Illusion* (1987), and been replaced as director by Richard T. Heffron and William Tannen. *Best Seller* (1987), a witty cop/psycho team-up thriller starring Brian Dennehy and James Woods, directed by John Flynn from an ingenious Cohen screenplay, rated another marginal release and wound up buried during a complex lawsuit over the residual rights to *Platoon*.

Q is less ambitious than *God Told Me To* in its sacrilege, if only because, contrary to the film, there are far fewer offence-taking Quetzalcoatl worshippers than there are Christian groups who wouldn't care for the suggestion that Jesus was a bisexual psycho from outer space. Nicholas's tortured Catholicism is borrowed from the Harvey Keitel character ('you pay for your sins on the street, not in church') in *Mean Streets*, and *Q* develops the Scorsese connection by dreaming up a split level world that is part *King Kong* and part *Mean Streets*. The film opens with the death of a window washer on the site of Kong's last stand, the Empire State Building. For ten minutes, the camera soars breathlessly around Kong's world of giant skyscrapers and God monsters. Then the film alights in the streets, where a cheery giant chicken perches on a fast-food concession, and a group of Scorsese-talking Italian-American criminals are trying to rope Quinn into a jewel heist. After bungling the robbery, Quinn drops the loot in the street and heads for a hidey-hole in the disused upper stories of the Chrysler Building, which is adorned with art deco eagle heads. 'A few minutes ago I was in the gutter, now I'm on top of the world. Funny, I'm afraid of almost everything, but I've never been afraid of heights.' His refuge in the sky also contains a shredded corpse and a giant egg. Quinn and Quetzalcoatl both attempt to defy the city, which is run by one of Cohen's committees. Quetzalcoatl is mown down by the fuzz and dies clutching a building that looks suspiciously like an Aztec pyramid. Quinn gets screwed out of his million on a technicality and is then attacked by the human sacrifice fanatic. Cohen closes the film with twinned acts of revolt. Quinn refuses to lend weight to his own sacrifice by saying a little prayer for Quetzalcoatl and, in the process of getting himself half-killed, learns that he isn't afraid any more. In defiance of Shepard's good old-fashioned monster ruling, the plumed serpent is reborn.

After Q, Cohen shot two Hitchcockian thrillers back-to-back in New York's SoHo, Perfect Strangers (1984) and Special Effects, in both cases building the film around an unusually strong actress fresh from an unrepeatable cult triumph. Anne Carlisle of Liquid Sky (1983) is less happily cast as a normal housewife ('She wanted to do something to prove she wasn't a freak or a drug addict') in Perfect Strangers than Zoe Tamerlis of Ms .45 is in the complex multiple role of the heroine(s) of Special Effects. Perfect Strangers, with Brad Rijn as a Mafia hit man who falls in love with the mother of the toddler witness he has been ordered to rub out, is perhaps the most conventional of Cohen's films as a director, although it has a few asides about feminism ('men don't realise that the kitchen they've locked us into is full of weapons') and some competent suspense to add threadbare frills to a very ordinary narrative. Special Effects, with its echoes of Vertigo, is close to being his best, spotlighting an extremely tight little plot about a mad movie director who kills would-be actress Andrea (Zoe Tamerlis) and then decides to make a movie about the unsolved murder both as a way of getting back into the Hollywood big time after a recent flop and as a way of framing the dead

girl's husband (Brad Rijn) for the original killing. The director casts lookalike Elaine (Tamerlis again) in the lead role, and tries to recreate Andrea's personality. Meanwhile, cop on the case Delroy (Kevin O'Connor) gets wrapped up in his role as a technical adviser on the movie-within-a-movie and finally takes over from the director as the auteur of events. The finale is marvellously twisted and chilling, with Elaine traumatised so deeply that Rijn tries to palm her off on his child as the original wife and mother, thus dooming a vibrant, intelligent woman to the mid-Western mediocrity from which Andrea was trying to escape in the first place. A final caption identifies Special Effects as 'A Phillip Delroy Film'.

Since then, Cohen has been back with the monsters, turning out The Stuff for New World and A Return to Salem's Lot and Island of the Alive for Warner Brothers in his usual scattershot style, then talking Bette Davies into starring in and as Wicked Stepmother (1988), all the while juggling script assignments for William Lustig's Maniac Cop (1987) and TV properties like Earthquake Los Angeles: The Big One and Return of Columbo. Cohen has always been capable of being a prolific film-maker and is forever juggling a string of projects. He even makes movies quickly enough to be able to get away with topical references – to Rupert Murdoch's press empire in Q, to resurgent militarism in The Stuff, to post-Heaven's Gate Hollywood in Special Effects, to AIDS in A Return to Salem's Lot and to a stock market crash in Deadly Illusion. The emergence of video as a primary release market may well provide the immediacy and tolerance his peculiar vision requires. The Stuff, Full Moon High and A Return to Salem's Lot are sometimes so haphazardly assembled that the director seems to be on holiday but all Cohen's movies are lively, packed with off-beat and unusual ideas, well acted and laced with quotable dialogue. In an age when his more immediately successful contemporaries are being turned into sub-Spielbergs, Cohen's movies can still not be mistaken for anyone else's. He is still a developing, surprising talent, and it is unlikely that he will restrict himself to the horror genre in

● *The new flesh.* Jeff Goldblum, **The Fly**

future, but the Messianic monsters of his films are too strong to be entirely deserted.

3. David Cronenberg

It's my conceit that perhaps some diseases perceived as diseases which destroy a well-functioning machine, in fact change the machine into a machine that does something else, and we have to figure out what it is that the machine now does. Instead of having a defective machine, we have a nicely functioning machine that just has a different purpose. Part of it is a self-deceptive way of coping with the possibilities of disease, but on the other hand I can imagine what it feels like to be a virus. The AIDS virus: look at it from his point of view – very vital, very excited, really having a good time. It's made the front page, and is really flexing its muscles and doing what it does. It's really a triumph, if you're a virus. It's really good stuff that's happening, it's not bad at all. A virus is a living creature – actually, sometimes they go crystalline on you, which is what's interesting. See the movies from the point of view of the disease. You can see why they would resist all attempts to destroy them. These are all cerebral games, but they have emotional correlatives as well.

David Cronenberg

David Cronenberg's breakthough movie, *Shivers* (1976), makes a strong first impression. The titles come up over a slide show, accompanied by an offscreen hard-sell spiel for Starliner Towers, an antiseptic, self-contained apartment block in some Canadian wilderness. Maybe it's the trace of eerie music behind the insincere pitch, maybe it's the washed-out colour scheme, but a few views of the Towers are enough to convince you that you wouldn't want to live there. This is confirmed immediately when the film cuts into the middle of a domestic quarrel. Dr Emil Hobbes (Fred

Doederlin) opens his unfaithful mistress and pours acid into her steaming belly. Then he cuts his throat with a scalpel. By now the audience is bludgeoned (we know this film is going to be tough, but we at least expect an establishing scene or two before the red meat) and confused (what the hell is going on?). The film does manage to explain itself in a few hurried scientific chats between the rising tide of anarchic carnage, but the plot is swamped by carnal nightmares.

Shivers is one of the few sick films that can be sold in its premise rather than its gross-out moments. The dead returning to life and a little girl possessed by the Devil are horror movie commonplaces, so *Night of the Living Dead* and *The Exorcist* need the feast of entrails and the crucifix masturbation to gain notoriety. *Shivers* is about Hobbes's monsters; creeping parasites that look like phallic turds. They infect people with a combination of venereal disease and aphrodisiac. By sleeping around, Hobbes's mistress has become the Typhoid Mary of an epidemic of rampant polymorphous perversion. The *Night of the Living Dead* ghouls only want to eat you; what Cronenberg's parasites intend is unthinkable. The most deeply shocking scenes in the film have geriatrics and children making lewd advances. The distinction between sex and horror has completely disappeared. An undisciplined film, *Shivers* gains from its scattershot approach. Cronenberg has since proved himself capable of more control but, in a movie about the encroachment of chaos upon order, it's appropriate that the narrative itself should break down. Dr Roger St Luc (Paul Hampton) seems like a conventional movie hero, but his only real purpose is to be there when Rollo Linsky (Joe Silver) explains the connection between Hobbes and the parasites. St Luc tries to curb the epidemic, but is never very sympathetic. The uptight doctor fails to notice that Nurse Forsythe (Lynn Lowry) is in love with him, symptomising everything wrong with life in Starliner Towers. The orgiastic solution of the blood parasites may be too extreme, but the soulless routine they replace suggests the straight world deserves to be eaten away from within. Predictably, inevitably, St

Luc is taken over and ends the film calmly leading the sex-crazed zombies out of the underground car park towards Montreal.

Shivers is memorable because of its *ugh* moments, when a parasite worms around in a victim's stomach, or crawls out of the plughole with disgusting designs on bathing Betts (Barbara Steele), but the film is gripping because of an almost subtle unity of purpose beneath the ground-breaking horrors. Of all current genre *auteurs*, Cronenberg has the most instantly recognisable private universe. His Canadian settings turn the country into a gigantic, wintry University of Sussex. The architecture is of the kind which wins design awards by blending red brick, concrete and slabs of glass into the landscape, but is somehow unsettling to live inside. Based in Canada, Cronenberg has the advantages of underused movie locations and psychological distance from Hollywood. In *Escape From New York*, John Carpenter exercises a penchant for in-joke *hommages* by naming supporting characters Romero and Cronenberg. Romero repays the compliment in *Creepshow* by feeding Mrs Carpenter to a fanged ape, but Cronenberg is unlikely to respond in kind. *Shivers* borrows cleverly from *Night of the Living Dead* and *Invasion of the Body Snatchers*, but never in the lazy, superficial way that others crib from Hitchcock to fill a gap.

Like Brian DePalma, Cronenberg came to the commercial cinema from the underground film movement. But while *Sisters* is a radical step away from the Godardian freewheeling of *Greetings* and *Hi, Mom!*, *Shivers* is a conscious extension of ideas from Cronenberg's fringe features, *Stereo* (1969) and *Crimes of the Future* (1970). *Stereo* is a black-and-white spoof documentary that covers the never-seen Dr Luther Stringfellow's research programme at the Canadian Academy of Erotic Inquiry. A Dracula-caped test subject (Ron Mlodzik) arrives by helicopter at the first of Cronenberg's plausible pseudo-scientific institutes, and has his natural telepathic ability surgically enhanced. In *Stereo*, the psi faculty can only be exercised during moments of sensual excitement, and so Stringfellow's experiments encourage a general air of sexual pioneering. While the sex in *Shivers* is interchangeable with the violence,

Stereo is oddly touching. Cronenberg has his telepaths stimulated by a luxurious tomato-eating session or a charming tea ceremony. It is only when the unseen scientists, disturbed by the exclusive bond growing between the telepaths, isolate the subjects that violence erupts. Robbed of the opportunity to use their heightened awareness, the telepaths become suicidal. One attempts to kill himself with an electric drill. *Crimes of the Future* follows the meandering odyssey of Adrian Tripod (Ron Mlodzik), a disciple of the absent dermatologist Dr Antoine Rouge of the Institute of Neo-Venereal Diseases, through a desolate world where all post-pubertal females have succumbed to Rouge's Malady. This grotesque affliction causes the victim to ooze chocolate syrup from all orifices, and the chief crime of the future is an irresistible desire to lick the stuff off the dying. After encountering groups of despairing foot and underwear fetishists, Tripod joins a paedophile organisation whose members realise their cherished perversion has become the only way to ensure humanity's survival. The task of impregnating a 5-year-old falls to Tripod, but he is unable to do the deed. The girl starts to leak gooey substances.

Cronenberg's underground films are more fun to read about in synopsis than to watch. 'I would imagine a double billing of those two would take a lot of sitting through,' Cronenberg told *Cinefantastique*. 'The direction I was taking came from the New York underground tradition of long and obscure art films.' They were shot silent, with a spoken commentary and music track added later. The monotony is increased by the use of extended static shots. Some of the mime in *Stereo* is extraordinary enough to deserve this reverential treatment, but after a reel or two of aimless drifting *Crimes of the Future* starts to drag. If nothing else, these movies prove it's possible to be boring and interesting at the same time. The pressures of commercial production prompted Cronenberg to reject the underground and give *Shivers* a helter-skelter pacing that adds visceral excitement to his cerebral concerns. If the parasites of *Shivers* can be read as unregenerate physicality overwhelming a repressed intellect, then the film also stands as an example of overreaction. *Stereo* depends too much on nuances and the willingness of an audience to interpret (the difference between what we see and what we are told by the voice-over is crucial), but *Shivers* is so unswervingly gripping that rational thought is impossible.

Rabid (1977) is as fast and direct as *Shivers*. Rose (Marilyn Chambers) enters Dr Dan Keloid's private hospital after a motorcycle accident. Keloid (Howard Ryshpan), who is worried by his image as 'the Colonel Sanders of plastic surgery', saves her life but turns her into a rabies-spreading vampire with a penile barb in her armpit. She spreads the plague through Montreal and is lost amid escalating violence. A workman uses a pneumatic drill to get into a limousine and gore the chauffeur. In a department store shoot-out, Santa Claus gets caught in the cross-fire. While Chambers is affecting as rabid Rose ('I have to have blood, but I'm still *me!*'), the film suffers a little from its son-of-*Shivers* place in Cronenberg's career. Like *Crimes of the Future*, *Rabid* seems to be a slightly more elaborate, slightly less startling footnote to its immediate predecessor. The rabies takes out a whole city rather than one building, but, although weird, Chambers's armpit is no match for the sex slugs. However, *Rabid* does find Cronenberg more in control of his material, and relaxed enough to work in odd vignettes – an Indian being finger-printed in a police station, little details about the staff and patients at the clinic – that suggest a fragile, normal world at once more rounded and threatened than the glossy suburban vacuum of Starliner Towers.

The Brood (1979) takes up the hints of sensitivity found between the blood-letting, and presents a smaller, intimate story, more in-depth characterisations and less gore. Dr Hal Raglan (Oliver Reed), author of the best-selling *The Shape of Rage*, runs the Somafree Institute of Psychoplasmics, a self-help therapy clinic where patients purge themselves of their neuroses by manifesting them as physical changes in their bodies. Raglan's star subject is Nola Carveth (Samantha Eggar), a woman capable of externalising her many resentments as a pack of monstrous dwarves. The film follows Frank (Art Hindle), Nola's ex, in his attempt to gain custody of their daughter Candy (Cindy Hinds). Frank gradually realises that everyone who has ever been seen as a threat by Nola is being killed by midgets in brightly coloured snowsuits. Although infinitely less violent than *Shivers* or *Rabid*, *The Brood* is far more painful. Perhaps because he regards it as a manifestation of the frustration he felt during his own divorce and custody case, Cronenberg uses the overstatement of *The Brood* to more concentrated, cathartic ends, much as Raglan's encounter sessions bring his patients to an emotional crisis in order to effect a cure. Again, bodily imbalance is the central image. Jan Hartog (Robert Silverman), who has nauseating exploded lymph sacs on his neck, is suing Raglan for urging his body to revolt against him. However, the film does manage to attain the balance that eludes its characters. Nola releases the latest of the brood from her exo-womb with some sickening biting and clawing but she immediately begins to lick the monster clean with the tenderness of a mother cat; and one shot juxtaposes monstrosity with calm innocence as two of the brood lead Candy down an autumnal highway. But, for all its icy grip as an emotional drama, *The Brood* still delivers the monster movie goods, most memorably in the moment that fulfils a universal childhood nightmare when a pair of hideous hands shoot out from underneath a bed to grab a victim's ankles.

There is little calm in *Scanners* (1981), but it is also a progression from the venereal apocalypse. The film reaches back to *Stereo* for its artificially created telepaths. The self-reference is made specific by the third eye scar on the forehead of Darrell Revok (Michael Ironside), the result of his 1969 suicide attempt with an electric drill. Dr Paul Ruth (Patrick McGoohan) is responsible for the scanners, whose birth was a side effect of the indiscriminate use of Ephemerol, a pre-natal drug, in the 1940s. Ruth is sponsored by ConSec, a sinister corporation that proves to have been infiltrated by Revok, charismatic leader of the evil scanners. The villain is unforgettably introduced as he comes forward as a volunteer in a telepathy experiment. During the demonstration, Revok makes another scanner's head explode. Revok is Ruth's son, as is Cameron Vale (Stephen Lack), a psychic derelict picked out of the gutter and groomed as a nemesis for the psychopath. Vale is found stealing leftovers from a fast food emporium designed by the same sadist who inflicted the CAEI, Starliner Towers and the Somafree Institute on the human race. The battle between Vale and Revok, and their supporters, develops in a series of slam-bang sequences. *Fast Company* (1977), Cronenberg's single non-genre film to date, is an action movie about drag-racing, and *Scanners* confirms his skills with conventional excitement. There is one fine car chase which ends when the sides of a dormobile open up like a pirate ship, and a cannonade of gunfire destroys Vale's van. Revok is backed up by a paranoia movie conspiracy of politicos, businessmen and security operatives, while Vale joins a commune of alternative scanners who go in for *Stereo*-style empathising. Vale locks into the ConSec computer to delve into the intrigue, and the programmers try to shut him down. 'There. No fireworks', says a switch-flicking technician before the place blows up. 'I'm one of you', says Vale to Pierce (Robert Silverman), an unhinged scanner who lives inside a model of his own head. 'You're one of *me*?' is the oblique reply. *Scanners* has the typical Cronenberg construction: it crams in more ideas than it can possibly deal with and tears through its overly complex plot so quickly that the holes only become apparent when it's all over. For the first time since *Stereo*, the tone is upbeat. The unrelenting action of *Shivers* and *Rabid* shows a society tearing itself apart; and, given the break-up of Nola's family, the incestuous cruelty of *The Brood* is inevitable; but *Scanners* follows a purposeful conflict between opposing, highly motivated sides, out of which a new world will emerge. The issue is settled in an eye-popping, vein-bursting special effects duel between Vale and Revok. Vale is burned to a cinder, but he completely takes over Revok's body. If *The Brood* finds a balance between mind and body, *Scanners* finally achieves a hard-won harmony. *Crimes of the Future*, *Shivers*, *Rabid* and *The Brood* all end with the persistent disease threatening to spread. In *Scanners*, for the first time in a David Cronenberg film, the Good Guys win.

In Cronenberg's next movie, however, the battle for the mind of North America is still being fought, and according to media prophet Dr Brian O'Blivion, the arena for the conflict is the *Videodrome* (1982). Structurally reminiscent of *Shivers*, the film follows Max Renn (James Woods), a cable TV hustler in a near-future Toronto whose justification for his channel's output of 'softcore pornography and hardcore violence' is 'better on television than in the streets'. Renn is trying to track down a pirate station that's transmitting *Videodrome*, 'a show that's just torture and murder. No plot. No characters. Very realistic', because he thinks 'it's the coming thing'. The detective story, as the rumpled Renn digs into the video mystery, eventually breaks down into narrative anarchy. Underneath the stimulating images of sex and violence is a signal which causes a tumour in Renn's brain that makes him subject to hallucinations which increasingly take over the flow of the film. A sado-masochist affair with phone-in psychiatrist Nicki Brand (Deborah Harry), during which Renn pierces her ears while they make love in front of a flickering screen and sees his mistress's name illustrated on her body with knife-nicks on her shoulder and a cigarette brand on her breast, may or may not be a perverse imagining, but later sequences completely fracture reality with disturbing developments of Cronenberg's by-now familiar bodily evolutions. A television set pulses with life and Renn buries his head in its mammary screen as he kisses the image of Nicki. A vaginal slot grows from a rash on his stomach and the villains plunge living video cassettes into it which program him as an assassin. His hand and gun grow together to create a sickening bio-mechanical synthesis.

The opening of *Videodrome* is a satire of a future video nasty business along the lines of Bertrand Tavernier's *La Mort en Direct* (*Death Watch*) (1979) – with Woods doing a marvellously seedy act as a producer dragged out of bed by his video wake-up call to liaise in a ghastly motel with a Japanese porno dealer who offers him a series of boring, tasteful sex shows that drive him to *Videodrome*. 'I am my father's screen', announces Bianca (Sonja Smits), ethereal daughter of the late Dr O'Blivion, who runs a mission where derelicts are given soup and a chance to watch television ('to patch them back into the world's mixing board'). Once Renn has been exposed to *Videodrome*, the film cannot hope to sustain its storyline, and, as Paul Taylor wrote in *The Monthly Film Bulletin* 'becomes most akin to sitting before a TV screen while someone else switches channels at random'. The hallucinatory sequences do have a basic plot, as Renn is used to kill his partners and then turns on his manipulators, but this is more or less swamped by Cronenberg's flesh-twisting horrors and flashes of a dozen different films. There is a spectacularly tacky musical number, a conspiracy movie about a corporate world take-over scheme, a private eye/vigilante/hero-on-the-run tale, a discourse on the nature of the medium and the message (Marshall McLuhan in *Stereo?*) and the near-future thriller *Videodrome* at first seemed to be. Any ending would be unsatisfying, but Cronenberg gives us one anyway as Renn commits suicide at the prompting of a disembowelled television set. Perhaps Renn's death is the only way to give a viewer a way out of *Videodrome*, but since the last three-quarters of the film appears to take place inside its main character's head it is difficult not to interpret the final blackout as another part of the ongoing illusion.

Videodrome is a brave move after the success of the near-conventional *Scanners*. It juggles so many ideas successfully that it can be forgiven for dropping a few of them. However, it was not a commercial success. The presence of Deborah Harry as Renn's kinky dream girl should make it eligible for cult status, but its cerebral, enquiring tone and Woods's uncomfortably good performance have won it too few friends. After travelling so far into his own personal nightmare, Cronenberg felt the need to ease off by tackling an uncomplicated commercial project. *The Dead Zone* (1983), with a screenplay by Jeffrey Boam from Stephen King's novel, is the only film he has directed without having been involved in the writing. Although Johnny Smith (Christopher Walken), a schoolteacher who awakens from a five-year crash-induced coma with the unnerving power to visualise potential disasters, is recognisable as one of Cronenberg's

tortured psychic heroes, the Everyman stamp of his name marks him as a far more straightforward protagonist than Adrian Tripod, Cameron Vale or Max Renn. Boam's screenplay condenses the novel's tapestry into a rather clumsily strung procession of episodes as Johnny discovers his powers, becomes embittered, helps the police track down the Castle Rock killer, and confronts the power-hungry, folksy presidential candidate (Martin Sheen) he knows will start World War III if elected. The Cronenberg elements are diluted – snowy Canadian locations double for King's New England, but the bleak landscape is given a homey horror movie character by old wooden houses; Johnny's visions punctuate the story, but never intrude upon the film's reality as Renn's do, so that, even before the plot reveals that the horrors can be averted, it is obvious they are 'safe'; and Johnny's ESP-driven *angst* is reduced to banality by an introductory sequence showing him as a happy-go-lucky ordinary guy before the accident ruins his life. While it is a slick, watchable, tactfully acted, thoroughly professional film, *The Dead Zone* is finally a failure, while *Scanners* and *Videodrome*, which leave more loose ends than a bucket of spaghetti, are successes.

Cronenberg has proved he can work in the mainstream, but his best films show that he doesn't need to. *The Fly* (1986), a major studio remake of the 1958 monster movie, is, despite its budget and lavish special effects, a step back towards the director's personal concerns. Seth Brundle (Jeff Goldblum), a gawky scientist who suffers from chronic motion sickness, invents a teleportion device, but mainly uses it as a means of impressing journalist Veronica Quaife (Geena Davis), with whom he is commencing an affair. When he tries the process out himself he fails to notice a fly in the telepod, and emerges not as an insect-headed monstrosity like David Hedison in the original film but as a super-improved version of himself. However, after he has demonstrated his prowess as a sexual athlete and a bar-room arm-wrestler, he finds himself gradually transforming, decomposing and otherwise losing his humanity ('Do you know that insects have no politics?') as the inner fly emerges through cancerous human flesh. *The Fly* is an even more concentrated, intimate movie than *The Brood*, with only three main characters and one major setting. Like Rose and Max Renn , Brundle remains himself as he changes – tossing away nervous remarks about his collection of dropped-off body parts, giving an amusingly disgusting TV chef-style demonstration of the fly-like manner in which the new creature eats a doughnut, humming 'I Know an Old Lady Who Swallowed a Fly', and treating his mutation as a voyage of discovery. While it contains one dream sequence involving a maggot baby that is rather clumsily inserted into the generally tight structure, *The Fly* is an uncompromised work that suggests Cronenberg could emerge as a major league director without abandoning his intelligent approach and mind-and-flesh-stretching concerns.

4. *Brian DePalma*

It's hard to make movies where you put women in peril any more. You can't really stalk women around any more. It's very difficult. It's sort of unsettling to field a lot of hostile questions about why you keep doing this and why you dislike women so much. You say 'it's a murder mystery, I'm running out of victims.' It's all right to kill men, but women are out. No one complained when I killed a man in *Sisters*.

Brian DePalma

In the 1970s, Hollywood became the Glitz Castle. Ageing moguls kow-towed to the youthful kings of megabuck success, Francis Ford Coppola, Steven Spielberg and George Lucas. Brian DePalma, initially a humble thane on the New York underground scene, is the Macbeth of the movies. He murdered his way to a throne with increasingly brilliant, increasingly callous horror thrillers. The New York films, *The Wedding Party* (1964), *Murder à la Mod* (1966), *Greetings* (1968), *Hi, Mom!* (1970) and *Dionysius in '69* (1970), established DePalma as a coffee house hero and incidentally

introduced talents like Robert DeNiro and Jill Clayburgh. DePalma's first bid for the Hollywood crown jewels, *Get to Know Your Rabbit* (1972), is a progression from the eccentric comedy of the New York films, a vehicle for Tom Smothers, co-starring Katharine Ross and Orson Welles. The film was backed by Warner Brothers, who saw DePalma as a promising combination of Frank Capra and Jean-Luc Godard, but *Get to Know Your Rabbit* was scuppered by what the trade papers describe as 'creative differences' (i.e. the director, the star, the writer and the producers wound up hating each other). After the film's negligible distribution, DePalma returned to New York, presumably under the impression that he had blown his chance. With *Sisters* (1972), DePalma moved into a commercially more comfortable genre and began the build-up to his second stab at a throne. While George A. Romero, Larry Cohen and David Cronenberg cherished their independence, DePalma blitzed Hollywood until, with *Carrie* (1976), he had a success big enough to elevate him to the movie brat pantheon.

Discounting an episode of the almost-unseen *Murder à la Mod*, *Sisters* is the first of DePalma's obsessive *hommages* to Alfred Hitchcock. It is also the most distinctive, original and satisfying, as secure in its assimilation of Hitchcock's ideas into the director's own vision as the best of Claude Chabrol. The story echoes *Psycho* and *Rear Window*, but the subversive humour of *Greetings* is still recognisable, and DePalma is visibly developing his own gruesome preoccupations. The opening is a brilliant piece of misdirection, treating the typically Hitchcockian theme of voyeurism in a lightly satirical manner. The approach is cleverly misleading, and makes the sudden plunge into serious, graphic horror extremely shocking. Phillip Woode (Lisle Wilson), a decent young man, is in a men's washroom when Danielle (Margot Kidder), an attractive blind girl, taps her way in and begins to undress. After a moment's hesitation, Woode does what we all hope we'd do, and leaves. The situation turns out to be a stunt arranged for *Peeping Toms*, a TV game show, and, feeling guilty, Danielle makes a date with Woode. He spends the

● *Sharp practice.* Nancy Allen, **Dressed to Kill.**

night in her apartment, and next morning is murdered by Dominique, Danielle's insane twin.

The early death of the apparent hero, and the consequent scene in which Dr Emil Breton (William Finley), Danielle's ex-husband, clears up after Dominique, are obvious reminders of *Psycho*. They probably give away too early the revelation that Dominique is dead and that the schizophrenic Danielle is the murderess, but at that point the split screen wittily switches to another plot. The killing has been witnessed *à la Rear Window* by journalist Grace Collier (Jennifer Salt), and she becomes the central character. Since she is the author of an article entitled 'Why We Call Them "Pigs"', the police are not inclined to take her seriously, and the private eye (Charles Durning) she hires proves similarly useless. Grace is left to solve the mystery herself, and it proves less simple than we had thought. The *Psycho* connection is cunningly used to conceal the twists – once we've guessed that Danielle and Dominique are the same person, we don't feel the need to think any more, and so are properly surprised to learn that they were Siamese twins, and that Danielle's trauma stems from Dominique's death during Dr Breton's surgical attempt to separate them. After an un-Hitchcockian nightmare climax (reminiscent of the bad dreams in *The House of Usher* and *Seconds*) has disposed of most of the major characters, DePalma delivers two final ironies. The cops who have so far disbelieved the now-brainwashed Grace try to get a statement out of her only to be confronted with a blank repetition 'there is no body because there was no murder', and an elegant shot finds Durning up a telegraph pole in the Canadian wilderness, staking out the dumped sofa in which Woode's dead body is stashed, waiting to pick up the now-dead culprits who will never claim it.

The public acceptance of *Sisters* encouraged DePalma to make *The Phantom of the Paradise* (1974), a self-indulgent bizarrie that retells the barnstorming melodrama of *The Phantom of the Opera* in a rock 'n' roll setting. Here DePalma finds subjects perfectly suited to his eclectic stylishness and anything-goes technical decadence, and creates his most personal synthesis of comedy and horror.

The film opens with a narration by Rod Serling in the teeth-clenched style of his *Twilight Zone* introductions: 'this is the story of the man who made the music, the girl who sang it, and the monster who took it away . . .' With a few jokey nods to *Citizen Kane* and *The Picture of Dorian Gray*, the film proceeds to follow the story of Terence Fisher's Hammer *Phantom* rather than the Gaston Leroux novel and the Lon Chaney vehicle. The Monster is not the disfigured Winslow Leach (William Finley), transformed into a bird-masked disco Dr Phibes by a fall into a record press, but Swan (Paul Williams), a multi-media entrepreneur who has sold his soul to the Devil for rock 'n' roll immortality. Enraged when he finds Swan has transformed his rock cantata *Faust* into a beach-party, drag-race musical ('carburetors, man, that's what life is all about'), the Phantom terrorises Swan's Xanadu, the Paradise. He is duped into further work on his masterpiece by the promise that Phoenix (Jessica Harper), his protégée, will star, but Swan proceeds to entomb him in a recording studio and replace the girl with his transvestite creation, Beef (Gerrit Graham). In the finale, Swan plans to have Phoenix assasinated during their televised wedding. Why? 'That's entertainment!' The Phantom escapes and burns Swan's videotaped Satanic contract. All Hell breaks loose in a typical DePalma climax.

Fisher's *Phantom* is an unsensational, surprisingly downbeat romance, but DePalma's is a dazzling, cynical charade. The misogyny that has become a prominent part of DePalma's world since the very pro-woman *Sisters* is first revealed in his in-adequately scripted heroine. Jessica Harper is sensational in the role, but Phoenix is made unworthy of the Phantom's love by her willingness to sell out very cheaply to Swan, and is almost forgotten in the apocalypse. While the death throes of Swan and the Phantom are being interpreted as a new dance craze, Phoenix is reduced to a traditional horror movie heroine bit, standing in the corner and screaming. DePalma's kinetic style is too much even for a subject as extraordinary as *Carrie* but *The Phantom of the Paradise* is irresistible. Its insane mixture of glamour and tat gets a lot closer to the gothic horrors of the rock world than realistic films like *Stardust* and *The Rose*. Sadly, the rock world has since got closer to the gothic horrors of *The Phantom of the Paradise*. In 1975, DePalma told *Cinefantastique*: 'I truly believe that ultimately some rock singer is going to be assassinated.' Swan is the end-of-the-road development of the hustlers played by Allen Garfield in *Greetings* and *Hi, Mom!*. It is impossible to take Paul Williams's boyish charm at face value after his venomous performance, cooing 'ink isn't good enough for me, Winslow' as he entreats the composer to sign his recording contract in blood.

But *The Phantom of the Paradise* flopped. So did *Obsession* (1976), an elaboration of *Vertigo*, from a Paul Schrader screenplay. Swan couldn't stand the idea of being 30, and, at, 36, DePalma might have been thinking he was getting too old for superstardom. George Lucas and Steven Spielberg, both younger men, had broken into the *Variety* All-Time Box-office Greats list. In order to feel good with his friends, DePalma had to find a solid gold winner for his next film. *Carrie*, Stephen King's first best-seller, was his shrewd choice; it provides him with a strong, unfamiliar plot to hang his show-off style on. Strangely, the auditions for *Carrie* were held in tandem with those for *Star Wars*. George Lucas may have had the bigger hit, but DePalma spotted the stars. Not only did he secure Sissy Spacek as his Carrie, but he gave a minor role to John Travolta and cast Amy Irving and Nancy Allen as Carrie's classmates.

Carrie is so successfully manipulative that its essential callousness is obvious only after its bravura cinematic impact has worn off. Despite Sissy Spacek's outstanding performance, the film is unsympathetic, blurring the dividing line between King's story about cruelty and DePalma's actual cruelty. After an hour of sharing Carrie White's humiliation, the audience is compelled to share DePalma's delight in blowing up the school. The busy frame splits in two, hordes of extras are crushed, Spacek stares through the orange flames, and the small-town high school becomes a vision of Hell. DePalma has set us up for the pretty holocaust with a depiction of the petty nastiness of peer group persecution that makes his cheerleaders seem as ripe for the Wrath of God as any of DeMille's Babylonians, and then stands back to watch the carnival. But why don't we ever learn whether Tommy Ross (William Katt), the likeable hero, survives being conked with a bucket of pigs' blood or not? And why does Carrie's only caring, sympathetic teacher (Betty Buckley), an apparently major character, have to be killed off in a meaningless split screen aside? DePalma gets so caught up in his multicoloured explosions that he forgets the people he burns to a crisp, and expects us to as well.

Everything is buried under DePalma's pyrokinetics – slow motion, fast motion, split screen, reversed sequences, tricky lighting, soft focus, gliding camerawork and an echt-*Psycho* score by Pino Donaggio that underlines all the scary moments with screeching strings. Finally, the film obliterates itself with its most powerful moment. Sue Snell (Amy Irving) floats in slow motion to Carrie White's grave. She kneels down to lay a wreath, and the earth opens so that a bloody hand can clutch at her. It's the old hand-through-the-window shock tactic, but never has it been as devastatingly executed as it is here. It may well be the best cheap shot in the cinema, but it cancels out the film that precedes it. Until the fade-out, audiences have been 100% involved with Carrie White. The violence has only been tolerable because Spacek has made the religion-ridden, put-upon, persecuted and ungainly girl sympathetic enough for us to understand her need to explode. Suddenly, her allegiance is transferred to Sue, at best a neutral character, and Carrie becomes the horrifying, malevolent witch the rest of the film has demonstrated she definitely isn't. Of course, It's All A Dream, but the powerful shock stays with you long after everything else in *Carrie* has faded.

DePalma tries to repeat the trick in *The Fury* (1978), in which telepath Amy Irving makes villain John Cassavetes explode in slow motion, a process observed from several angles in loving detail. It's an appalling joke, half-inspired by *Zabriskie Point* and far less effective than the comparatively restrained *Scanners* exploded head. The wandering plot of John Farris's *The Fury*, another telekinetic best-seller, lacks King's concentrated charge, and encourages DePalma to explode all over the place. There is a superb car chase in the fog, which turns the screen into a light show and reveals the director as at his happiest when working in the abstract, and a handful of stunning single shots, like the high angle dissolve as day replaces night in the city, but the most entertaining flourishes are also the least relevant to whatever it is that is going on. *The Fury* is capable of supremely unpleasant moments, like the whirling, blood-spattered death of Fiona Lewis, and supremely stupid moments, like the much-remarked plot device that requires a character with the power of levitation to die in a fall, but it still has more invention and energy than most popcorn movies. DePalma has always been aware of his indifference to the human aspects of his exercises, and casts his films strongly in order to retain humanity. Jessica Harper and Sissy Spacek stay alive amid the mechanics, but Kirk Douglas, John Cassavetes and Carrie Snodgress are overwhelmed by *The Fury*. For DePalma, even the leading characters are expendable.

The history of Macbeth is a tragedy, and there are hints in DePalma's later films that he bitterly regrets the qualities he has lost. The messy *Home Movies* (1980), made in collaboration with film students, evidences nostalgia for the wild improvisation of the 1960s New York movies. *Dressed to Kill* (1980) is another disguised remake of *Psycho*, with a very sinuous, un-Hitchcockian style that combines chilliness and eroticism to prove that even heartlessness can be put to good use. A bored housewife (Angie Dickinson) allows herself to be casually picked up in an art gallery and, after an adulterous afternoon, is razor-slashed to death in a lift by a mad transvestite. A high-class call girl (Nancy Allen) and the dead woman's gadget-minded son (Keith Gordon) investigate and discover the secret life of Dickinson's smooth, self-involved psychiatrist (Michael Caine). With its dream-like atmosphere and Argento-ish insistence on the importance of wordless, apparently irrelevent sequences like the menacing/sexy gallery stalking,

Dressed to Kill betrays its sources and suggests that Antonioni, not Hitchcock, is the real inspiration for much of DePalma's work. Ultimately, the film is only about psycho killings in the limited sense that *L'Avventura* is about missing persons.

Blow Out (1981) furthers the Antonioni connection by combining *Blowup* with Coppola's *The Conversation* as a semi-confessional. An exploitation film-maker (John Travolta) accidentally records a murder while compiling eerie night-time noises for *Coed Frenzy*, a cheap slasher movie, and is forced to become a responsible, concerned citizen by investigating a political conspiracy. In these films, there are signs that the continuous cruelty is beginning to wear thin, and, although he shows more understanding for his male psychopaths (Michael Caine, John Lithgow) than their whorish victims (Angie Dickinson, Nancy Allen), DePalma is starting to like his characters. *Dressed to Kill* winds up with another *Carrie* shock, but *Blow Out* finishes with a disquieting ambiguity. The mystery has been solved at the expense of the heroine's life, and Travolta dubs her dying scream on to *Coed Frenzy* in an act either of frozen-hearted callousness or deeply felt tribute. Nancy Allen, the victim, was then Mrs Brian DePalma, a frequent star in her husband's films, usually as a happy hooker. Her death in *Blow Out* is the first in DePalma's filmography he seems to care about.

In the 1980s, DePalma is still struggling, uncomfortable with his own established screen persona but unable to find a worthy new one. Since *Blow Out*, he has largely abandoned the thriller genre he feels he has done to death and found some measure of success in the gangster field. The comic *Wise Guys* (1986) is an unqualified failure, but *Scarface* (1983) and *The Untouchables* (1987) are splashy, bold, epic entertainments in the grand manner. With strong script imput from Oliver Stone and David Mamet, and monolithic casts including Al Pacino as the Cuban petty crook who plays Macbeth in *Scarface* and Sean Connery and Robert DeNiro as Eliot Ness's street cop mentor and Al Capone in *The Untouchables*, these are less identifiable as DePalma movies than most of his work, but find room for his habitual overblown holocausts and set pieces. The finale of *Scarface*, with Pacino going down amid a hail of bullets as his ghastly mansion is attacked by an assault force, and the Odessa Steps parody in *The Untouchables*, with a baby serenely bouncing down the stairs in a huge station while feds and crooks shoot it out in slow motion around him, are superb pieces of simple styling. However, *Body Double* (1984), which DePalma scripted and directed, is yet another Hitchcock reworking, returning to *Rear Window* and *Vertigo* to wring a few more twists out of the voyeuristic material. Despite a studied cheesiness — the hero (Craig Wasson) is a claustrophobic Peeping Tom duped in a murder scheme involving a drill killing and porno star Holly Body (Melanie Griffith) — and competent performances, *Body Double* is all empty gestures and third-hand business. Here, DePalma is not so much imitating Hitchcock as imitating himself imitating Hitchcock, suggesting that he has followed the example of Norman Bates and built his own private trap.

the weirdo horror film

or: *Cult, Kitsch, Camp, Sick, Punk and Pornography*

To me, bad taste is what entertainment is all about. If someone vomits watching one of my films, it's like getting a standing ovation. But one must remember that there is such a thing as good bad taste and bad bad taste.

John Waters, *Shock Value*

In the 1960s, Andy Warhol discovered that he could squash his critics by admitting that, of course, his art was trash; it was supposed to be. To Warhol's rather quaint 1890s, decadent sensibility, art is, by definition, useless and wasteful. And so is garbage. The faintly patronising concept of kitsch allows that trash art can be relished because of, not despite, its pretensions, inferior standards and poor taste. Certain sophisticates value the horror film as kitsch, much as their predecessors, the Marquis de Sade and Lord Byron, used to prize sentimental gothic novels for unconscious implications their own works would belabour. *Midi-Minuit Fantastique*, the French magazine of the early 1960s, was full of serious pieces on the surreal delirium of *The Most Dangerous Game*, *Peeping Tom* and the films of Barbara Steele. Even today, the publication springs inescapably to mind whenever Lucio Fulci refers to flesh-eating zombies and Antonin Artaud in the same breath. Less endearing are the Brothers Medved, whose *The 50 Worst Movies of All Time*, *The Golden Turkey Awards* and *Son of Golden*

Turkey Awards sneer from a great height at the defencelessly dreadful likes of *Robot Monster*, *Plan Nine From Outer Space* and *The Horror of Party Beach*. To my mind, the siren lure of the redeemably bad is better analysed in the chapter of Stephen King's *Danse Macabre* which considers 'The Horror Movie as Junk Food': 'Films that are just bad can be dismissed impatiently, with never a backward glance, but real fans of the genre look back on a film like *The Brain From Planet Arous* with something like real love. It is the love one spares for an idiot child, true, but love is love, right? Right.' In a related vein, here is Andrew Sarris on *cinéaste maudit* Edgar G. Ulmer: 'anyone who loves the cinema must be moved by *Daughter of Dr Jekyll*, a film with a scenario so atrocious that it takes forty minutes to establish that the daughter of Dr Jekyll is indeed the daughter of Dr Jekyll. Ulmer's camera never falters even when his characters disintegrate.'

It is barely possible to see Roger Corman's horror comedies *A Bucket of Blood* (1959), *Little Shop of Horrors* (1960) and *Creature From the Haunted Sea* (1960) as kitsch, but the director is too sharp to live down to the label. True kitsch-cultivators need to feel superior to the people who take the trash they wish to regard as Art at face value. In *A Bucket of Blood* they are mercilessly parodied as the beatniks who worship statues with titles like 'Dead Cat', 'Murdered Man' and 'Severed Head'. These are literally clay-coated

● *Man-made*. Monique Van Voore, Srdjan Zelenovic, **Flesh for Frankenstein**.

detritus passed off as Art. False sophisticates are happier with Al Adamson's dire *Blood of Dracula's Castle* (1969), one of the first deliberate kitsch movies. It's a very bad 1940s Dracula movie, with some tame violence and a few miniskirts as concessions to the passing years. The performances of the fifth-rate cast are terrible (gigolo-type Alex D'Arcy is a chubby, prissy Dracula), the early scenes are needlessly padded with dolphinarium footage and much of the film is out of focus. One of the victims chained up in the cellar is too short to reach the manacles, and so she perches on the box that Adamson's for-hire cine-camera came in. However, Dracula's butler (John Carradine) is given a handful of half-humorous lines that would have been rejected by the Crypt Keeper as too corny. 'Type double-O negative. A very good year'. The feeble jokes prove Adamson has given up. He realises that he lacks the talent and resources to make his film exciting or titillating, so he throws in a few knowing Warholian winks. In the cheat finale, we hear that Dracula is disintegrating, but don't see the process because it would have been too expensive. But *Blood of Dracula's Castle* is supposed to be trash, so why complain?

To compound his crimes, Adamson didn't even limit himself to this one atrocity. In fact, it's one of his *better* films. Armed with a lack of talent, John Carradine (sometimes Lon Chaney Jr, Russ Tamblyn and/or Scott Brady), repeated footage of car crashes and that bloody dolphinarium, the services of soon-to-be-acclaimed cinematographers like Vilmos Zsigmond and Laszlo Kovacs, portions of old Filipino movies, a stock company of has-beens and never-weres (including Vicki Volante, Robert Dix, Kent Taylor, Zandor Vorkov, John Bloom and directors-to-be John Bud Cardos and Greydon Clark), the heroine services of his peculiar wife Regina Carroll, and a weird desire to mix and match bits from series Westerns, Universal horrors, biker flicks, psychedelia and Ritz Brothers slapstick, Adamson has also put his name to *Horror of the Blood Monsters* (1970), *Dracula Vs. Frankenstein* (1971), *Brain of Blood* (1971) and *Blood of Ghastly Horror* (1971). The dating of these movies is approximate, at best, because Adamson usually filmed them in bits and pieces over up to five years, incorporating or deleting plot elements — like the bikers and the psychedelia — as they went in and out of fashion, and changing the title accordingly. Adamson is by no means unique in the 'Z'-feature field: David L. Hewitt (*Dr Terror's Gallery of Horrors*, 1967; *The Mighty Gorga*, 1970), Larry Buchanan (*Creature of Destruction*, 1967; *The Loch Ness Horror*, 1979), Ray Dennis Steckler (*The Incredibly Strange Creatures Who Stopped Living and Became Mixed-Up Zombies!!?*, 1963; *Blood Shack*, 1980) make films just as excruciatingly dull, and comparative newcomers like Don Dohler and Fred Olen Ray are passing the torch along. Aside from keeping John Carradine and Scott Brady in work, all these film-makers — despite the fair amount of *auteurist* control they exercise over their micro-budgeted quickies — have really succeeded in doing is staying in business against the odds and inflicting unendurable boredom upon audiences. Any fool who thinks bad films are uproarious fun would be cured if locked in a cinema during an all-night Al Adamson retrospective.

Appropriately, it was the Warhol Factory that changed the emphasis from finding kitsch horror movies (Warhol listed *Creation of the Humanoids* as one of the best films of 1962) to making them. *Sleep* (1963), *Kiss* (1964) and *Blow Job* (1964), the artist's early films, are found subjects. Ordinary, downright boring events become Art simply because they have been filmed. The idea is clever, but the films are unwatchable. With *Trash* (1970) and *Heat* (1973), Warhol handed the director's chore to Paul Morrissey and the Factory began to make 'real movies', complete with narrative, script, performances and increasing technical polish. In 1973, Morrissey directed the definitive trash/kitsch horror movies, *Flesh for Frankenstein* and *Blood for Dracula*. No way are these mainstream movies, but they were the first Factory productions to break out of the underground and play the regular cinema circuits. Shooting back-to-back in Italy, Morrissey was assisted by the directorial imput of Italian schlockman Antonio Margheriti (Anthony Dawson) and helped enormously by the professionalism of his technicians. In *Frankenstein*, the Baron (Udo Kier) is a necrophile whose philosophy is 'to know death you have to fuck life in the gall bladder'. Intent on creating a Serbian master race, he is foiled when he accidentally uses the brain of an impotent would-be monk for his supposedly superpotent Perfect Man (Srdjan Zelenovic). In *Dracula*, the Count (Kier again) is wheelchair ridden and unable to find virgin blood in an aristocratic family because the handyman (Joe Dallesandro) keeps deflowering the daughters before the vampire can get to them. Whenever Dracula slurps tainted blood, he has to stagger into an art deco bathroom and heave.

Morrissey is an infinitely better director than Al Adamson. The deliberately 'bad' aspects (Dallesandro's wooden acting, extremely excessive gore and lines like 'That Count Dracula is no good for anyone and he never was!') integrate perfectly with the films' witty reinterpretations of horror movie legendry. Instead of pathetic blood bank jokes, Morrissey uses pointed, inventive sight gags. Frankenstein advances on an unwary head donor with a gigantic pair of 3-D garden shears. Dracula travels through *mittel* Europe with a coffin on the roofrack of his Oldsmobile. Even the violence is funny: *Frankenstein* climaxes with a Jacobean massacre as all the characters converge on the laboratory and lay each other out, and after a limb-lopping battle there is little left of Dracula worth staking. Warhol always wanted beautiful people in his trash films: Morrissey extends the idea to a sumptuous romanticism that borrows equally from the 1950s Hammer remakes and the 1930s Universal originals. Amid the depravity, there's even room for a little sentiment. The Baron's *Tannhäuser*-scored dream of an ideal of physical beauty and the Count's cold turkey torment as he fails to find solace in 'a nice green salad' are funny, horrible and moving. Sadly, Morrissey's *Hound of the Baskervilles* (1977), with Peter Cook and Dudley Moore as Holmes and Watson and a distinguished cast of character comedians, is a witless bore, dedicated with misguided affection to the *Carry On* series. Morrissey's gothic horror double bill finds the underground striving to make real movies. They look professional, the stories make weird sense and they feature star names (*Blood for Dracula* has cameos by Vittorio De Sica and Roman Polanski). Udo Kier later found a niche in arty European horror films, from a cameo in *Suspiria* to a grim Dr Jekyll in Walerian Borowczyk's dark, misanthropic and interestingly offensive *Dr Jekyll et les Femmes* (*Blood of Dr Jekyll*) (1981).

John Waters is the reverse angle, a film-maker so comically depraved the underground can look down on him. For the Baltimore-based *auteur* of *Mondo Trasho* (1969), *Multiple Maniacs* (1970), *Pink Flamingoes* (1973), *Female Trouble* (1974), *Desperate Living* (1977), *Polyester* (1981) and *Hairspray* (1987), bad is good, ugly is beautiful and sick is funny. Waters claims his first films were financed by shoplifting, and his favourite star used to be Divine, a 400lb. transvestite sometimes described as 'the world's most beautiful person' or 'America's most eligible gay bachelor'. Waters's early films are technically worse than those of his idol, Herschell Gordon Lewis, but *Pink Flamingoes* is unforgettable. With disarming candour, Waters described his thinking to *Fangoria*: 'I had $10,000 to make a film. I had to compete with *Shampoo* and the big Hollywood films . . . I had to go out on a limb. I had to do something that people might not like, but they wouldn't ever be able to forget.' The final scene has the camera shakily zero in on a defecating dog and, without a cut, observes as Divine scoops up the shit, eats it, licks her lips and smiles. Waters was right. It's a for-the-first-and-only-time screen moment, a joke at the expense of Warhol's art films that will outlive them, and a lot funnier and more offensive than Warren Beatty impersonating a rabbit. 'I've never tried to top that, never tried to do anything that was more hideous, and that was the only thing of that sort anyone's been asked to do in my films that was real . . . I would never ask anyone to do anything that might cause them to be hurt, nor would I like to see anything like that.' So there. Even John Waters draws a line somewhere, even if it does happen to be on the other side of eating dog shit.

Since *Pink Flamingoes*, Waters has been raising larger budgets and getting a more professional effect. *Polyester* is his first in 35mm. and casts Divine opposite a name actor (well, Tab Hunter), while *Hairspray* not only has Deborah Harry and Pia Zadora but the sort of setting – a music TV show of the early 1960s – one would expect from Baltimore's other resident director, Barry Levinson (*Diner*, *Tin Men*). In truth, his cinema functions best at its rattiest, and *Pink Flamingoes* is his disposable masterpiece. Unlike *Mondo Trasho* and *Multiple Maniacs*, it is in colour and has synchronised sound, but technically it's got nothing else going for it. Babs Johnson (Divine) and Connie Marble (Mink Stole), aided by their disgusting entourages, fight for the title of 'The World's Filthiest Person'. This is less a plot than a good-humoured excuse for a checklist of perversions. Connie kidnaps girls, has the chauffeur impregnate them through rape or DIY artificial insemination, and sells the babies to lesbian couples, using the profits to finance a chain of porno bookstores and an elementary-school drug-pushing concern. The film also includes a sex act with a slaughtered chicken; an overweight, half-naked grandmother (Edy Massey – yeccch!) sucking eggs in her playpen; Divine smuggling stolen meat out of the butcher's shop in the crotch of her underwear (and later serving it up for dinner); incestuous, and debatably homosexual (the actor is a gay man, but the character is a woman) fellatio; a cannibal orgy modelled on *Night of the Living Dead*; Raymond Marble (David Lochary) exposing himself in the park, with a turkey neck tied to his penis; foot-fetishism; assorted minor cruelties; just-plain-old-fashioned murder; and the man with the elasticated anus (whose turn comes a close second behind the dog doody dinner for sheer vomitousness). In his autobiography, Waters writes 'I pride myself on the fact that my work has no socially redeeming value', but underneath it all he's an All-American Boy seeing how far he can go before his parents send him up to his room. At best, Waters's revolting obsessions are life-affirming in the way Tom Lehrer's gleefully cheery songs, 'Poisoning Pigeons in the Park' and 'Oedipus Rex', are.

Waters is a disarming, necessary film-maker, but *Pink Flamingoes* is enough. Sitting through the entire pre-*Hairspray* oeuvre is a wearisome task that proves how few of our remaining taboos are worth breaking. Prolonged exposure to Waters's topsy-turvy universe inures one to the childish obscenities ('I blew Richard Speck!' Divine shouts in *Female Trouble*), and highlights the moments when his pose as an amoral pervert slips. The references to *Cinderella* (the villainess of *Desperate Living* dresses like the wicked stepmother) and *The Wizard of Oz* (which in hippier times Waters tried to remake as *Dorothy, The Kansas City Pothead*) do not degrade the fairy tales, but import some of their innocence into his squalor. In some sense, Waters is the perfect pre-adolescent film-maker, getting every child's worst ideas out of his system. 'I would love to make a movie for very neurotic children. But then, perhaps, I've already done that. I've shown my films at children's birthday parties; they just love 'em, like Punch and Judy shows'. As the slightly tame *Polyester* indicates, the rise of sadistic pornography has made Waters's bad taste obsolete. When, in *Desperate Living*, a lesbian decides her sex change wasn't a good idea after all and cuts her new penis off with a pair of kitchen scissors, Waters's jolly decadence is too near the dead-straight nastiness of *Ilsa, She-Wolf of the SS* (1972) or *Appointment with Agony* (1979) to laugh at. In his own writings, collected in *Shock Value* and *Crackpot*, Waters has even shown himself up as a witty moralist, and *Hairspray* goes so far as to have – gasp! – a socially redeeming, anti-racist sub-plot, not to mention actual technical competence and considerable charm.

In *Shock Value*, Waters pays homage to his favourite directors, H.G. Lewis, the Wizard of Gore, and Russ Meyer, the first *auteur* to emerge from the skinflick industry. Meyer is like Waters in that one of his films is enough. Individually, they are dazzling, but the repetition palls with the carry-over from film to film, especially since Meyer's reuse of the same basic material often borders on self-plagiarism. Otherwise, he is Waters's exact opposite. Waters has consistent

● Edith Massey, *(yecch!)*. **Female Trouble.**

ideas, but no technique; Meyer is one of the most inventive low-budget directors of the age, but ruthlessly lampoons any pretensions that his films might actually be about something. The minimal requirements of the porno audience allow Meyer to get away with anything as long as a mammary freak strips every few minutes. Meyer's style is immediately recognisable – cartoonish blocks of primary colour; intricate, brilliantly paced editing; punctured melodramatics; out-of-place marching band scores (usually the 'Horst Wessel Song'); in-jokes like naming the villain of *Beyond the Valley of the Dolls* (1970) Porter Hall, after the sneaky 1940s character actor; pretentious narrations full of meaningless meanings; religious, sexual and violent frenzy; and girls with very, very big tits. Like Waters, Meyer is attracted by the possibilities of the horror film but is unwilling to commit himself to the genre. *Kiss Me Quick* (1963) has alien sexologists and a sub-plot about the love life of the Frankenstein Monster, but is less distinctive than a quartet which anticipates the down-home gothic of the rural massacre movie: *Lorna* (1964), *MudHoney* (1965), *Motor Psycho!* (1965) and *Faster, Pussycat! Kill! KILL!* (1966).

In *Kings of the Bs*, Roger Ebert, Meyer's frequent collaborator, describes this phase as 'the period when he went out into the woods and filmed stark (but semi-tongue-in-cheek) melodramas about demented hillbillies, religious fanatics, over-sexed baby dolls, violent woodsmen, and obscene grandmothers'. This group contains Meyer's best work. *Lorna* is the nearest thing to a serious film he has ever attempted, alternately bleak and wistful, with Lorna Maitland giving an evocative performance as the unfulfilled rural wife who has a steamy affair with an ex-convict while her decent but useless husband digs salt in a field with a sadistic local Iago. And *Faster, Pussycat* is some kind of a classic. Having just karate-chopped an All-American drag-racer to death and kidnapped his sweet teenage girlfriend, Varla (Tura Satana), a psychotic go-go dancer, leads her two equally crazy sidekicks to the run-down desert homestead of a crippled miser and his hulking, retarded son. The thrill-kill kittens kick up plenty of dust as they double-cross each other, search for the old man's hidden fortune and explode with the kind of hyperactivity that suggests they are headed for early graves. Like all four films, *Faster, Pussycat* is relatively restrained in the nudity department (the leather blouses are cut low, but never come off), and benefits from a driving jazz/sleaze score (the theme song was covered by the Cramps), overdrive melodramatics, hilarious dialogue and performances pitched so broad they make the Marx Brothers seem restrained. The film is the ultimate expression of the American cinema's fetishist enthusiasm for big breasts, fast cars, tight jeans and sudden death.

Since 20th Century-Fox backed *Beyond the Valley of the Dolls* (which they sold as 'the first exploitation-horror-camp-musical'), Meyer has neglected brooding gothics in favour of violent comic books like *Supervixens* (1975), *Up!* (1976) and *Beneath the Valley of the Ultravixens* (1979). In 1972, however, he directed the nearest thing yet to a Russ Meyer horror movie in *Slaves*, a spoof of the *Mandingo*-style plantation saga that borrows its stars (Anouska Hempel, David Warbeck, Dave Prowse) and its mealy mouthed mix of sadism and moralising from Hammer Films. Our titled hero's home is introduced with a caption that reads 'Maxwell House, England'. Concerned at his brother's disappearance in the Caribbean, David Warbeck disguises himself as a commoner and travels to the island of San Cristobal. The colony is run by Lady Susan Walker (Hempel), whose favourite pastime is flogging, maiming, crucifying and generally abusing her slaves. Her evil regime is supported by a troop of mincing francophone mulattos who, for no discernible reason, are all named after French politicians. The brother (Prowse) turns up as a castrated zombie. The blacks finally rebel with an orgy of bloodshed that, if we are to believe the narrator, leads to the state of interracial harmony that prevails in the world today, as symbolised by naked black and white people running along the beach. Some of *Slaves* is awfully funny (as when Hempel unzips her 1836 riding boots), and all of it is exciting to watch, but it's still pointless. In Meyer's later films, nothing leads anywhere except to more sex, violence and showy technique. Finally, he is more irritating than Waters. Since the disaster of his anti-censorship diatribe, *The Seven Minutes* (1971), he has been unwilling to stick his neck out with anything more than pure exploitation. Russ Meyer knows how to make good films, but refuses to do so.

Waters is so *outré* he has had no imitators (one hardly dares imagine the plague of rip-offs we'd have suffered if *Pink Flamingoes* had made as much money as *Halloween*), but several contemporary directors are recognisably working in the same outfield. George Kuchar and Curt McDowell collaborated on the screenplay of the McDowell-directed *Thundercrack!* (1975), a polymorphously perverse return to *The House on Haunted Hill*. A group of driven characters are stranded for the night in a creepy old homestead during a raging thunderstorm. They have various kinds of for-real sex with each other, occasionally taking time out from sweating, grunting and trying to keep their genitalia in shot to reveal their dark secrets in flashback. Bing (Kuchar), a zookeeper, searches for his lost love, an escaped gorilla. In a hidden room, the son of the house, victim of an Asiatic curse, drags his hideously enlarged genitals around. The grim pastiche dialogue is nicely written, but dreadfully delivered. Obviously, willingness to copulate, masturbate or sodomise on camera was more important than acting ability when *Thunder-crack!* was being cast. The film is further crippled by its cheapness: the old dark house is limited to a tiny kitchen, a few cosy rooms and a cramped basement, and the exterior revealed in lightning flashes is a drawing. The best thing about the movie is the soundtrack, an eerie collage of whistling winds, pounding rain, rumbling thunder and Mark Ellinger's hypnotic silent movie piano score. The film is too doom haunted to appeal to a gay or straight porno audience, and yet its two hours plus of penetrations, perversions and come-shots make it all but unbearable for anybody else. Since it joined *Pink Flamingoes* on the late-night cult circuit, *Thundercrack!* has become the most walked-out-of film this side of Michael Snow's *La Région Centrale*.

Although *Thundercrack!* is more extreme than most weirdies, it does operate in a recognisable tradition of zero-budget Hollywood gothics. Sharing McDowell and Kuchar's roots in 1930s old-dark-house movies is Jack Hill's *Spider Baby; or: The Maddest Story Ever Told* (1964), a luridly advertised ('The SEDUCTIVE INNOCENCE of LOLITA! The SAVAGE HUNGER of a BLACK WIDOW!') item about a houseful of freaks reverting to savagery. With a rock 'n' roll title song sung by Lon Chaney Jr, and some very creepy performances from Jill Banner and Sid Haig as degenerates and Carol Ohmart as a scheming bitch/coquette, *Spider Baby* is sort of a more perverse *Addams Family*, with genuinely grotesque humour and a unique cheesiness. Nick Zoed's *Geek Maggot Bingo* (1983) tries to match Hill's tone with its pantomime sets, punk singing cowboy (Richard Hell), vampire queen called Scumbalina (Donna Death), ranting mad scientist, inventively distorted no-budget monster make-up, a cameo by the then-editor of *Fangoria* indulging a private feud by purporting to imitate the then-editor of *Sleazoid Express*, and narration by TV horror host Zacherle. Zoed, also responsible for *They Eat Scum!* (1982), tries too hard and comes up with a movie that makes Al Adamson look like Martin Scorsese – it's difficult to tell whether the dialogue is witty because it's practically inaudible, but an all-too-accurate sign half-way through the film reads 'Leave Now, It Isn't Going To Get Any Better!'. More worthwhile is Rufus Butler Seder's *Screamplay* (1985), which features George Kuchar of *Thundercrack!* as yet another psycho and comes on in black and white with painted sets like the last German Expressionist Horror Movie. A hopeful screenwriter played by Seder himself in an imitation of Dwight Frye's fly-eating maniac from *Dracula* arrives in Hollywood, USA, and writes his frustrations out in a screenplay. However, the unpleasant real-life characters he writes horrible death scenes for in his movie soon start falling victim to a real mad murderer. *Screamplay* actually has a plot worth talking about, but still doesn't skimp on its neo-underground peculiarity.

It took the Warhol Factory to demonstrate the

kind of movie Waters or Curt McDowell might make if they had resources of talent, budget and moral responsibility to balance their psycho-sexual urges. *Andy Warhol's Bad* (1976), directed by Jed Johnson, stars Carroll Baker as Mrs Aiken, an electrolysis expert who runs a murder-by-contract agency on the side. The film's unforgettably gross moment has an end-of-her-tether housewife drop a screaming baby out of the window. The camera follows its twenty-storey plunge, and closes on the blood-spattered face of an upset passer-by. Almost every scene is built around motiveless cruelty: one of Mrs Aiken's hit-ladies shoves a severed finger into a bottle of ketchup, another pair firebomb a cinema because they don't like the movie and Mrs Aiken scatters broken glass in front of the fridge she knows the barefoot L.T. (Perry King) will raid. These antisocial characters often make Divine's filth crusade seem easygoing. Waters's people enjoy perversions for their own sake; the characters of *Bad* like victimising each other. The more hurtful they can be, the more fun they have. Fat Estelle (Brigid Polk) hires Mrs Aiken not just to kill her neighbour's beloved dog but to torture it first. A dissatisfied customer quibbles whether a crushed limb is as much value for money as an amputation. Waters's characters don't care about right and wrong, and their director agrees with them. Johnson's people know what Good is, but choose to be *Bad*, and are properly criticised for it. In a crucial scene, L.T. is assigned to terminate a rich couple's retarded son, but is unable to go through with it. When he tells the cowardly parents to kill their child themselves, Johnson at last gives the audience someone to root for. L.T.'s seriously held moral position comes as a welcome catharsis after an hour and a half of undiluted evil. Lest the sincerity seem out of place, Johnson reinforces the point with a comic comeuppance for Mrs Aiken. A corrupt black cop drowns her in the kitchen sink.

The Rocky Horror Picture Show (1976) is less interesting as a movie than as a social phenomenon. The filming of a successful British fringe musical, it flopped on its original release, but rose from the dead as a late-night attraction across America. The fancy-dress fanatics who patronise the film indulge in an unprecedented interaction with the on-screen events, interpolating new lines as footnotes to the dialogue, and generally challenging the passive nature of the cinema-going experience. The film itself is a less satisfying blend of horror pastiche and rock 'n' roll than *The Phantom of the Paradise* and only its advocacy of outrageously camp behaviour hints at a possible appeal to millions of Americans who don't pick up on the s-f movie in-jokes of 'Science Fiction Double Feature' (the opening song, delivered by a pair of disembodied lips) and were never exposed to the 1950s Edgar Lustgarten True-Life Crime shorts lampooned by the cutaway scenes of criminologist Charles Gray explaining the plot and the dance steps. *The Rocky Horror Picture Show* needs its sloppiness and deadwood jokes to give its fans lee-way for their elaborations. If the film were any better, the audience participation would be annoying; if it were any worse, there'd be nothing to play with.

The plot is a more colourful, more innocent version of *Thundercrack!* : Brad (Barry Bostwick) and Janet (Susan Sarandon) are forced by a flat tyre and a rainstorm to spend the night in a Middle American castle, and are seduced by bisexuals from outer space. The fun-loving Dr Frank N. Furter (Tim Curry) minces around in a corset and fishnet stockings belting out a torch song, 'I'm a Sweet Transvestite From Transsexual, Transylvania', a camp icon and over-the-top enough to be unthreatening. Expressing a British affection for American monster movies and rock 'n' roll music, the film carries over the best of the stage show – an energetic cast and catchy songs from composer-lyricist-hunchbacked assistant Richard O'Brien. As directed by Jim Sharman, an Australian who has flirted with fantasy in *Shirley Thompson Versus the Aliens* (1972) and *Summer of Secrets* (1976), *The Rocky Horror Picture Show* is a modest film. Its creators seem as bemused by the fuss as anyone else, and proved unable to do it again with *Shock Treatment* (1981), which has a better score and Jessica Harper but is otherwise a painfully obvious satire on American TV soaps and game shows.

● 135

Dr Frank N. Furter's 'Don't dream it, be it!' philosophy is quoted by the parti-coloured Jordan in the considerably less endearing *Jubilee* (1977). Richard O'Brien makes a brief appearance as Dr John Dee, the alchemist, opposite Jenny Runacre's Queen Elizabeth I and Adam Ant's camp Ariel, in the pidgin-Shakespeare prologue to Derek Jarman's tour of a post-breakdown London. The world of *Jubilee* is lifted from Michael Moorcock's Romances of Entropy, but for the author's restraint, humour and deft characterisations Jarman substitutes an orgy of pram-burning and barbed-wire tightrope-walking. A man with a garden full of plastic flowers eats a cockroach because it is full of protein; Adolf Hitler is alive and well (as in Meyer's *Up!*) and living in Devon; Buckingham Palace and St Paul's Cathedral are owned by Borgia Ginz (Orlando), a recording industry tycoon who makes Swan look ethical; and, in the course of turning in the most amateurish perform-ance in 1970s art cinema, Toyah Willcox graphically castrates a Special Branch man. Doing horrid things to policemen is understandably a recurrent theme in the film fringes, as witness the cop cannibal orgies of *Pink Flamingoes* and *Themroc* (1973), but this particular sequence goes beyond even *I Spit on Your Grave* in its hysterical goriness, invoking John Waters's distinction between Good Bad Taste and Bad Bad Taste.

Before *Jubilee*, Jarman had made *Sebastiane* (1975), a gay religious epic with dialogue in Latin, and his pretensions hang over the punk spirit of 1977 like a Scotch mist over a blasted heath. The film is as harsh, nasty and ill-mannered as it is supposed to be. and a few of its personalities (Runacre – from the film of Moorcock's *The Final Program*, Orlando, Little Nell from *The Rocky Horror Picture Show*) can act, but its unrelieved anarchy and violence miss Waters's light touch. There's plenty of sex, but, as one of the film's too-many sweeping statements has it, 'love snuffed it with the hippies'. The only good joke in *Jubilee* is a cruel one at the expense of the punk audiences: the film is cast with rock stars, but the only song we hear all the way through is an *a capella* version of 'My Love Is Like a Red, Red Rose'. When Jarman has his punks scream a few stanzas of 'Jerusalem', one suspects his sympathies are with William Blake. He was probably a lot happier, although no more conventional, filming *The Tempest* (1979) – his best movie – and *Caravaggio* (1986). Ten years after *Jubilee* , he returned to its vision of the United Kingdom going to Hell in *The Last of England* (1987), and produced a monotonous grumble that could give Nick Zoed or Al Adamson a run for their money in the tedium front. A ten-minute sequence features a shivering naked man on a building site trying to eat a raw cauliflower.

Although often lumped in with Jarman, Peter Greenaway is a far less dilettante film artist, even if his films are, on occasion, just as difficult to put up with. Formerly (and, occasionally, still) a documentarist, Greenaway first expanded into fiction with *Vertical Features Remake* (1978), a pseudo-documentary about an elusive and fake film undertaken for ambiguous reasons, and *The Falls* (1980), a very long series of interviews with people whose name begins with the prefix 'Fall' and who have been affected by the mysterious Violent Unknown Event. Greenaway then had some surprising measure of commercial success with *The Draughtsman's Contract* (1982), an Age of Reason murder mystery set in formally elegant surroundings, and followed up with the enigmatic and irksome *A Zed and Two Noughts* (1985), which is almost a caricature of a downbeat art film set in a derelict zoo, featuring an obsession with symmetry and decay. His strongest, easiest film is *The Belly of an Architect* (1987), with Brian Dennehy as an American architect dying of stomach trouble in Rome while being deceived by everyone around him. Beautiful and enigmatic, the film resembles some weird mutation of a Dario Argento *giallo*. Greenaway's cinema is uncategoris-able, which is perhaps (along with his sly humour) his most attractive feature, but images of death, decay and an incipient apocalypse recur. Without the fuss of *Jubilee*, Greenaway has captured a deep-frozen, very English flavour of horror that makes him uncomfortable but essential.

Few films are as committed to the nightmarish

as *Eraserhead* (1978). Other directors filter their nightmares through the surrealist movement (*Un Chien Andalou*) or horror movie mannerisms (*Night of the Living Dead*), but David Lynch's bad dream is unadulterated. Even though it defecates on conventional ideas of narrative, *Eraserhead* attracts more than the art film crowds who go for Jarman and Greenaway. Like *Pink Flamingoes* and *The Rocky Horror Picture Show*, it is a cult film. It plays late-night shows and repertory cinemas to a clientele which thinks Ingmar Bergman is the star of *Casablanca*, but which prides itself on an ability to take weirdness beyond the capacity of a general audience. Henry Spencer (John Nance), an Oliver Hardy lookalike with a *Bride of Frankenstein* quiff, lives in a bed-sitting-room of unparalleled seediness. His single window affords an expansive view of a brick wall. *Eraserhead* is set in the slums of Oz, a fantasy that is more drab, grey and grimy than the real world. It's a place you've dreamed about for years, but never expected to see in the movies. And it's depressing. Henry marries a repulsive girl who has borne his hideously mutated baby, a creature the parents of the *It's Alive* children wouldn't want their kids to play with. Behind the radiator, there is a wonderland where a woman with fungus-rotted cheeks monotones a downbeat ditty entitled 'In Heaven Everything Is Fine' while stomping on writhing unpleasantnesses. In a dream within the nightmare, Henry imagines his severed head being mined for indiarubbers in a pencil factory. When his wife leaves him, Henry is left in his room with the squealing monster. He stabs it, and the thing cascades a roomful of excrement into which Henry disappears. *Eraserhead* defies criticism. It is impossible to enjoy, but Lynch has used his paltry resources brilliantly and realised an effect no other film has even attempted.

It was arresting enough to convince Mel Brooks to offer Lynch the prestigious *The Elephant Man* (1980). With a budget, a traditional storyline, name actors and a professional crew, Lynch still managed to return to his dreams and surrounded John Hurt's Victorian freak with steam-disgorging Industrial Revolution equipment and some black-and-white surgical gore. He was Oscar-nominated for his unconventional efforts, and that hasn't happened to John Waters or Derek Jarman. Lynch was stuck out in the desert by Dino de Laurentiis, an intractable source novel and a gargantuan production for *Dune* (1984), but survived the experience and turned out *Blue Velvet* (1986), a twisted small-town mystery that opens with gloomy Kyle MacLachlan poking around in the grass and discovering an ant-covered severed ear. Surprisingly, the plot of *Blue Velvet* does finally add up, but it's the weird sado-eroticism, crazed characterisations and stylishly bizarre visuals that make an impact. Lynch stages marvellously evocative, subtly chilling sequences in which Isabella Rossellini and Dean Stockwell respectively find new nuances in Bobby Vinton's title song and Roy Orbison's 'In Dreams'. The nightmare film-maker *par-excellence*, Lynch may develop into the major influence on the horror movies of the 1990s. The only directors who can match him have abandoned physical reality altogether and make films with puppets – the Czech Jan Svankmajer (*Moznosti Dialogu/Dimensions of Dialogue*, 1982; *Jama, Kivdalo a Nadeje/The Pit, The Pendulum and Hope*, 1983) and the English-resident Americans, the Brothers Quay (*The Street of Crocodiles*, 1986).

The least appetising kitsch films are not badly made or in poor taste, but pretentious. And yet, personally, I like Adrzej Zulawski's *Possession* (1981) more than *Eraserhead*. Zulawski takes his film too seriously, but it's fun all the same. Marc (Sam Neill) is a secret agent at the dreaded beck and call of his paranoia movie superior, The Man With Pink Socks. He is distracted from his spying by personal problems: not only has his wife Anna (Isabelle Adjani) taken a trendy lover, but she has also spontaneously generated a tentacled monster in a subway tunnel. Samantha Eggar acts in an equally unlikely reproductive manner in *The Brood*, but Adjani goes further by having an affair with her beastie. Zulawski goes mad with his swooping camera, has everything in shot painted blue and encourages his stars to attack their roles with a kind of stylised hysteria rare outside the Japanese theatre, but *Possession* is compulsive all the same.

Also pretension ridden but interesting, especially

● *As far as an image can go.* **Moznosti Dialogu/Dimensions of Dialogue.**

fifteen years after the fact, are the wave of what might be termed 'Weird Hippie Shit' flicks that flooded out in the wake of the freak success of *Easy Rider*. This category includes acid-trip idiocies like *Is This Trip Really Necessary?* (1970), turn-of-the-century biker vs witchcraft movies like *Hex* (1973), message-ridden post-'Nam psycho movies like *Americana* (1981), and monkeying-around-in-the-desert Buddhist/electric Westerns like *Zachariah* (1971) and Alexandro Jodorowsky's *El Topo* (1972). Typical of the way these films flirt with horror (among other genre categories) are Alan Gadney's *Moonchild* (1971), Alan Rudolph's *Premonition* (1972) and Silvio Narizzano's *The Sky Is Falling/The Sky Is Falling* (1975). Gadney mixes John Carradine (it wasn't a real Weird Hippie Shit movie unless you had at least one of the Carradines in it) and Victor Buono into an incomprehensible oddity set in the 1920s with homonulci and reincarnation in a desert inn. Meanwhile Rudolph deals with a red flower known to the Indians that causes hallucinatory premonitions when smoked in joints and then has a rock group broken up by an irreversible doom amid much colour-negative psychedelia and music footage. And Narizzano's hilarious Spanish/Lichtenstein production has boozy, whiskery slob Dennis Hopper — a staple of the weirdo film from *Easy Rider* through to *Blue Velvet* — and washed-up Hollywoodian Carroll Baker indulge in bizarre perversions like cracking eggs on a black girl's head while forcing her to sing 'Shortnin' Bread' until some hippie angels of vengeance turn up to bring their decadent group to a gory finish. Lots of young talent turned up in these movies, but they soon moved into the mainstream or were attracted by the more controlled weirdness being practised by the likes of Henry Jaglom, Bob Rafelson or Robert Altman at around the same time. Still, even Altman made *Brewster McCloud* (1972), a Weird Hippie Shit film if ever there was, and there were straggling entries as late as Richard Rush's *The Stunt Man* (1980) and Eli Hollander's *Out* (1982).

The most engaging director to emerge from the underground-trash-horror nexus is Paul Bartel, who shares his taste for sleaze with Waters and McDowell, but displays a tolerant, tasteful charm in his approach that is, given his subject matter, incredible. Originally a New York-based fringe film-maker, his first serious short — which he later remade for Steven Spielberg's *Amazing Stories* TV show — is *The Secret Cinema* (1966), a paranoid curiosity whose heroine discovers that her life is the subject of a peep-show film directed by the Mysterious They. In 1972, MGM and Gene Corman sponsored Bartel's first feature, an echt-kinky mock horror film, *Private Parts*, about a runaway girl who unwisely takes refuge in her crazy aunt's old dark hotel. Although the script was originally set in New York, the MGM deal required that the story be relocated to Los Angeles, and Bartel's cross-country trip to a tawdry Hollywood is one he has been making ever since. 'The terrible problem with *Private Parts*', explained Bartel to *Fangoria*, 'was that the title could not be advertised in a number of cities, so when you have a title you can't print in the paper, it's a big problem. Secondly, MGM was not sure how to market it. They didn't know whether to market it as a horror film or a sex film.'

Actually, *Private Parts* is a blacker-than-sick comedy. When perverted George (John Ventantonio) spies Norman Bates-style on the young heroine Cheryl (Ann Ruymen), she is not disgusted but touched. The weirdo inhabitants of the hotel are all somehow likeable, from the Reverend Moon (Laurie Main), who sometime swaps his dog collar for black leathers and drapes his man-size crucifix with bicycle chains and pin-ups clipped from muscle magazines, to Aunt Martha (Lucille Benson), who keeps a pet rat and is obsessed with photographing the recently dead in the hope of catching the image of the departing spirit. The film's most notorious scene has George sleeping with an inflatable doll, but Bartel is less taken with the *Thundercrack!* depravity of the act than with the strange image of the plastic woman filling out with a flood of tapwater. Bartel characterises his people through the clutter with which they surround themselves. Cheryl is forever nosing around other people's rooms and lingering with the camera over an Antonioni-like assortment of photographic enlargements, some Kenneth Anger-style fetish gear, or the more traditional horror movie inner sanctums and corpses.

Despite a few creative differences, Bartel was well served by a stay at Roger Corman's New World. The outfit then existed in the borderline between the major studios and poverty row. Corman's films usually have *everything* – blood, naked girls, action, car crashes, laughs, monsters and . . . oh yes . . . a little social significance for the college crowds. After second-unit work on the car chases of Steve Carver's *Big Bad Mama* (1974), Bartel made *Death Race 2000* (1975), which covers a future trans-American road race in which points are scored for the number of pedestrians run over (women and children count extra, hence lines like 'if they scatter, go for the baby!'). It's the closest real movies have come to Chuck Jones's Road Runner cartons: the rebels out to sabotage the race devise schemes that would do Wile E. Coyote proud, like a cardboard cut-out tunnel mouth on the edge of a precipice. The hero is Frankenstein (David Carradine), a government-bred racer who has had so many limb and organ transplants he doesn't know who he is any more; and the villain is Machine Gun Joe Viterbo (Sylvester Stallone), a black shirt/white tie hoodlum so rotten he'd even run over his own pit crew to rack up a few bonus points. The race coverage is complete with gushing commentaries about the finer points of the Great American sport and star prizes presented to the grieving relatives of the victims.

Bartel can turn serious for the scene in which the lady president of Frankenstein's fan club sacrifices herself to her idol, but mostly he jokes about the moralising. The rebels – all typical 1970s college liberals – are led by a white-haired granny called Thomasina Paine, and the creepy Mr President blames all acts of internal terrorism on the perfidious French. Finally, Frankenstein turns out to be an OK guy, although not before delivering the cinema's very worst joke (a pun about a hand grenade). He assassinates Mr President, restores all civil liberties, replaces his monster suit with an all-white get-up, marries his spunky mechanic (Simone Griffeth) and enters the White House. Junior Bruce ('The Real' Don Steele), the commentator, complains about the abolition of the death race. 'Of course it's violent. We love it violent, violent, violent! That's the American way!' Bruce has been an irritant throughout the film and, in the last shot, Frankenstein runs over him with a white limousine and heads off on his honeymoon.

Bartel followed *Death Race 2000* with *Cannonball* (1976), a modern day version of the same plot also starring Carradine, with guest appearances from New World personnel like Dick Miller, Jonathan Kaplan, Martin Scorsese, Joe Dante, Allan Arkush, Roger Corman and Bartel himself as a singing gangster. Since then, he has mainly been visible as a comic performer in his friends' films: *Rock 'n' Roll High School* (1979) and *Heartbeeps* (1981) for Arkush, *Piranha* for Dante, *Heart Like a Wheel* (1983) for Kaplan, *Into the Night* (1985) and *Amazon Women on the Moon* for John Landis and *Mortuary Academy* (1987) for Michael Schroeder. Dante and Arkush, graduates of New World's trailer department, collaborated on *Hollywood Boulevard* (1976), an incredibly cheap satire padded with footage lifted from every New World picture they could get their scissors to. Hollywood Boulevard is a block up from Sunset Boulevard and sleazier, and the film concerns a murderous maniac who terrorises the production of a low-budget exploitation epic called *Atomic War Brides*. Bartel plays Erich von Leppe, the riding-booted director. 'What we're trying to do here is combine the legend of Romeo and Juliet with high-speed car action and a sincere plea for international atomic controls in our time', von Leppe tells an interviewer. Then he gives a Godzilla-suited actor his motivation, 'to step on as many people as possible'. At one point he instructs a topless actress working on *Machete Maidens of Mora Tau* to deliver a line which sums up the philosophical essence of the film: she puts a knife to a Filippino extra's throat and sneers 'get it up or I cut it off!'

In the 1980s, Bartel made a return to directing with a pair of disappointing comedies – *Not for*

Publication (1984), a screwball farce set in the world of tabloid journalism, and *Lust in the Dust* (1985), a spoof Spaghetti Western that reunites Tab Hunter and Divine. However, before this decline, he made his most achieved film, *Eating Raoul* (1982). The film is distantly related to *The Corpse Grinders*, *Fun With Dick and Jane* and *Motel Hell*, but is really unlike anything in the movies since *Kind Hearts and Coronets* and *The Ladykillers*.

I wanted to make a film about two greedy, uptight people who are at the same time not too unlike you and me and Nancy and Ronnie, to keep it funny and yet communicate something about the perversity of these values. My movie touches on many things: the perversion of middle-class values, the resurgence of Nixonism, Latin machismo versus WASP fastidiousness, *film noir*. Finally, however, it's about how financial considerations overpower emotional ones.

Paul Bartel

And, no doubt, it is a sincere plea for international atomic controls in our time.

Actually, *Eating Raoul* manages to deal with all its issues, and reach back beyond the weirdo horror film to rediscover romantic comedy. Self-financed, it is also the only Bartel film in which his concerns have not been smudged by producer-insisted-on gore, action and smut. Murder is bloodlessly executed with a kitchen utensil ('Will you buy me a new frying pan? I don't feel good about cooking in the one we're using to kill people.'). The film is a return to the sleazy Los Angeles of *Private Parts* and *Hollywood Boulevard*, where kids amuse themselves by sandbagging the mailman with a TV set, and 'the line between food and sex has completely dissolved'. This ratty world is viewed through the chaste outrage of Paul and Mary Bland (Bartel and former Warhol superstar Mary Woronov), who live among a collection of delicious 1950s furnishings (stuffed wine bottles, cloud-shaped mirrors, rubber mice, pastel wallpaper), and dream of escaping the city of decadent swingers to open a tasteful restaurant in the country. Realising Los Angeles is full of rich perverts no one will miss, the Blands hit on the scheme of luring them to their apartment with ads in the underground press, and killing them for their money. The small-scale wallet-looting enterprise is organised into an efficient business by Raoul (Robert Beltran), a Chicano housebreaker who arranges to dispose profitably of the swingers' cars, clothes and bodies. His best customer is a canning company that produces 'Doggie King': Bartel finds in perversion a kind of inverted decency. Doris the Dominatrix (Susan Saiger), a whip-and-leather specialist, is actually a chatty housewife only too pleased to take a rest from bringing up her toddler to give the Blands some advice on how to make it in the degeneracy business. One of the cinema's sickest belly-laughs comes when the disgusted Paul hurls an electric lantern into a hot tub full of naked swingers led by the ever-obnoxious Don Steele. The film's charm can be measured by a sweetly happy ending in which the Blands finally achieve the restaurant of their dreams – after Raoul has been eaten, of course.

● *Beware the bogey man.* Nancy Loomis, **Halloween.**

psycho movies

psycho movies

or: 'I Didn't Raise My Girl to be a Severed Head!'

You can't kill the boogey man!

> ***Halloween***

It's apt that the exploitation film, a field whose cultural legacy includes the beach party musical, should run on the surfing principle. Way out on the ocean, some nothing movie surfaces. A ripple starts. Then, an unexpected success. Alerted by the distant crash of overwhelming profits, the independent producers leave off sunning themselves, grab their boards, and streak down to the water. The wave picks up, a peak is hit, and then ... wipe out. The producers flounder back to the sand, drink beer, eye bikinis, and wait for the next Big One. Banking on the next Big One has always been a popular Hollywood parlour game. The odds are less favourable than those of Russian roulette, and the forfeits nearly as inconvenient. The major characteristic of the trend system is its unpredictability. A producer claiming that his latest epic is the next Big One is liable to be a desperate man hyping a tax write-off like *Logan's Run* or *Swamp Thing*.

Halloween had its American première on 31 October 1978. The modestly budgeted quickie went on to earn $18,500,000 in the domestic market alone, becoming financially one of the most successful independent films of the 1970s. As night follows day, and the rivers flow into the sea, and Isis raised Osiris from the dead, *Halloween* would initiate a trend.

Halloween began life as *The Babysitter Murders*, a 'concept' devised by independent producer Irwin Yablans. *The Babysitter Murders* was about an escaped homicidal maniac who murders babysitters. Yablans was possibly familiar with Peter Collinson's *Fright* (1971), in which an escaped homicidal maniac (Ian Bannen) nearly murders a babysitter (Susan George). Then again, he could have been thinking of William Castle's *I Saw What You Did* (1965), in which a homicidal maniac (John Ireland) goes after the babysitter he thinks has seen him murder Joan Crawford. Then there was Fred Walton's short *The Sitter* (1977), later expanded as *When a Stranger Calls* (1979), in which an escaped homicidal maniac (Tony Beckley) nearly murders a babysitter (Carol Kane), and Brian Clemens's TV series *Thriller* which, in the early 1970s, used the plot every other week. On paper, *The Babysitter Murders* did not sound like the kind of film that would stretch the horror genre overmuch.

Although thrown away on their original US releases, *Dark Star* and *Assault on Precinct 13*, director John Carpenter's first two films, had been well received, if not exactly box-office dynamite, in the United Kingdom. Noticing how *Assault* excited the London Film Festival crowd, Yablans offered his concept to Carpenter. He also came up with the idea of having the story take place on Hallowe'en night in order to provide the film with a) a title better than *The Babysitter Murders*; b) an excuse for spooky horror movie atmospherics; and c) a gimmick-releasing strategy during the post-summer, pre-Christmas period when cinemas are traditionally short of products. In *Overexposures*, David Thomson remarks upon the effectiveness of the title: 'You could easily give a twenty-five word synopsis for John Carpenter's compulsive B picture. But the one word is all we need, and brevity is always more intriguing. Halloween cannot promise anything sedate, and Halloween is to menace as sugar is to gratification'. At that stage in his career, Carpenter would probably have been happy to make anything from *Rebecca of Sunnybrook Farm* to *Elephant Girls in Bondage*. Although he sanctioned the use of the Panavision wide-screen format (unusual in a cheap horror film, and vital to *Halloween*'s shock tactics) and the prowling Pana-glide camera, Yablans seems to have expected little more than an efficient massacre movie.

Although the ingredients of *Halloween* hadn't been used in a feature film for some time, they were familiar from the despised fields of the theatrical short and the made-for-TV movie. Supporting pro-grammes have long been cluttered with humdrum variations on the maniac-menaces-girl-in-a-claustro-phobic-situation formula, like *The Dumb Waiter* (1979), *Deep End* (1979) and *Dead End* (1981). Paradoxically, in view of the trenchant feminist critiques of the big screen psycho movie, the made-for-TV equivalents have usually been vehicles for strong leading women like Valerie Harper in *Night Terror* (1977), Lauren Hutton in *Someone is Watching Me* (1978) or Suzanne Pleshette in *Fantasies* (1982) and *A Stranger Waits* (1986); or adventurous starlets like Sally Struthers in *A Gun in the House* (1981) and thrice-menaced Kathleen Beller in *Are You in the House Alone* (1978), *No Place to Hide* (1981) and *Deadly Messages* (1985). *Someone is Watching Me* is a fairly clever reworking of *Rear Window*, directed from his own script by John Carpenter, while he was sitting around waiting for his big screen break.

The closest recent cinema had come to *Halloween* was Bob Clark's engrossing, if over-plotted, *Black Christmas* (1975). A subjective camera heavy-breather who could well be, but isn't, Keir Dullea, John Saxon or Art Hindle, stalks co-eds Olivia Hussey, Margot Kidder and Andrea Martin around a Canadian sorority house. Like *Halloween* , *Black Christmas* uses a holiday as a backdrop: the end-of-term setting excuses the characters' failure to notice that the people around them are disappearing one by one, and also provides a logical reason why the old dark house should be empty. Whereas Carpenter uses Hallow-e'en to epitomise his childlike boogey man, Clark plays with the contrast between Christmas and the horrors, intercutting a Dario Argento-style murder (Kidder stabbed with a crystal ornament) with an angelic troupe of carol singers. The most heavily criticised aspect of *Black Christmas* – the transformation of its unknown psycho villain into a quasi-supernatural presence – would be seen as *Halloween*'s strongest suit.

In short, *Halloween* was about as original as an Italian Western remake of a *samurai* epic, a Chinese imitation thereof or a private eye film in blackface. Yet, like *A Fistful of Dollars*, *Fist of Fury* and *Shaft*, *Halloween* went down well with the American exploitation movie-going public: the rural drive-in patrons, ethnic ghetto audiences and college kids. Intriguingly, and, given the later controversy, ironically, *Halloween* differs from the other trend-setters in that it's a film men and women respond to equally, whereas the earlier movies – with their violent action, cool machismo and all-male conflicts – were definitely boys' pictures. It might not seem like much of an advance for feminism to get women on the screen at last only to kill them off, but the post-*Halloween* psycho craze was the first exploitation trend to deal to any extent with women's lives. In Spaghetti Westerns, kungfu flicks or blaxploitation pictures, women die only to motivate the heroes' revenge sprees. If – like Angela Mao Ying, Pam Grier or Tamara Dobson – they are elevated to the hero role, they function as simple reversals of Bruce Lee or Richard Roundtree, kungfu-kicking or gun-totin' pseudo-men. Psycho movies contain plenty of bimbos, but the better entries in the cycle spotlight female presences as strong and interesting as Jamie Lee Curtis, Carol Kane, Linda

Hamilton, Meg Tilly and Nancy Allen. Invariably, the female lead is top-billed and locked in conflict with the male killer, who is frequently overcome by her gutsiness and resourcefulness with little help from any cops, boyfriends or male sidekicks who happen to be cluttering up the supporting cast.

Halloween is the perfect machine movie. Its only message is 'boo!' and, seen in the cinema for the first time, with a receptive audience, it really works. It's sort of silly, full of seat-clutching scare moments, and, most of all, fun. Carpenter has distilled the essence of what a drive-in audience wants from a no-think horror movie and served it up in a triple portion without the trimmings. Michael Myers is a psycho. He has no deep mother-hating motivations, he just enjoys frightening people. On Hallowe'en night, Michael busts out of the nut house and heads for Haddonfield, Illinois, where, as a precocious pre-teen, he once murdered his babysitting sister. Dr Loomis (Donald Pleasence), Michael's slightly cracked shrink, sets off on a one-man crusade to stop his former charge from killing again. Once Michael gets home, he scares a lot of passers-by, kills three high-school kids, and relentlessly tries to kill Laurie Strode (Jamie Lee Curtis). The situation is all that matters; plot inconsistencies are blithely glossed over with a few snappy put-downs (when the sheriff reasons that a man who has been institutionalised since he was 5 years old shouldn't be able to drive a car, Loomis replies 'he was doing a pretty good job of it last night' and lets the loose-end drop), characterisations are purely functional (although Curtis, P.J. Soles, and, particularly, Nancy Loomis, are among the most convincing teens in the cinema), and nothing, but nothing, is allowed to get in the way of the next hand-through-the-window scare.

Carpenter is by no means an unsophisticated film-maker. He gives the film an eerie Jack O'Lantern mood and a terrific pace that defuse all objections on the grounds of logic. *Halloween* seems to be set in a conventional, realistic small town, but actually it takes place in a poetic fantasy world somewhere between the 'B' picture and the fairytale, where different natural laws obtain.

The nearest the film comes to an idea is the metamorphosis of Michael into the Shape, an unkillable incarnation of the darkest of all childhood myths, the boogey man. The boogey man doesn't have to make sense, all he has to do is be scary. Just as Carpenter is less cruel to his high-school girls than Brian DePalma (in *Carrie*, P.J. Soles is an absolute bitch, but in *Halloween* she is merely kittenish), he is less cruel to his audience. DePalma has no compunction about callously killing his cast off, but Carpenter insists the boogey man can't really hurt Jamie Lee Curtis. After all, she is the heroine of a horror film, and the genre owes her family a favour after the way it let her mother, Janet Leigh, slip unexpectedly into the *Psycho* swamp. Carpenter's most favoured scare trick has something leap out of the corner of the frame, a jolting effect that also serves as a reminder that this is, after all, only a movie. Although Michael survives the fade-out, the film implies that the horror isn't serious.

In itself, *Halloween* is fine. Few horror films are as well made or as inoffensive. It's somehow reassuring to chuckle at Pleasence's mock-serious blather about the absolute incarnation of Evil, and because the tension is so powerfully built up, the final release is that much more relieving. William Castle, producer-director-showman of, among others, *The House on Haunted Hill* and *I Saw What You Did*, proved there was a case for the 'fun' horror movie. His output was distinguished by the loving use of cheap shocks, half-satirical spooky settings, and a plethora of publicity stunts. With *Halloween*, Irwin Yablans, John Carpenter and line producer Debra Hill revived this harmless tradition. Then came *Friday the 13th* (1980), and psycho movies started to go nastily wrong.

Sam Goldwyn once said 'what we need are some brand new clichés'. *Halloween* provided *Friday the 13th*, and the subsequent flood of imitations, with a set of ready-made conventions that immediately became as predictable and ritualised as the plots of ladies' magazine romances. Usually, a significant date is referred to in the title, marking some past atrocity that will be replayed in the present. *Prom Night* (1980), *My Bloody*

Valentine (1981), *Happy Birthday to Me* (1981), *Mother's Day, Hell Night, Graduation Day* (1981), *New Year's Evil* (1982), *Silent Night, Deadly Night* (1984), *Home, Sweet Home* (1985) – about a Thanksgiving killer – and two competing *April Fools' Day* movies leave very little of the calendar unused, unless any enterprising producers would care to have a stab at *Burns Night* or *The Bank Holiday Monday Massacre*. (It has been suggested that the failure of the small-town drama *Independence Day* (1983) was due to the fact that people mistook it for a cheap slasher, which may be why it eventually got retitled *Follow Your Dreams*.) The chief stylistic flourish is the use of the subjective camera to stand in for the lurking killer, often encouraging the audience to share the psycho's voyeurism, but sometimes to disguise his identity in preparation for a surprise ending most cinemagoers will be able to guess in reel 2. If you can't spot the 'mystery' murderers in *The Toolbox Murders* (1978), *Mil Gritos Tiene la Noche* (*Pieces*) (1981) or *The Prowler* (1981), you should turn in your deerstalker and magnifying glass at the popcorn concession and go home.

The victims are invariably a parade of dumb American kids, marked for death by predilections for drink, soft drugs, stupid practical jokes and giggly making-out. The casting department draws on the pool of adolescent types employed in the rash of post-*National Lampoon's Animal House* teenage farces. *Friday the 13th*, with its doomed Summer Camp counsellors, is basically *Meatballs* with red meat, and the group of stoned kids playing 'Strip Monopoly' would certainly not be out of place in a *Porky's* sequel. The narrative usually depends heavily upon the Idiot Plot, a device occasionally featured in big-budget horrors like *Alien* or *Predator*, but more at home in the *Friday the 13th* end of the market. The Idiot Plot demands that, in order to build up suspense and justify the horror sequences, all the characters act like idiots. *Halloween* shrewdly justifies its absurdities with engaging cheek, but *Friday the 13th* is full of people wandering off into the darkness on the lookout for a nice, secluded spot where the killer can polish them off. While the suggestion that the

subjective camera encourages the audience to gloat over the characters' deaths is debatable, it is true one tends to feel anyone who decides to take a midnight stroll down by the lake, after Crazy Ralph has told them what to expect and half their friends have disappeared only to turn up again as colourfully butchered carcases, deserves the consequences. Audiences subjected to these films will yield more groans as airhead teens do stupid things than screams of terror as they get hacked to death.

Friday the 13th is a jackdaw of a film, it steals not only from *Halloween*, but also from *Jaws*, *Carrie* and, most problematically, the superficially similar *Texas Chainsaw* school of splatter. John Carpenter doesn't spill a drop of blood. He doesn't have to; his film succeeds through suspense and atmosphere, not through the comparatively few scenes of actual violence. Michael Myers seems to enjoy scaring people more than killing them. However, *Friday the 13th*'s Sean S. Cunningham, and most of his followers, aren't talented enough to direct a hosepipe. They can't scare with good film-making, so they batter the viewer with a stream of explicit, blood-drenched slayings. Scripts may be uninspired, but a range of invention is shown in finding murderous uses for a variety of kitchen, garden and workbench implements. 'John will never eat shish-kebab again', cackles the poster for *Happy Birthday to Me*, a movie whose selling points are 'the six most bizarre murders you will ever see'. Also memorable are the nail guns of *The Toolbox Murders* and *Nail Gun Massacre* (1987), the power drills of *The Driller Killer* and *The Slumber Party Massacre*, the miner's pick of *My Bloody Valentine*, the garden shears of *The Burning*, the pitchfork of *Friday the 13th , Part 2* (1981) and *The Slayer* (1981), the kiddie-toy bows and arrows of *Bloody Birthday, Sleepaway Camp* and *Five Corners* (1987), the bayonet of *The Prowler*, and the first-aid kits employed by the villains of *X-Ray* (1981), *Visiting Hours* (1982), *Terminal Choice* (1985) and the disappointingly nasty *Halloween II* (1981). The pumpkin-masked lawnmower murderer of the skit *Wacko!* (1981) would have been a lot funnier if it hadn't been done for real in *The Love Butcher*. During the 1930s craze for Busby Berkeley's insane flesh kaleidoscopes, it was suggested that a suitable theme song for mothers of film-struck daughters might be 'I Didn't Raise My Girl to be a Human Harp'. Today's advances in special effects make-up mean that young actresses have to go through a lot worse to pay the rent.

Friday the 13th was released in Britain on Friday the 13th, in June 1980. Oddly, Paramount overlooked the obvious and let it out a month earlier in the US. Part of the controversy that surrounded the film arose because it was distributed by a major studio rather than one of the usual exploitation outfits. It was a runaway success ($17,113,000 on the *Variety* scale), and , that autumn saw the British releases of a plague of similar slaughterhouses: *When a Stranger Calls, Terror Train, Don't Go Into the House* (1979), *Don't Answer the Phone, Prom Night, Silent Scream* (1980) and *He Knows You're Alone*. The Yorkshire Ripper was still at large, and a psycho who kills women seemed a lot less like a good idea for a 'fun' movie than it had at the time of *Halloween*. Feminist groups organised a nationwide protest, singling out Brian DePalma's accomplished but heartless *Dressed to Kill* and a double billing of *When a Stranger Calls* with *Humanoids From the Deep*. Ironically, the most offensive of the bunch, *Humanoids*, in which naked girls are clawed and raped by scaly monsters, was directed by a woman, Barbara Peeters, although she claims producer Roger Corman cut in all the tits and gore without telling her. Red paint was splattered across screens. Suddenly, trash movies were an issue.

He Knows You're Alone (1980), a fair-to-mediocre thriller that would have been lucky to get a slot at the bottom of a grindhouse double bill in any other year, benefited in 1980 from a major release and saturation publicity. The film opens with a sequence set in a cinema. Two young girls are watching a psycho movie. One girl is upset and refuses to look at the screen during a scary murder scene; the other takes a delight in the stalking of the heroine, continually chortling 'she's gonna get it now!' The sadistic horror film fan is dumpy and unattractive, while her squeamish friend is a willowy blonde. The sensitive girl is stabbed to death by a psycho in the audience. The other girl stops laughing at the movie violence, and screams in real terror. The reason for the inclusion of this scene is that it allows director Armand Mastroianni to kick the film off with an arbitrary horror sequence and then pull back to reveal it's only a movie, neatly putting the audience off balance. The reactions of the characters show that Mastroianni is at least aware of the debate surrounding the ethics of the psycho movie. However, a crucial issue is dodged by making the death-loving voyeur a woman motivated by female envy, rather than a man identifying with the male killer out of sexual hostility, and the film smugly justifies itself by reassuring us that, while we might relish safely unreal horrors, we would be as shocked as the surviving girl if faced with a genuine murder. The director has continued his nothing-in-particular career with slicker movies – *The Killing Hour* (1982), *The Supernaturals* (1986), *Cameron's Closet* (1987) – that lack even the occasional scariness of his début feature.

The most popular wellspring for movie psychosis is twisted sex, from gay Bruno (Robert Walker) in *Strangers on a Train* and oedipal Norman (Anthony Perkins) in *Psycho* onwards. In *Halloween, Friday the 13th* and *Dressed to Kill*, the psycho murders anyone who gets laid, while, in *The Centerfold Girls, Don't Answer the Phone, Eyes of a Stranger, Angel* and *The Majorettes*, Jack the Ripper-types pick on pin-ups, prostitutes, nude dancers, models, cheerleaders and other sexual surrogates. But the psycho movie's puritanism is not as simple as it seems. Michael Myers kills four promiscuous teenagers, three girls and a boy. Laurie, the one virgin in the group, escapes, but crucially Michael was after her all the time. The implication is not that he doesn't want to kill 'nice' girls, but that the heroine's purity is a defence against Evil in an almost mystic sense. Other films have even more bizarre anti-sex motivations – the *Friday the 13th* killer is actually a woman, Mrs Voorhees (Betsy Palmer), avenging the death of her retarded son

● John DiSanti, Jennifer Jason Leigh. **Eyes of a Stranger.**

by slaughtering the kind of camp counsellors who were too busy having sex to notice the kid drowning. (Incredibly, in the sequels, the killer is Jason, the supposedly drowned mongoloid, avenging the death of his mother at the hands of the heroine of the first film.) The *He Knows You're Alone* psycho was jilted at the altar, and so picks mainly on brides, although he is not above killing the tailor who makes the wedding dresses and a few bridesmaids to underline the core of his neuroses. *My Bloody Valentine* and *The Prowler* both revolve around social affairs suspended for many years because of a past tragedy. When the respective towns decide it's time to have a Valentine's Day dance or a graduation ball again, the killings start anew. In these films, the sex keeps a comparatively low profile, and the killer is triggered off by the trappings of *romance* – paper hearts, ball gowns, dance music, *billets doux* and sighing sentiment.

Gender confusion is a particularly popular psycho kink, again going all the way back to Norman Bates. In a deliberate attempt to outdo *Psycho*, William Castle made the killer in his *Homicidal!* (1961) a girl (Jean Arless) raised as a boy: she was followed by the rock star monster of *Beyond the Valley of the Dolls*, the mad slasher of *Private Parts* and the narrator of Iain Banks's novel *The Wasp Factory*, while boy-raised-as-girl psychos feature in *A Reflection of Fear* (1971), *Deadly Blessing*, *Sleepaway Camp* – not to mention the last named's back-to-back sequels *Sleepaway Camp 2: Unhappy Campers* (1988) and *Sleepaway Camp 3: Teenage Wasteland* (1988) – and *Unhinged* (1982). In a related vein, we have Tom Berenger as a gay singles bar murderer in *Looking for Mr Goodbar* (1977), Richard Cox as a gay leather bar murderer in *Cruising* (1980), Michael Caine as a would-be transsexual slasher in *Dressed to Kill* and Sally Kirkland as an actual transsexual slasher in *Fatal Games* (1983). In the spoof *Pandemonium*, Tab Hunter is a football hero who murders cheerleaders because he was never allowed to be one. Surprisingly, there has never been an organised gay protest against the sub-genre – although the New York opening of *Cruising* was picketed by

local homosexual activists and the NYPD in protest at the way William Friedkin depicted them in the film – for the prevailing attitude towards any kind of deviation from the hetero norm is consistently hysterical, ill-informed and ridiculous.

It's too much to ask trash to be consistent in anything. If screenwriters cannot come up with plots that make sense above the slice 'n' dice level, how can they be expected to have a coherent ideology? Films like *The Toolbox Murders* and *Friday the 13th, Part 2*, which expose teenage female flesh and then carve it up, are sexist in a particularly unpleasant way. But the nasty sexism of the psycho movie co-exists with a vein of equally nasty feminism. The image of Woman varies from the submissive bubbleheads and tawdry hookers (unliberated types who pander to masculine fantasies) who fall victim, to the ivory tower princesses and self-motivated career girls (independent, assertive, positive female role models) who turn the tables and survive. In *Eyes of a Stranger* (1981), a *Cosmopolitan* fantasy lady breadwinner (Lauren Tewes) discovers the identity of the male psycho and sets about persecuting him with anonymous telephone calls and midnight prowls around his apartment. For a while, he strikes back by terrorising her blind sister (Jennifer Jason Leigh), but at the finish the two girls blast the killer out of the window with a handy magnum. The wimp hero turns up just too late to be of any use. The film endorses female violence against men. Murder in self-defence has the beneficial side-effect of curing the sister's traumatic disability (see also *The Spiral Staircase*). It's not such a big step from 'get laid and die' to 'get liberated or die'.

There is a deep callousness behind these films; for the human race *in toto*, not just the female half of it. Characters are nine-pins, set up to be bloodily knocked down. We are sometimes called upon to identify with the psycho, but more often the massacres are used to justify a deplorable, lynch mob attitude to the mentally ill. In *When a Stranger Calls*, Tony Beckley is not just a walking killing machine, but a pathetic, displaced street wino trying to get back at the affluent society by bringing terror into comfortable suburbs. The fascist cop on the case (Charles Durning) is not out to send him back to the home, but to kill him in cold blood so he won't have a chance to get loose again. *When a Stranger Calls* is a shade more self-aware than most of its kind, which are better represented by the dreadful, ratty *Don't Answer the Phone* and the glossy, cheesy *Ten to Midnight* (1982). In these, liberal heroines try to sympathise with unredeemable lunatics, but change their minds when the killers come after them, and cheer on heroes who gun down the unarmed killers rather than have them cop an insanity plea. *Don't Answer the Phone* has Nicholas Worth as a father-fixated, religious fanatic, overweight, impotent, voyeurist photographer, Vietnam veteran murderer. The man has more than his share of personal problems, but the tough cop hero shoots him in the back with a valedictory sneer of 'Adios, creep!' Gene Davis in *Ten to Midnight* is a macho swine who commits his murders in the buff, Lizzie Borden-fashion, and is condemned by Charles Bronson's heartfelt 'the way the law protects these maggots, you'd think they were an endangered species'.

The secret of psycho movies, and the reason why they outlasted the mile-long-spaceship films that followed *Star Wars*, is that they're incredibly cheap to make. They have a no-name director, frequently a first-time-out-of-film-school grad who needs the work or a mildly respected figure taking refuge from recent disasters (Kenneth Hughes, J. Lee Thompson); an amateur theatrical reject cast top-lined by a promising young screamer in the Jamie Lee Curtis tradition and an old-timer who could do with the money (Glenn Ford, Cameron Mitchell, Leslie Nielsen); the kind of production values and *mise-en-scène* usually found only in underground art movies or hardcore pornography; a droning, whining score whipped up by someone musically unskilled who knows how to switch on a synthesiser; a script that borrows bits of *Halloween* and *Friday the 13th* along with 'B' movie clichés unheard since the 1930s; and editing executed with all the panache of a chainsaw turkey-carving.

All the successful psycho movie needs is a make-up man who can pop an eyeball with a reasonable amount of conviction, a basic lack of human feeling and greed. If even *Fall Break* (1984), *Splatter University* (1985) and *Girls School Screamers* (1986) can make money, then there's no reason to give up yet. Budgets are so low that a film doesn't even have to be a big success to turn in a vast profit. Given the need to use young actors, it's hardly surprising that some future names first appeared with arrows through them in psycho flicks: among the teens wiped out in the post-*Halloween* shockers, the sharp-eyed will be able to spot Mickey Rourke, Kevin Bacon, Crispin Glover, Tom Hanks, Rachel Ward, Holly Hunter, Daryl Hannah, Tanya Roberts, Elizabeth Daily, Vanity and Ally Sheedy.

Occasionally, something will accidentally go right and a half-way decent film will turn up. Roger Spottiswoode's *Terror Train* (1979) and Tom De Simone's *Hell Night* (1981) might not score much for originality, but they have been mounted with comparative luxury (manifested in an imaginatively detailed setting for their frat party slayings – an antique train and a haunted house), and capably directed by men on their way to better things: De Simone is a style-conscious porno grad, and Spottiswoode was headed, via *Under Fire* (1983), to the mainstream. The casts feature fairly talented unknowns, with a sprinkling of solidly professional old timers like Ben Johnson and Linda Blair (who, having started early, was a horror veteran when barely out of her teens). *Terror Train* boasts one of the few surprising surprise endings in the genre, and *Hell Night* has more credible college kids than most, but these programmers only look good because the psycho movie rut is so deep and muddy. Any film which is nicely acted, moderately restrained in its throat-slashing and keeps the boom microphone out of the frame looks like a classic. Even so, by the time competent pictures like *The Scaremaker* (1982), *The Initiation* (1984), *Appointment With Fear* (1985) and *Sorority House Massacre* (1986) came along, the whole genre was so predictable, boring and irritating that these well-made, well-acted, decently-characterised films seemed overwhelmingly pointless.

Psycho movies have proliferated like a school of piranha fish, taking bites out of each other until they finally coalesce into one endless film. Any stray ideas are likely to crop up all over the place at once, as film-makers imitate each other like unbalanced pod creatures from *Invasion of the Body Snatchers*, often with results about as graceful as the human-headed dog in the 1978 version. *He Knows You're Alone* ripped off *The Silent Partner* for a scene where a severed head is discovered in a fish tank. By the time of *Night School* (1981), released a scant four months later, the trope was hackneyed enough for a cop to refer to 'the old head in a fish tank bit'. Finally, in *The House on Sorority Row* (1982), the business had mutated to the extent of giving us not only a 'head in the toilet bowl' sequence, but a nightmare variation in which the bloodily severed head winks at the heroine. *Night School* actually spins the image into a whole plot, concerning Papua New Guinean headhunting rituals in Boston. Neither the best nor the worst of its type, *Night School* can claim to be the most unashamedly imitative. The splashing red paint in a shower scene turns out to be paint used in an aboriginal sex ritual – which would be a lot cleverer had the famous *Psycho* showerbath scene not already been kicked around by *High Anxiety*, *Dressed to Kill*, *The Funhouse*, *He Knows You're Alone*, *Eyes of a Stranger* and *Fade to Black*. Even more strikingly, director Kenneth Hughes restages shot-for-shot the famous stalking-in-the-park sequence from *Cat People*. And the film is a cheat – the flat-chested killer in skin-tight leathers is ultimately unmasked as busty Rachel Ward.

During the psycho movie's 1980–2 heyday some interesting directors found themselves forced into the worthless genre. Tobe Hooper's *The Funhouse*, Wes Craven's *Deadly Blessing* and Vernon Zimmerman's *Fade to Black* (1980) are more dispiriting than soulless hack works like *The Burning* because, in many scenes, talent shines through. *The Funhouse* has a marvellously garish, unsettling look, blending punk with carnival gaudiness; *Deadly Blessing* has an interesting sub-text about Ernest Borgnine's repressive religion, and features lovely images of black-clad Hittites toiling in pinkish wheat fields; and *Fade to Black* cleverly inverts the movie-consciousness of its rivals by constructing a rickety story around a film buff murderer (Dennis Christopher) who dresses up as film fantasy figures (Hopalong Cassidy, the Mummy, Richard Widmark, Dracula, Laurence Olivier) to eliminate his enemies. The films have endearing, well-played characters but, every ten minutes or so, are compelled to get back to the business of killing them off. In contrast, the real rubbish only comes alive when drawing blood: make-up artist Tom Savini (death-man on *Friday the 13th*, *Maniac*, *Eyes of a Stranger*, *The Prowler*, *Alone in the Dark* and *Friday the 13th – The Final Chapter*) insists on having control over the staging of the shots in which his gore effects appear, and he is a better film-maker than the clods who string the murders together.

While the North American psycho flick was descending to rehashes like *Humungous* (1982), an acromegalic-on-an-island opus, and *Unhinged*, a sickle-slicker slasher so inept that the clapperboard can twice be discerned in the grey murk during a slow fade, New Zealand came up with a series of oddities which tangentially relate to the trend if only because they are otherwise unclassifiable. Sam Pillsbury's *The Scarecrow* (1981) seems to be a sensitive study of adolescent trauma in a 1950s small town, rich in well-observed eccentricity, but gaunt John Carradine wanders through the anecdotes as a murderous magician who is untidily disposed of in a double-take flashback near the end. Slightly more approachable is Tony Williams's *Next of Kin* (1982), whose heroine inherits an old peoples' home full of crotchety characters who tend to turn up drowned in the bath. *The Lost Tribe* (1983), a tale of identity shifts between an anthropologist and his twin brother, uniquely makes use of its remote New Zealand Setting; *Mr Wrong* (1984), from a story by Elizabeth Jane Howard, has a car haunted by the spirit of a murdered girl trying to protect her killer's next would-be victim; and *Trial Run* (1984) has an independent lady jogger terrorised by her own son for neglecting her family. There was also an odd rash of Australian psycho films – *Snap-Shot* (1979), *Nightmares* (1980), *Early Frost* (1981), *Lady, Stay Dead* (1982) – all of which lack a certain urgency. Jack Fisk's Stateside *Raggedy Man* (1981) is similar in its aimless tone, the story of a menaced telephonist in 1941 Texas, helped by Fisk's pretty-pretty Americana and Sissy Spacek's careful performance, but hindered by the spectre of *Halloween*.

Attendant upon the death throes of the psycho movie – which are admittedly still going on – were a handful of satires. *Bloody Birthday* (1982) and *Alone in the Dark* (1982) aren't sure whether they're supposed to be funny, but crack a few jokes to conceal threadbare plots. *Bloody Birthday* concerns three children, born without souls during an eclipse, who spend their tenth birthday murdering anyone they don't particularly like. *Alone in the Dark* has Jack Palance, Martin Landau and gigantic Erland Van Lidth escaping from libertarian Donald Pleasence's funny farm during a power cut, and terrorising the family of a doctor they don't particularly like. The nicely titled *Student Bodies* (1982), Alfred Sole's *Pandemonium*, *Saturday the 14th* (1982), *National Lampoon's Class Reunion* (1982) and *Wacko!* are broader parodies that largely fall flat, despite the genre's obvious potential for sending up. Nevertheless, anyone who has felt compelled to sit through as many *Friday the 13th* clones as I have can't help but chuckle at the way Sole spoofs the Canadian-shot but American-set psycho movie by having a Royal Canadian Mounted Policeman in full uniform investigate a series of murders in a US small town, or the sneering dialogue of *Wacko!*, in which a supporting character whines 'so this is the obligatory cast-suspicion-on-the-perverted-gardener scene?'

Amy Jones's *The Slumber Party Massacre* (1982), Roger Corman's uncharacteristically tardy entry in the psycho stakes, is a cheap, funny pastiche of the genre, worthwhile for the breathtakingly blatant symbolism of the scene in which the neon-eyed psycho gets his drill-bit lopped off by an enraged co-ed. Written by feminist Rita Mae Brown with

only vestigial socially redeeming content, the film features such sick jokes as a girl asking the psycho, who is disguised as a pizza delivery boy, 'what's the damage?' only to be told 'Six, so far!' *Slumber Party Massacre 2* (1987) is an inevitable disappointment despite its psycho, a rock star with a power drill built into his guitar. Fred Walton's *April Fools' Day* (1986) goes so far into the practical joke theme as to have *none* of its murders turn out to be the real thing, which is at once refreshingly surprising and ultimately pointless. Bill Froelich's *Return to Horror High* (1987) further deconstructs the psycho movie by being about the shooting of a film based on a real-life mass murder, in which flashbacks get mixed up with clips from the film-in-progress. An intense teenage rape scene is interrupted by a sleazy producer trying to ensure that an actress's breasts are in shot and then by the leading lady, who protests at the mistreatment of women in schlock films like this. The genre's moribundity was also displayed in *Silent Rage* (1982), which starts off as a straight psycho thriller, but rationalises its killer's *Halloween*-indestructibility with some Frankensteinian mad science, and throws in karate chopper Chuck Norris for a knock-down, drag-out finish.

Mark Rosman's *The House on Sorority Row* is perhaps the best of the formula co-ed killer pictures, thanks to a well-worked-out plot; inventively bizarre touches like having the heroine confront the murderer while under the influence of a hallucinogen and seeing the world as a Mario Bava-esque nightmare; and bits of witty Hitchcock-and-bull, like the scene in which a campus cop finds two sorority girls in bedraggled party frocks pushing a corpse-laden garbage skip across the lawn at dead of night, or a pan through a graduation party that picks out the haunted faces of the guilty girls amid the revellers. Nick Castle's *TAG: The Assassination Game* (1982) amusingly extrapolates the student psycho craze into a popular college pastime, staging elaborate duels with rubber arrow guns, that gets out of hand. Castle, who plays the Shape in *Halloween*, spoofs not only the psycho films but superspy supercools as well, in the figure of Bruce Abbott, an unshaven

● *Window of the soul.* Anthony Perkins, **Psycho II.**

slob who becomes more presentable with each killing, transforming from Travis Bickle into Napoleon Solo (the same material is played boringly straight as an in-the-woods townies-vs-mutants picture, *The Zero Boys*, 1986, by Greece's own splatter specialist, Niko Mastorakis). Robert Vincent O'Neill's *Angel* (1983), set among Hollywood Boulevard's weirdos, mercilessly mocks its traditional murderer, who is forced to disguise himself as a bald, robed *hare krishna*, tries to vent his macho hostility upon a woman only to find he's menacing a transvestite, and finally runs screaming with a 14-year-old gun-waving hooker in hot pursuit.

Obviously, the psycho movie soon became viable only if linked to some other gimmick. In 1982, the owners of *Halloween* and *Friday the 13th* had to offer more than a rehashed plot to make second generation sequels to their gold mines. Tommy Lee Wallace's *Halloween III: Season of the Witch* refrains from giving us 'still more of the night HE came home' and ditches all the characters and situations from the original in favour of a completely new storyline, devised by the uncredited Nigel Kneale. Celtic toymaker Conal Cochran (Dan O'Herlihy) plans to revive the pagan significance of All Hallows' Eve by playing a vast sick joke on the hordes of brats who defame the ancient holiday by dressing up in dumb costumes and begging for sweets. His scheme involves mass-produced masks that contain slivers of a stolen Stonehenge monolith, and an insidious television signal which will turn any childish head inside a Silver Shamrock novelty hood into a writhing pile of snakes, bugs and worms (heh heh heh). While O'Herlihy and his evil plot are great fun, the film perhaps has too many redundant borrowings from *Invasion of the Body Snatchers* to capitalise on the originality of the concept. *Friday the 13th, Part III* has even less in the way of plot and characters than the first two instalments, and lacks whatever tension and horror they could muster. However, it is in eyeball-bursting 3-D. Splat!

Of course, the ultimate psycho-sequel is *Psycho II* (1983), a twenty-two-years-after job which cunningly cuts up and reassembles the key images of Hitchcock's seminal movie in the service of screenwriter Tom Holland's unusually clever and convoluted plot. Norman Bates (Anthony Perkins) is judged sane and released, despite the protest petitions of Leila Loomis (Vera Miles), a survivor of the original film, the sister of murdered Marion. Norman returns to the dilapidated Bates Motel, puritanically fires the manager (Dennis Franz), who has been getting the place a reputation with the sex 'n' drugs crowd, and tries to make a life for himself in the real world. Richard Franklin, director of the loosely Hitchcockian *Road Games* (1981), swoops over the familiar Universal backlot with his Louma crane, and plays perplexing games with taken-for-granted images like Meg Tilly's shower, the pinprick hole in the bathroom wall, and the crossed hands sculpture. Perkins's Norman is again the most humane and sympathetic character in the film, but this time he is also a persecuted hero trying to cling to his precious, dearly earned sanity despite several plots against him and the nagging suspicion that his murdering mother might be alive and watching over him. The devilish finale brings the story, and the whole psycho genre, full circle, with Norman's dead mother in her rocking chair, and the Bates Motel reopening for business. Sadly, Universal could not leave well enough alone. They had Perkins himself direct (very well) *Psycho III* (1986) from a much less satisfactory storyline – with only the romance between Norman and a nervous nun (Diana Scarwid) to recommend it – and then turned out a TV pilot *Bates Motel* (1987), with Bud Cort as the new proprietor, which resembles nothing so much as a horror redressing for *Fantasy Island* or *The Love Boat*.

The leanest of the post-*Halloween* psycho pictures is Robert Harmon's *The Hitcher* (1986), which distils modern myths of the dangers of long-distance driving, the perils faced by big-city boys in the boondocks and the strangers who shouldn't be given a lift. 'My mother told me never to do this', sleepy teenage motorist C. Thomas Howell admits as he invites Rutger Hauer into his car one rainy night. The driver realises his mistake as soon as his passenger produces a switchblade and makes conversational openings like 'have you ever wondered just how much blood comes out of a burst eyeball?' The hero gets rid of the hitcher with deceptive ease, but soon finds himself pursued by the motiveless psychopath – who frames him for multiple murder, puts severed fingers in his portion of fries and kills off anyone who makes a move to help him. 'Why are you doing this?' Howell asks. 'You figure it out', the Hitcher replies. Hauer is a far more interesting reading of the psycho-as-monster figure than the Shape or Jason, in that he has cruel dialogue to go along with his horrififc deeds. We see the Hitcher's face, but he remains as beyond our understanding as any supernatural force. Towards the end, Harmon gets a little too heavy-handed about the relationship between hero and villain, but while he is concentrating on irrational violence on lonely roads his deceptively simple film works on as many levels as the Road Runner cartoons of which it's so weirdly reminiscent.

While the *Halloween* series suspended trading after three outings – there have been various proposals by Debra Hill, John Carpenter, Dennis Etchison and Moustapha Akkad for a *Halloween IV*, and Akkad finally got it into production in 1988 – the *Friday the 13th* saga has ground on well beyond the death or transmutation of the rest of the sub-genre. After the 3-D outing, which is only memorable for adding the now-trademark hockey mask to the mad Jason's outfit, Tom Savini was brought back to pour on the ketchup for the promisingly titled *Friday the 13th – The Final Chapter* (1984), in which 12-year-old Tommy Jarvis (Corey Feldman) finally kills the previously invulnerable Jason with an apparently irreversible machete to the head. However, the film was successful enough to excite Paramount's Cupidity Circuits, and an excuse was whipped up for *Friday the 13th , Part V – A New Beginning* (1985) in which the teenaged Tommy (John Shepherd) is still institutionalised after his traumatic brush with Jason and a new killer impersonates the dead psycho superstar to no good effect. Not only was the film down to the level of the rest of the series, but the legions of nutcase Jason fans called

for their hero's return from the grave. By now, the mad-killer-as-monster concept had been done completely into the ground, and one or two movies like *The Slayer* and *One Dark Night* were experimenting with more interesting, supernaturally flavoured slashers. Thus, in *Friday the 13th , Part VI – Jason Lives!* (1986), the much-abused Tommy (Thom Matthews) exhumes Jason to make sure the bastard is still dead. Lightning strikes the rotted corpse and Jason is soon up and killing as an honest-to-God zombie. *Friday the 13th* was then used as a blanket title for a series of trashy TV horror items shot in Canada (surprisingly, David Cronenberg directed one episode, 'Faith Healer'), linked by an antique-shop setting out of Amicus's *From Beyond the Grave*, but Jason seems set to go on splattering the big screen for ever. Some people at Paramount have even been heard muttering that it would be a good idea to make *thirteen Friday the 13th* movies: not bad for a series that run out of ideas one and a half reels into the original film.

Jason's reincarnation as a supernatural creature probably has something to do with the success of rival psycho Freddy Krueger (Robert Englund), a child murderer who lives on in the dreams of the children of the lynch mob who burned him to death. Freddy made his debut in Wes Craven's *A Nightmare on Elm Street*, and was responsible for the resurrection of the just-petered-out psycho trend. Like *Halloween*, *A Nightmare on Elm Street* is a well-crafted, scary movie set in a Middle American teenage milieu that happened to click with the movie-going public. It has a witty, resourceful heroine in Heather Langenkamp (at one point during her ordeal, she looks into a mirror and remarks 'God, I look 20 years old!'), some Donald Pleasence-style comfortably familiar hamming from John Saxon and Ronee Blakely as her parents, a wonderfully menacing, lewd and horror-comic villain in Freddy, and a whole barrel of the tricky is-it-a-dream-or-isn't-it sequences Craven had used to good effect in his earlier movies. If it finally seems a less satisfying film than *Halloween*, it may be because its interplay between dream and reality entails a lot of off-and-on mood

● *Heeeeere's Freddy!* Robert Englund, **A Nightmare on Elm Street, Part 2: Freddy's Revenge.**

reversals that doesn't work up the cumulative suspense of Carpenter's film.

Uniquely in the psycho field, Freddy Krueger is a monster with a personality to go with his trademarks (a clawed gardening glove, a battered hat, a stripey jersey and a fried face): the actors who created the roles of Leatherface, Michael Myers and Jason haven't returned in the sequels, but only Englund could play Freddy. He has been back in the disappointing, unusually gay-themed *A Nightmare on Elm Street Part 2 – Freddy's Revenge* (1985), directed by Jack Sholder of *Alone in the Dark*, and the flamboyant, effects-laden, three-ring circus *A Nightmare on Elm Street , Part 3 – Dream Warriors* (1987), directed by Chuck Russell with most of the surviving cast of the original film and some story imput from Craven. The *Elm Street* films use the dream theme to have fun with surreal images of the sort sometimes found on comic book covers – the clawed hand coming out of the bath, the telephone receiver with a tongue, the monster leaning out of a wall in *A Nightmare on Elm Street*, or the old-dark-house-of-the-psyche finale of *Dream Warriors* which seems to take place inside Freddy's head. The series typifies the horror film of the 1980s – obsessed with make-up effects, loaded down with crowd-pleasing humour, fundamentally safe and silly – and a comparison with Craven's earlier works suggests the decade has fostered an unfortunate tendency to settle for less. The dream theme, however, has become a psycho commonplace thanks to Freddy; in 1988, *The Dream Demon, Dream Invaders, Bad Dreams* and *Deadly Dreams* were all announced or in production.

The basic situation of *Halloween* – a girl on her own and a menacing older man – turns up again in the powerful finale of Joyce Chopra's *Smooth Talk* (1985), an adaption of Joyce Carol Oates's unforgettably scary short story 'Where Are You Going, Where Have You Been?' Here, there are no psycho slashings and no horror movie paraphernalia to get in the way of the strange relationship between awkward, frankly rather irritating 15-year-old Connie (Laura Dern) and the smooth-talking, coolly shaded Arnold Friend (Treat Williams). Left alone one Sunday afternoon by her family, Connie opens the door to find Arnold waiting, and he launches into an astonishing tirade – seductive, cajoling, threatening, sinister, funny – designed to get her into his streamlined car. He wants her to go for a ride with him, a euphemism that betokens a whole range of sexual, violent and mystical possibilities the story (and the film) wisely leaves vague. *Smooth Talk* plays with conventions from the 1980s teenage comedy as well as the psycho picture, and the devilish Arnold Friend ('that's what I want to be to you, A. Friend'), while he doesn't have the kills Michael, Freddy, the Hitcher or Jason can notch up on their machetes, has an insidious approach to the destruction of innocence that perhaps suggests the ultimate distillation of the coming-of-age, getting-laid, getting-killed, death-of-childhood themes that run throughout the whole teenage body-count genre.

● *Crawling the walls.* JoBeth Williams, **Poltergeist.**

ghost stories

A haunted house is a special place; the laws of nature do not apply. Similarly, haunted house films defy whatever rules can be formulated to account for the rest of the horror genre. Their popularity is perennial rather than cyclical. If a *The Amityville Horror* (1979) is a big success or a *The Shining* (1980) gets a lot of publicity, there will be a trickle of similar cheapies, but never a cascade like the exorcism or psycho fads. In *Danse Macabre*, Stephen King points out that Shirley Jackson's *The Haunting of Hill House* is the only horror novel of the century to achieve unembarrassed critical acclaim, and that *The Amityville Horror* successfully appeals to an older, more conservative audience than most horror movies. In a genre often represented by the likes of *Vampire Hookers* (1979) or *Sorority Babes in the Slime Ball Bowl-a-Rama* (1987), and where even outstanding works are triumphs of excess rather than restraint, a house which is merely haunted seems almost respectable.

It is essential that a haunted house should have a Past, and the history of the sub-genre stretches back beyond the cinema to the Victorian ghost story and the eighteenth-century gothic novel. Whenever a mainstream author decides on horror, he is likely to be drawn to the semi-respectable ghost story (Kingsley Amis's *The Green Man*, Paul Theroux's *The Black House*, Susan Hill's *The Woman in Black*). Consequently, haunted house films are more tied up with literature than most horror movies. *Alien* or *Scanners* may turn up as paperback novelisations, but the books don't work. The subjects have been conceived solely in terms of cinematic as opposed to literary effects. Ghost stories sell better as books than as films, but the years since *Rosemary's Baby* have seen adaptions of prose hauntings by Thomas Tryon (*The Other*, 1972), Daphne du Maurier (*Don't Look Now*, 1973), Richard Matheson (*The Legend of Hell House*, 1974), Max Ehrlich (*The Reincarnation of Peter Proud*, 1975), Robert Marasco (*Burnt Offerings*, 1976), Roland Topor (*Le Locataire* (*The Tenant*), 1976), Peter Straub (*Full Circle*, 1976; *Ghost Story*, 1981), Jeffrey Konvitz (*The Sentinel*, 1977), James Herbert (*The Survivor*, 1980), and Stephen King (*The Shining*); plus a few stabs at the it's-all-true authenticated case histories of Frank DeFelitta (*Audrey Rose*, 1977; *The Entity*, 1982) and Jay Anson (*The Amityville Horror*). The books and films are of variable quality, from du Maurier to Konvitz and from Stanley Kubrick to Michael Winner, but they all set out to capture the mass appeal market rather than minority interest cult curiosity.

Until the 1970s, haunted house films were a once-in-a-while genre, with memorable items like *The Uninvited* (1944) materialising every so often. In 1963, Robert Wise turned Shirley Jackson's delicate masterpiece into a fine film, *The Haunting*, but the ghost story lay dormant for a decade, existing only as a sub-text for Devil movies. *Rosemary's Baby* gains a lot from the sinister characterisation of the Bramford, the New York brownstone into which the Woodhouses move. There is no ghost, except the angry shade of Beethoven invoked by the unseen pianist's stumbling attempts to get through *Für Elise*, but the Bramford does have a Past. Ira Levin refined the parallel plot, a device that has been used in most subsequent haunted house films. While the protagonist is being overwhelmed by the supernatural forces clinging to his/her new home, he/she does a little detective work and pieces the place's evil past together from newspaper morgues, friendly occultist know-alls, and ageing eyewitnesses. Usually, the root of the present haunting lies in some long-forgotten, unavenged wrong. In addition to its evil past, the Bramford had an evil future: John Lennon was murdered outside the house used in the film. *The Exorcist* needlessly tries to pass itself off as a haunted house film during its slow build-up. Few audiences are fooled by the poltergeist phenomena but *The Exorcist* started the haunted housing boom. It proved that best-selling horror could also be box-office horror, and its much-reproduced poster silhouetted the exorcist against the ominous facade of an old house, dark but for a ghostly light in one window.

One of Steven Spielberg's earliest assignments was *Something Evil* (1971), a CBS Movie of the Week. Sandy Dennis, Darren McGavin and their young son move into their ideal home, an old ranch. Slow-motion flashbacks, supernatural winds and whiskery old-timer Jeff Corey muttering convince the family the place is haunted. Friendly occultist know-all Ralph Bellamy confirms the diagnosis. The parallel plot comes into play as the parents investigate the evil past while the son is possessed by a malevolent ghost. For a TV movie, *Something Evil* is excellent. Idiosyncracies in dialogue, performance and direction bring to life a storyline which is as bland as can be expected from a medium which institutionalises mediocrity. Good horror is rare on network television. The scarier it is, the more likely it is to make the ungripped half of the population switch to another channel and take in some other sponsor's commercials. Even the best made-for-TV horrors, *Duel* and *The*

Night Stalker, are tense and witty, not frightening and disturbing. TV haunted houses are rather familiar, comforting places. In *The House That Wouldn't Die* (1970), *Crowhaven Farm* (1970), *She Waits* (1971), *Don't Be Afraid of the Dark* (1973), *The Strange and Deadly Occurrence* (1974), *This House Possessed* (1981), *Don't Go to Sleep* (1982) and *Cry for the Strangers* (1982), there are plenty of secrets, but few surprises.

There are also batches of hero-with-ESP-gets-into-dull-plot (*Daughter of the Mind*, 1969; *Baffled!*, 1972, *Visions . . .*, 1972; *The Eyes of Charles Sand*, 1972; *Mind Over Murder*, 1979) and psychic-investigator-vs-witchiness (*Sweet, Sweet Rachel*, 1971; *Conspiracy of Terror*, 1975; *The Norliss Tapes*; *Good Against Evil*; *Curse of the Black Widow*; and even episodes of *McMillan and Wife* and *Starsky and Hutch*) TV movies with barely a shudder between them. Discerning TV buffs might find more to interest them in Paul Wendkos's *Fear No Evil* and Robert Day's *Ritual of Evil* (1970): Louis Jourdan plays Dr David Sorel, a suave para-psychologist who gets involved in better mysteries than usual. Plans to spin Sorel off into a series called *Bedevilled* never came to anything, which was probably just as well considering what happened to his colleague, Carl Kolchak. Occasionally, television has varied the haunting by having an evil force curse an aeroplane (*Sole Survivor*, 1969; *The Horror at 37,000 Feet*, 1973; *The Ghost of Flight 401*, 1977) or a pleasure boat (*Cruise into Terror*, 1977) with silly results. *The Horror at 37,000 Feet* has Captain Chuck Connors's plane halted in mid-air when Roy Thinnes tries to export an ancient Druid stone to America. Tammy Grimes, Buddy Ebsen, Jane Merrow and Lyn Loring are also on the passenger list, with William Shatner as an alcoholic priest who is losing his faith. Unfortunately, the promising blend of disaster soap opera and Lovecraftian lore is let down by some exceedingly boring manifestations (the usual strong winds, indoor fog and Latin chants). *Cruise into Terror* is much the same, with Ray Milland, Christopher George, Lynda Day George and Hugh O'Brian becalmed off the Gulf of Mexico under the evil influence of a breathing sarcophagus. John Forsythe, an alcoholic priest who is losing his faith, reveals that the sarcophagus contains the 2,000-year-old Son of Satan, who has already destroyed two civilisations (ancient Egypt and the Mayans) and is limbering up for his third.

While the very best US TV horror movies aspire to the big screen, the medium does sometimes turn out off-beat ghost stories that work within its climax-every-twelve-minutes, no-sex-no-violence-no-controversy limits. *Black Noon* (1971) has the same old faces (Roy Thinnes, Lyn Loring, Ray Milland) but for once turns up an interesting, perverse plot. Preacher Thinnes moves to a Western township in the 1880s to build a church, and is sacrificed to the Devil by the locals, who prove to be the ghosts of the Salem witches. The project reads like a combination of *Bonanza*, *Crowhaven Farm* and *The Wicker Man*, but director Bernard L. Kowalski and writer Andrew J. Fenady play the film like a double-edged game of cowboys. In preparation for the sacrifice, Thinnes must be corrupted and this is accomplished by luring him into an archetypal Western scenario. To save the heroine (Yvette Mimieux in flowing white) for whom he has adulterous desires, Thinnes must kill a tyrannical gunslinger (Henry Silva in black leather). Thus tainted by lust and blood, he is fit to be hanged upside-down in his newly built, burning church.

British TV is sometimes less restrained that its American counterpart when it comes to terrifying people, and one of the key ghost stories of the 1970s is the BBC's *The Stone Tape* (1972), brilliantly written by Nigel Kneale and outstandingly directed by Peter Sasdy. When an electronics company buys a haunted house in order to turn it into a research laboratory, the head of the team (Michael Bryant) decides to investigate the haunting with the aid of all the high-tech equipment at his disposal. They are supposed to be developing a new recording medium, and it seems as if the stones of the old house, which 'playback' the death of a Victorian servant girl, might function as such. The play elaborates on the scientific/supernatural concerns of Kneale's serial, *Quatermass and the Pit* (1959) and prefigures *Legend of Hell House*,

Poltergeist and *Prince of Darkness* in its opposition of a group of well-equipped, scientific ghostbusters and a monstrously irrational haunting. The experiment starts out in a light-hearted manner, but the manifestations turn out to be more serious and dangerous than they seem. Mixing film and videotape, Sasdy creates a genuinely unsettling atmosphere in the haunted room, and, coaxing high-strung performances from a strong cast, plays up every nuance of Kneale's typically subtle, detailed script. Finally, the ghost is wiped off the stone tape, but that only serves to bring the monstrous primeval spirits which killed the maid in the first place to the surface and computer programmer/medium Jane Asher must die in order to suppress the ancient evil. Less influential, but equally daring and even more frightening, is Don Taylor's 'The Exorcism' (1974), an hour-long play for a series called *Dead of Night*, which has a bourgeois dinner party in a converted farmhouse afflicted by the ghosts of the starved peasant previous tenants.

The supernatural elements of *Don't Look Now* are veiled by director Nicolas Roeg's anti-literal sensibility and author Daphne du Maurier's classical fascination with doom-haunted Venice. Donald Sutherland and Julie Christie lose their daughter in a drowning accident. They retreat to Venice, where Sutherland has psychic flashes of a funeral and glimpses a small figure in a red raincoat whom he takes for his daughter's ghost. Sutherland pursues the apparition, only to be confronted by a hideous, homicidal dwarf who has been terrorising the city. The foreseen funeral is his own. Richard Loncraine's *Full Circle*, from Peter Straub's novel *Julia*, has a very similar story: Mia Farrow is murdered by the evil little girl ghost she confuses with her own dead child. Straub and Loncraine play the game with their haunted house, parallel plot, *Omen* freak accidents and Mia Farrow's Rosemary Woodhouse victim act. Roeg, however, rejects genre conventions and distorts the simple story: the fragmentation of images and Roeg's love of juxtaposing incidents distanced in narrative time make the whole film seem like one of Sutherland's incomprehensible-until-it's-too-late visions. *Don't*

Look Now is less a ghost story than a peek behind the curtain of reality that reveals a barely accessible phantom zone 'beyond the fragile geometry of space'.

Only Roeg successfully uses this elliptical approach to the supernatural. Other literary adaptions tend to be earthbound by their plots. *Legend of Hell House*, from Richard Matheson's *Hell House*, has a team of psychic investigators funded by dying millionaire Roland Culver, who wants to know by the end of the week whether or not there is life after death. The scientists move into the super-haunted house of the late Emeric Belasco – mass murderer, sadist, degenerate, diabolist, necrophile and generally not-nice person. Physicist Clive Revill trundles a huge machine into the house. It is supposed to dispel all the psychic residue and disprove the theory of personal survival beyond the grave, but it doesn't work. Roddy McDowell, a burnt-out hotshot medium, figures it all out when he realises the house likes to cripple its victims. McDowell defeats Belasco's army of spooks and confronts the mummified corpse of the old man himself, revealing that his colossal grudge against the world is a result of having being born a midget. The anticlimax is helped by the clever casting of Michael Gough, whose screen image from *Horrors of the Black Museum* to *The Corpse* corresponds exactly with what we are told of Belasco. The film is entertaining, sometimes conceptually daring, but its cool, scientific detective story mitigates against irrational fear.

Although less neatly comprehensible that *Legend of Hell House*, Dan Curtis's *Burnt Offerings* is equally strangled by its plot. Robert Marasco's compulsive characterisations and nicely ambiguous horrors are handled well in Sidney Lumet's film of his Broadway success, *Child's Play*, but rendering *Burnt Offerings* on celluloid diminishes it to a more generously budgeted version of the Made-for-TV haunted house movie. Curtis, who is best known for his TV work (*The Night Strangler*, *The Norliss Tapes*, the Jack Palance versions of *Dracula* (1972) and *The Strange Case of Dr Jekyll and Mr Hyde* (1968), the *Dark Shadows* gothic soap), can here afford Karen Black and Oliver Reed rather than

Stella Stevens and Roy Thinnes, and finds a bigger, better-designed haunted mansion for them to move into. Otherwise, the formula is the same, with Lee Harcourt Montgomery as their happy-go-lucky, pain-in-the-neck kid, and special guest star Bette Davis as Aunt Elizabeth. The family should know what to expect as soon as the infantile landlord (Burgess Meredith) tells them they can have the house for the summer at a suspiciously low rent, providing they look after an old lady on the top floor who never leaves her room.

Meredith is also one of the residents of the New York brownstone erected over the gateway to Hell in *The Sentinel*, an even more confused and confusing haunted house movie. Model Christina Raines moves in, despite the blind priest (John Carradine) on the top floor who never leaves his room. All the other tenants are dead murderers, and Raines's sleep is disturbed by her deceased dad. She slices his nose off with a breadknife. After learning that her boyfriend (Chris Sarandon) is a murderer, attempting suicide and confronting the freakshow legions of Hell, Raines is recruited by the Catholic Church (Arthur Kennedy and Ava Gardner) and given Carradine's job as Guardian of the Abyss. Director Michael Winner and novelist Jeffrey Konvitz have been blaming *The Sentinel* on each other ever since its release. Actually, they are an ideal match, executing their tasks with equal tastelessness and pretension.

Burnt Offerings and *The Sentinel* are the dregs of a genre more or less created by Roman Polanski in *Repulsion* (1965) and *Rosemary's Baby*. Polanski's *Le Locutaire* completes the circle by presenting a *Dance of the Vampires* pastiche of the post-*Rosemary's Baby* haunted house film. Carol (Catherine Deneuve) in *Repulsion* and Rosemary are both tenants. Carol is already going mad, and imagines that her London flat is persecuting her; Rosemary really is being conspired against by her Satanic neighbours and the devil-ridden apartment house she lives in. Trelkovsky (Polanski himself) is the ultimate put-upon victim. He moves into a Paris apartment vacated by the previous tenant's suicidal plunge out of the window. The building is haunted by the ghosts of Polanski's previous films – the unseen piano player from *Rosemary's Baby*, the psychotic visions from *Repulsion*, the transvestite urges from *Cul-de-Sac* (1966) – and Trelkovsky comes across as Alfred from *Dance of the Vampires* grown older and even more introverted. Trelkovsky's approach to the world is to give in to even its most unreasonable demands, but when he senses a conspiracy to force him into the dead girl's identity, he at least tries to struggle, even if he is finally driven to get himself up in her clothes and make-up and throw himself out of the window. He survives the first fall, so he drags himself back upstairs and tries again. *Le Locataire* is nastier and funnier than *Rosemary's Baby*, presenting a cartoonish nightmare world in which the merely obnoxious becomes, in the hero's eyes, actually demonic. Shelley Winters's sluttish concierge, Melvyn Douglas's senile landlord and Jo Van Fleet's spiteful neighbour are overbearing, unfair and selfish. Trelkovsky's vision gives them glowing *The Exorcist* eyeballs and flicking serpent tongues, but it is impossible to share his nightmare because he is an unsympathetic wimp, continually bullied even by his friends, humiliated by his neighbours, presumed upon by beggars and cheated by tradesmen. He is picked up, thrown away, robbed, ignored and finally forced to become someone else entirely.

A very different haunted Paris appears in Jacques Rivette's *Céline et Julie vont en bateau* (*Céline and Julie Go Boating*) (1974), which is an optimist's humane vision of the world of magic which Argento summons up in *Suspiria* and *Inferno*. It's a long film, but such is its charm and ingenuity that one wishes it were actually longer. Librarian Julie (Dominique Labourier) and magician Céline (Juliet Berto) play role-swapping games in the streets of the city, and are repeatedly drawn to a haunted house which functions as a kind of interactive cinema. Inside, ghosts Bulle Ogier, Marie-France Pisier and Barbet Schroeder are playing out over and over again a 1920s melodrama which will end with the death of a child. The heroines enter the house and assume the minor roles of maids in the story, eventually twisting the solemn mystery into a farce with a happy ending. *Céline et Julie* is much more than a ghost story, and delights in the possibilities of the cinema as a succession of conjuring tricks, harking back to the very roots of French *film fantastique* with Georges Méliès; and the Théâtre Robert-Houdin. Catherine Binet's *Les Jeux de la Comtesse Dolingen de Graz* (1981), with its echoes of Verne and Stoker and elliptical interpretation of an adolescent girl's longings in terms of a series of (imagined?) horror stories, has much the same tone. Eduardo de Gregorio, Rivette's screenwriter, returns solemnly to the haunting in *Sérail* (1976), in which writer Corin Redgrave finds himself in a plot that echoes *Céline and Julie* and *Seizure*, and *Aspern* (1981), an adaption of the subtlest of Henry James's ghost stories (because it has no ghost), *The Aspern Papers*.

The most labyrinthine of the arty haunted houses is Harry Kumel's decaying, decadent and Belgian *Malpertuis* (1972), from the novel by Jean Ray, where a dying Orson Welles has had survivors from ancient Greek mythology sewn into human skins and bound to his unreasonable will. Sailor-suited blond beauty Mathieu Carriere ventures into Malpertuis and falls for Euryale (Susan Hampshire), the last of the Gorgons. There are several different endings, as in *Céline and Julie*, but the incomprehensible games never stop. Also from the Low Countries is Paul Verhoeven's provoking Dutch *De Vierde Man* (1983), with gay writer Jeroen Krabbé plagued by *Don't Look Now* premonitions. A gouged eyeball drips from a spyhole in a hotel door, and it becomes obvious that blonde minx Renée Soutendijk is a witch who has cremated three previous husbands and has her sights set on either Krabbé or the hunky young man he is after as the next on her death list. Finally, the worst happens, but our hero is saved by the intervention of none other than the Virgin Mary, who is living out her life as a nurse in Flushing just as quietly as Kumel's Titans and demigods are in Malpertuis. Like most of these Continental ghost stories, Verhoeven's film has a pleasantly black sense of humour and an erotic charge unusual in the traditionally staid sub-genre.

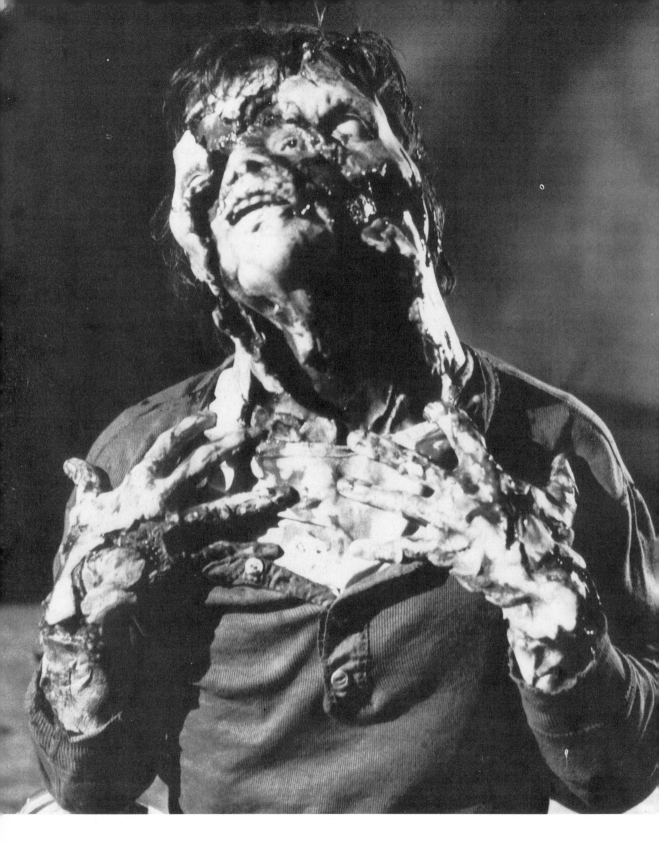

● *Symptoms.* Jack Magner, **Amityville II: The Possession.**

The based-on-fact horror film was born when William Peter Blatty modelled *The Exorcist* on a documented case history of twentieth-century possession, but the form only hit big when Jay Anson's heavily fictionalised account of the pestering of George and Kathy Lutz in their new home, *The Amityville Horror*, became a surprise best-seller and was duly filmed. James Brolin and Margot Kidder buy a creaky old house on Amity Island for a surprisingly reasonable price. Slime creeps down the walls, a child's imaginary playmate makes startling appearances, a babysitter is locked in a cupboard, a nun throws up, $1,500 in cash vanishes (smart ghost, huh?) and Father Rod Steiger is attacked by flies while trying to bless the house. Anson makes an attempt to structure the random haunting with a parallel plot – the family discover that the house is the site of a pre-credits mass murder and an Indian burial ground – while Brolin starts brooding and leering like the murderous former tenant. Because it's all supposed to be true, *The Amityville Horror* has to waste time on possible explanations without settling for one. *Don't Look Now* and *Inferno* are similarly difficult, but they don't even try to make sense on a story level; *The Amityville Horror* plods TV movie-like from incident to incident. Underneath Lalo Schifrin's scary score, Stuart Rosenberg's battering ram direction and Rod Steiger's terrible performance, all *The Amityville Horror* wants to do is stop you switching channels. Sidney J. Furie's *The Entity*, from a factional book by Frank DeFelitta, has all the same problems. Single parent Barbara Hershey is raped by an invisible incubus, and her case is studied by a psychiatrist and some parapsychologists. Hershey's performance is good enough to make you feel uncomfortable about the way she is treated by the camera, which lingers over her naked body as unseen hands knead her breasts. Again, realism is attempted by neglecting concise story-telling in favour of an open-ended muddle. The based-on-fact horror film may name names, give dates and cite statistics, but that doesn't make it any more credible than *The House That Wouldn't Die*.

Although nominally supposed to deal with the original mass murder, Damiano Damiani's *Amityville II: The Possession* (1982) is a complete fabrication, which makes it a lot more like trashy fun than its square predecessor. Damiano's creeping camera-work makes more of the mock gothic house and its eye-like gable windows, and cheerfully borrows bits from *The Exorcist*, *The Shining* and a dozen other movies to beef up a lopsided plot. An Italian-American family, plagued by the method-acting tics of Burt Young and Rutanya Alda, moves into the house, and the teenage son is possessed by something slimy from the cellar that gives him orders through his Walkman headphones. The devil kid starts unambitiously by walking out of his birthday party and seducing his sister, but works his way up to wiping out the whole family with dad's shotgun. The story gets wildly out of hand as renegade exorcist James Olsen kidnaps the possessee from jail and drags him to the house for a climactic display of head-splitting make-up effects and noisy ritual chanting. Like *The Amityville Horror*, *Amityville II* doesn't make sense, but at least it uses its puerility as an excuse for over-the-top entertainment. The possibilities (and perhaps the patience) of the Catholic Church having been exhausted by Rod Steiger and James Olson, the second sequel, Richard Fleischer's *Amityville 3-D* (1983), brings sharp-nosed sceptic Tony Roberts and a scientific team of *Stone Tape* fans into the house. They vow to get to the bottom of the hauntings, but, unsurprisingly, all Hell breaks loose, and no answers are forthcoming from the resident bug-eyed demon. A potentially fascinating footnote to the *Amityville* industry is provided by 'The House That Bled to Death', a 1980 segment of the *Hammer House of Horror* TV show, in which a financially beleaguered couple *fake* a haunting in their new house in order to get big bucks from the paperback and the movie deal, but in the process turn their daughter into a homicidal killer. The idea is great, but the execution is pedestrian on every level.

The most eagerly awaited horror movie of the decade was *The Shining*. The project united Stephen King, America's foremost modern horror writer, Jack Nicholson, the world's highest-paid actor, and Stanley Kubrick, the galactically re-nowned, trend-setting director who has surrounded himself with a mystique of colossal independence. After the usual three years of multiple takes, precision editing and nit-picking craftsmanship, Kubrick allowed *The Shining* to be released, only to face audience and critical incomprehension. Jack Torrance (Nicholson), a frustrated writer, Wendy (Shelley Duvall), his jittery wife, and Danny (Danny Lloyd), their psychic son, spend the winter looking after the Overlook, a snowbound Colorado luxury hotel with an evil past. Jack, already an unstable dried-up drunk with a history of child abuse, is driven completely psycho by the place and becomes a murderous menace to his family. King's novel is densely plotted and multi-layered, establishing the Overlook's essential evil with a recital of the various atrocities that have happened in the place. Kubrick prunes this background, leaving in only the story of Grady, the previous caretaker, who chopped up his wife and two children in a fit of cabin fever. For Kubrick, King's plot and carefully established motivation are only devices to coop up his characters and have them tear each other to pieces.

The build-up is tense and uneasy. The camera soars through the Colorado mountains and homes in on the Overlook. Nicholson's eyebrows arch alarmingly. Danny has glimpses of the twin ghosts of Grady's little girls. Our expectations that *The Shining* will turn out to be the most superterrifying horror film of all time seem to be confirmed; but when the descent into chaos begins, so does the laughter. King's horrifying ghost in Room 237, which appears as a leggy blonde nude but turns into a bloated, leprous hag, is curiously unimpressive. When Jack goes off the wall, the film turns into one of Kubrick's nightmare comedies, and Nicholson easily matches the grinning grotesques of Sterling Hayden, Peter Sellers and George C. Scott in *Dr Strangelove*, Malcolm McDowell and Patrick Magee in *A Clockwork Orange* and Lee Ermey and Vincent D'Onofrio in *Full Metal Jacket*. Much of *The Shining* comes on like a *grand guignol* remake of *I Love Lucy*, as Jack snickers and bares his teeth like

the Big Bad Wolf ('little pigs, little pigs, let me come in!') and hacks through a door with a demented howl of 'Heeeere's *Johnny!* With Wendy turned into a whimpering cartoon (appropriately, Duvall's next role was Olive Oyl), Danny serving as an almost irrelevant, sensible stand-in for the audience, and Hallorann (Scatman Crothers), the black psychic whom King has save Wendy and Danny, disposed of with an axe in his stomach, *The Shining* becomes a love story between Jack and the Overlook.

Kubrick makes conscious use of previous screen hauntings, particularly that of Eleanor (Julie Harris), who finds in Hill House the home she has never had, but has to die to stay there. Jack is approached by Lloyd (Joe Turkel), a deferential ('Anything you say, sir!') bartender who serves him in the cavernous 1920s ballroom, and Grady (Philip Stone), the politely racist mass murderer who gives him a few words of advice in the art deco lavatories. They represent the management, and offer Jack the permanent position of caretaker. Like Eleanor, he has to die to take up residence. After his frozen demise in the hotel maze, the film ends with a slow zoom into a 1921 photograph which finds a smiling, dinner-jacketed Jack among the 4 July guests.

The shot refers to *Repulsion*, with the suggestion that it has all been in Jack's mind, but also to *Burnt Offerings*, where the finale finds the framed photos of Oliver Reed, Bette Davis and Lee Harcourt Montgomery added to the house's collection of previous kills. The idea that *The Shining* is a large-scale *Repulsion* doesn't work. Kubrick may not go into the gangland killings, political corruption or the death of the woman in Room 237, but his Overlook is genuinely haunted. Some of the ghosts come from the book, some from Kubrick's previous films (the room Keir Dullea shares with the *2001* monolith must be off one of the Overlook's corridors) and some (the tidal wave of blood that comes out of the elevators) are never explained. *The Shining* is a labyrinth through which there are many routes. The film and the novel take different paths, intersecting at some junctures, occasionally passing the same landmarks on opposite sides, and heading towards roughly the same centre. Mazes are supposed to be confusing and incomplete – that's their attraction – and it is only right that those moments when we are given a godlike overview of the whole map (a stunning shot has Jack examine a model of the hotel's maze and see his wife and son wandering through it) should be infrequent.

Sadly, John Irvin's film of Peter Straub's *Ghost Story* is less likely than *The Shining* to be a fruitful critical rediscovery. The novel is as wrapped up in its genre as the basic title suggests. Among the ghosts that haunt Straub's Milburn are the deliberately invoked shades of Henry James, M.R. James and Nathaniel Hawthorne. The complicated plot covers every possible permutation of the classical ghost story, missing only its simplicity. Lawrence D. Cohen, who also adapted *Carrie* for the screen, fails to cope with the novel's intricate structure. Straub's immortal succubus is replaced with the spirit of a girl drowned in the 1920s by a group of young men who have sat around ever since spinning scary yarns as a kind of conscience-flagellation. The ghostly Eva Galli is unsettling when represented by Alice Krige's smile, but less impressive when turned by Dick Smith's make-up crew into a dissolving corpse. After the ravenous zombie hordes of Romero and Lucio Fulci, it's a bit much to ask an audience to be afraid of a plain old walking corpse who does little except loiter about while her geriatric victims fall off high places. *Ghost Story* is a green-tinged film, forever lingering on moonlit mirrors, sheets of glass and stretches of water. It's pretty enough, but infuriatingly neglects the more powerful cinematic ideas in the book. Straub parallels the ghost's thrall over Milburn with the icy grip of a Maine winter, emphasising the crippling effect of 20-ft snowdrifts on the town's routine and the bone-freezing cold on its doddering heroes. *The Shining* exploits the Overlook's snowy siege, but *Ghost Story* throws this particular horror away.

Ghosts work better in short stories than novels, and Peter Medak's *The Changeling* (1979) is nothing more than a well-told anecdote. Composer George C. Scott moves into an old mansion to recover from the death of his family in a snowbound car accident. This is familiar enough, but the supernatural disturbances are genuinely unnerving, from a manic wheelchair that makes sudden appearances to a devastating Dolby stereo soundtrack. The parallel plot finally unearths a nastier-than-usual dark secret: years earlier, a tyrannical father had drowned his crippled son and replaced him with a hardy foundling who has grown up to be rich and powerful Senator Melvyn Douglas. It's all to do with that old melodramatic contrivance, the zillionaire's unreasonable will, as it is in the awful film of Virginia Andrews's slushy horror best-seller *Flowers in the Attic* (1987), in which four unnaturally pale and stupid children are locked up in an old dark house so their mean-spirited momma can poison them and come into a fortune. There isn't a ghost, although the children do their best to haunt the house, but Jeffrey Bloom's film does manage one moment of high camp dreadfulness as pasty-faced Kristy Swanson disrupts Victoria Tennant's wedding waving a half-eaten, arsenic-flavoured biscuit shrieking 'eat the cookie, Momma!'

The turn of the decade saw a surprising number of hack ghost stories. Gus Trikonis's *The Evil* (1978), with Richard Crenna, Joanna Pettet and Andrew Prine discovering a chubby Devil (Victor Buono) in their basement, was quite properly followed by Herb Freed's *Beyond Evil* (1980), a possession-by-ghost saga with John Saxon and Lynda Day George. *The Survivor*, David Hemmings's good-taste version of James Herbert's gruesome novel, has pilot Robert Powell walk away from a crash and, urged by the ghosts of the dead, track down the rotter who planted the bomb. Despite Jenny Agutter as a psychic in Victorian black lace, *The Survivor* is a crashing bore. Powell turns out to be a ghost himself, an ending that would fit a 15-minute *Night Gallery* sketch better than it does an 82-minute movie, but was still reused for Ellen Barkin in the astonishingly silly and pretentious *Siesta* (1988). For some strange reason, Thom Eberhardt gave *The Survivor* another spin of the wheel when he reworked Herbert's story without credit for the dreary *Sole Survivor* (1983). Trish

● *Old soldiers never die.* Curt Wilmot, **House.**

Van Devere moved out of *The Changeling* into *The Hearse* (1980), in which she is an eligible widow courted by a funeral carriage. The inevitable John Carradine potters around *The Nesting* (1981), a superior cheapie in which a lady novelist is bothered by massacre victims who date back to the days when her gothic pile was a cat-house; this theme was later recycled by Roberta Findlay for *Blood Sisters* (1987), another haunted-whorehouse-of-horrors number. *Death Ship* (1980) is a floating SS torture chamber that roams the Caribbean, doing in anyone stupid enough to board her, like Richard Crenna and George Kennedy. Eugenio Martin's *Sobreonatural* (1980) is a sombre Spanish haunted house movie, John Hough's *The Watcher in the Woods* (1982) is one of Disney's early, disastrous attempts to ditch the family image, and Kevin Connor's *The House Where Evil Dwells* (1982) has Susan George and Doug McClure re-enacting a *samurai* love triangle in Japan. Even John Cassavetes's *Opening Night* (1978) has neurotic actress Gena Rowlands plagued by the imaginary spirit of an adoring fan run over in front of the theatre. And *Satan War* (1980) deserves to be remembered as the most minimalist, boring zero-budget ghost story of all time – the chief manifestations of this 70-minute ordeal are an out-of-shot hand slowly turning a crucifix upside-down and coloured porridge seeping from kitchen cabinets.

John Carpenter's *The Fog* (1980) opens as if it's going to be a return to the campfire ghost story. 'Five minutes to midnight', a watch snaps shut, 'time for one more story.' The camera pans around a circle of excited children, and grizzled sea-captain John Houseman scares them with the tale of the wreck of the *Elizabeth Dane*. The prosperity of Antonio Bay has grown from salvage looted from a clipper the town elders let run aground in the fog. A hundred years to the day later, the drowned seamen return with the fog to get their revenge. Sadly, the promising idea is diffused by a screenplay that never finds any underlying coherence for its episodes. The victims are selected arbitrarily. A little old lady and a matey weatherman die, but the bitchy chairperson of the centennial committee (who could easily stand in for the grasping town founders) is spared. Carpenter manages individual sequences with his customary skill, and has his excellent cast fill out his too many characters with a few apparently effortless touches, but *The Fog* runs aground on its erratic plot and gaps in logic. It is ultimately disappointing to find that the eerie fog contains a crowd of wormy shambling zombies who are good for some *Night of the Living Dead* imitations, but fail to inspire sustained dread. Carpenter's later *Prince of Darkness* (1987), heavily influenced by *The Stone Tape*, has much the same problems and virtues, with a particle-physics-based apocalyptic haunting of such magnitude that individual manifestations (corpses reanimated by bugs, squirted green goo turning scientists into zombies, Alice Cooper as a wino who wields a deadly half-bicycle) can't hope to live up to it. As in *The Fog*, one of the odd features is Carpenter's insistence on having four or five climaxes taking place simultaneously and intercutting the perils of various unrelated characters. In both films, it's Carpenter's *technique* – the prowling steadicam, his own driving score, nervous dialogue, widescreen compositions – that conveys a sense of an omnipresent supernatural force.

For no apparent reason, 1986–7 saw a flurry of haunted prison movies. *Force of Darkness* (1986) and *Slaughterhouse Rock* (1987) just use the abandoned facilities as a handy location for formula demonic manifestations, but Renny Harlin's *Prison* (1987) is a genuine attempt to combine the ghost story with the old-fashioned prison picture. When hard-assed warden Lane Slate reopens the run-down penitentiary where he once allowed an innocent man to be electrocuted, the vengeful ghost of his victim possesses the entire concrete hellhole and starts killing people off. Although it's at heart just another stringing together of bizarre death scenes – victims are punctured by animated bars, burned up in solitary or mummified in barbed wire – *Prison* does make good use of its oppressive background. Old Hollywood elements like the attempted break-out, the mess hall disturbance and the climactic riot are cleverly reinterpreted in horror film terms, and Slate stays just this side of camp as the monomaniac villain. It's unlikely that the film will be influential – *The Chair* (1987), although released after *Prison*, was made earlier – and it's difficult to see precisely why this particular set of ingredients should suddenly become so viable. Producer Irwin Yablans suggests 'just as *Halloween* took advantage of a very obvious, neglected fact that the most horrific night of the year had never been used for a horror movie, it stands to reason that a prison, the most horrific place imaginable, ought to be used in that way, as well'.

The 1980s' most elaborate attempt at an original haunted house movie is *Poltergeist*, an unlikely collaboration between co-producer/co-writer Steven Spielberg and director Tobe Hooper. The film comes on like a supernaturally inclined treatise on the State of the Union, with 'The Star-Spangled Banner' playing under the credits, and a deliberately archetypal suburban setting. The whitebread Freeling Family – Craig T. Nelson, JoBeth Williams and their three cute kids – discover various supernatural forces in their newly built home. At first, they play games with them, almost delighted by the fun of apports and poltergeist phenomena; then darker spirits intrude from the twilight zone (specifically from Richard Matheson's 'Little Girl Lost' episode) and the youngest child is sucked into the void inside the television set. Spielberg's amused tolerance of suburban triviality jostles with Hooper's grouchy view of city slickers treading on the countryside. The trouble turns out to have been caused by Everyman Nelson's real-estate bosses, who have built a housing development over a rural cemetery without bothering to shift the corpses. There's a nasty EC comics story, 'Graft in Concrete', in which a bunch of crooked contractors do the same thing – the bodies crawl out of their graves and shove the crooks under a steamroller before embedding them in their own tarmac. *Poltergeist's* supernatural complainants are more childish: a cyclone and a grumpy tree from the *Wizard of Oz*, and a fantasy land beyond the bedroom closet from *The Lion, the Witch and the Wardrobe*. *Poltergeist* may well be the only successful, non-spoof horror film in which nobody gets killed.

Poltergeist tries too hard to be as serious about psychic phenomena as *Close Encounters of the Third Kind* thinks it is about UFOs. Both films have sermonising scientists with all the technical jargon they can muster, and both films bury them under the pyrotechnics provided by the Industrial Light and Magic effects facility. Spielberg dominates the partnership, with phantoms in the living-room and Nelson and Williams as his usual suburban clowns, but one misses the viciousness of Hooper's monstrosities when a sub-*Outer Limits* goblin evilly looms out of nowhere just to say 'boo!'. Hooper does manage to make the animated playthings from *Close Encounters* take on the malevolence of the carnival dolls of *The Funhouse* when a grinning toy attacks its cherubic owner. The haunting in *Poltergeist* makes less sense than the one in *Something Evil*, but the film does stand as the horror equivalent of the exuberant, harmless, greatest show on Earth genre blockbusters (*Star Wars*, *Raiders of the Lost Ark*, *E.T.*) currently ensconced as the most successful films of all time. Its successful juggling act in keeping so many disparate elements up in the air is underlined by the unpalatable muddle of Brian Gibson's elaborately pointless *Poltergeist II: The Other Side* (1986), which spectacularly drops every ball.

return to the past

return to the past

Although they did actually begin in 1950 . . . what we ordinarily think of as a 1950s-type science fiction movie didn't end when the fifties actually did; trends don't watch calendars.

Bill Warren, *Keep Watching the Skies*

For George Lucas, the 1950s end in the summer of 1962; when the kids of *American Graffiti* leave high school for college, adulthood, responsibility and Vietnam. Bill Warren's definitive study of American science fiction movies in the 1950s also uses 1962 as a full stop for the decade. Warren, at least, is premature. In the late 1980s, teddy boys, hula hoops and *Your Show of Shows* exist only as nostalgia, but the 1950s s-f monster movie is passing itself off as the contemporary item at your local theatre. *Invasion of the Body Snatchers* (1978), *The Incredible Shrinking Woman* (1981), *The Thing* (1982), *Godzilla 1985* (1985), *Invaders From Mars* (1986), *The Fly* (1986), *Little Shop of Horrors* (1986) and *The Blob* (1988) are expensive, colourful remakes of cheap, mainly black-and-white 1950s greats and *Not of This Earth* (1988) is a cheap remake of Roger Corman's cheap original. New versions of *The Day the Earth Stood Still* (1951), *The Creature From the Black Lagoon* (1954) and – as predicted in the original edition of this book – *The Amazing Colossal Man* (1957) have been mooted, and I wouldn't be surprised to learn

that a producer somewhere is blowing the cobwebs off *Attack of the Crab Monsters* (1957) or *Fiend Without a Face* (1958). A close look at *Alien* (1979) and *Alligator* (1981) will reveal the Howdy-Doody-badge-wearing, crew-cut, canasta-playing spirit of a bygone age beneath the modish superficials. Even Ken Russell's ultra-hip, druggy mind-blower *Altered States* (1981) is only a jazzed-up remake of *The Neanderthal Man* (1953) and the 'Expanding Human' episode of *The Outer Limits*.

The 1950s s-f film went into low-budget hiding in the 1960s, but persisted with *The Day Mars Invaded Earth* (1962), *The Wizard of Mars* (1964) and *Destination Inner Space* (1966) from the US; and *Unearthly Stranger* (1964), *The Projected Man* (1967) and *Night of the Big Heat* (1968) from the UK; not to mention the repeated demolition of Japan by mushroom people, giant turtles, Xs from outer space and bodysnatchers from Hell in the likes of *Matango (Attack of the Mushroom People)* (1963), *Daikuju Gamera (Gammera the Invincible)* (1966), *Uchu Daikuji Guilala (The X From Outer Space)* (1967) – disappointingly, the X is a giant chicken lizard – and *Kyuketsuki Gokemidoro (Goké – Bodysnatcher From Hell)* (1968). *Night of the Living Dead* takes a lot from the 1950s: a documentary-style graininess from *Them!* (1954), an army of walking corpses from the terrible but not entirely negligible *Invisible Invaders* (1958), and a catch-all explanation from almost everything:

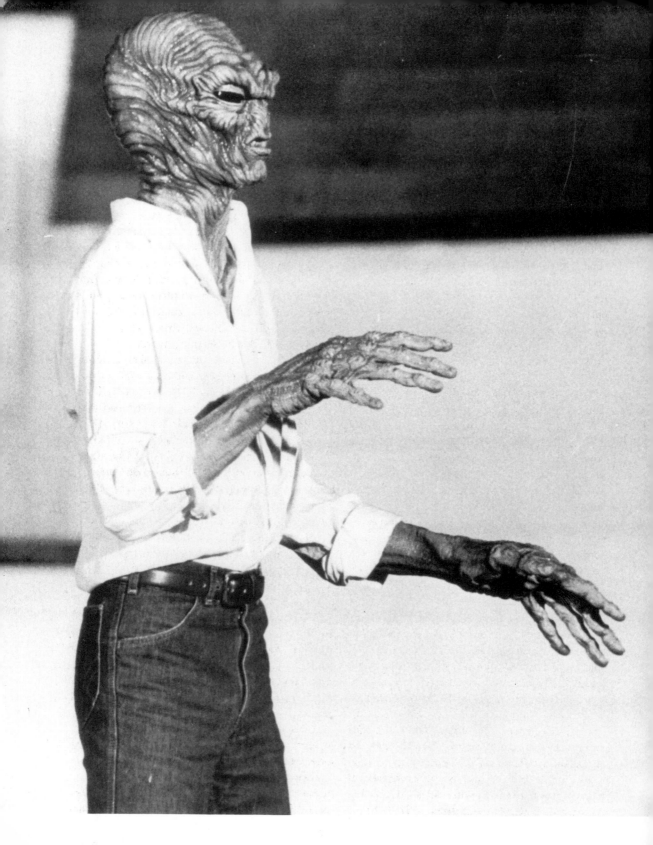

● *'Of all the worlds in all the galaxies, why did they have to pick this one?'* **Strange Invaders.**

'You mean the tree got up on its roots and started killing people?'
'Yep, must be the radiation.'

Although the panicky characters of Romero's film are worlds away from the starched scientists and soldiers who represented Our Side in the 1950s (Morris Ankrum, John Agar, Faith Domergue), the success of *Night of the Living Dead* gave a fillip to the dying strain. How else to account for the deadly serious *Night of the Lepus* (the one about giant killer rabbits mistaking Rory Calhoun, Janet Leigh and Stuart Whitman for nibblesome sticks of celery) as late as 1972? During *detente*, radiation was replaced by ecological macguffins in movies like *Gojira tai Hedora* (*Godzilla Vs the Smog Monster*) (1971), *Doomwatch*, *The Milpitas Monster* (1976) and *Spawn of the Slithis* (1978):

'You mean the garbage heap got up on its pseudopods and started killing people?'
'Yep, must be the pollution.'

Otherwise, *Night of the Lepus* and a handful of generally dull minor films like *The Cremators* (1972) and *The Crater Lake Monster* (1977) follow the same formula as *The Deadly Mantis* (1957) and *The Beginning of the End* (1957). The monsters attack. A scientific explanation is discovered. The monsters attack more extensively. Our Side finds the monsters' weakness. The monsters get blasted off the face of the planet. And serves them right for being so predictable.

After *Night of the Living Dead* it became difficult to take the 1950s monster movie seriously. The form was not helped by *The Octaman* (1971), which discovers the dumbest of all evolutionary dead ends in a man with an octopus for a head, or *The Mutations* (1975), in which Donald Pleasence turns students into Venus flytraps. As the 1970s progressed, seriously intended films like the boring *Track of the Moonbeast* (1972) and the competent *Sssssssss* (1973) became extinct; low-budget film-makers threw in some intentional laughs to cover for the unintentional ones. In *The Incredible Two-Headed Transplant* (1970), Bruce

Dern combines a psychopath with a hulking retard. 'Shut up', says one head to the other, 'I'm running this monster!' The theme song is 'It's Incredible!' Even more incredibly, the idea was reused in the more expensive but no less stupid *The Thing With Two Heads* (1972), in which racist Dr Ray Milland is grafted on to a giant black convict (Rosy Grier). Alex Rebar returns from Saturn as *The Incredible Melting Man* (1978) and takes off across the countryside leaving a trail of corpses and goo. 'Oh my God', cries Burr DeBenning, 'it's his ear!' Finally, Rebar dissolves into a puddle of putrescence and is dumped into the nearest trashcan by a whistling janitor, which doesn't leave out-and-out comedies like John Landis's *Schlock* (1973) and *Attack of the Killer Tomatoes* (1977) with much to spoof.

One of the 1950s' best-remembered things from another world returned in a semi-satirical sequel, *Beware! The Blob* (1971), directed by Larry Hagman. A chip off the old blob is retrieved from the Arctic (where 'Steven' McQueen had sent it in 1958) and goes on a devouring spree. Guest star comedians Shelley Berman, Godfrey Cambridge and Burgess Meredith are allowed to do their acts before the creeping strawberry jelly gets them. Hagman makes more extensive use of the monster than Irvin S. Yeaworth did in the *el cheapo* original, and it has to do some endearing lurking, oozing and absorbing before Robert Walker Jr catches it on the ice-rink. There are a few clever jokes, like the extra vainly waving a crucifix at the globbering mass as he goes under; and an amusing, shivery score by Mort Garson that plays variations on Burt Bacharach's immortal standard 'Beware the Blob' ('. . . it creeps into your living room! Be careful of the blob!') The Blob itself, at once the simplest and most satisfying of all movie monsters, returns again in its own high-tech remake, courtesy of producer Jack H. Harris and director Chuck Russell, and is spoofed in Larry Cohen's *The Stuff*, in which the glutinous killer mass is also edible.

Alien revisits the 1950s without a trace of humour. It seems like an advance to bring the spaceship movie out of the New Deal Flash

Gordon swashbuckling of *Star Wars* into the Eisenhower era of 'Keep watching the skies'; but *Alien* is as much an overdressed cheapie as George Lucas's Saturday Morning Picture Show. The special effects 'Flying Purple People Eater' and directorial overenthusiasm lend lustre to a receding plotline. The hand-picked cast of strong American and British non-stars (Yaphet Kotto, Harry Dean Stanton, Ian Holm, John Hurt) and the realistic, profane dialogue (one draft of the script even had a foulmouth computer), bring alive a screenplay that staggers under stereotypes, obscurities and muddy thinking. Sigourney Weaver may be an independent, gutsy heroine, but the spaceship *Nostromo* also carries Veronica Cartwright as a representative of red-nosed sniffing and feminine panic at their most demeaning. With the exception of the character who turns out to be a scheming robot, all the men on the ship are the kind of dorks who loiter in dark corners waiting to be pounced on. It's impossible to resist the 'I wonder who's gonna get it next?' game while watching *Alien* . The film's few surprises arise from the unexpected grossness of the expected fates dropped on expected individuals at expected intervals. Much (including a lawsuit) has been made of *Alien*'s relationship with *It! The Terror From Beyond Space* (1958), but it's actually more like an outer space blueprint for the *Friday the 13th* bloodbaths.

Alien is an original screenplay by Dan O'Bannon and Ronald Shusett, rewritten amid much acrimony by David Giler and Walter Hill, and directed by Ridley Scott, *auteur* of innumerable Strongbow cider and Hovis bread commercials. O'Bannon develops from his *Dark Star* script the grimy space freighter crewed by bitching incompetents who've obviously signed up for the trip because no one on Earth can stand them. The film's overdrive pacing probably comes from Hill and Giler, whose background is in lean action pictures like *The Warriors* and *Southern Comfort*. Scott's contribution is an extension of his TV adverts – an accumulation of telling details that obscures illogicality. Sliced bread tastes vile and *Alien* is a dumb film, but you'd never guess that from

watching Scott's foggy, prettified·visuals. *Alien* is a fortuitous combination of disparate, mutually hostile talents who have knocked each other off their hobby-horses for the betterment of the film. It may not be great, but it's at least good – unlike, say, Scott's *Legend*. The real star of *Alien* is H.R. Giger's obscenely masculine man-in-a-suit monster, in incarnations that vary from an exploding egg to a salivating, steel-fanged adult. For the first time in the cinema, the special effects department conceal the zip, and show a creature who is not only convincingly alien but convincingly alive.

The only purpose of the Alien is procreation. Its spawn include *The Dark* (1979), *Scared to Death* (1980), *The Intruder Within* (1981), *Alien 2 sulla terra (Alien Terror)* (1981), *Galaxy of Terror* (1981), *The Deadly Spawn* (1981), *The Being* (1983), *The Falling* (1984), *Biohazard* (1984), *The Titan Find* (1985), *Star Crystal* (1986), *Breeders* (1986), *Creepozoids* (1987), *The Kindred* (1987) and *Blue Monkey* (1987). With that kind of concentrated obnoxiousness falling weekly from the skies, Steven Spielberg's *E.T.* shouldn't have been surprised to find the generality of mankind unwilling to put out the welcome mat. Since spaceships are expensive to construct, most cut-price aliens do their intruding and inseminating in caverns, oil rigs, sewers or other corridor-ridden substitutes. Not only is the running around in tunnels reminiscent of *Dr Who* , the whole plots of most of these had been anticipated by a 1974 serial, 'The Ark in Space', in which Tom Baker confronted some galactic locusts using cryogenic corpsicles as incubators. Most of the rip-offs are dull, but Norman J. Warren's *Inseminoid* (1980) aspires to hectic lunacy by having its cast (which includes a heavy feminine complement – Stephanie Beacham, Jennifer Ashley, Victoria Tennant and Judy Geeson) rush around some offworld catacombs with the enthusiasm of a crowd of schoolkids with plastic bags over their heads playing spacemen. The best of the Italian *Alien* pseudo-sequels is Luigi Cozzi's *Contamination – alien arriva sulla terra (Contamination)* (1980), which is mainly concerned with the literally gut-rupturing effects of a close encounter with its alien eggs and is unique in choosing to rip

● *Bathtime for blondie.* Peter Mandell, Maryam D'Abo, **XTRO.**

off *Quatermass 2* (1958) with its unscrupulous capitalists from outer space.

All *Alien* has really added to the genre is its graphic vision of the monster tearing its way out of a human shell. In 1982, the image was used in films as different as *Amityville II: The Possession, Cat People* and *The Sword and the Sorcerer*. Mild satire of the form is attempted in *Galaxina* (1980), *The Creature Wasn't Nice* (1982), *The Ice Pirates* (1984) and *Eat and Run* (1986), and New World put a few jokes into their uncharacteristically grim *Humanoids From the Deep* (1980): a bunch of rednecks corner a straggling monster and stomp him to death. More typical of the Corman approach is Allan Holzman's *Forbidden World* (1981), in which an omnivorous monstrosity that replicates the tissues of whatever it eats is done in when hero Jesse Vint performs a do-it-yourself operation on a sick scientist and feeds the thing a cancerous liver. The monster literally pukes itself to death. By the time of *Xtro*, the field was so exhausted the film chooses to throw its womb-rupturing alien away early and explore more interesting side-tracks. A reconstructed human returns to Earth after three years on a flying saucer, and his wife doesn't believe his story. His son is fascinated, especially when dad gives him the power to plant eggs in the *au pair*'s stomach. In the film's best scene, a lifesize Action Man commando doll raids the downstairs flat and ices a nosy neighbour.

With its naturalistic dialogue and monster preying on characters in an isolated setting, *Alien* is obviously indebted to *The Thing From Another World* (1951). The most elaborate *Alien* follow-up presents itself as a remake of the Howard Hawks production, going back beyond Christian Nyby's film to John W. Campbell's original novella 'Who Goes There?' John Carpenter pays tribute to the earlier film by restaging two of its key images: a circle of men on the ice outlining the embedded flying saucer, and the melting ice-block in which the hideous Thing is trapped. But enough is enough, and Carpenter otherwise avoids parroting his idol, returning instead to the aspects of Campbell's story that Hawks discarded. Hawks's

monster is a vampiric vegetable biped; Carpenter's is a mimic who can look like any human or animal it chooses to absorb. Despite the reactionary mood of Hollywood at the time of *The Thing*, Carpenter does not revive the cold war sub-text. In 1951, the Thing attacks an installation in the Arctic that is part of the Distant Early Warning system, and the message is 'keep watching the skies!' In 1982, the story is set in Campbell's Antarctic, the victims are all civilians and the moral appears to be 'keep watching the slime!'

While Hawks has Our Side going professionally into action in defence of the Earth, Carpenter is darker and more downbeat. Everybody in the Hawks film knows what to do and gets on with it. Courses of action are proposed, weighed and taken up or rejected in a few terse sentences. Conflicts arise, but no one doubts his own rectitude. The 1980s characters are justly suspicious of each other, do nothing but bicker and stand back while their comrades sprout tentacles. Macready (Kurt Russell) is obviously a graduate of the Duane Jones school of horror movie heroism. He takes a lot of decisive action, but usually has sketchily developed ideas like tying everyone else up while he tests their blood. Exposed by its treacherous blood sample, the Thing explodes out of its tethered host and finds its potential victims conveniently roped to their chairs. The finish is remarkably understated, perhaps contributing to *The Thing*'s so-so box-office. Two survivors squat in the ruins of the base, unsure of each other's humanity, waiting to freeze to death.

Carpenter has his 70mm camera prowl around the ice-floes and the corridors of the base, and handles a few quietly uneasy scenes as the characters try to put off any action by talking through their insoluble problem ('I know that I'm human, and you can't all be monsters or you'd jump me, so . . . '). But the Main Attraction of *The Thing* is its brilliant, horrible, disgusting special effects. A severed head grows spider's legs and scuttles out of the room. A cardiac arrest case opens a toothy mouth in his chest and bites off the hands of the doctor trying to administer heart massage. For all its side-show-has-taken-over-the-

Big-Top sequences, *The Thing* is a more honest, less hokey film than *Alien*. Its characters may do all the wrong things, but they never act like the suicidal idiot Harry Dean Stanton must be for wandering under the Alien. Nervous, intellectual players like Donald Moffat, Richard Dysart, Charles Hallahan and Wilford Brimley are convincingly out of their depth as the woolly, flabby, crotchety men of the ice station and, of course, literally poles apart from Hawks's efficiently functioning group of military men. And Kurt Russell sneers his way through another grouchy hero role, pouring whisky into the smug chess-playing mini-computer that is the film's only female character, or looking up at the roaring, towering Thing and unloosing his flamethrower with a bitter, resigned 'yeah, fuck you too!'

James Cameron's *Aliens* (1986), the official follow-up to *Alien*, surprisingly caps the original by opting to imitate another earthbound genre. If Scott's film is a body-count picture, then Cameron's is an outer space equivalent of one of Sam Fuller's on-patrol war movies – *The Steel Helmet* or *Merrill's Marauders*. Sigourney Weaver is drafted by the creepy corporation that set her up as a monster munchie in the first place and shipped back to the planet where the *Nostromo* found the alien egg. This time, she's given some back-up in a team of US colonial marines who correspond exactly to the kind of gung-ho platoons found in World War II or Korean War pictures, only the future allows for a mix of men and women and the inclusion of an android (Lance Henriksen) along with the blacks, Hispanics and other token ethnic minorities. While Cameron is cynical enough to put an incompetent officer in charge and have Bill Paxton along as the traditional war movie coward who snaps under pressure, part of the piledriver scariness of *Aliens* is down to the fact that, this time, most of the characters are well equipped and well trained – one marine's comment on the mission is 'not another bug hunt!' – but still vulnerable. In a quietly scary moment Ripley reassures the blank-faced little girl who has survived one alien attack by telling her that she is protected by professional soldiers, only to have

the child calmly bleat 'that won't make any difference'. *Aliens* is an optimistic, individualist rereading of the genre: Ripley is softened from the hard-nosed bitch she was in the first film, and it's her humanity that makes her stronger than the heavily armed soldiers who fail where she succeeds. In the finale, Ripley gets into a suit that turns her into a combination Japanese warrior robot and futuristic forklift truck and goes one-on-one with the screeching, egg-laying alien queen.

. . . the fact is there hasn't been a good werewolf movie in ten or fifteen years.
Stephen King, *Danse Macabre*

Writing in 1982, Stephen King was immediately contradicted by the on-screen arrival of a pack of werewolves, *The Howling* (1981), *An American Werewolf in London* (1981), *Full Moon High*, *The Beast Within* (1982), *Cat People*, *The Company of Wolves*, the King-scripted *Silver Bullet* (1985), *Monster Dog* (1986), *Teen Wolf* (1985) and *Teen Wolf Too* (1987) and the TV series *Werewolf*. Even Daryl Hannah as a mermaid in *Splash!* (1984) has a transformation trick or two. These shapeshifters are the children of *Alien*, arriving at the same time not because the *Zeitgeist* was somehow suddenly favourable to lycanthropy, but because of advances in special effects technology. Henry Hull in *The WereWolf of London* (1937), Lon Chaney Jr in *The Wolf Man* (1941), Michael Landon in *I Was a Teenage Werewolf* and Oliver Reed in *Curse of the Werewolf* all become beastly, courtesy of lap dissolves and plenty of yak hair. *Moon of the Wolf* (1972), *The Boy Who Cried Werewolf* (1973), *Legend of the Werewolf* and a whiskery slew of Paul Naschy vehicles all use the same 1930s trickery. With only these outmoded flesh-creeping devices, the genre had atrophied. After *Alien*, men like Rick Baker, Rob Bottin and Stan Winston realised there was more to monstrosity than furry opticals. They have perfected make-up appliances which allow us to see faces elongate and become wolfish, the human body twist into lupine shape and teeth and fangs flick like switchblade knives. By the time of *The Thing*, unbelievable transformations were commonplace: some audiences remain unimpressed when a husky turns into a many-mouthed hellspawn.

The first of the new breed of werewolf movies, *The Howling*, spotlights Rob Bottin's effects work but does not completely rely on it. Joe Dante and John Sayles, director and writer of *Piranha*, surround the set piece transformations with a monster movie specifically tailored to film buffs. Most of the characters are named after the directors of previous werewolf films – Terry Fisher, Fred Francis, R. William Neill, Erle C. Kenton, even Jerry Warren. In an age of Hawks and Hitchcock homages, it takes intestinal fortitude to pay tribute to Warren, the creator of *The Incredible Petrified World* (1957), *Teenage Zombies* (1958) and, of course, *Face of the Screaming Werewolf* (1959). *The Howling* is cast with familiar old faces: Kevin McCarthy, Slim Pickens, Kenneth Tobey, Forrest J. Ackerman and, as a sinister figure checking a phone booth for loose change, Roger Corman. Sayles takes a few ideas from the trash best-seller the film is supposed to be based on, and then constructs his own, considerably neater plot. Karen White (Dee Wallace), a TV reporter, has a nasty experience tracking down Eddie the Mad Rapist (Robert Picardo) in a sleazy, neon-lit, Scorsese-style city. Soon, she's having nightmares that look like s-m porno loops and has to recover from her ordeal in The Colony, a restful clinic way out in the peaceful woodland. The setting is idyllic, but Karen can't get much sleep because of the howling in the woods. Run by an avuncular talk-show pundit, Dr George Waggner (Patrick MacNee), The Colony turns out to be a front for a group of neurotic werewolves. Waggner's self-help therapy is helping them adjust to the modern world, but there are dissenters. Crazy Erle (John Carradine) represents old guard lycanthropy, sneering at Waggner, 'you can't tame what's meant to be wild, doc . . . it ain't natural'.

Karen is particularly impressed when she runs into Eddie again. He digs the bullet that's supposed to have killed him out of his brain and offers it to her with 'let me give you a piece of my mind', and then goes through his astounding transformation routine, turning into the movies' most impressive werewolf monster. Hero Chris Halloran (Dennis Dugan) has picked up some silver bullets at Dick Miller's occult shop ('Werewolves? They're worse than cockroaches!') and he gets our sadly bitten heroine out of The Colony. Determined to expose the menace, Karen comes on TV to speak out and goes wolf on camera. We cut to some typical audiences – a kid enthuses 'Hey Mom, a lady on television just turned into a wolf!' and is ignored, and a cynic in a bar yawns 'it's amazing what they can do with special effects these days'. One of Dante's trademarks is a fondness for triple punch-lines. After the hairy parody of *Network*, we discover nymphomaniac werewolf Marsha Quist (Elisabeth Brooks) ordering rare hamburgers; and after the credits, Dante rewards all of us who sat through to the very end with a clip from *The Wolf Man*.

The Howling is a brisk chiller that effortlessly revives the prowling-through-misty-forests genre with enough zip and spectacle to play to a general audience and plenty of sly in-jokes to pander to genre *cognoscenti*. Inevitably, it has suffered from sequels. Philippe Mora first demonstrated his skill with shapeshifters in *The Beast Within*, which has Paul Clemens impressively but stupidly turning into a giant cicada amid some murky melodramatics. He was then recruited for *Howling II* (1985), variously sub-titled *My Sister is a Werewolf* and *Stirba – Werewolf Bitch*, in which Christopher Lee and Sybil Danning are involved with a cult of Transylvanian lycanthropes who are so powerful they can only be wiped out with *titanium* bullets. As if that weren't silly enough, Mora then returned to his native Australia to shoot *Howling III: The Marsupials* (1987), which deals with the hitherto unknown, pouched antipodean branch of the monster family-tree. In 1988, John Hough – who had Kerrie Keane turn into a demonic satyr rapist in *Incubus* (1982) – has just started directing *Howling IV: The Original Nightmare*. If films as bad as Mora's campy pair can keep a series going, there's no end in sight.

John Landis's *An American Werewolf in London* is

● *Old-worlde monster.* **An American Werewolf in London.**

a more ambitious blend of character comedy and horror than *The Howling*. While Dante and Sayles give their werewolves concise contemporary footnotes, Landis chances everything by going back to the basic plot of *The Wolf Man*. An American in Britain is bitten by a werewolf, and is horrified to find that he has become an olde worlde monster. Surprisingly, Landis does not use the story for a Mel Brooks-style spoof, opting instead for an authentic pop-tragic monster movie. Landis made his name with knockabout comedy, but although *An American Werewolf* contains plenty of good jokes and amusing observations, its scary and/or tear-stained scenes are played for real. David Kessler (David Naughton) and Jack Goodman (Griffin Dunne) are hiking across the photogenic but unwelcoming Yorkshire moors when the beast attacks. David, the survivor, wakes up in a London hospital and falls in love with his nurse — quite understandably, since Jenny Agutter plays her as the incarnation of everything nice about England. He is soon tormented by dreams in which machine-gun-toting Nazi demons massacre his family in front of *The Muppet Show*, and the periodical appearance of the decaying Jack who, as well as copping all the best lines ('Have you ever talked to a corpse? It's *boring*!'), warns him what will happen when the full moon rises. And what does happen is a display of Rick Baker's seamless effects work, scored with one of the several versions of 'Blue Moon' that plays throughout the film, as David dwindles into a ravenous monster.

The film's blend of panicky humour and pathos is extremely adroit. Deciding to commit suicide, David phones his parents in America from a call-box, only to find his bratty kid sister alone in the house ('Mom and Dad would never have left me alone when I was ten') and uninterested in his final declaration of love for his family. *An American Werewolf* is the first horror film since *Death Line* (directed by another American, Gary Sherman) to puncture British feelings of superiority over our Transatlantic cousins. When David tries to find something worth watching on the much-vaunted 'best television service in the world' he gets a choice between a darts match, the test card and an advert for the *News of the World*. The final confrontation between the werewolf and the gory ghosts of his victims is set in the all-too-real Eros Theatre, Piccadilly Circus, which is showing *See You Next Wednesday* — a make-believe movie Landis refers to in all his films, here incarnated as a plausibly terrible British skinflick. The film slips slightly with some unnecessarily splattery werewolf slayings, and strangely avoids the climax it seems to be building towards. The script has resurrected the nugget of Universal Pictures lore that states a werewolf can only be killed by one who truly loves him, but in the end, Jenny Agutter dolefully stands aside while the police shoot the creature and the Marcels scat-sing another reprise of 'Blue Moon'.

Paul Schrader's *Cat People*, a remake of the Jacques Tourneur/Val Lewton classic, is one of the few totally serious horror films of the 1980s. *The Howling* and *An American Werewolf* incorporate enough deliberate comedy to take care of the more ridiculous, but necessary, sides of their stories, but *Cat People* is almost solemn. Irena Gallier (Nastassia Kinski) and her clergyman brother Paul (Malcolm McDowell) are supposedly the last descendents of a tribe who, when sexually aroused, metamorphose into black panthers and can only resume human shape by killing. According to Paul, the only safe sex the siblings can have is with each other. *Cat People* is certainly perverse, and it is to Schrader's credit that there are as few giggles as there are, for the film has an astonishingly slapdash plot. Some of the transitions are so abrupt one assumes scenes have been censored out or the projectionist has got the reels in the wrong order. Schrader and screenwriter Alan Ormsby feel compelled to restage the best-remembered sequences from the first film, even though they disrupt the new story. When, in 1942, Simone Simon chances across another cat woman (Elizabeth Russell) in a restaurant, it is a magical moment; but Schrader resets the scene in a New Orleans bar as a fumbled throwaway that makes nonsense of the 'last of the cat people' angle. If there is at least one other cat person prowling around, McDowell's sex problems can easily be solved without all the mutilations, *Angst* and incest. Similarly, the revamping of the famous scenes in which the heroine's romantic rival is stalked in a park and a deserted swimming pool are stupid because they take place when we know Irena has not yet turned into a panther. Still, *Cat People* has an almost hypnotic fascination. Red sand blows away from a pile of bones under the credits, a beautiful image later echoed by a cascade of blood lapping at Irena's feet. It is some measure of the film's weirdness that the hero, Oliver Yates (John Heard) is as sexually hung up as the cat people, a Dante-obsessed zookeeper who prefers animals to human beings. In an extraordinarily kinky, offbeat wind-up, Oliver is driven to tie Irena down and make love to her. She permanently becomes a panther and is caged as an exhibit in his Victorian zoo. The final freeze-frame of Irena as a panther is an unexpected, achingly melancholy alternative to the silver-bullet shoot-outs that traditionally finish werewolf films. *Cat People* is literally dreamy, unconcerned with convincing its audience, but a refreshing, if strained touch of seriousness amid so many flip, jokey monster movies.

Wolfen is a pot-pourri of ideas tangentially related to the werewolf revival. A pair of hedonist, coke-snorting socialites and their chauffeur are torn to pieces, and New York's most rumpled homicide dick, Dewey Wilson (Albert Finney), footles around the decaying Bronx looking for likely culprits among dissatisfied urban Red Indians. Low-lifes and bums are regularly slaughtered by something that prowls like a steadicam and sees the world in electric-tinted opticals. Wilson rejects his superiors' terrorist theory and pins the deaths on a pack of superwolves. It turns out the Indians have always known about the Wolfen, but never bothered to tell whitey. After much head-severing, Wilson reaches some sort of truce with the beasts. As directed by Mike Wadleigh of *Woodstock*, with uncredited post-production restructuring by John Hancock of *Let's Scare Jessica to Death*, *Wolfen* is top-heavy with issue-consciousness. Most of the supporting characters are grudge-holding minority spokesmen who rant about the unjust treatment of Indians, wolves or human flotsam, and Wadleigh nourishes a healthy anti-Establishment fury about the state of the Bronx. The radical stuff is tempered with dollops of sheer grue and a good deal of imaginative imagery. The opening murders take place near a creaking miniature windmill, and the subsequent Wolfen attacks are cued by visual and aural echoes — sound sculptures, a burned-out organ in a roofless church or shattering sheets of plate glass shutter. The 'alienvision' effect used to depict the Wolfen's heightened senses is an advance over the red filter of *Legend of the Werewolf*, and is cleverly 'explained' via a parallel with a heat-sensitive video lie detector. However, the Wolfen themselves are disappointingly ordinary when they finally make their appearance. They look like the cuddly, real-life animals of *Never Cry Wolf* who wouldn't dream of ripping anybody's head off.

Even more perverse in its blend of art and commerce than *Cat People* and *Wolfen* is Neil Jordan's *The Company of Wolves*. Taking menstrual pretension, Hammer films and the story of Little Red Riding Hood as starting points, the movie weaves in and out of reality and its various anecdotes with a complexity worthy of an eighteenth-century gothic novel. In her dreams, the little girl heroine (Sarah Patterson) lives in a haunted forest, and is told a series of fairytales by her eccentric grandmother (Angela Lansbury). These stories-within-stories highlight a series of werewolf transformations designed and executed by Christopher Tucker with a horrific panache that outdoes anything in *The Howling* or *An American Werewolf* — a gypsy bridegroom claws his flesh away, and we see the skeleton and musculature of a wolf emerge from the gory mess; a sinister but suave huntsman opens his mouth too wide, and a furry, fanged snout bursts through; a wronged peasant girl curses the wedding party of her high-born seducer, and, while the footmen stand impassively about, the powdered and peri-wigged aristocrats explode as frisky animals from their elaborate costumes. It adds up to little more than an Amicus anthology shot through with elementary psychiatry, but *The Company of Wolves* deserves credit for its sustained peculiarity, and certainly buries alive the werewolf skit on Red Riding Hood in *Freaky Fairy Tales* (1986).

While the werewolf boom was taking the 1950s creature feature into unfamiliar areas, one film had the wit to be an unassuming, good old-fashioned monster movie. *Alligator*, directed by Lewis Teague from another neat John Sayles script, may not be as expensive as *Cat People* or *An American Werewolf*, but it makes ninety-one minutes pass painlessly. Ramon, a little girl's pet baby alligator, is flushed down the toilet in 1969 by her tyrannical father. In the sewers, he feeds on dogs dumped after illegal experiments by Dean Jagger's Unscrupulous Chemical Company and grows to giant size. Balding cop Robert Forster loses a partner to the reptile while they are investigating the case of the disappearing sewer workers and the unidentified severed limbs. Forster enlists the aid of a pretty lady herpetologist (Robin Riker) who happens to be Ramon's long-lost owner grown up. Thanks to nice performances and Sayles's cute dialogue, they make a good team; but the real hero is Ramon, who wins the audience over by chewing his way through the more unsympathetic members of the supporting cast. Henry Silva makes an especially funny supercool snack as an arrogant big-game hunter who stalks the 'gator through the slums with a trio of jive-talking ghetto blacks as 'native bearers'. Finally, Ramon comes out of the water during a pool-side reception for Jagger's daughter. He proceeds to eat the Establishment, swallowing all the corrupt cops, politicians and industrialists responsible for his freakish fate. The clip-on radical sub-text should stand as a model of economy for heavy-going preachers like Mike Wadleigh and David Selzer, allowing the film to end with a combination of King Kong's assault on a hostile city and the Marx Brothers' destruction of a stuffy social event. *Alligator* has its inevitable clichés (Sayles always uses the it's-starting-all-over-again pay-off; here, another baby 'gator plops down the drain after Ramon has been blown up), but it is a disarming work with more accessible in-jokes than

usual (a graffito in the sewer reads 'Harry Lime Lives') and enough energy and action to fill a dozen other quickies.

John Sayles, who divides his time between writing genre movies and directing more personal dramas, combines his two specialities in *The Brother From Another Planet* (1984), in which a black extraterrestrial (Joe Morton) is stranded in Harlem: although it has fun with its alien bounty hunters, who've learned English from watching *Dragnet*, the film is happier with its vignettes of everyday peculiarity than with the muddled s-f stuff. Too often films made by rabid fans of *Famous Monsters of Filmland* wind up choking on their own in-references and third-hand plots, whether cheaply and unwatchably as in Fred Olen Ray's *The Alien Dead* (1979) and Don Dohler's *The Alien Factor* (1978), or with some vague entertainment value, as in Stephen Herek's *Critters* (1986) and Fred Dekker's *Night of the Creeps* (1986). These films are stuck with cutesy ideas like giving all the characters the names of the Roger Corman 1950s repertory company (*The Alien Dead*) or of 1980s horror movie directors (*Night of the Creeps*) and it's eventually difficult even to put up with such throwaway *hommages* as the patterning of *Critters* on a couple of old *Outer Limits* episodes down to the use of alien names borrowed from the old series. The in-jokes of *The Howling* are part of a mosaic approach that adds a lot to the film's appeal, and even the use of 'Moon' songs in *An American Werewolf* has a certain relevant charm, but too often one gets the feeling that the director is merely trying to ingratiate himself with the fans. Other symptoms of the fan-turned-pro movie are an over-reliance on special effects (*The Deadly Spawn* has astonishingly good all-mouth toothy monsters and *nothing* else) and a tendency to cast Forrest J. Ackerman, John Carradine or Dick Miller in cameo roles.

Chris Windsor's *Big Meat Eater* (1982) manages to work this vein of nostalgia quite distinctively, although it misses its chance as a cult movie by refusing to leaven its esoteric humour and multi-genre pastiche with kinky sex and (apart from an unnecesary finger-shredding) graphic gore. The story of Burquitlam, a 1950s small town imperilled by aliens who raise the murdered mayor from the dead and have designs on radioactive chemicals festering in the septic tank of the local butcher's shop, suggests the film is supposed to be a musical remake of *Plan Nine From Outer Space*. However, the many plot complications are nothing more than a thin excuse for a series of *non sequiturs* made endearing by their complete incongruity. Abdullah (Big Miller), the mayor's mountainous murderer and the big meat eater of the title, is introduced stoking the furnace into which he will feed his first victim, but his status as an EC horror comic monster is undermined when he launches into 'Baghdad Boogie', a completely irrelevent song, accompanied by three belly dancers who appear from nowhere and promptly vanish when the number is over. The alien effects are deliberately and charmingly dire, with a cupcake spaceship bobbing over a Toytown model, and two plastic robots conversing in perfectly intelligible, though sub-titled, English. Alongside the larger weirdness of these sustained absurdities are any number of unexpected gags like the zombie mayor's use of a kitchen whisk to replace his severed hand, and the inventor hero's literal use of a fishbowl space-helmet.

While expensive remakes and reworkings like Tobe Hooper's *Lifeforce* and *Invaders From Mars* pile on the special effects horrors in a bludgeoning attempt to apply the collective horrors of one decade to the subtly different neuroses of another, and barbed amusements like *Alligator* and *Q* extend their throwback subjects into contemporary areas of concern, the Steven Spielberg/John Landis-produced *Twilight Zone: The Movie* (1983) and Michael Laughlin's *Strange Behavior* (1981) and *Strange Invaders* (1983) attempt, not only to update old television and film genre material, but, in Laughlin's words, 'to recapture the sense of fun and emotional response' characteristic of Hollywood in the 1950s. *Twilight Zone* deftly establishes its cultural sub-text with an apparently improvised skit, directed by John Landis, in which Albert Brooks and Dan Aykroyd drive through the night, reminiscing about the days of *Sea Hunt*, *Bonanza*,

Car 54, Where Are You? and Rod Serling's well-remembered anthology series, while *Strange Invaders* opens with a caption that describes the 1950s as a decade when 'the only things we had to worry about were the Communists and rock 'n' roll', aptly summing up the fears of conformity and anarchy represented respectively by *Invaders From Mars* and *I Was a Teenage Werewolf*.

Unfortunately, *Twilight Zone* is emasculated by the squeaky clean influence of St Spielberg, who had already turned 1950s paranoid fantasies into the benevolent reveries of *Close Encounters* and *E.T.*, whose episode is a sugary anachronism about old folk learning not to be embittered by a brush with magic (see also *Cocoon* and *Batteries Not Included*), and whose softheartedness blights the whole production. Joe Dante contributes a brilliantly designed segment based on Jerome Bixby's 'It's a *Good* Life' that seems like a malicious allegory of Spielberg's deadening childishness. Anthony (Jeremy Licht), a 12-year-old psichopath, makes his wishes come true, and entraps a surrogate family in a phony cartoon world where everyone is forced to be lovable and happy. Dante pulls off great shocks as the results of Anthony's tantrums are seen — his sister has her mouth wiped away, and Uncle Walt (Kevin McCarthy) pulls a towering, fanged, Bugs Bunny monster from a hat. Bixby's story and Serling's original *Zone* episode present Anthony as an irredeemably cruel 6-year-old tyrant, but, unable to brook such an uncharitable view of childhood, the film turns him into a confused, lonely superkid who, in a smarmy happy ending, reforms under the guidance of teacher Kathleen Quinlan and spreads peace and love wherever he goes. The only part of the movie to crawl out of the marshmallow swamp is George Miller's paranoid reading of Richard Matheson's 'Nightmare at 20,000 Feet', with John Lithgow as an airborne neurotic who spots a gremlin tearing at the plane's wing during a storm. Briefly, Miller fulfils the promise of introductory rhetoric, 'Do you want to see something *really* scary?'

While the *Twilight Zone* film falters because of its inability to understand the mechanics of its inspirations, *Strange Invaders* wittily turns *It Came From Outer Space* (1953) and *North By Northwest* (1958) inside-out through zippy homages to Eisenhower-era kitsch. The combination of affectionate recreation and amused distancing with which Laughlin approaches his sources is exemplified by the 1958 prologue, in which an archetypal flying saucer hovers over a Norman Rockwell small town, and the *American Graffiti* pastel glow is replaced by an *Outer Limits* ambience of dark shadows and clutching alien hands, while 'My Special Angel' on the soundtrack gives way to John Addison's ominously Herrmannesque orchestral score. The mood is authentically shivery for a moment, but undercut when Centerville's Marie Celeste depopulation is conveyed through close-ups of abandoned artefacts like a clockwork frog still kicking in the bathtub. The cleverest of the film's jokes is the inversion of the liberal s-f scenario represented by *The Day the Earth Stood Still* and *It Came From Outer Space*, in which the plot hinges on the inability of imperfect mankind to understand ambiguously benevolent aliens. Here, the visitors from out there are a survey team intent on studying Earth culture, but they make the elementary mistake of assuming the clothes, hairstyles and cultural furniture that make a perfect human disguise in 1958 will last until 1983. Led by erstwhile *Thing*-fighter Kenneth Tobey and hysterically *fatale* Avon lady Fiona Lewis, the invaders stalk through the film in spotted bow ties and American gothic stares, listening to the Skyliners, driving finned cars, racking up incredible scores on video games, and generally acting in the approved creature-from-another-world fashion. The joke is capped by Diana Scarwid as an alien who follows Suzanne Pleshette of *The Invaders* by succumbing to human emotions. She goes native by responding to the lure of pendant jade earrings, culottes, cropped hair and green glitter make-up, passing for human when dressed up in the sort of oddments 1950s costume designers used to give the alien love interest in dreadfuls like *Cat Women of the Moon* (1954) and *Queen of Outer Space* (1958).

Laughlin's earlier *Strange Behavior*, shot weirdly in New Zealand although set in another archetypal American small town, is less well realised than *Strange Invaders*; it feels the need to dilute its 1950s fairytale feel — as exemplified again by Fiona Lewis as a slinky villainess — with 1980s-style gore, but it also has a wide variety of off-beat characterisations from stalwarts like Michael Murphy, Louise Fletcher, Arthur Dignam and Scott Brady, and a cleverly turned plot about a mad behaviourist's use of brainwashing to execute a revenge from beyond the grave. David Blyth's all-New Zealand movie, *Death Warmed Up* (1984), deals with similar subject matter — a mad scientist producing a race of mutants through unethical brain surgery — but singularly fails to find a style to suit it. Experimenting with sub-rock video posturing and throwing in clumsy humour, clumsier gore and an absurd mock-philosophical finale in which the avenging hero turns into a fascist and has to be electrocuted for his sins, Blyth attempts to come up with an 1980s approach to the mad science genre, in the way *Blade Runner* and *The Terminator* adopt a contemporary, cyberpunk s-f tone, but the essential banality of his material trips him up. Equally messy, but slightly more likeable, is *Night of the Creeps*, which opens with a black-and-white 1950s sequence, then cuts to the 1980s and has a crew-cut, alien-infested zombie menace a campusful of *National Lampoon* nerds. Tom Atkins steals the show as a suicidal detective, 'the good news is that your dates are here, the bad news is that they're *dead!*'

Thom Eberhardt's *Night of the Comet* (1984) and Charles Band's *Trancers* (1985) more successfully integrate the old and the new, blending bits of 1950s s-f with 1980s zombies, a cracking pace and a fine-tuned sense of humour. Eberhardt tackles the 'deserted city' genre of *Target: Earth* (1954) and *Day of the Triffids* (1963) with teens Catherine Mary Stewart and Kelli Maroney let loose in a Los Angeles depopulated by the passing of a comet. Most people have turned into piles of red dust, but a few survive as scarred zombies. Although scientists Mary Woronov and eyeballs-akimbo Geoffrey Lewis take the apocalypse seriously, Stewart and Maroney refreshingly see it as an opportunity to have a good time. They crawl out of their hiding places and head straight for the department stores to indulge in a scavenging spree to the tune of 'Girls Just Want to Have Fun'. *Trancers* has Trooper Jack Deth (Tim Thomerson), a cop in the city of Lost Angeles, tracking the eponymous creatures, Moonie-like followers of an evil psychic who 'aren't alive, but aren't dead enough'. Sent back in time into the body of his 1980s ancestor when his quarry takes refuge in the past, Deth gradually gets into the fun of the twentieth century, and snaps off one of the most memorable of s-f film catch phrases, 'dry hair is for squids!' *Trancers* — which has more ideas and inventions in its seventy-three minutes than you'll find in Ridley Scott's entire filmography — is the best 'B' picture of the decade, and Band's Empire Studios have never quite matched it in such hit-or-miss quickies as *Sword Kill* (1984), *Eliminators* (1986), *Terror Vision* (1986) and *Mutant Hunt* (1986). Danny Bilson and Paul De Meo, screenwriters of *Trancers*, directed and produced *Zone Troopers* (1986), with many of the same personnel and a story featuring an intrusion of aliens from outer space into a World War II battlefield, but the very clever script and acting are let down by a hasty production and minimal special effects.

Joe Dante followed his contribution to *Twilight Zone: The Movie* with a far more satisfactory collaboration with Steven Spielberg, *Gremlins* (1984), the brilliant and underrated *Explorers* (1985) and the disappointing comic re-run of *Fantastic Voyage* (1966), *Innerspace* (1987). Obviously, the history of the science fiction film is evoked time and again in Dante's work, but he rarely allows his affection for old movies to get in the way of his modern sensibilities. *Gremlins* is almost a struggle between the world views of Spielberg and Dante, the former with his belief in an apparent order that periodically tears itself apart in the face of a real (*Jaws*, *Duel*) or imagined (*1941*, *Close Encounters*) threat, while the latter presents a world in perpetual uproar invariably failing to take notice of the toothy monsters chewing away at the foundations. While Spielberg contributes the cuteness of the original *mogwai* and the Rod Serling-like moralities of Keye Luke's closing homily, Dante launches an anarchic attack on such sacred American institutions as the YMCA, Walt Disney, Smokey the Bear, *It's a Wonderful Life* and Phil Spector's *Christmas Album*. With monsters who become a parody of the riotous humans whose town they take over — brawling and breakdancing in a local bar, tampering with bits of machinery, or providing a rowdy audience for *Snow White and the Seven Dwarfs* — and a hilariously appalling 'Why I Hate Christmas' keynote speech from Phoebe Cates, *Gremlins* is a wide-eyed conflation of the tinsel of Christmas with the gleeful excess of Saturnalia. *Explorers* is Dante's deepest work to date, and perfectly integrates its obsession with old monster movies to demonstrate how essential a sense of wonder is for the future of mankind, as a trio of misfit kids venture into outer space in a spaceship they have made in their backyard and encounter their alien equivalents, a pair of neglected teenage bug-eyed monsters who are besotted with Earth television.

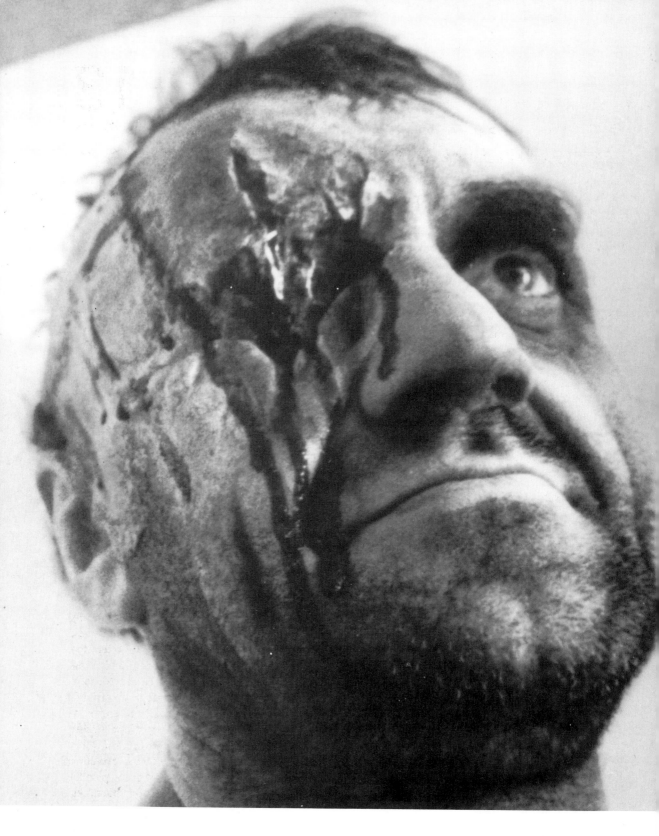

● *Pasta-eating zombie.* **E tu vivrai nel terrore . . . L'Aldila.**

cannibal zombie gut-crunchers —
cannibal zombie gut-crunchers —

italian style!
italian style!

Since the end of the romance between art houses and the Italian cinema, Rome has become the Taiwan of the international film industry. The patron saint of pasta production is Dino de Laurentiis, the expatriot mogul who touted his remake of *King Kong* (1976) as 'the most original screen spectacle of all time!' Dino's $24,000,000 rip-off is a Mount Rushmore achievement lesser producers can only dream of matching. The ideal of the Italian exploitation huckster is Chico Marx, a small-time swindler selling the same product over and over again at inflationary prices, delighting in his own unashamed greed and vulgarity, and continually reasserting his pride in his work with cries of 'At'sa fine, boss!' Italy may make rip-offs, but at least it can claim to make the best, most lively, most audacious rip-offs in the world. It is accepted practice to produce official-sounding sequels to American hits. When *The Deer Hunter* was put out in Italy as *Il Cacciatore*, Antonio Margheriti (a.k.a. Anthony Dawson) made an *Il Cacciatore 2 (The Last Hunter)* (1980), which, ironically, is a rip-off of *Apocalypse Now* (1979). Naturally, Margheriti's *Apocalisse domani (Cannibal Apocalypse)* (1980) is his version of *Dawn of the Dead*. Scarcely two months after *Dawn of the Dead* had been successfully released in Italy as *Zombi*, Lucio Fulci had *Zombi 2* in the cinemas, and since then — amid an entire horde of flesh-eating *morti viventi* movies — there have been at least three different films under the title *Zombi 3*. Strangest

of all, perhaps, is the case of Marlo Landi's *Patrick vive ancora* (1980), a spurious sequel to Richard Franklin's hardly earth-shattering *Patrick*. Obviously, films don't even have to be big hits to rate an Italian imitation.

Historically, the pattern of Italian commercial cinema has been an overlapping succession of genre cycles. Usually, but not invariably, triggered by the domestic popularity either of a specific American film or of a traditional Hollywood genre, these cycles come and go in a few years. During the short lifespan of any individual cycle, an incredible number of similar films are rushed through production and into distribution before the format wears thin and the popularity fades. The period of overlap between cycles often accounts for intriguing hybrids like the horror/ *peplum* (Mario Bava's *Ercole al centro della terra (Hercules in the Haunted World)*, 1961; Riccardo Freda's *Maciste all' inferno (The Witch's Curse)*, 1962) or the disco/*giallo* (Lucio Fulci's *Murderock, uccide a passo di danza*, 1984). Too often the relationship between Italian cycles and their (mainly) American 'originals' is perceived as one of simple imitation. Thanks to Christopher Frayling's *Spaghetti Westerns*, it is now a critical commonplace to assert that the rash of Italian/Spanish Westerns that followed Sergio Leone's Clint Eastwood trilogy are a vital stage in the evolution of the genre as a whole. However, there is still a tendency to overlook the way Italian spectacles, horror films, murder mysteries, science fiction pictures, superspy thrillers and jungle adventures do exactly the same things with the trappings of their Hollywood models that Leone does with the legacy left him by John Ford, Budd Boetticher and Anthony Mann. While many Italian genre films are simply worthless carbon copies with a few baroque trimmings, the best examples of most cycles are surprisingly sophisticated mixes of imitation, pastiche, parody, deconstruction, reinterpretation and operatic inflation.

Italy first became known for horror movies in the early 1960s with the unexpected critical championing of the early films of Riccardo Freda (*I Vampiri* (Lust of the Vampire), 1957, *Lo Spettro* (The Ghost), 1963) and Mario Bava (*La Frusta e il corpo* (Night Is the Phantom), 1962, *I Tre volti della paura* (Black Sabbath), 1963) in France, Great Britain and the United States. These films have a distinctively Italian style, but there was thought to be a feeling at home that only the British and Americans could make good horror movies. This led Freda and Bava to sign their films with anglicised pseudonyms, Robert Hampton and John M. Old (later, Lamberto Bava would call himself John M. Old Jr), and give the leading roles in their films to Italian-speaking foreigners. The happiest result of this curious anglophilia was the career of Barbara Steele, who became typecast as a witchlike *femme fatale* after her performances in Bava's *La Maschera del demonio* (Mask of Satan) (1960) and Freda's *L'Orrible segretto del Dr Hichcock* (The Horrible Dr Hitchcock) (1962). Blessed with a haunted face and a dry-ice sensuality, Steele is one of the screen's great vampires, although since she was once quoted as never wanting 'to climb out of another fucking coffin again' she is probably unhappy with the distinction. After the decadent blossoming of these operatic, overblown horrors in the early 1960s, the Italian horror film was eclipsed by the crazes for Herculean muscle epics (called *peplum* films, after a short classical garment worn by all the extras), *Mondo cane*-style mock/sick documentaries, Spaghetti Westerns and James Bondian spy thrillers.

The international success of Dario Argento's

L'Uccello dalle piume di cristallo revived the genre of Bava's *Sei donne per l'assassino*, and let loose a plague of masked, black-gloved homicidal maniacs with twisted motivations and surprising identities, and *The Exorcist*'s wallow in Catholic guilt encouraged a legion of Italian rivals, but from the late 1960s through to the mid-1970s, Italian horror was underground. Argento was making hooded killer thrillers that didn't have to be labelled *orrore*, and Bava was forced to follow suit or enter into beleaguered international co-productions. One of the drawbacks of the cycle system is that any director who happens to find his *métier* is liable to be stranded when his speciality goes out of fashion and he's forced to make something else, as witness Bava's lame attempts at Spaghetti Western (*La Strada per Fort Alamo* (Arizona Bill), 1965) or spy spoof (*Le Spie vengono dal semifreddo*, (Dr Goldfoot and the Girl Bombs), 1966). In this period, there was a brief cycle of sex/horror movies with Nazi themes, of which the most notorious is Sergio Garrone's *Lager SSadis kastrat Kommandantur* (S.S. Experiment Camp) (1976), which mix the women-in-prison sexploitation movie with mad science, fascist fetishism and misogynist torture. Garrone's film was followed by the likes of *Le Lunghi notti della Gestapo* (Red Nights of the Gestapo) (1976), *L'Ultima orgia del III reich* (The Gestapo's Last Orgy) (1977) and *La Deportate della sezione speciale SS* (Deported Women of the SS Special Section) (1977). The inspiration for these unredeemable nasties would seem to have come equally from American-made sado-quickies like *Ilsa, She Wolf of the SS* (1974) and *Love Camp 7* (1968) and from solemnly hypocritical, expensively furnished Italian prestige productions like Luchino Visconti's *La Caduta degli dei* (The Damned) (1969), Liliana Cavani's *Il Portiere di notte* (The Night Porter) (1974) and Tinto Brass's *Salon Kitty* (1976).

Meanwhile, there was a very minor trend of adaptions of popular Continental comic strips, often emphasising mild sado-masochism and late 1960s fetish gear. De Laurentiis's productions of Roger Vadim's *Barbarella* (1968) and Bava's *Diabolik* (Danger, Diabolik) (1968) set the style, but they were soon followed by silly horror comics like Piero Vivarelli's *Satanik* (1968), Bruno Corbucci's *Isabella, Duchessa dei diavoli* (1969) and Corrado Farina's enormously boring *Baba Yaga* (*Baba Yaga — Devil Witch*) (1973). Margheriti kept banging away at any genre to hand, but his horror output of the late 1960s and early 1970s has a distinctly tarnished feel: *Contronatura* (*The Unnaturals*) (1969) and *La Morte negli occhi del gatto* (*Seven Dead in the Cat's Eyes*) (1973) are old dark house murder mysteries with gore, and *Nella stretta morsa del ragno* (*Web of the Spider*) (1970), despite Klaus Kinski as Edgar Allan Poe, is a merely competent remake of his own, superior *La Danza macabra* (*Castle of Blood*) (1964). The vampire episode of Bava's *I Tre volti della paura* was remade with a modern setting as *La Notte dei diavoli* (*Night of the Devils*) (1972), and other old ideas are rehashed in such gothics as *La Notte che Evelyn usci dalla tomba* (*The Night Evelyn Came out of the Grave*) (1971), *La Notte dei dannati* (*Night of the Damned*) (1971), *L'Etrusco uccide ancora* (*The Dead Are Alive*) (1972), *Il Castello delle donne maledette* (*Frankenstein's Castle of Freaks*) (1973), *Il Pleniluno delle vergine* (*The Devil's Wedding Night*) (1973) and *Frankenstein all'Italiana* (*Frankenstein — Italian Style*) (1974). As with the Nazi cycle, the main frill here is the combination of sexploitation and violence, dressed up with leftovers from the Universal and Hammer horrors that had inspired Bava and Freda in the first place.

Dawn of the Dead revived the Italian horror film with a bloody vengeance. George A. Romero's Pennsylvania-based film is actually a co-production with Italy's Dario Argento, with a manic score by the Goblins, whose earsplitting rock is prominently featured in a batch of Italian movies. The success of the film created a new Italian horror cycle, and 1980 saw, in rapid succession: Marino Girolami's ridiculous *Zombi holocaust*, Bruno Mattei's *Virus — inferno dei morti viventi* (*Zombie Creeping Flesh*), Aristide Massaccesi's porno quickie *La Notte erotiche dei morti viventi* (*Island of the Zombies*), Andrea Bianchi's tackily gory *Le Notti del terrore* (*Zombi 3*), and Umberto Lenzi's nuclear-powered *Incubo sulla città contaminata* (*Nightmare City*).

Mattei's *Virus* is fairly representative: it steals outtakes from the Goblins' *Dawn of the Dead* score, a South-East Asian locale from *Apocalypse Now* and a chunk of its title from Argento's *Inferno*. Typical of the sleazy contrivances of the genre is the sequence (repeated in *Zombi holocaust*) in which the heroine wins over some natives by taking her clothes off and painting her body, but the film also has a surprisingly apposite (if stupidly expressed) message that unless the developed world feeds the Third World, the latter will eat the former.

Intimately related to the cycle are Margheriti's *Apocalisse domani*, about rabid cannibal Vietnam veterans led by John Saxon, and Massaccesi's *Antropophagus* (*The Anthropopagous Beast*) and its follow-up *Rosso sangue* (*Absurd*) (1981), in which mortal flesh-eaters act like Romero's zombies. Massaccesi, frequently billed as Joe D'Amato (or David Hills, Kevin Mancuso, Steven Benson, Peter Newton, Michael Wotruba and perhaps many more), has a well-earned reputation as the most boring film-maker in the world, but he also goes in for moments of gore more extreme even than those of Lucio Fulci. In the climax of *Antropophagus*, screenwriter/cannibal degenerate Luigi Montefiore (a.k.a. George Eastman) is punctured in the belly with a pickaxe by Tisa Farrow and messily eats his own entrails. However, the first 87 minutes of this interminable 90-minute film deal with dull characters wandering around a boat, a Greek island, some caves or an old dark house. The sort-of sequel, which has Edmond Purdom as a mad scientist priest tracking down a Frankensteinian cannibal killer (Montefiore again) created by the Church, is exactly the same, although it throws in its outrageous gore scenes one every fifteen minutes rather than cramming them all into the last reel. Since the end of the *morti viventi* cycle, Massaccesi has gone back to his old stamping grounds, and made yet more sex films with his perennial Emanuelle, Laura Gemser (a.k.a. Moira Chen), and had bashes at the barbarian *peplum* and the *Mad Max* rip-off. His filmography also includes the necrophile soap opera *Buio omega* (*Blue Holocaust*) (1979) and self-explanatory hybrids like *Emanuelle e gli ultimi cannibali*

(*Emanuelle and the Last Cannibals*) (1977).

The *morti viventi* craze brought Lucio Fulci to the fore much as the science fiction boom of the 1950s promoted Jack Arnold. Like Arnold, Fulci had been around for a while, making whatever was offered to him, and briefly found a genre to which he was ideally suited. Sadly, like Arnold, the passing of the genre has plunged him back into a morass of unchallenging 'assignments'. Fulci, a director since the early 1960s, at first specialised in slapstick comedy, flirting with science fiction and horror in such knockabout items as *Dos Cosmonautas a la fuerza* (1967) and *Il Cavaliere Costante Nicosia demoniaco ovvero Dracula in Brianza* (1975). He also found time to make Spaghetti Westerns (*Tempo di massacro* (*The Brute and the Beast*), 1966; *I Quattro dell' apocalisse*, 1976), blood-drenched historical epics (*Beatrice Cenci*, 1971), softcore *gialli* (*Una sull' altra* (*One on Top of the Other*), 1971), and cheapskate adaptions of out-of-copyright literary works (*Il Ritorno di Zanna Blanca* (*White Fang*), 1974). At his lowest, he even directed *All' Onoredel piaccionio le donne* (*The Eroticist*), (1971), an entire movie about the popular Italian pastime of bottom-pinching. He contributed minor films to minor horror trends, dashing off a rural psycho movie (*Non si sevizia un paperino* (*Don't Torture the Duckling*), 1972) and a *Don't Look Now* imitation (*Sette notte in nero* (*The Psychic*), 1977), but didn't make his mark until the trail-blazing, coat-tail-riding *Zombi 2* (1979). Released in America as *Zombie* and Britain (minus an eyeball piercing) as *Zombie Flesh Eaters*, *Zombi 2* is less an imitation Romero than a bloodier return to the zombie 'B' pictures of the 1940s. After a zombie-ridden yacht drifts into New York harbour, newshound Ian McCulloch and heiress Tisa Farrow track the epidemic back to a Caribbean island where whisky doctor Richard Johnson is trying to find a cure for a voodoo curse, and the *conquistadores* are crawling from their graves. There is a great action scene early in the film as an underwater zombie and a shark try to eat each other, but the rapid-fire, non-stop horror sequences that follow lose their ability to shock. Romero's restraint and sly wit make *Dawn of the Dead* cumulatively powerful, but Fulci approaches

Zombi 2 with a straight-faced hysteria that becomes tiresome. The punch-line is ludicrous, as a radio announcer keeps gabbing while the zombies get him, 'I have just been informed that zombies have entered the building ... they're at the door ... they're coming's in ... aarrgh!'

Fulci followed *Zombi 2* with *La Paura nella citta dei morti viventi* (*City of the Living Dead*) (1980) and *E tu vivrai nel terrore... L'Aldila* (*The Beyond*) (1981), stately gothics that lack the second-hand drive which keeps the earlier film exciting, but which hint at an individual personality emerging in his *oeuvre*. *La Paura* begins with the suicide of a priest in a New England churchyard, and *L'Aldila*, the crucifixion of a diabolist painter in a Louisiana hotel. Both horrors open doorways to Hell into which the dumb protagonists blunder and which, in lieu of more imaginative infernal manifestations, disgorge shambling hordes of flesh-eating zombies. *La Paura* has a suspenseful sequence where Christopher George, idling in a cemetery, realises heroine Catriona MacColl has been buried alive nearby and, in trying to rescue her from her coffin, repeatedly thrusts a pickaxe dangerously near her head. *L'Aldila* uses the character of the devil-worshipping artist to justify disquieting, painterly images like the sudden appearance of a blind girl standing alone on a causeway across a lake. Both films turn their Transatlantic locations into genuinely eerie, unworldly antechambers to Roman studio visions of Hell. But Fulci's gore scenes are unpleasant, unconvincing, and disastrously paced. In *La Paura*, the zombies like to tear the backs of people's heads off, and the demon priest makes a girl throw up her intestines, but both effects require the victim obligingly to stand still while the decidedly slow undead catch up with them and a cutaway dummy can be substituted. In *L'Aldila*, Fulci allows us to see daylight through a little girl's head, but also throws in a scene with a horde of infernal spiders that is simply bathetic, as a fistful of Woolworth's-reject novelty bugs mechanically crawl over their writhing victim.

After *Lo Squartatore di New York* (*The New York Ripper*) (1982), a razors-through-eyes-and/or-nipples *giallo* nauseatingly advertised to the trade with the line 'Fulvia Film proudly announces... Slashing Up Women Was His Pleasure!', Fulci toned down the splatter to fit his liking for image-oriented, lingering films. *Il Gatto nero di Park Lane (The Black Cat)* (1982) is a quiet version of the Poe tale, set in an English village, played almost entirely in facial close-ups of the evil cat and its demented master (Patrick Magee) for maximum claustrophobia. *Quella villa accanto il cimitero (The House By the Cemetery)* (1982) is another step away from the zombie flesh-eaters, although the cellar does contain Dr Freudstein, a mad scientist who has become a bloodthirsty, immortal monstrosity. As in *Il Gatto nero*, the horror murders are hung on a strong situation, with Freudstein's willingness to murder his wife and daughter to prolong his life paralleling the hero's willingness to endanger his wife and son to get to the bottom of the mystery. Fulci's oddball touches include the psychic little boy seeing his babysitter as a beheaded fashion mannequin in anticipation of her death, and a cracked gravestone set into the hallway through which Freudstein clutches at unwary ankles. Finally, Fulci elaborates on the trip-into-Hell finishes of *La Paura* and *L'Aldila* by having the child escape from the monster through the gravestone only to find himself in the Victorian limbo inhabited by the ghost of Freudstein's little girl.

If *Il Gatto nero* and *Quella villa* are a shade too leisurely for their own good — of Fulci's films, only *Zombi 2* has anything like pace — then *Manhattan Baby* (1983) is practically catatonic. And yet it is the culmination of his work in the horror field, dispensing altogether with logical plotting, characters and even (one bird attack apart) gory violence. What *Manhattan Baby* does have is a succession of oneiric images, as an ancient Egyptian supernatural force manifests itself in a New York apartment — Sahara sand drifting over herringbone tiles, scorpions scuttling from desk drawers. Also, as in *Il Gatto nero*, there is an obsession with eyes — a recurrent theme in Fulci's work (gouged in *Zombi 2* and *Lo Squartatore*, cataract covered in *L'Aldila*). The Egyptian eye medallion which is the focus of the curse is visually echoed by various blind characters, endless

extreme close-ups of twitching eyes and even a set of joke spectacles with bulging plastic eyeball attachments. Whereas earlier Fulci films either borrow from or refer explicitly to Lovecraft, Clark Ashton Smith and Henry James, *Manhattan Baby* retreats into childhood fantasies derived from C.S. Lewis and Ray Bradbury ('The Veldt') as the nursery becomes a children-only limbo into which adults venture at the risk of their lives. But, just as Fulci entered his minimalist phase, the Italian horror boom was gone, and he found himself having to add bizarre touches to the barbarian bicep epic *Mace il fuorilegge (Conquest)* (1983) and being lost entirely in the future game-show quickie *Roma 2033: I Centurioni del futuro (2033: The Fighter Centurions)* (1983).

If Lucio Fulci has the highest profile of the Italian rip-off artists, then Sergio Martino could perhaps claim to be the most endearing. Martino has dabbled with various genres, including a sexploitation reworking of Poe's 'The Black Cat' (*Tuo vizio e una stanza chiusa e solo io ne ho la chiave (Excite Me)*, 1972) a Polanski-esque woman-cracking-up fantasy (*Tutti i colori del buio (They're Coming to Get You)*, 1972) and a hooded killer thriller (*I Corpi presentano tracce di violenza carnale (Torso)*, 1973), but his most distinctive works are Boys' Own Paper adventures. *L'Isola degli uomini pesce (Island of the Mutations)* (1978) was intended as a rip-off of Don Taylor's listless *Island of Dr Moreau* (1977), but emerges as a much more entertaining film. In the 1890s, Claudio Cassinelli is shipwrecked on a mysterious island where Barbara Bach dashes about on horseback, Joseph Cotten toils amid bubbling retorts in his laboratory and Richard Johnson sneers as a vintage dastard named Edmund Rackham. The native population includes a tribe of superstitious savages with an exotic voodoo priestess (Beryl Cunningham) and a school of fishy mutants. When Cassinelli recognises one of his old shipmates under the scales, he discovers that the mutations are being created for the highest of scientific and humanitarian reasons by Cotten, but that Johnson is unethically using them as slaves in his scheme to steal some sunken treasure. Unlike *Island of Dr Moreau*, *L'Isola degli uomini pesce* accepts itself at face value and makes

● Ursula Andress *in trouble*. **La Montagna del dio cannibale.**

its clichés acceptable by serving them up as if Johnson were the first villain ever to think of locking a stalwart hero in a room which will slowly flood with the tide, and Cotten the first mad scientist to have a lovely daughter unaware of his loopy experiments. In the US, Martino's movie was mixed with new footage featuring Cameron Mitchell and Mel Ferrer shot by Joe Dante for release as *Screamers*. Martino returned to the jungle with Cassinelli in *La Montagna del dio cannibale* (*Prisoners of the Cannibal God*) (1978) and *Il Fiume del grande caimano* (*The Great Alligator*) (1980), and then set up shop in the future for *2019, dopo la caduta di New York* (*2019: After the Fall of New York*) (1982).

La Montagna del dio cannibale is primarily an old-fashioned jungle movie, with Cassinelli helping Ursula Andress and Stacy Keach penetrate the steaming undergrowth of New Guinea in search of Andress's missing husband and 'wealth beyond their wildest dreams' in uranium deposits. The cannibals turn up in the last reel, worshipping the dead husband (his rotting corpse has a ticking Geiger counter in its chest cavity), but their flesh-eating and human sacrifice are subordinate to an already complicated plot, merely thrown in to add a few sick touches to the standard adventuring. The Italian cannibal movie cycle is almost unique in that, although it assimilates influences as diverse as *A Man Called Horse*, *The Valley Obscured by Clouds*, *Aguirre – Wrath of God* and *Apocalypse Now*, it is actually an indigenous form whose brief popularity owes little to the box-office success of any of its foreign inspirations. Indeed, if anything, the Italian cannibal movie is a cross-breeding of the lurid pseudo-anthropology of the *Mondo* movie and the sub-Tarzan brand of jungle adventure that occasionally creeps out of Rome when the fluctuations of the lira make location shooting in the Third World possible. Considering the proximity of Italy to Africa and the brief craze in the 1960s for making films there, it's surprising that the cannibal movies of the 1970s and 1980s have invariably preferred to use South American or South-East Asian backdrops.

The genre proper seems to have been invented by Ruggero Deodato, whose Philippines-set *L'Ultimo mondo cannibale* (*Cannibal*) (1976) stars Ivan Rassimov and Me Me Lay, the performers who are the cycle's most recurrent feature. *L'Ultimo mondo*, however, is merely a dry run for Deodato's *Cannibal holocaust* (1979), which serves as the definitive cannibal movie and an auto-critique of the genre. Set in South America, it prefigures John Boorman's *The Emerald Forest* (1985) in its depiction of the first contact between savage intruders from the civilised world and a Stone Age tribe who are less primitive than they seem. In a pointed attack on the *Mondo cane* school of documentary imperialism, the intruders are a team of film-makers who force the tribe into greater and greater acts of savagery in order to get sensational footage for their next movie. They are overwhelmed and eaten, and the producers back in New York examine the footage in order to find out what happened to them in 'the green inferno'. While acting and script are rudimentary, Deodato's handling of the film-within-a-film technique and the oblique revelation of his 'message' are very impressive. He further demonstrated his talents with *La Casa sperduta nel parco*, a brutal *giallo*, and dissipated himself with a childish adventure *I Predatori d'Atlantide* (*The Atlantis Interceptors*) (1983), the jungle action *Inferno in diretta*, the body count picture *Body Count* (1986), the barbarian picture *Barbari* (*Barbarians*) (1986) and the tardy *Cannibal Holocaust 2* (1987).

If Deodato is responsible for the *ne plus ultra* of the cannibal movie in *Cannibal holocaust*, then long-time hack Umberto Lenzi takes the form about as far as it can go in the direction of gratuitous violence in his notoriously sickening *Cannibal ferox* (1980). This is a South American jungle travelogue enlivened by convincing scenes in which a cannibal hacks off a penis and eats it, a woman is hung from meat-hooks in her breasts, an eye is fished out with a knife, the villain's skull is sliced like a breakfast egg so his brains can be scooped out and eaten, human entrails are ripped out and consumed, and stock footage animals eat each other for real. John Morghen, the victim of the penis and brain atrocities, is the Italian cinema's

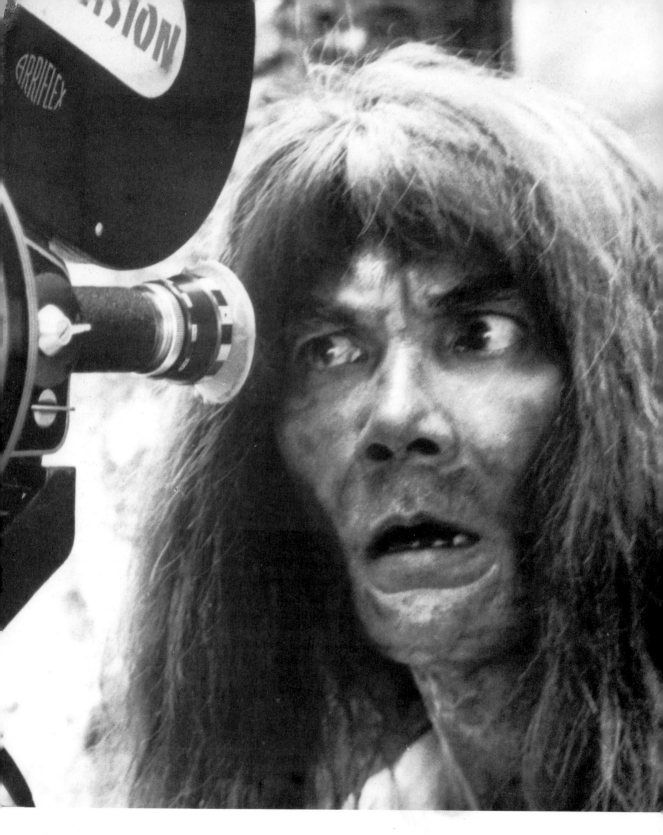

● *Third-world film-making. On the set of* **Cannibal.**

favourite whipping-boy: he has his head drilled in *La Paura nella citta dei morti viventi*, gets beaten and humiliated in *La Casa sperduta nel parco*, has a hole shotgunned through him in *Apocalisse domani* and gets offed by a psycho in *Deliria (StageFright — Aquarius)* (1987). Lenzi simply doesn't know where to stop, and as a result *Cannibal ferox* is the nastiest of the nasties, not least for its willingness (shared with many Italian films) to slaughter animals for real on camera because it's cheaper than staging special effects. In Asia, Lenzi was responsible for the pioneering *Il Paese del sesso selvaggio (Deep River Savages)* (1972) and *Mangiati vivi dai cannibale*, both of which team Rassimov and Lay. Here, cannibalism is spotlighted in a few comparatively mild scenes, but the films are more concerned with recreating the stories of *A Man Called Horse* and the Rev Jim Jones. Among Lenzi's other credits are the incomprehensible *giallo Spasmo* (1974) with Suzy Kendall and Ivan Rassimov, a film only notable because George A. Romero shot some wide-screen murders for insertion into American release prints, and the dullish *Poltergeist* imitation *Ghosthouse* (1987). He is sometimes billed as Humphrey Humbert, but has probably never heard of Nabokov.

Although Deodato and Lenzi more or less monopolise the cannibal movie, there are inevitable ventures into the field from Aristide Massaccesi (*Emanuelle e gli ultimi cannibale*) and Jesus Franco (*Mondo cannibale (Cannibals)*, 1979; *Il Cacciatore di uomini (Devil Hunter)*, 1980). Aside from stragglers like Franco Prosperi's *Il Cannibal* (1979), Giuseppe Maria Scotese's *Cannibal domani* (1983) and Roy Garrett's *Emerald Forest* rip-off *Amazonia* (1986), that just about accounts for the whole of the genre. However, there was a commercially useful overlap with the flesh-eating zombie genre, which was also prone from time to time to explore the rain forests of New Guinea and the Philippines. Marino Girolami's *Zombie holocaust* fills its jungles with zombies *and* cannibals, and boasts an alternate title (*La Regina dei cannibale*) to serve in areas where cannibals remained popular and zombies hadn't yet arrived. And *Virus — Inferno dei morti viventi* and *Apocalisse*

domani have a bizarre exchange scheme whereby the one has zombies in the traditionally cannibal-thronged jungles, while the other brings cannibalism home to downtown Atlanta.

While Lucio Fulci, Antonio Margheriti, Umberto Lenzi and Aristide Massaccesi have been around for decades, doing whatever is in fashion, times have been rougher on more individualist talents like Riccardo Freda and Mario Bava. Freda, happy enough in the 1960s with the gothics and the *peplum*, hasn't been prolific in the last twenty years. *L'Ossessione che uccide (Murder Obsession)* (1980) is an attempted horror come-back, saddled with the presence of Laura Gemser and some choppy gore inserts as gloomy characters meet their fates in an old dark house. The spectre of Dr Hichcock has truly been exorcised. The late Mario Bava never really lived up to the promise of the 1960s movies, but he did continue to develop as the languid stylist of the horror movie, even if his daring visual experiments are invariably compromised by his penny-dreadful scenarios. After the late masterpieces *Operazione paura (Curse of the Dead)* (1965) and *Il Rosso segno della follia (A Hatchet for the Honeymoon)* (1969), Bava seemed doomed in the 1970s to repeat himself. *Ten Little Indians* reruns like *Cinque bambole per la luno d'agosto (Five Dolls for an August Moon)* (1970) and stalk-and-slash fables like *Antefatto (Blood Bath)* (1970) hardly stretch Bava's talents, and he falls back in the former on his practised pictorialism and in the latter on extremely explicit gore killings. These are mean-spirited *gialli* with contrived plots and uniformly grasping, ridiculously unsympathetic characters. *Cinque bambole* keeps cutting back to the walk-in freezer as yet another polythene-shrouded corpse is hung up alongside an obscenely raw side of beef to obscure the fact that the borrowed plot has been mangled, and *Antefatto* sets the rules ten years too early for the *Friday the 13th* series and bests them with a cynical, cyclical plot whereby everyone murders someone else in a domino chain. It's hard to tell just how seriously Bava is taking these films, which are afflicted by zoom-happy camerawork and bizarre early 1970s fashions.

Gli Orrori del castello di Norimberga (Baron Blood) (1972), shot in Germany just after the Madrid trip that yielded the martyred *Lisa e il diavolo*, is further evidence of Bava in decline. Elke Sommer, Bava's Lisa, is an innocent bystander while a resurrected, disfigured nobleman takes over his old castle and begins anew his sadistic reign, only to be undone by a witch's curse and the killer zombies of his victims. The screenplay borrows its obvious surprise villain from *Mystery of the Wax Museum* with such a lack of conviction that even the traditionally boneheaded hero guesses the identity of Baron Blood's current incarnation long before Joseph Cotten climbs out of his wheelchair and dissolves. A good rule of thumb in these movies is not to trust a) anyone in a wheelchair or b) any American 'name' actor who doesn't appear to have much to do with the plot. Cotten and Sommer have been abandoned by their director and give non-committal performances, unsure whether to underplay or overplay the material. But *Norimberga* is fascinating to watch. Bava's endless zooms in and out of every niche in the castle never transcend the pulp script, but one is always aware that the camera, the lighting and the editing are moving, even if the story isn't. Bava plays with light, backlighting a chase through the fog so it seems to take place in an unreal world of oranges, reds and blues, and making the real castle seem like a stylised studio set. This is simply too much for *Norimberga*, but Bava makes moments of an awful movie seem magnificent.

Originally a cameraman, Bava was allowed to make *La Maschera del demonio* as a reward for completing *I Vampiri* when Freda fell ill. With a cyclical elegance worthy of one of Baron Blood's family curses, Lamberto Bava made his debut as a director on the strength of his contribution to his ailing father's *Shock transfert — suspence — hypnos (Shock)* (1977). Lamberto — who also co-directed *La Venere d'ille* (1978) with his father for Italian TV — had a hand in the multi-authored screenplay of *Shock*, giving Mario an intensely characterised ghost story upon which to build his brilliant mise-en-scène . Mario does not need to fall back on the

overcompensations of *Norimberga*, and is thus more subtle than usual. The distracting images (a porcelain hand poking up between sofa cushions, a razor blade lodged between piano keys) and tricky shots (the heroine's hair turns into Medusa tendrils in a dream) are there, but this time they mean something in the context of the screen story. Previously, the only memorable characters in Bava's films have been masked (either literally, or, in the case of Barbara Steele, by a sphinx-like face) mysteries. *Shock* has a genuine performance from Daria Nicolodi as a controlled hysteric who believes her young son to be the malevolent spirit of his father. Nicolodi's hidden core of guilty madness is physically manifested as the murdered corpse of her husband, bricked up in the cellar. When the wall is breached, the equilibrium she has found in her madness is broken and she becomes a raving lunatic.

Lamberto Bava's *Macabro (Macabre)* (1980), his own directorial debut, is a stronger, non-supernatural version of *Shock*. Bernice Stegers keeps the head of her lover in the fridge and is driven to violence by the well-intentioned curiosity of her caring but obsessive landlord (Stanko Molnar) and the incredible, ice-cold malice of her young daughter (Veronica Zinny). The spectre of Mario lurks in the shadowy recesses of Molnar's New Orleans home with its bric-à-brac and prowling camera, and Zinny's child monster is a development of the creepy kids who figure in many of Mario's films, from *Operation paura* to *Shock*. Whereas the typical Mario film has a wandering plot that serves as an excuse for the set pieces much as a formula backstage musical might string together a series of outstanding production numbers, *Macabro* has a story as tight and inner directed as its heroine. The three characters are confined to the old dark house with very little contrivance, and their unnatural obsessions (Stegers's with the head, Zinny's with her parents' failed marriage and Molnar's with Stegers) feed into and exacerbate each other. *Macabro* is, of course, the seminal head-in-the-fridge movie, and the image is used far more creatively than the Poe-style concealed corpse of *Shock*. Molnar is blind, so he can never be sure whether the ghastly objects he finds are what he fears they are. Sadly, the spell of *Macabro* is broken by a freeze-frame twist that has the head come to homicidal life for the sake of a *Friday the 13th* kick in the teeth and a spurious 'it's all true' announcement.

Lamberto Bava's post-*Macabro* career hasn't quite lived up to his debut, finding him caught between the cyclical trap of the Italian exploitation merry-go-round and the increasingly erratic influence of Dario Argento. *La Casa con la scala nel buio* (*A Blade in the Dark*) (1983) is a *giallo* in the Argento vein, with a composer hero working on the score of a film murder mystery becoming haunted by strange events that appear to have seeped out of the movie-in-progress. After that, the director felt the need to turn out efficient, unspectacular imitations of *First Blood* and *Jaws*, *Blastfighter* (1984) and *Shark — rosso nell' oceano* (*Devouring Waves*) (1984) before returning to Argento's orbit and developing the theme of *La Casa con la scala nel buio* in *Demoni* (1986). Produced by Argento and set in Berlin, *Demoni* features a group of characters trapped in a cinema which is overwhelmed by demonic ghouls who escape from the horror film unreeling on screen. The promising subject matter is rather botched as Bava opts for a misjudged *Night of the Living Dead* rerun, throws in an inept selection of Heavy Metal hits on the soundtrack and fails to find any ironic angles in the story. The film-within-a-film is a hackneyed gothic, but the 'real' movie is mounted in exactly the same style. Giuliano Montaldo's *Circuito chiuso* (*Closed Circuit*) (1978) is a subtler, more arresting variation on the theme as a murder investigation into a shooting in a cinema finally upturns a supernatural solution as the killing is pinned on a Spaghetti Western gunman. *Demoni*, a triumph of illogicality run riot, was a smash hit in Italy, and Argento and Bava responded with the

even less inspired *Demoni 2* (1987), in which a block of flats is the site of chaos when demon glove-puppets spill out of television screens in a combined imitation of *Shivers*, *Poltergeist* and *Videodrome*. On his own, Bava turned to television and made his worst movie to date, the uninspired spoof *Dentro al cimitero* (*Graveyard Disturbance*) (1986).

In the late 1980s, Italian horror is again in retreat. The currently popular cycles have been triggered by non-*fantastique* movies like *First Blood*, *Rambo: First Blood, Part 2* and *Platoon*, and so Antonio Margheriti and his colleagues are turning out militaristic action/explosion films which lack even the fantasy-horror frills that dress up the mythic barbarian or future warrior genres. However, with Argento — a major director in Italy, and thus not yoked to any passing genre — committed to his *giallo* mode and exerting his influence, it seems likely that the strain will continue. Indeed, Argento is one of the few Italian film-makers who warrants quickie imitations of his own films. Lucio Fulci thuddingly turns out a xerox *Phenomena* in *Ænigma* (1987), which substitutes slugs for insects, and the promising Maurizio Tedesco duly rips off *Demoni* in the pointless *Spettri* (*Specters*) (1987). The *giallo* is a staple Italian genre rather than being linked to a cycle, and masked mystery murderers still stalk the screens in the likes of Carlo Vanzina's *Sotto il vestito niente* (*Nothing Underneath*) (1986), an acceptable DePalma imitation astonishingly mooted originally as a project for Michaelangelo Antonioni. Michele Soavi, an actor in films for Fulci, an assistant to Argento and the younger Bava, and the director of a documentary about Argento, made his debut with *Deliria*, produced by Aristide Massaccesi from a story by Luigi Montefiore, and wrings a few more drops of blood from the standard story of a troupe of actors stuck in a theatre with an owl-headed psycho killer.

● *He bought the company.* Howard Sherman, **Day of the Dead.**

fun with the living dead
fun with the living dead

A hand reaches into the frame to shake Fran (Gaylen Ross) out of her dreams. As the girl wakes up, the main title is imposed: *Dawn of the Dead*. With his opening shot, George A. Romero establishes that the sequel to *Night of the Living Dead* will be a radical revision of the original nightmare movie. The intruding hand belongs not to a zombie kick-starting the film with a gnawing attack, but to a TV technician rousing Fran so she can get back to the job of keeping a collapsing Philadelphia station on the air throughout the Living Dead apocalypse. The black-and-white cemetery at the beginning of *Night* signals that, although horror clichés may be inverted, the film is still going all out for terror. *Dawn* is a different kind of movie. The control room with its overlapping, cross-purposes dialogue is not a horror movie setting but a hectic microcosm of the American media jungle, like the studios in the State of the Union black comedies *Nashville* and *Network*. Romero and the assistant director, Christine Forrest, are seen at messy consoles, trying to keep a disintegrating chat show together. Fran is marked as the heroine when she blanks out a list of inoperative rescue stations her boss wants on screen every minute. He doesn't want the audience to tune out: like Robert Duvall in *Network*, he is willing to murder people to get good ratings. Steven (David Emge), Fran's helicopter pilot boyfriend, proposes they escape together, on the grounds that 'somebody's got to survive'.

On the air, a scientific expert antagonises his interviewer: 'it's precisely because of incitement by irresponsible public figures like you that this situation is being dealt with irresponsibly by the public at large'. For those who missed *Night of the Living Dead*, the scientist helpfully provides a punchy rundown of the situation, 'Every dead body that is not exterminated becomes one of them! It gets up and kills. The people it kills get up and kill... They kill for food!'

The nightmare of the Living Dead is over, and the sequel is wide awake, blinking at an apocalypse brightly coloured by the dawn's early light. The zombies first appear as a distraction during a tensely edited battle between SWAT troopers and a group of ethnic ghetto types who refuse to come under martial law and hand over their dead for incineration. Roger (Scott Reininger) looks the other way while another trooper, Peter (Ken Foree), scrags a SWAT team member who has gone apeshit and is indiscriminately gunning down the surrendering citizenry. Someone shouts 'don't open that door!' But someone else opens the door, and a groping crowd of mutilated, blue-faced zombies pile out. Aside from a few plummy pronouncements from the Trinidadian Peter ('When there's no more room in Hell, the dead will walk the Earth') and a Puerto Rican priest ('When the dead walk... we must stop the killing or lose the war!'), the film doesn't attempt to surround the zombies with any aura of frightening mystique, or even make them particularly danger-ous. The first victim hugs her dead husband, only to have him bite a chunk out of her neck. Everyone who falls to the Living Dead dies because of sheer stupidity (Roger's gung-ho playfulness) or a retention of outmoded values (the woman's refusal to accept her husband's death, Steven's possessiveness over the useless goods he has looted). The main dangers in the film come from violent humans: the racist SWAT psycho, the redneck posse from *Night* and a mindless gang of motorcycle crazies who destroy the ghoul-free haven the four central characters establish in a huge shopping mall.

After deftly sketching in the collapse of civilisation in Philadelphia, Romero removes his heroes from the mess and has them play Robinson Crusoe in the isolated mall. When Steven huffily insists he is entitled to commandeer the TV station's helicopter, Peter underlines the break with lawful society: 'And we're out here doing traffic reports? Wake up, sucker. We're thieves and we're bad guys ... And we gotta find our own way.' Having used grim violence to batter the audience during the ghetto shoot-out, Romero lightens the tone with sick slapstick. A zombie blunders into a helicoptor rotor and has the top of his head neatly sliced off. An undead handyman has his own screwdriver shoved into his ear. By the time the survivors get to the mall, the zombie hordes have been reduced to the status of amusing nuisances. The Living Dead dodder up escalators, fall into fountains, and seem lulled by the tinkle of musak. A fully robed nun and a saffron-swathed krishna kid are seen among their ranks. With few edible humans around, the zombies' consumer frenzy is manifested in the childish acquisitiveness with which they cradle now-useless items and their instinctive wish to get into the mall. 'It was an important place to them.'

The unreal environment of the arcade distracts the heroes from the rigours of simple survival. When they break in, Roger and Peter are enthused by the opportunities for plunder. 'Let's get the stuff we need first; I'll get a television and a radio!' Later, Steven and Peter find an overflow-ing cash register and dip in with wry grins, '... you never know'. In a series of exuberant, zombie-dodging action scenes, the survivors fortify the mall. Happy-go-lucky Roger gets off on whopping ghouls and is bitten. Once the place is sealed off, the living get themselves up in a Wild West assortment of guns, holsters and bandoliers from the sports department and clear out all the indoor zombies. Romero pulls another switch by cutting away from the massacre to the sobering aftermath. Bodies are stacked in the freezer, the zombies wait outside like Victorian orphans in the snow at Christmas, Fran throws away her guns, and Roger dies pathetically, shouting 'We whipped 'em. We whipped 'em good!' Before he goes, Roger gasps that he will try not to come back, but Peter still has to shoot his corpse in the brain as it sits up.

With the zombies out of the way, the survivors find themselves at something of a loose end. They toy idly with an abundance of luxuries they don't really want, and start getting on each other's nerves. Like the gun fetishism and the exploding heads that surround it, the slow movement of *Dawn of the Dead* is vital to Romero's cartoon of American culture. Peter and Steven no longer have zombies to shoot at, so they blast away at imaginary ducks and spaceships on video games. Fran applies elaborately tarty make-up, scoops handfuls of sweets from the confectionery count-ers, and skates alone on the ice rink. Dissatisfied with the traditionally supportive and/or victimised heroine role, Fran's key line is 'I'm not gonna be den mother for you guys.' Romero forsakes fast editing and dynamic camera movements for extended takes and stately pans that convey the stasis of life in the mall. The heroes' survival has become a parody of the vanished society rather than an outlaw alternative. The characters dress up in expensive clothes, play poker with real money that means less than matchsticks and spread caviar on their cream crackers, but soon get bored stiff. The pregnant Fran refuses Steven's offer of a symbolic ring, and the distance between the couple is poignantly encapsulated in a still life of them in bed: Steven slumped asleep; Fran upright, awake and blank faced. When reality, in the shape of the violent bikers, intrudes, it is almost a relief. Peter strips his smart tracksuit and gets back into his SWAT uniform.

The sick comedy of the early scenes explodes into bloody knockabout for the finale. The bikers are a fun-loving version of the culturally confused youth gang from *Assault on Precinct 13*. They attack to US cavalry bugle calls, and carry oddments of mediaeval and Wild West weaponry. Peter is impressed: 'They been survivin' out on the road through this thing . . . that's a professional army, man!' But the sniggering thugs in mustachios and sombreros act more like the inept wolves in Tex Avery's Droopy cartoons. When reminded that there isn't anything to watch on a TV set, a looter smashes it in with a sledge-hammer instead of stealing it. One biker shoves a cream pie into a zombie's face, another leaves a severed arm in a test-your-blood-pressure machine. Colourful blood and guts are strewn across the screen by make-up supremo Tom Savini, who also plays the leather-jacketed leader of the pack. No one wins the battles, but the ending is curiously upbeat for a post-*Night of the Living Dead* horror movie. Steven returns from the dead and leads the zombies to his former hiding place, hinting at a dawning intelligence in the hitherto moronic hordes. The decadent idyll of the mall is destroyed, and the Living Dead overrun the place. Peter contemplates suicide, but changes his mind and fights his way through the ghouls with a show-off display of martial arts to join the escaping Fran in the helicopter. With a touch of hope, they fly off into the sunrise.

Dawn of the Dead is a transitional film, full of people waking up, becoming aware, working things out, rising from the dead. Romero develops this fragile optimism in *Knightriders* (1981), which also deals with the viability of alternative lifestyles. The film, which doesn't feel the need to destroy straight society in order to find a replacement, chronicles the struggles of a crowd of Arthurian bike freaks who stage motorised jousts at mediaeval fairs. The knightriders include several players from *Dawn of the Dead*, and echo both the heroic survivors and the anarchic marauders of the earlier

film. The dilemma of an independent film-maker like Romero, caught between artistic integrity and commercialism, is also kicked about in the very personal screenplay, as represented by the noble, mystic, slightly cracked King Billy (Ed Harris) and the flashy, wealth-and-fame-minded Morgan (Tom Savini).

Knightriders' lack of box-office and critical acceptance probably drove Romero to *Creepshow* (1982), an entertainment that uses the frame of 1950s horror comics as an end in itself rather than as a means towards the grisly trenchancy of the Living Dead films. Written by Stephen King, who also appears as a retarded farmer turned into a walking weed by a mysterious meteor, *Creepshow* is an omnibus of slight horror stories. The episodes tend to set up interesting situations, but fail to come up with the necessary funny/horrible punch-lines. However, Romero has fun producing the celluloid equivalent of a comic, with animated splash panels, think bubbles, Charles Atlas ads, mail order voodoo doll offers and a decaying host to introduce each tale with cackling blurbs. A cast of semi-name actors are spurred into providing appropriately caricatured, unpleasant performances which sit nicely against the garish, primary colour backgrounds. Leslie Nielsen chuckles as he watches the tide come in over his buried wife and her lover via cable television, E.G. Marshall is a bullying, fastidious multimillionaire persecuted by creeping cockroaches in his pristine penthouse, and Adrienne Barbeau is incredibly vulgar and embarrassing as a faculty wife whose hubby (Hal Holbrook) dreams of doing her in. Although frequently funny, *Creepshow* is an evident relaxation which inevitably disappoints after Romero's run of probing, innovative films, and a second issue, *Creepshow 2* (1987), directed by Romero's cinematographer Michael Gornick, is a fumbling disaster. Among the properties the director has committed himself to are *Monkey Shines* (1988), a thriller about a deranged spider monkey with near-human intelligence, *Apartment Living*, a comic horror about an apartment which eats people, and two Stephen King properties, *The Stand* and *Pet Sematary*. *The Stand*, an epic clash between the forces of Good and Evil in a post-holocaust America, shares many things – including an independent, pregnant heroine called Fran – with the Living Dead films.

The H.G. Lewis-style gore movie declined originally when major studio productions like *The Wild Bunch* and *Taxi Driver* gave *Bloodthirsty Butchers* and *The Wizard of Gore* competition in the explicit violence field, with the added attractions of competent film-making, good stories and prestige stars and directors. Thanks to Tom Savini's developments in special effects make-up for *Dawn of the Dead*, the genre made a comeback in the early 1980s. Paramount might be willing to make a fortune distributing *Friday the 13th*, but no major studio would actually produce a film using Tom Savini's high-tech splatter at its most graphic. Romero's thoroughly valid use of extreme carnage in *Dawn* opened the way for the return of the objectionable, consciousless meat movie. Joel M. Reed's *The Incredible Torture Show* (1978) was reissued during the splatter boom under an assumed name, *Bloodsucking Freaks*, that loses the risqué acronym the distributors evidently find more offensive than the scene in which a poor schmuck is given a blow job with a severed head. The Great Sardu, a disciple of Lewis's *Wizard of Gore*, hosts the incredible torture show with a few words about the violence they're about to see: 'If you're bored by it, pretend it's real, but if you're excited by it, pretend it's fake.'

The Great Sardu's philosophy was put into unethical practice by Alan Shackleton, distributor of *Snuff*, hyped as 'an overwhelming assault on the senses too real to be simulated, too shocking to be ignored', and snappily advertised as 'the film that could only be made in South America, where life is CHEAP!' *Snuff* was originally *Slaughter* (1974), an incredibly dire, excruciatingly dull movie about a Charles Manson-type called Satan (pronounced 'Suh-tarn') who orders his girlfriends to kill some movie makers. The film is so cheap the police investigation of the crimes is conducted from a desk plonked Monty Python-style in a farmyard, and the five minutes' worth of plot is padded out with endless footage of the girls posing in now outdated modish gear (flowery dresses, bees'-eye sunglasses). The violence is far too mild to relieve the tedium. At the climax of *Slaughter*, Satan's girls kill a businessman and his mistress. *Snuff* cuts from this to a scene of the film-makers supposedly shooting the movie. The girl who plays the killer has been 'turned on' by the violence, and so the film crew dutifully pin her down, while the director seduces, mutilates and disembowels her. The scene, supposedly done for real, is executed with extremely tacky sub-Savini gore effects and performed by embarrassed players visibly stifling laughter. Although *Slaughter* is an Argentinian film made by Americans Michael and Roberta Findlay, the snuff scene was shot ten years later in New York. The victim bears only a vague resemblance to the actress she replaces. The hoax deserves a place in film history as an example of the appalling contempt some people in the business have for their audiences. As well as assuming that the world is full of bloodthirsty sadists who want to see a genuine murder on the screen, *Snuff* insults the four people out there who have been interested in the plot of *Slaughter*. The additional scene replaces the original ending, so we never find out whether Satan and his girls get what they deserve.

Despite protests and pickets – some arranged by Shackleton himself – New York D.A. Robert Morgenthau recognised *Snuff* as an obvious boondoggle, and refused to prosecute, but the early 1980s did see the mobilisation of a pro-censorship lobby against the massacre movie. *Friday the 13th* slipped past the MPAA ratings board with its Tom Savini-engineered decapitations intact. *Friday the 13th, Part 2* originally contained a similar batch of atrocities created by Carl Fullerton, but had to be drastically pruned before its release, and most of the later entries in the series are almost tame in their butchery. The sterling efforts of such worthies as Roger Ebert and British MP Graham Bright have forced the gore film into a period of retrenchment. In America, Ebert hounded distributor Jerry Gross in an attempt to get *I Spit on Your Grave* ('Hunted, captured, stripped and raped by a gang of grungy guys, Jennifer slashes, gashes, and mashes her attackers to a bloody, palpitating pulp!') from distribution. And in the UK, Bright sponsored the Video Recordings Act — the so-called 'Video Nasties Bill' — which instituted a system of censorship and certification for home video far in excess of anything inflicted upon theatrical films. Some splatter films currently circulate in hard-gore and soft-gore versions. Even the abbreviated *Basket Case* is worth watching, but *Maniac*, shorn of Tom Savini's pump-shotgun-exploded heads and scalpings, is almost up to *Snuff* for unwatchable boredom.

An interesting, unexpected addition to the exclusive ranks of gore film directors is the expatriot German Ulli Lommel. *Die Zärtlichkeit der Wolfe* (*The Tenderness of Wolves*) (1973), Lommel's first film, produced by the late Rainer Werner Fassbinder, is an arty, boring biography of a real life vampire murderer; and *Cocaine Cowboys* (1979), his first American production, is a weird art movie with Jack Palance, filmed at Andy Warhol's house. Suzanna Love, a writer-actress who appears in *Cocaine Cowboys*, hitched up with Lommel, and together they created *The Boogeyman* (1980), which opens like a stalk-and-slash psycho movie and closes like an exorcism exploitationer, but has a gripping mid-section about the properties of a haunted mirror. When smashed, the shards of mirror bring most of the film's peripheral characters to gory deaths. A young couple necking in a car have their heads pinned together with a breadknife. Lommel and Love's follow-up, *Olivia* (1981), has a similarly gross moment when a bloody electric toothbrush vibrates through the back of Robert Walker Jr's neck. Otherwise, *Olivia* is a clever and pointed psychological thriller about a psychotic housewife who follows London Bridge to Arizona but cannot escape the deadening grip of her British lout husband. Corpses are dumped into the Thames and the Colorado rivers, and the plots of *Vertigo* and *Marnie* are played with, but finally *Olivia* is inescapably drawn into the fairytale world beyond the bathroom mirror where her dead mother lives.

The mirror's evil influence persists in *Boogey-*

man 2 (1982), a very cheapskate (about half of it consists of repeat footage of the highlights of the first film) but somehow compelling movie in which the Love character goes to Hollywood to sell her story to some sleazy movie types who fall victim to the mirror. It's an odd, vanity production that seems to be constructed around echt-Fassbinder sequences in which Lommel (playing the director, of course) and his friends gripe about the state of modern Hollywood. *The Devonsville Terror*, with Love as the reincarnation of a martyred witch bringing justice to a blighted small town, and *Brainwaves* (1982), in which she undergoes a revolutionary medical treatment that gives her some of the memories of the victim of a local psychotic, are more conventional, but still bristle with weird kinks. Lommel makes short, snappy films — even the elaborate, well-cast *Brainwaves* is less than eighty minutes long — and isn't very interested in exploitation values. He has advanced from having to co-star Love with the ubiquitous John Carradine in *The Boogeyman* to the point where he can rope in Donald Pleasence, who gets to pull maggots out of his arms in *The Devonsville Terror*, or an ensemble including Kier Dullea, Tony Curtis and Vera Miles in *Brainwaves*.

Frank Henenlotter's *Basket Case* (1981), shot and set in the worst area of New York, wears its sleaze with pride. The end titles dedicate the film to H.G. Lewis, the characters are socially handicapped to such an extent that the leads of *Trash* could look down on them, and the nearest the script comes to romance is 'you're cute when you slobber'. Duane (Kevin VanHentenryck) checks into the grotty Hotel Broslin with a wicker basket that contains Belial, a small, misshapen creature who is mostly head and claws. Closely related to the protagonist(s) of 'The Mannikin', one of Robert Bloch's more unpleasant short stories, Duane and Belial were born as Siamese twins and have been separated by an intolerant father. Unfortunately, the film establishes the situation with more invention than it develops it. The flashback that explains the monster's origins contains not only the film's best sick joke (the father's legs falling out of the frame after he has been sawn in half) but the most imaginative and affecting images (Belial weakly clawing his way out of a twist-tie garbage bag; an understanding aunt cradling the creature as she reads aloud to the brothers). Sadly, Belial's revenge against the quack doctors who performed the separation, and his jealous frustration of Duane's attempts to get laid are not strong enough to sustain the film beyond the resolution of its mystery. The main problem is the overstated performances of all concerned: satirically feigned badness all too easily turns into genuine badness.

Henenlotter's delayed follow-up, *Brain Damage* (1987), again has a marvellous monster — a brain-eating parasite called Elmer with a suavely snide George Sanders personality — and again fails to find a plot worthy of it. Intended as a tribute to William Castle's *The Tingler*, *Brain Damage* evokes the plot of Chuck Jones's cartoon *One Froggy Evening* as the monster suckers Brian (Rick Herbst), an unwary young man, into supplying it with human brains by getting him hooked on a hallucinogenic secretion it injects direct into the kid's brain. The film is stuck with sub-*Liquid Sky* psychedelic sequences, but is worth it for the cold turkey sequence as Brian dreams he's pulling his brain out through his ear in a bloody string while Elmer croons the Tommey Dorsey hit 'Elmer's Tune' at him. Backing up Henenlotter with a steadicam on *Brain Damage* is Jim Muro, a kindred spirit NYC sleazemaker whose accomplished but unstructured *Street Trash* (1986) marks a promising début. A case of 60-year-old hootch sold off cheap by a skid row liquor store makes winos melt down or explode in a series of graphic set pieces. These scenes are triumphs of cartoonish make-up splatter, but are hardly integrated into a film which straggles all over the place, roping in Vietnam veteran psychopaths, a hardboiled killer cop, junkyard hi-jinx out of Kurosawa's *Dodes'ka-den*, unworkable gang-rape-and-necrophilia jokes, a mafia don who does a Sinatra take-off under the end credits and a tasteless slapstick gag with a ripped-off penis. Henenlotter and Muro — like Jackie Kong, who turned an H.G. Lewis tribute script for *Blood Feast 2* into *Blood Diner* (1987) —

reveal the pitfalls of setting out to make a cult gore movie without even a trace of serious intent.

Don Coscarelli's *Phantasm* (1979) is more slick than sleaze, although its main selling-point is a flying bauble which fastens on to a victim's forehead and redistributes his entire blood supply through a garden sprinkler attachment. Unlike the poverty row gore film directors, Coscarelli tries for gloss rather than gross, and achieves some of the EC comic delirium of *Dawn of the Dead*. Borrowing its structure from *Invaders From Mars* and *The 5,000 Fingers of Dr T*, *Phantasm* is an adolescent nightmare, and prefigures the 1980s trend for pitting mid-teens against monsters (*The Deadly Spawn*, *Neon Maniacs* (1985), *The Gate*, *The Lost Boys*). The hero is a young boy (Mike Baldwin), obsessed with monsters and horror films, who dreams himself into an outrageous, incomprehensible pulp plot. A group of beings from another dimension kill people, shrink the corpses to dwarf size, and put them in plastic barrels for transportation home, where they are revived and used as slave labour. The plot makes even less sense in the film, which is a minefield of false turns, silly ideas and illogical scare scenes. Coscarelli is capable of ludicrous weirdness like the inhuman severed finger in a matchbox that wriggles, bleeds yellow and turns into a buzzing creepy-crawly, and gets a lot out of his principal location, a spacious mausoleum. *Phantasm* is stolen by Angus Scrimm as the Tall Man, a loping Karloffian undertaker who represents the aliens on Earth, sometimes in the transsexual form of the equally bizarre Lady in Lavender (Kathy Lester). The Tall Man has the best scare moments, turning to leer out of a Victorian photograph, or suddenly lunging into the frame from hidden chasms, and is a good old-fashioned monster who deserves his own glow-in-the-dark Aurora hobby kit.

The best of the post-*Dawn of the Dead* EC comics is Sam Raimi's *The Evil Dead* (1983). The film opens with a flourish of omens that clearly signposts the horrors to come as five teenagers travel to an isolated Tennessee cabin for the weekend: the dangerous old bridge that connects them with the outside world crumbles as it is crossed; a subjective camera demon crashes through the woods; a torn poster for *The Hills Have Eyes* decorates the cellar; and endlessly swirling dry-ice fog gives way to a crackling storm which punctuates the previous victim's tape-recorded testament with ominous rumbles. An ancient book bound in human skin summons a pack of Sumerian devils, and all hell breaks loose. The reversal of recent genre clichés has the macho hero, Ash (Bruce Campbell), reduced to a display of whimpering collapse in the Jamie Lee Curtis manner, while all the girls in the party turn into screeching witches as given to infantile taunts ('we're going to get you!') as to actual clawing attacks. Unlike *Phantasm*, *The Evil Dead* acknowledges that narrative economy is as important as off-the-wall surrealism and races through its story with no time-outs to set up the next special effect. Finally, the film bows out with a display of spectacular putrefaction that goes as far beyond the similar finale of *The Devil's Rain* as that had surpassed the comparatively tame dissolutions of Hammer's Dracula films. Without the serious intent of *The Texas Chainsaw Massacre* or the satire of *Dawn*, the film is an enjoyable catch-all roller-coaster ride through the splatter genre, and is probably justified in straight-facedly advertising itself (in its own credits) as 'the ultimate experience in gruelling terror'.

If *The Evil Dead* shifts the horror film into overdrive, then *Evil Dead II* (1987) puts its foot through the floor and goes insane. Sam Raimi and Bruce Campbell actually followed their first hit with the underrated *Crimewave* (1984), which owes as much to EC's 1950s *MAD Magazine* as its predecessor does to *Tales From the Crypt*. With Paul L. Smith and Brion James as cartoonish exterminators who deal in assassinations with all the finesse of Wile E. Coyote and the Tasmanian Devil, *Crimewave* revels in its slapstick strangeness. When its failure drove its creators back to that deserted shack in the woods, the Three Stooges/Looney Tunes/Scenes We'd Like to See craziness went with them. The movie opens with a scaled-down remake of the first film, and heaps even

more indignities upon Ash (Campbell again), who periodically turns into a possessed monster and has hassles from not only his ballet-dancing dead girlfriend and her chainsaw but also his own sadistic, possessed hand as it smashes crockery over his head. Driven to Biblical measures, Ash jams his wrist on to the buzzing chainsaw and cackles 'who's laughing now?' to his recalcitrant member as it scuttles away to make more trouble. The answer is, practically everyone, for, apart from a few sudden shocks, there is no real horror in *Evil Dead II*. If the first film was a horror comic, then the sequel is a slapstick comedy that uses gore for gags. A popped eyeball flies into a girl's mouth, the dead girlfriend's dances are made awkward by the way her head tends to fall off, gallons and gallons of blood gout from holes in the walls, the hand is trapped under a bucket weighed down with a groan-making copy of *A Farewell to Arms*, Ash prepares to face down the ultimate evil by strapping on a chainsaw in place of his missing hand ('groovy!'), and the hero winds up trapped in the Middle Ages with his chainsaw and his custom car, hailed as a hero by the knights who have been waiting for a saviour from the skies to fend off the Deadites.

Less pacy than the *Evil Dead* films, but even more concentrated in its *grand guignol* chuckles, is Stuart Gordon's *Re-Animator* (1985), a low-budget adaption of a series of short pieces even H.P. Lovecraft didn't take very seriously, sponsored by Charles Band's schlock factory, Empire Pictures. Herbert West (Jeffrey Combs), a creepy student at the Miskatonic Medical School, has developed a glowing green reagent which can restore the dead to life. Unfortunately, most of his reanimatees are too traumatised by their deaths to be sane. West's greatest success is Dr Hill (David Gale), a decapitated faculty member who tries to take over the reanimation business. 'Don't be silly,' West snaps as Hill expounds grandiose schemes, 'who's going to believe a talking head?' *Re-Animator* is a dyed-in-the-wool sickie, designed mainly in black and white so the huge splashes of red in the set piece zombie mutilation scenes really stand out. Gordon's cast have fun with such

● *Mad scientist, before . . .* ● *and after.* David Gale, **Re-Animator.**

coarse jokes as the zombie who head-butts the living head, the python-coils of living intestine which constrict West to his deserved death, and Hill's bodiless slobbering over the naked heroine (Barbara Crampton) as he pokes his bloody tongue in her ear. It takes an inferior follow-up, *From Beyond* (1986) — also from Lovecraft, with many of the personnel from *Re-Animator* retained, along with the basic theme of a clash between two equally mad scientists — to reveal the first film's weaknesses. In his second stab, Gordon goes even further into bizarre grotesquerie as interference with another dimension turns one scientist into a twisted monstrosity out of *The Thing* and another into a bald zombie with a brain-eating tendril poking from his forehead. However, while *Re-Animator* is a model of economy, with every potentially flabby sequence cut back to the bone, *From Beyond* has a rambling, suspenseless non-story laced with calculated kinkiness and general pointlessness. If you laugh at everything, what's the point?

The pitfalls of the broadly comic approach which entirely swamped the genre in the mid-1980s are demonstrated by Dan O'Bannon's opportunist *Return of the Living Dead* (1985). Based loosely on John Russo's novel sequel to *Night of the Living Dead*, the film parodies Romero's vision, poking fun at such conventions as the shoot-'em-in-the-brain solution and the traditional slow, dim-witted dead. O'Bannon's zombies are fast moving, fast talking creatures who party in a graveyard and love to snack off freshly splattered brains. The living characters strap a half-zombie down and get it to explain that being dead hurts, but eating brains eases the pain. While it is funny in parts, thanks to audacious characters like the Tarman, an oily tatterdemalion whose catchphrase is 'I want to eat your *brainssss*!', or the nude punkette zombie (Linnea Quigley), *Return of the Living Dead* is a movie that is self-destructed by its cynicism. In the early reels, O'Bannon manages a few genuinely creepy/funny touches, as when the reanimating gas floods a medical warehouse and revives a caseful of flapping, pinned-down butterflies and a cut-in-half-and-mounted dog (the

counterpart of *Re-Animator*'s half-cat), but, when he drags in a load of stereotyped punk rockers to be victimised and ladles inappropriate deathrock music over its action, the movie gets too hip and spoofy for its own good. The finale suggests everyone has given up on taking anything seriously, as a very downbeat twist finish (the authorities calmly nuke most of Kentucky to solve the problem) is lost amid lazy repetition of footage and a general inability to do anything with the full head of steam that has been worked up. It hardly needed to go the *Evil Dead* route and be remade as a total comedy, but Ken Wiederhorn set out to do such a thing in the bungled *Return of the Living Dead, Part 2* (1987), a film whose *reductio ad absurdam* cannibalising of its antecedents is aptly summed up by its sequel-to-a-sequel, parodying-a-parody title.

Before *Re-Animator*, Charles Band had seen the way things were going, and reacted by producing Luca Bercovici's *Ghoulies* (1984), a slapdash skit inspired by the comic tone of *Gremlins* that tries to do for horror what his masterpiece, *Trancers*, does for science fiction. With its cheap-but-endearing special effects, colourfully silly victims and confident use of black magic and old dark house clichés, *Ghoulies* is lightly likeable, a guilty pleasure that showcases Empire's assets — the crisp, comic-book style of cinematographer Mac Ahlberg, the full-throttle scoring of Richard Band (who provides a disco remix of the *Psycho* theme for *Re-Animator*), the instant recycling of a fistful of themes from other films, offbeat character comedy and the muppet-like monstrosities of John Buechler. However, *Ghoulies 2* (1987), which concentrates on having better special effects than the original, is in every other way much worse, lacking the quirks the first film uses to compensate for its immobile furry freaks. Having hit a formula, Empire proceeded to run it aground with a series of occasionally amusing lookalikes: *Rage War* (1985), *Troll* (1985), Stuart Gordon's pleasant quickie *Dolls* (1987) and *Cellar Dweller* (1987). Prolific enough to issue a pack of cards, with a current project for each card in the deck, as a promotional item at Cannes, Empire have tried to upgrade their image with the occasional 'straight' item, like *Crawlspace* (1986) or *Prison*, but have never lived up to comparisons with the Roger Corman heyday of New World. Weirdly, *Ghoulies* has had some influence, at least on the titles of *Spookies* (1986) and *Munchies* (1987), which are otherwise copies of *The Evil Dead* and *Gremlins*.

However, Empire looks like a class outfit when set beside Troma, the Hell's Kitchen grindhouse responsible for *Girls School Screamers*, *Splatter University*, *The Toxic Avenger*, *Class of Nuke 'Em High*, *Monster in the Closet* (1986), *Surf Nazis Must Die!* (1987) *Redneck Zombies* (1987) *Starworms II: Attack of the Pleasure Pods* (1987) and such often-announced dodos as *Deadly Daphne's Revenge*, *Curse of the Cannibal Confederates*, *Fat Guy Goes Nutzoid*, *I Was a Teenage TV Terrorist* and *Demented Death Farm Massacre — The Movie*. Troma are best known for their irksomely self-conscious camp titles and outrageously dumb promotional stunts: actually making the movies is an afterthought to securing pre-sales deals to get them into video shops throughout the world. Given that Troma set out to produce films that can charitably be described as crap, it might perhaps be unfair to chastise them for succeeding, but their output is among the most unwatchable in the history of the cinema. Their best-known films are *The Toxic Avenger* ('a film packed full of unnecessary sex and violence') and *Class of Nuke 'Em High* ('they learned the three Rs — readin', 'ritin' and radiation!'), which deal with mutations in the fictional community of Tromaville, 'the toxic waste capital of the world', and demonstrate you can't manufacture a cult movie. The problem is Troma films are never serious but also have no idea how to go about being funny. The mixture of teenage tits and ass, dead-straight nastiness (a girl masturbating over pictures of road accident victims in *The Toxic Avenger*) and slapstick stupidity is unpalatable, but beside the point in a business where the creative process is over once the poster has been designed. If a film with the Troma tag has any redeeming qualities at all, as with *Screamplay* and *Combat Shock*, the chances are that it's a buy-in they're releasing rather than the home-grown product.

Less offensive, blander, but just about as worthless are the *House* films put out by the sanitised, post-Roger Corman New World; Steve Miner's *House* (1985), produced by *Friday the 13th* mogul Sean S. Cunningham, is a cut-and-paste non-threatening horror film. Best-selling William Katt moves into a spooky house to write a book, and is pestered by monsters that lunge from closets, gardening tools that fly around on their own, a bloated toad-woman who impersonates his ex-wife, and his dead army buddy. With a few scraps of content — Katt's traditional Vietnam trauma — to go with its sit-com cameos, snatches of inapt pop music and wholesale borrowings from *Poltergeist*, the film could almost be a generic product, *Horror Movie* or *Scary Film*. The follow-up, *House 2: The Second Story* (1986), is even less coherent and tries even harder to be a kiddie comedy rather than a horror movie, despite its impressive 9ft-tall cowboy zombie. These movies — along with such big-budget, major studio films as *Fright Night* and *The Lost Boys*, and such cheapies as *Trick or Treat* and *The Gate* — reduce the genre to the level of *Scooby Doo, Where Are You?* With children, adolescents or childish young men in the leads, and with one scene of knockabout looning for every dose of effects-dripping monstrousness, the films provide the MTV generation with something to watch every three minutes but are unable to get seriously scary, or even seriously funny. All they prove is that nobody needs a safe horror picture.

In 1985 — briefly — things got serious again, when George A. Romero returned with a third report from the developing story of the end of human civilisation. Although *Night of the Living Dead* and *Dawn of the Dead* were intended as the first two-thirds of a trilogy, *Day of the Dead* is not necessarily the final chapter. Harking back to *I Am Legend*, in which the old world is destroyed and replaced by a functioning society of the undead, the game plan was for *Night* to deal with the beginnings of the holocaust; *Dawn* to follow the complete breakdown of society; and *Day* to depict a future world where living and dead have come to terms, and trained zombies fight wars on behalf of sybaritic humans who live in subterranean city states. Facetiously announced under the title *Zombies in the White House*, Romero's original outline ends with the passing of the Living Dead plague and the establishment of an ambiguously utopian new normality after the overthrow of the repressive old order. However, Romero was unable to make the film he had scripted. It was important to release the film unrated in the US to avoid the stigma of an X-rating — which is synonymous with hardcore porn — but that would curtail the film's commercial chances to the point whereby Romero's elaborate screenplay was economically unfeasible. Instead of scaling down his script, the writer-director backtracked in the history of the zombie apocalypse to a point when — following the hints dropped in the finale of *Dawn* — it is generally acknowledged that the Living Dead retain some species of conscious thought and science, in the shape of the Frankensteinian Dr Logan (Richard Liberty), who is pioneering the domestication and socialisation of the zombie hordes.

Like *Dawn of the Dead*, *Day of the Dead* opens with its heroine waking up. However, Sarah (Lori Cardille) is waking up to a nightmare of clutching zombie hands, and then has to wake up again, in a helicopter circling over Fort Myers, Florida. Sarah is with a military-scientific group holed up in an underground silo, and is primarily concerned with looking for other survivors and finding a solution for the problem. Things have deteriorated since *Dawn*: the Living Dead now outnumber the living by 400,000 to 1, and — owing perhaps as much to the development of Tom Savini's make-up artistry as to continuity — the ghouls are more visibly decayed. Although physically more monstrous than ever — the first creature we see lacks a lower jaw but still waggles its tongue — they are otherwise more human. Whereas the monsters of the earlier films were silent and implacable, the zombies of *Day* wail in hunger and despair, are mainly bullied and abused by the living, and begin to exhibit individual personality traits. Back in the silo, Logan blathers about his researches and family background, and gives patronisingly schoolmasterish speeches to his tethered zombie subjects.

When one misbehaves, he turns off the lights in the room with 'you can just sit there in the dark and think about what you've done'. Logan's star subject is Bub (Howard Sherman), a zombie who half-remembers his pre-death life in the military with mocking salutes, and who is pacified by Beethoven's *Ode to Joy* on a walkman and by the choice chunks of dead soldier Logan feeds to him. 'They can be tricked into being good little girls and boys', Logan concludes, 'the same way we were tricked, on the promise of some reward to come.'

Throughout, the series has been influenced by the black comedy and blacker worldview of EC comics. The traditional EC plot, demonstrated by practically all the episodes of *Tales From the Crypt* and *The Vault of Horror*, has a dastardly villain commit more and more outrageous crimes until he is given an ironically apt come-uppance by supernatural means. Typically, a murderer will be confronted by the walking, rotting, vengeful corpse of his victim and be gruesomely killed. 'Trick or Treat', the pilot segment Romero wrote for the television series *Tales From the Darkside*, uses this structure, as do the 'Something to Tide You Over', 'They're Creeping Up On You' and 'The Hitch-Hiker' episodes of the *Creepshow* movies. In the *Dead* films, American society is cast in the role usually given to an individually hatable character. A rotten social order suffers its just desserts in the shape of the Living Dead, who at once epitomise and chastise any number of vices: conservative complacency, consumerist frenzy, mindlessly instinctive political positions, random violence, pointless greed. In *Day of the Dead*, Romero reverts to the purest form of the 'poetic justice' story and presents a collection of thoroughly despicable characters who stand in for greater evils and are graphically pulled apart in the style of EC's famous gross-out final panels. Rhodes (Joe Pilato), the military head of the installation, is a kill-happy despot with a penchant for summary executions who, at one point, threatens to have Sarah shot for failing to sit down during one of his lectures to the assembled survivors. When Rhodes machine-guns Logan, Bub comes after His Master's Killer in an implacable, shuffling chase that is effectively a panel-for-panel reshoot of the EC comic finish. Bub becomes the first zombie to learn how to use a firearm on his enemy, and Rhodes goes out in a manner that would warm the Crypt Keeper's heart, screaming 'choke on 'em' to the zombies gobbling away at his intestines.

The dissecting-room humour of *Dawn of the Dead* is further refined, and occasionally matches *Re-Animator* in its ghoulish glee. Logan demonstrates an ideal way of rendering the dead docile by pruning away all of a zombie's head save for a fragment of bloodied brain. The doctor also proves his theory that the Living Dead are anthropophagous by instinct, rather than by a need for sustenance, by disconnecting all the internal digestive organs of a ghoul who continues to snap feebly at a dangled hand. Of course, this test subject then tries to sit up and deposits its stomach and sundry other messes on the laboratory floor. Elsewhere, we get such strange 'gags' as the up-ended half-head whose eyes still swivel or the soldier whose head becomes a gory bowling-ball with eyesocket fingerholes. *Day of the Dead* needs these slapstick horrors because it is otherwise an unrelievedly intense, grim movie. Although the bunker is larger than the locales of the earlier films, and purpose built for such a calamity, it is an even more claustrophobic and uncomfortable setting. The scientists and soldiers live in bare concrete rooms with spartan cots, because only the group's civilians — Jamaican helicopter pilot John (Terry Alexander) and drunken Irish radio operator McDermott (Jarlath Conroy) — have the time or inclination even to try and make themselves at home by putting up wall-posters of the seaside in their garden-furniture and plastic-foliage-strewn corner of the silo. Logan continually complains 'How are we going to set an example for them if we behave barbarically ourselves?' and the film repeatedly shows that these people don't need to be raised from the dead to have an excuse for tearing each other apart.

The movie is full of explosive tensions, with petty quarrels blowing up into murderous feuds. The characters spend more time pointing guns at each other than worrying about the threat of the zombies at the gates. The film slips once or twice in John's amplification of the throwaway mysticism of *Dawn of the Dead*, as he philosophises wistfully about the futility of all human endeavour and the causes of the crisis. 'We been punished by the creator, punished for our sins. He visited a curse on us so we might get a look at what Hell was like. Maybe He didn't wanna see us blow ourselves up and put a big hole in His sky. Maybe He just wanted to show us He was still the boss man.' While *Day of the Dead* is in the main the best characterised and acted of the three films, Terry Alexander's overdone accent comes perilously near to turning the laid-back but macho John — whose dearest wish, fulfilled in the end, is to escape 'to the islands' and soak up some sun — into the modern equivalent of the superstitious black characters played by Willie Best or Mantan Moreland in 1940s Caribbean voodoo movies like *The Ghost Breakers* (1941) and *King of the Zombies* (1941). But, for the most part, Romero reveals not only his proven skills as a director of action and personal unease, but a command of poetically profane language that makes many of the dialogue scenes more forcefully shocking than the special effects horrors. Particularly uncomfortable is the series of explicit and roundabout threats made by Rhodes and his men against Sarah, the only woman in the group, who is sexually unavailable thanks to her deteriorating and plainly doomed relationship with Miguel (Antoné DiLeo), the cracked soldier who finally brings about an end to the stasis of life underground by letting the dead into the bunker. In an age of weak xerox horror films, *Day of the Dead* is the real thing — red, raw and dripping.

the post-modern horror film

the post-modern horror film

Day of the Dead failed to repeat the box-office success of its predecessors. *Return of the Living Dead*, which was released shortly after Romero's film, was far more profitable. This may partially be down to the publicity muscle a semi-major company (Orion) was able to put behind Dan O'Bannon's R-rated film, but it also suggests comic horror has all but driven the real stuff out of the market-place. *Day of the Dead* stretches the zombie film just about as far as it can go — and the film Romero wanted to make could have been even more challenging — but the horror movie audience is more interested in the partying hi-jinx of trendy monsters like O'Bannon's funky zombies, Freddy Krueger or Herbert West. Other significant failures of the 1980s include *Videodrome, The Keep, The Sender* and *The Thing*. Obviously, the non-camp horror movie is currently an endangered species.

It's not a new situation. In the mid-1940s, American horror films turned into childish monster mashes like *House of Frankenstein* and finally wound up dragging in Abbott and Costello just as the *Friday the 13th* films combine slasher material with sub-*Porky's* nerd jokes. When horror cinema descends through repetition and spoof to ridiculousness, the mantle of the genre is passed on to other types of movie. The *films noirs* of the 1940s deal far more effectively with the underlying horrors of the decade — war traumas, alienation, psychological imbalance, social upheaval — than

any of the contemporary outings of Boris Karloff, Bela Lugosi or Lon Chaney Jr. Val Lewton led the way by taking horror themes into *noir* territory in *Cat People* and *The Seventh Victim* (1943), but pure *noir* cinema doesn't even need the Serbian curses and chic diabolist circles Lewton and his collaborators imported to the familiar milieu of rainswept city streets and neon-lit diners. The true horror greats of the years between 1941 and 1956 are not *The Wolf Man* (1941), *Strangler of the Swamp* (1945), *The Beast With Five Fingers* (1948) and *House of Wax* (1953), but *Phantom Lady* (1944), *Detour* (1945), *Brute Force* (1947) and *Kiss Me Deadly* (1955).

Now, there is no handy new genre waiting to step in and temporarily take the place of the old, as *film noir* did for horror in the 1940s, or the rural road movie for the Western in the 1970s. The horrors and neuroses of the age have had to percolate through the entire spectrum of cinema. Genre holocaust set in about the time of Francis Ford Coppola's folly *Apocalypse Now* (1979). As Martin Sheen travels up-river towards the Cambodian domain of mad Colonel Walter E. Kurtz (as the name suggests: half-Disney, half-Joseph Conrad), the cinema crumbles around him. *Apocalypse Now* touches on every possible film type: the conspiracy movie, with George Lucas (Harrison Ford) and Roger Corman (G.D. Spradlin) assigning Sheen to 'terminate with extreme prejudice'; the Western, with Robert Duvall in a Union Army

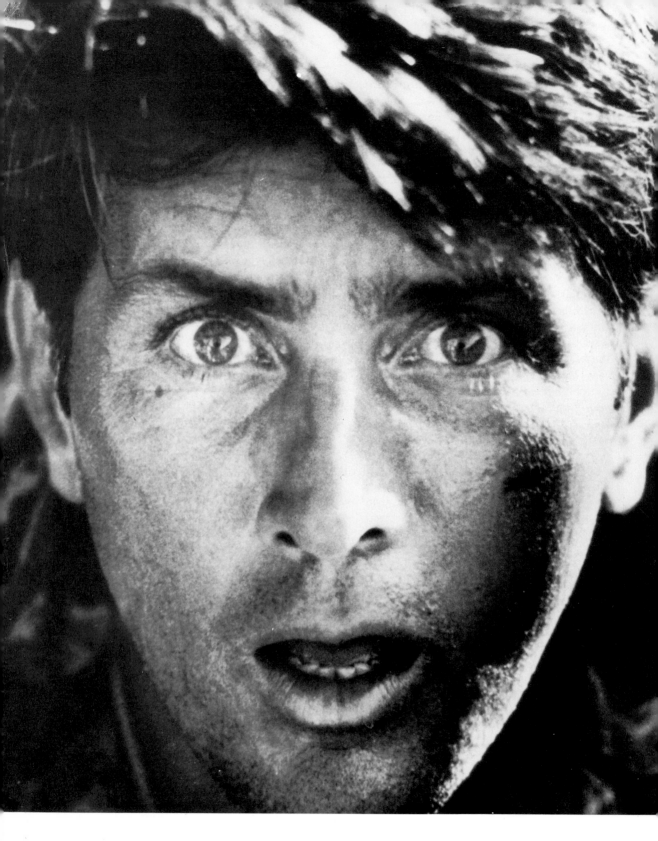

● *The End.* Martin Sheen, **Apocalypse Now.**

stetson leading the air cavalry in a raid; psychedelia, with old hairy Dennis Hopper still tripping; literary adaption, with Coppola and John Milius carefully adapting the plot of *Heart of Darkness*; *film noir*, courtesy of Michael Herr's hardboiled narration, closer in spirit to Chandler's Marlowe than Conrad's Marlow; the Hollywood musical, as *Playboy* playmates stage a rowdy dance number in a literal combat theatre; the Godardian avant-garde as the camera pans across iconic Brando's collection of signifying texts; and, of course, the complex myths and legends built up around the war film itself from gung-ho patriotism to hell-no rebellion. Duvall's raid on a Cong-held village in order to capture some quality beach-front ('Charlie don't *surf!*') even recalls the AIP beach-party musical.

The horror film is never far off the jungle track. A tiger bursts out of the undergrowth with all the impact of a *Halloween* knee-jerk shock. The point of no return is a nightmare battle for a bridge eternally built by day and wrecked by night. Here the command structure has collapsed and the war is fought with apparently mystic powers. A mortar operator, tripping on LSD and raucous rock, fires into the darkness with unerring accuracy. Beyond this is the horror movie world of the Montagnard tribesmen ruled by bald-pated sacred monster Kurtz. The surreal jungle and white tyrant recall the early 1930s of *The Most Dangerous Game*, and the Angkor Wat ruins suggest a return to *Revolt of the Zombies* (1936). Mutilated corpses are tossed about with all the relish of an Italian cannibal epic; Hopper interrupts his praise of the visionary Kurtz by referring to a scattering of Umberto Lenzi-style severed native heads with 'Oh, he goes too far sometimes . . . he'd be the first to admit that.' Brando monologises on the meaning of horror, and the conventional horror movie becomes obsolete. The physical and emotional overstatements of the genre have exploded into the mainstream. If Romero's Living Dead movies depict the Beginning of the End, *Apocalypse Now* comes close to being the End of the End.

Since *Apocalypse Now*, genre ghettos have been burning down. Film-makers obviously attracted to

horror have avoided the straitjacket of the monster movie and taken what they want from the horror film without feeling the need to plunge in wholeheartedly. Joel and Ethan Coen — Sam Raimi's associates on *The Evil Dead* — set out to make a James M. Cain-style passion murder thriller in *Blood Simple* (1984), but find the trappings of the post-*Halloween* monster/psycho movie come in handy for a finale in which the monstrously bloated villain M. Emmet Walsh menaces Fran McDormand. This sequence deploys a perfect mix of Argento-style bizarre violence and sweaty irony as Walsh, his hand nailed to a windowsill, shoots holes through the wall, while McDormand believes she is being menaced by her husband (Dan Hedaya) who has, in fact, been disposed of earlier by several unrelated hands. If *Blood Simple* stayed within the boundaries of its domestic murder genre, it would only have its convoluted plot and gritty characterisations to recommend it. Considerable impact is gained by the Coens' willingness to move from the overheated naturalism of the early sequences through the *grand guignol* bravura of the scene in which John Getz tries to bury the still-feebly-alive Hedaya in a field to the outright horror of the climax. Audiences in previous decades might have found such shifts confusing and have tuned out, but the climate of the 1980s is loose enough to accommodate even such radical leaps as those of the Coens' second film, *Raising Arizona* (1986). This crazy comedy yanks in a 'warthog from Hell' demon biker who'd be perfectly at home in Wes Craven's filmography, and embroiders its visual and verbal wit with genre images like a pair of screaming, mud-covered characters erupting from the ground during a thunderstorm and the final destruction of the villain as he is literally blown to pieces.

The most important of the post-genre horror films is Martin Scorsese's *After Hours* (1985), an ostensible comedy that is as indebted to the structure, logic and horrific grip of your worst nightmares as *Night of the Living Dead*, *The Texas Chainsaw Massacre* or *Halloween*. Returning to the 'Hell is a city' theme of *Taxi Driver*, Scorsese puts his protagonist — Paul Hackett (Griffin Dunne), a shallow but pleasant computer operator — through a series of ironic ordeals that suggest God, screenwriter Joseph Minion and the mechanics of a brilliantly assembled *conte cruel* have it in for him. *After Hours* touches on genre horror briefly in a nod to *A Bucket of Blood* as Paul is put inside a Munchian papier mâché sculpture, but otherwise achieves its unparalleled effects without recourse to *grand guignol*. Indeed, in its use of narrative as a means of either punishing or martyring its central character ('All I wanted to do was meet a nice girl, do I have to die for that?'), the film is closer to classical farce. Paul flirts with Marcy (Rosanna Arquette) in a café, and winds up invited to a SoHo loft flat for a night of conversation and, it is implied, unparalleled sex. From hints dropped by Arquette's flatmate (Linda Fiorentino), he deduces that the apparently flawless girl is covered with hideous burn scars, then she herself turns out to be prone to astonishingly unsettling mood shifts. Paul decides it's time he got the hell out, but his single $20 bill was whipped out of the taxi by a freak wind and the subway fare went up at midnight. He is forced to hustle from late-night bar to all-night diner and from crazy character to crazy character, at first in an attempt to get enough small change to go home but eventually to stay ahead of the impromptu lynch mob who have decided he's the thief terrorising the neighbourhood. Returning to apologise to Marcy, Paul finds the rejected girl has added to his load of miseries by committing suicide, and proceeds to fall into the clutches of a succession of dangerous women — beehived waitress Teri Garr, psychopathic ice-cream lady Catherine O'Hara, and burn-out Verna Bloom. Like all great nightmare movies, *After Hours* demonstrates the existence of a world of utter horror just a few short steps away from prosaic normality. Scorsese's all-night SoHo is a less blatant inferno than the country of the Living Dead, the Old Franklin Place, Dario Argento's witch-haunted cellars or Haddonfield on Hallowe'en night, but it's the true locale of the horror cinema in the late 1980s.

The descent into Hell, either of a personal or societal nature, is a dominant theme in current films, from comedy (*Adventures in Babysitting*, 1987) through musical (*Pink Floyd: The Wall*, 1982), gangster movie (*Mona Lisa*, 1986) and political consciousness-raising (*Salvador*, 1986) to action-adventure (*Indiana Jones and the Temple of Doom*, 1984). Meanwhile, the horror influence has permeated the entire spectrum of the cinema: Jerzy Skolimowski reworks in art cinema terms the basic structure of *Last House on the Left* — itself derived from Bergman — in *The Lightship* (1985), with Captain Klaus Maria Brandauer forced to take a stand when his vessel is invaded by epicene thug Robert Duvall and his degenerate henchmen; *After Hours* has paved the way for a cycle of so-called 'yuppie nightmare' films like Jonathan Demme's accomplished *Something Wild* (1986) and the banal *Fatal Attraction*, in which smug, secure, affluent and complacent men are dragged into a morass of violence and danger when they pursue casual affairs; Jean-Jacques Beneix, who made his début with the modish thriller *Diva* (1982) takes the romantic psycho-drama into surreal, perversely erotic areas in *La Lune dans le caniveau* (*The Moon in the Gutter*) (1983) and *Betty Blue* (1986), which suggest the sort of films Dario Argento might make if he didn't feel the need to stay within his self-created genre; the war film yields such visions of Hell on Earth as *Platoon* (1986), with its Herman Melville overtones, *Full Metal Jacket* (1987), in which basic training creates monsters, and *Empire of the Sun* (1987), with its occupation and apocalypse; and the cop thriller increasingly focuses on alienated policemen competing with psychotic creatures for the attention of elusive heroines — a formula followed in 1987 by movies as varied as the good-natured *Stake-Out*, the glossily superficial *Someone to Watch Over Me*, and the obsessive, twisted *Cop*.

In 1968, horror movies were changing. There were areas that could only be dealt with comfortably in a film like *Night of the Living Dead*. In 1988, horror films are static, even stagnant. Good work is being done, and will continue to be done, within the genre, but it has lost the edge it has had for most of the last twenty years. It is not alone: all genre cinema is mutating. While few films tackle as many different forms as *Apocalypse Now*, a majority seem to be hybrids as complex as *The Witches of Eastwick* (horror/comedy/romance/small town drama/fantasy), *Angel Heart* (horror/private eye/1950s nostalgia/Southern melodrama), *Off Limits* (Vietnam/cop/psycho/1960s nostalgia), *Wall Street* (exposé/thriller/soap opera/Faustian parable), *Fatal Attraction* (horror/thriller/romance/morality/lifestyle) or *Dudes* (comedy/punk/Western/road movie/action/ghost/fantasy). The dominant strain of horror just now is teen/horror/comedy, as represented by the *Nightmare on Elm Street* movies, *Fright Night*, the *Friday the 13th* series, the *Evil Dead* films and *The Lost Boys*. One of the most symptomatic horror films of recent years is *Michael Jackson's Thriller* (1984), an 11-minute rock video directed by John Landis that consists solely of special effects and posing, in support of an incredibly popular but particularly duff pop song. *Thriller*, like all music promos, is essentially a combination of TV commercial and showing off — by definition, it has no content whatsoever. Sadly, it is not only typical, but actually superior: at least it has good special effects and posing. At the other end of the spectrum is something as disposable, crass and pointless as *Halloween Party* (1987), which stretches lesser-quality variants of the same ingredients out for ninety-five minutes. The teen/horror/comedy configuration has been around long enough to solidify and become predictable. Nobody needs another camp kids-vs-creepies film, but that's what we're likely to get for the foreseeable future. Yet, withal, horror remains a vital, potentially and actually exciting facet of the cinema. If generic horror is dying or dead, it is at least as active as its zombies and vampires. And, the horror film — like many of its characters — has a habit of returning from the dead.

bibliography

Books
(important texts or reference works are marked with an asterisk)

NIGEL ANDREWS: *Horror Films* (1985)

CHAS BALUN: *Horror Holocaust* (1986), *The Gore Score* (1987)

MARTIN BARKER (ed.): *The Video Nasties: Freedom and Censorship in the Media** (1984)

JOHN BAXTER: *Science Fiction in the Cinema* (1970)

CALVIN THOMAS BECK: *Scream Queens: Heroines of the Horrors* (1978)

PETER BISKIND: *Seeing is Believing: How Hollywood Taught Us to Stop Worrying and Love the Fifties** (1983)

JOHN BLOOM: *Joe Bob Goes to the Movies* (1987)

JOHN BROSNAN: *The Horror People* (1976), *Future Tense: The Cinema of Science Fiction* (1978)

IVAN BUTLER: *Horror in the Cinema* (1970), *The Cinema of Roman Polanski* (1970)

MICHEL CIMENT: *Kubrick* (1980)

CARLOS CLARENS: *An Illustrated History of the Horror Film** (1967)

JEAN-PIERRE COURSODON: *American Directors* (2 vols, 1983)

TONY CRAWLEY: *The Steven Spielberg Story* (1983)

CHARLES DERRY: *Dark Dreams: A Psychological History of the Modern Horror Film** (1977)

PHILIP DiFRANCO (ed.): *The Movie World of Roger Corman* (1979)

R.H.W. DILLARD: *Horror Films* (1976)

WAYNE DREW (ed.): *BFI Dossier 21: David Cronenberg* (1984)

PHIL EDWARDS: *Shocking Cinema* (1987)

WILLIAM K. EVERSON: *Classics of the Horror Film* (1974), *More Classics of the Horror Film* (1986)

ALLEN EYLES, ROBERT ADKINSON and NICHOLAS FRY (eds.): *The House of Horror* (1973)

ALAN FRANK: *The Horror Film Handbook* (1982)

CHRISTOPHER FRAYLING: *Spaghetti Westerns: Cowboys and Europeans From Karl May to Sergio Leone** (1981)

PAUL R. GAGNE: *The Zombies That Ate Pittsburgh: The Films of George A. Romero** (1987)

NEIL GAIMAN and KIM NEWMAN (eds.): *Ghastly Beyond Belief: The Science Fiction and Fantasy Book of Quotations* (1985)

BILL GEORGE: *Eroticism in the Fantasy Cinema* (1984)

DENIS GIFFORD: *A Pictorial History of Horror Films* (1973)

PIERS HANDLING (ed.): *The Shape of Rage: The Films of David Cronenberg* (1983)

PHIL HARDY (ed.): *The Aurum Film Encyclopedia: Science Fiction** (1984), *The Aurum Film Encyclopedia: Horror Films** (1986)

JIM HILLIER and AARON LIPSTADT (eds.): *BFI Dossier Number 7: Roger Corman's New World* (1981)

J. HOBERMAN and JONATHAN ROSENBAUM: *Midnight Movies** (1983)

DAVID J. HOGAN: *Who's Who of the Horrors and Other Fantasy Films* (1980), *Dark Romance: Sexuality in the Horror Film* (1986)

JESSIE HORSTING: *Stephen King at the Movies* (1986)

ROY HUSS and T.J. ROSS (eds.): *Focus on the Horror Film* (1972)

TOM HUTCHINSON: *Horror and Fantasy in the Cinema* (1974), *Horrors: A History of Horror Movies* (with ROY PICKARD, 1983)

STEPHEN JONES and KIM NEWMAN (eds.): *Horror: 100 Best Books* (1988)

EPHRAIM KATZ: *International Film Encyclopedia** (1979)

STEPHEN KING: *Danse Macabre** (1981)

DANIEL KROGH with JOHN McCARTY: *The Amazing Herschell Gordon Lewis and His World of Exploitation Films* (1983)

WALT LEE: *Reference Guide to Fantastic Films** (3 vols, 1972–74)

GERARD LENNE: *Le Cinéma 'Fantastique' et ses Mythologies** (1970)

HARRIS M. LENTZ: *Science Fiction, Horror & Fantasy Film and Television Credits** (2 vols, 1983)

LEONARD MALTIN: *TV Movies** (annual)

PASCAL MARTINET: *Mario Bava** (1984)

TODD MCCARTY and CHARLES FLYNN: *Kings of the Bs** (1975)

JOHN MCCARTY: *Splatter Movies** (1981), *Psychos* (1986)

HARRY and MICHAEL MEDVED: *The Fifty Worst Films of All Time* (1978, with RANDY DREYFUSS), *The Golden Turkey Awards* (1980), *Son of Golden Turkey Awards* (1986)

RICHARD MEYERS: *For One Week Only: The World of Exploitation Films* (1983)

RICHARD MEYERS, AMY HARLIB, BILL and KAREN PALMER: *Martial Arts Movies: From Bruce Lee to the Ninjas** (1985)

JAMES MONACO: *How to Read a Film** (1977)

DARRELL MOORE: *The Best, Worst and Most Unusual Horror Films* (1983)

JIM MORTON (ed.): *ReSearch # 10: Incredibly Strange Films** (1986)

ED NAHA: *Horrors From Screen to Scream* (1975), *The Films of Roger Corman: Brilliance on a Budget* (1982)

PETER NICHOLLS: *The Encyclopedia of Science Fiction* (ed., 1979), *Fantastic Cinema: An Illustrated Survey** (1984)

BARRIE PATTISON: *The Seal of Dracula* (1975)

DANNY PEARY: *Cult Movies** (1981), *Cult Movies 2** (1983), *Omni's Screen Flights/Screen Fantasies* (ed., 1984), *Guide for the Film Fanatic* (1986)

BAXTER PHILLIPS: *Cut: The Unseen Cinema* (1975)

DAVID PIRIE: *A Heritage of Horror: The English Gothic Cinema, 1946–1972** (1973), *The Vampire Cinema* (1977)

S.S. PRAWER: *Caligari's Children: The Film as Tale of Terror* (1980)

JOHN RUSSO: *The Complete Night of the Living Dead Filmbook* (1985)

STUART SAMUELS: *Midnight Movies* (1983)

ANDREW SARRIS: *The American Cinema* (1967)

WILLIAM SCHOELL: *Stay Out of the Shower: 25 Years of Shocker Films Beginning with 'Psycho'* (1985)

DAVID J. SCHOW and JEFFREY FRENTZEN: *The Outer Limits: The Official Companion* (1986)

JACK G. SHAHEEN (ed.): *Nuclear War Films* (1978)

ALAIN SILVER and ELIZABETH WARD (eds.): *Film Noir* (1979)

JULIAN SMITH: *Looking Away: Hollywood and Vietnam** (1975)

DAVID SOREN: *The Rise and Fall of the Horror Film: An Art Historical Approach to Fantasy Cinema* (1977)

JOHN STANLEY: *Creature Feature Movie Guide* (1981, 1984)

PHILIP STRICK: *Science Fiction Movies** (1976)

JACK SULLIVAN (ed.): *The Penguin Encyclopedia of Horror and the Supernatural* (1986)

DAVID THOMSON: *A Biographical Dictionary of the Cinema** (1975, 1980), *Overexposures: The Crisis in American Filmmaking** (1981)

JAMES B. TWITCHELL: *Dreadful Pleasures: An Anatomy of Modern Horror* (1985)

PARKER TYLER: *Magic and Myth of the Movies* (1947)

JAMES URSINI and ALAIN SILVER: *The Vampire Film* (1975)

JAN VAN GENECHTEN (ed.): *Fandom's Film Gallery 2: Night of the Living Dead** (1976)

GREGORY A. WALLER: *The Living and the Undead: From Stoker's Dracula to Romero's Dawn of the Dead* (1985)

BILL WARREN: *Keep Watching the Skies: American Science Fiction Movies of the Fifties, Volume One: 1950–1957** (1982), *Volume Two: 1958–1962** (1986)

JOHN WATERS: *Shock Value: A Tasteful Book About Bad Taste* (1981), *Crackpot: The Obsessions of John Waters* (1987)

MICHAEL WELDON: *The Psychotronic Encyclopedia of Film** (1983)

RICK TRADER WHITCOMBE: *Savage Cinema* (1975)

CHRIS WICKING and TISE VAHIMAGI: *The American Vein* (1979)

DAVID WILL and PAUL WILLEMEN (eds.): *Roger Corman: the Millenic Vision* (1970)

DON WILLIS: *Horror and Science Fiction Films I* (1972), *II** (1982), *III** (1983), *Variety's Complete Science Fiction Reviews* (ed., 1985)

DOUGLAS E. WINTER: *Faces of Fear: Encounters with the Creators of Modern Horror** (1985)

ROBIN WOOD and RICHARD LIPPE (eds.): *American Nightmare: Essays on the Horror Film** (1979)

GENE WRIGHT: *Horrorshows: The A to Z of Horror in Film, TV, Radio and Theatre* (1986)

MARC SCOTT ZICREE: *The Twilight Zone Companion* (1982)

Periodicals

CineFan (US)

Cinefantastique (US)

CinéShock (France)

City Limits (UK)

Crimson Celluloid (Australia)

Deep Red (US)

L'Ecran fantastique (France)

Fangoria (US)

Fear (UK)

Gore Gazette (US)

Grandelinquence (UK)

Halls of Horror (formerly House of Hammer) (UK)

Mad Movies (France)

Midnight Marquee (formerly Gore Creatures) (US)

The Monthly Film Bulletin (UK)

Nostalgia (formerly Heretic) (France)

Photon (US)

Pretty Poison (UK)

Samhain (UK)

Shock Xpress (UK)

Sleazoid Express (US)

Slime Time (US)

Splatter Times (US)

Starburst (UK)

Star Ciné Video (France)

Variety (US)

World of Horror (UK)

acknowledgements

Authors are like the Mercury astronauts in *The Right Stuff* (1983). They may get all the credit, but in fact they are perched atop a vast engine that has been constructed through the efforts of a dedicated team of coffee-makers, editors, typesetters, researchers and friends. I not only wrote this book, but typed it as well and, for the most part, made my own coffee. However, I still owe a lot to the men and women at Mission Control.

I've drawn freely on my own scattered writings. Chapter Ten first appeared, in a shorter form, in David Tiffen's magazine, *Certain Gestures*; Chapter Thirteen can be found, in a different (longer) form in the January through to March 1986 issues of the *Monthly Film Bulletin*; and much other material comes from reviews and essays published in various magazines. Thanks for help with these are due to the glamorous editors of the *City Limits* cinema section — Fiona Ferguson, Saskia Baron, Amanda Lipman — under whom I have worked, and to Richard Combs of the *Monthly Film Bulletin*, Stefan Jaworzyn of *Shock Xpress*, Eugene Byrne of *Venue* and Brian Smedley of *Sheep Worrying*.

Invaluable assistance in the form of letters, videos, advice, complaints, books, magazines, general support and just plain decency came from Lucas Balbo, Clive Barker, Ruth Baumgarten, Clive Bennett, Lynda Bennett, Angela Berthiaume, Anne ('put the baby in the blender') Billson, Scott Bradfield, Faith Brooker, the staff of the BFI Library ('... Miss Newman? Oh, I'm sorry ...'), John Brosnan, Ramsey Campbell, Dave Carson, Pam Cook, David Cross, Colin Davis, Meg (sigh) Davis, Phil Day, Alex Dunn, Barry Edson, Terry Ellacott, Angie Errigo, Dennis Etchison, Mark Finch, Jo Fletcher, Nigel Floyd, the staff at Forbidden Planet 2, Barry Forshaw, Neil Gaiman, Kathy Gale, the Gothique Film Society, Colin Greenland, Tim (Master of Martial Arts) Greenwood, Rob Hackwill, Mick Hamer, my agent Antony Harwood, Janet Hawken, Susannah Hickling, Kate Hughes, Sheila Johnston, Steve Jones, Roz Kidd, Stephen Laws, Kate Leys, John McCarty, Norman MacKenzie, Tim Mander, Nigel Matheson, Barry Maurice, Tony Michele, Tom Milne, Geoff (the King of Comedy) Myers, Sasha Newman, Peter Nicholls, Phil Nutman, Catriona O'Gallaghan, the Peace and Love Corporation, Julian Petley, David Pirie, Matt (Barry Backhander) Preston, Mike Prickett, David Pringle, Dave Reeder, Steve Roe, Geoff Ryman, JoAnne (Ms .45) Sellar, Dean and Patty Skilton, Dave Simpson, Alex Stewart, Jack Sullivan, Dave Taylor, Tom ('help me get his boots T.C.!') Tunney, Lisa Tuttle, the University of Sussex Crypt patrons, Tise Vahimagi, Mark Valen, Mike and Di Wathen, Susan Webster, Club Whoopee and Robin Wood. Above all, absolutely the most help this book has had as far back as the first edition we don't want to talk about has come and continues to come from the invaluable Alan Jones.

index of alternative titles

The biggest headache in writing *Nightmare Movies* has been titles. I hold that a film is really called by whatever appears on screen in its country of origin. I have made an effort to get titles right, which is not as easy as it sounds — this will be the first book to list *Matthew Hopkins — Witchfinder General* as a title for the film widely known as (but not actually called) *Witchfinder General* and to make a distinction between *Friday the 13th, Part VI: Jason Lives* (American title) and *Jason Lives — Friday the 13th, Part VI* (British title). Various ethnocentric types have carped about my use of foreign language titles, and so I have yielded my snobbish earlier position and put English language titles in the text. If two or more English alternates exist I've used the British release title and shunted the American one into this appendix, because I get fed up with American (or even British) books that smugly refer to *Horror of Dracula* and *Die, Die, My Darling* when they're really British films called *Dracula* and *Fanatic*. To be fair, I've reciprocated by using *Dawn of the Dead* and *Sisters* rather than

Zombies and *Blood Sisters* whenever the retitling has been done for Britain. Given the choice between two alternates in country of origin — *God Told Me To* or *Demon, Shivers* or *The Parasite Murders* — I've unashamedly picked the title I like best. I've tried to make this listing reasonably comprehensive, but it would be a full-time job to keep track of all retitling (I've only sampled the retitlings done by fly-by-night video distributors and for Australian release, for example, and God only knows what's going on down in those Southern drive-ins). I've been fairly selective when dealing with such phantoms as pre-release titles or advertising titles: *The Ultimate Warrior* was made as *The Barony*, for instance, and the video packaging of *Butcher, Baker, Nightmare Maker* calls it *Nightmare Maker*, but neither title has ever — so far as I can ascertain — seen the light of a projector lamp. I've also not bothered to list the Portuguese, Lichtensteinean or Andorran titles if a film is a Portugal/Lichtenstein/Andorra/Italy co-production.

nightmare movies

A

The Abduction of Saint Anne: alt: *They've Kidnapped Anne Benedict*
Adventures in Babysitting: Br: *A Night on the Town*
The Affair: see: *There's Always Vanilla*
Alice, Sweet Alice: alt: *Communion*
Alien Contamination: see: *Contamination — alien arriva sulla terra*
The Alien Dead: pre-r: *It Fell from the Sky*
Alien Predator: see: *The Falling*
Alien Warning: alt: *Without Warning*
Almost Human: see: *Shock Waves*
Il Altro inferno: vid: *The Presence;* US: *Guardian of Hell*
Amityville 3: The Demon: see: *Amityville 3-D*
Amityville 3-D: TV: *Amityville 3: The Demon*
Amuck: see: *Schizo*
Anatomy of a Horror: see: *Deadline*
Andy Warhol's Dracula: see: *Blood for Dracula*
Andy Warhol's Frankenstein: see: *Flesh for Frankenstein*
Angel of Vengeance: see: *Ms .45*
Antechristo: US: *The Tempter*
Antefatto: alt: *Ecologia del Delitto;* US: *Last House on the Left 2;* US: *Twitch of the Death Nerve;* alt: *Bay of Blood*
Anthropophagous: see: *Antropophagus*
Antropophagus: Eng: *Anthropophagus;* US: *The Grim Reaper*
Antropophagus 2: see: *Rosso Sangue*
Ants: see: *Panic at Lakewood Manor*
Apocalisse domani: US: *The Cannibals are in the Streets;* alt: *Savage Apocalypse;* alt: *The Slaughterers;* vid: *Invasion of the Flesh Hunters*
April Fools' Day: alt: *Slaughter High*
The Arizona Ripper : see: *Bridge Across Time*
The Arousers: see: *Sweet Kill*
Asylum: alt: *House of Crazies*
At Play With the Angels: see: *There's Always Vanilla*
Autostop rosso sangue: alt: *Hitch Hike*
Axe!: Br: *The California Axe Massacre*

B

The Ballad of Hillbilly John: see: *Legend of Hillbilly John*
The Banana Monster: see: *Schlock*
The Barbaric Beast of Boggy Creek, Part II: alt: *Boggy Creek II*
Barn of the Naked Dead: see: *Terror Circus*
Battletruck: US: *Warlords of the 21st Century*
Bay of Blood: see: *Antefatto*
Beiss Mich, Liebling: alt: *Love — Vampire Style*
Beverly Hills Housewife: see: *Dial Rat for Terror*
Beverly Hills Nightmare: see: *Dial Rat for Terror*
Beware My Brethren: see: *The Fiend*
Beware! The Blob: alt: *Son of Blob*

Beyond the Bridge: see: *Olivia*
Beyond the Door: see: *Chi sei?*
Beyond the Door II: see: *Shock transfert — suspence — hypnos*
Beyond the Darkness: see: *Buio omega*
Beyond the Fog: see: *Tower of Evil*
Beyond the Gate: see: *Human Experiments*
Beyond the Living: see: *Nurse Sherri*
Beyond the Living Dead: see: *La Orgia de los Muertos*
The Big Boss: see: *Fist of Fury*
Bigfoot and the Hendersons: see: *Harry and the Hendersons*
Bigfoot — The Mysterious Monster: see: *The Mysterious Monsters*
Black Caesar: Br: *The Godfather of Harlem*
Black Christmas: alt: *A Stranger in the House;* alt: *Silent Night, Evil Night*
Blacksnake!: see: *Slaves*
Blind Alley: see: *Perfect Strangers*
Bloodbath of Dr Jekyll: see: *Dr Jekyll et les femmes*
The Blood Beast Terror: US: *The Vampire Beast Craves Blood*
Blood Brides: see: *Il Rosso segno della follia*
Blood Butchers: see: *Bloodeaters*
Blood Couple: see: *Ganja and Hess*
Bloodeaters: Br: *Forest of Fear;* alt: *Blood Butchers;* alt: *Toxic Zombies*
Blood for Dracula: alt: *Andy Warhol's Dracula;* Italian title: *Dracula cerca sangue di vergine e... mori di sete*
Blood of Dr Jekyll: see: *Dr Jekyll et les femmes*
Blood of Frankenstein: see: *Dracula Vs. Frankenstein*
Blood of Ghastly Horror: alt: *The Man With the Synthetic Brain;* pre-r: *Psycho a-Go-Go*
Blood of the Iron Maiden: see: *Is This Trip Really Necessary?*
Blood of the Undead: see: *Schizo*
Blood on Satan's Claw: alt: *Satan's Skin*
Blood on the Moon: see: *Cop*
Blood Sisters: see: *Sisters*
Blood Suckers: see: *Dr Terror's Gallery of Horrors*
Bloodsuckers: see: *Incense for the Damned*
Bloodsucking Freaks: see: *The Incredible Torture Show*
The Blood Virgin: see: *Symptoms*
Bloody Bird: see: *Deliria*
The Bloody Judge: see: *El Proceso de las Brujas*
Bloody New Year: pre-r: *Time Warp Terror*
Bloody Spa: see: *Warlock Moon*
Blue Monkey: alt: *Insect*
The Body Stealers: alt: *Thin Air*
The Bogey Man: see: *The Boogeyman*
Boggy Creek II: see: *The Barbaric Beast of Boggy Creek, Part II*
Bone: see: *Dial Rat for Terror*
Booby Trap: alt: *Wired to Kill*
The Boogeyman: Br: *The Bogey Man*
Boogeyman 2: Br: *Revenge of the Boogeyman*
Brain of Blood: alt: *The Creature's Revenge*
Bridge Across Time: alt: *Terror at London Bridge;* alt: *The Arizona Ripper*
Broken Hearts and Noses: see: *Crimewave*
The Brute and the Beast: see: *Tempo di massacro*
Buio omega: Br: *Beyond the Darkness;* US: *Buried Alive*
Burial Ground: see: *Le Notti del terrore*
Buried Alive: see: *Buio omega*
The Butcher: see: *Psycho From Texas*
Butcher, Baker, Nightmare Maker: alt: *Night Warning;* alt: *Thrilled to Death*

C

The Cabinet of Dr Caligari: see: *Das Kabinett des Dr Caligari*
Caged Virgins: see: *Vierges et Vampires*
The California Axe Massacre: see: *Axe!*
The Campsite Massacre: pre-r: *The Forest Primevil*; alt: *The Final Terror*
Cannibal: see: *L'Ultimo mondo cannibale*
Cannibal ferox: US: *Make Them Die Slowly*; alt: *Woman From Deep River*
Cannibal Orgy: see: *Spider Baby; or: The Maddest Story Ever Told*
Cannibals: see: *Mondo cannibale*
The Cannibals are in the Streets: see: *Apocalisse domani*
Cannonball: Br: *Carquake*
Carnivorous: see: *L'Ultimo mondo cannibale*
Carquake: see: *Cannonball*
The Cars That Ate Paris: US: *The Cars That Eat People*
The Cars That Eat People: see: *The Cars That Ate Paris*
The Case of the Full Moon Murders: Br: *The Case of the Smiling Stiffs*; alt: *Sex on the Groove Tube*
The Case of the Smiling Stiffs: see: *The Case of the Full Moon Murders*
Castle of Blood: see: *La Danza macabra*
Castle of Terror: see: *La Danza macabra*
Cataclysm: alt: *Nightmare Never Ends*
Cemetery Girls: see: *El Gran Amor del Conde Dracula*
The Child: Br: *Zombie Child*; alt: *Kill and Go Hide*
The Children: alt: *The Children of Ravensback*
The Children of Ravensback: see: *The Children*
The Chilling: see: *Dead of Night*
Chi sei?: US: *Beyond the Door*
Chopping Mall: pre-r: *Killbots*
The Chosen: see: *Holocaust 2000*
Christmas Evil: see: *You Better Watch Out*
City of the Walking Dead: see: *Incubo Sulla Citta*
Code Name: Trixie: see: *The Crazies*
Colt Concert: see: *Tempo di massacro*
The Coming of Dracula's Bride: see: *Dracula Sucks*
Communion: alt: *Alice, Sweet Alice*; alt: *The Holy Terror*
The Computer Killers: see: *Horror Hospital*
La Comtesse aux seins nus: alt: *Sicarius — The Midnight Party*; alt: *The Naked Thrill*
Confessional: see: *House of Mortal Sin*
Contamination — alien arriva sulla terra: US: *Alien Contamination*
Cop: pre: *Blood on the Moon*
Cop Killer: see: *Order of Death*
The Corpse: pre-r: *Crucible of Horror*; US: *The Velvet House*
Corrupt: see: *Order of Death*
Count Dracula and His Vampire Brides: see: *The Satanic Rites of Dracula*
Crash!: alt: *Death Ride*
Crazed Vampire: see: *Vierges et Vampires*
The Crazies: alt: *Code Name: Trixie*
Crazy House: see: *House in Nightmare Park*
Creature: see: *The Titan Find*
Creatures of the Prehistoric Planet: see: *Horror of the Blood Monsters*
The Creature's Revenge: see: *Brain of Blood*
The Creature Wasn't Nice: Br: *Spaceship*
The Creeper: see: *Rituals*
Creepers: see: *Phenomena*
The Creeping Unknown: see: *The Quatermass Experiment*

Crimewave: alt: *Broken Hearts and Noses*; pre-r: *The XYZ Murders*
The Crimson Cult: see: *Curse of the Crimson Altar*
Critical List: see: *Terminal Choice*
Crucible of Horror: see: *The Corpse*
The Cursed Medallion: see: *Il Medaglione insanguinato*
Curse of the Crimson Altar: US: *The Crimson Cult*
Curse of the Dead: see: *Operazione paura*
Curse of the Demon: see: *Night of the Demon* (1958)
Curse of the Vampires: see: *Dugong Vampira*

D

Daddy's Deadly Darling: see: *Pigs*
Damnation Alley: pre-r: *Survival Run*
Dance of the Vampires: US: *The Fearless Vampire Killers*
Danse Macabre: see: *La Danza macabra*
La Danza macabra: Eng: *Castle of Blood*; alt: *Danse Macabre*; TV: *Castle of Terror*
Dark Shadows: see: *Mutant*
The Dark Side: see: *The Reincarnate*
Dawn of the Dead: Br: *Zombies*
The Day Before Halloween: see: *Snapshot*
Day of the Woman: see: *I Spit On Your Grave*
Dead Kids: see: *Strange Behavior*
Deadly Eyes: alt: *The Rats*
The Deadly Spawn: alt: *Return of the Aliens*
Dead of Night (1974): alt: *Deathdream*; pre-r: *The Veteran*; pre-r: *The Night Andy Came Home*; vid: *The Chilling*
Dead People: see: *Messiah of Evil*
Dead Time Stories: see: *Freaky Fairy Tales*
Death Bed: see: *Terminal Choice*
Death Bite: see: *Spasms*
Death Corps: see: *Shock Waves*
Deathdream: see: *Dead of Night* (1974)
Death Drive: see: *Autostop rosso sangue*
Death is Child's Play: see: *Quien puede matar un niño?*
Death Line: US: *Raw Meat*
Death List: see: *Terminal Choice*
Death Trap: alt: *Starlight Slaughter*; alt: *Eaten Alive*; alt: *Legend of the Bayou*; alt: *Horror Hotel*
Death Weekend: US: *The House By the Lake*
Deep in the Heart: see: *Handgun*
Deliria : alt: *StageFright*; alt: *Bloody Bird*
Demon: see: *God Told Me To*
Os Demonios: alt: *The Sex Demons*
Deranged: see: *Idaho Transfer*
The Devil's Commandment: see: *I Vampiri*
The Devil's Men: alt: *Land of the Minotaur*
The Devil's Obsession: see: *L'Ossessa*
Devil Within Her: see: *I Don't Want to Be Born*
Diabolique: see: *Les Diaboliques*
Les Diaboliques: Br: *Diabolique*: US: *The Fiends*
Dial Rat for Terror: alt: *Bone*; alt: *Beverly Hills Nightmare*; alt: *Beverly Hills Housewife*
Die, Monster, Die!: see: *Monster of Terror*
Digital Dreams: see: *RageWar*
Doctors Wear Scarlet: see: *Incense for the Damned*
Dogs of Hell: see: *Rottweiler*
Don't Answer the Phone: alt: *The Hollywood Strangler*
Doomed to Die: see: *Mangiati vivi dai cannibali*
Double Jeopardy: see: *Olivia*

Double Possession: see: Ganja and Hess

Dracula (1958): US: Horror of Dracula

Dracula cerca sangue di vergine e... mori di sete: see: Blood for Dracula

Dracula Exotica: Br: Love at First Gulp

Dracula's Bride: see: Dracula Sucks

Dracula's Dog: Br: Zoltan — Hound of Dracula

Dracula's Great Love: see: El Gran Amor del Conde Dracula

Dracula Sucks: alt: Dracula's Bride; alt: The Coming of Dracula's Bride; alt: Lust at First Bite

Dracula's Virgin Lovers: see: El Gran Amor del Conde Dracula

Dracula Vs. Frankenstein: alt: Blood of Frankenstein

Dr Black and Mr Hyde: alt: The Watts Monster: vid: Serum

Dr Breedlove: see: Kiss Me Quick

Dr Butcher, MD: see: Zombi holocaust

Dr Frankenstein on Campus: Br: Frankenstein on Campus: pre-r: Flick

Dr Jekyll et les femmes: Eng: Blood of Dr Jekyll; vid: Bloodbath of Dr Jekyll

Dr Terror's Gallery of Horrors: alt: Blood Suckers; alt: Return From the Past

Dripping Deep Red: see: Profondo rosso

2019, dopo la caduta di New York: Eng: 2019: After the Fall of New York

The Dungeonmaster: see: RageWar

Dynamite Women: see: The Great Texas Dynamite Chase

E

Eaten Alive: see: Death Trap

Ecologia del Delitto: see: Antefatto

The Eerie Midnight Horror Show: see: L'Ossessa

Emanuelle e gli ultimi cannibali: US: Trap Them and Kill Them

Enemy From Space: see: Quatermass 2

Entity Force: see: One Dark Night

Ercole al centro della terra: Br: Hercules in the Haunted World

Escape 2000: see: Turkey Shoot

L'Esorcista n.2: see: Un Urlo dalle tenebre

E tu vivrai nel terrore... L'Aldila: US: Seven Doors of Death

The Evil: vid: House of Evil

Evil + Hate = Killer: see: Psycho From Texas

Exorcist III: see: Un Urlo dalle tenebre

Exposé: pre-r: The House on Straw Mountain

Eye of the Evil Dead: see: Manhattan Baby

F

Faces of Fear: see: Olivia

Fall Break: alt: The Mutilator

The Falling: Br: Mutant 2; alt: Alien Predator

The Fall of the House of Usher: see: The House of Usher

Fantasies: Br: The Studio Murders

The Farm: alt: The Curse

Fatal Games: alt: The Killing Touch

The Fearless Vampire Killers: see: Dance of the Vampires

Fear No Evil: pre-r: Mark of the Beast

The Fiend: pre-r/US: Beware My Brethren

The Fiends: see: Les Diaboliques

Fight for Your Life: alt: Held Hostage

The Final Program: US: The Last Days of Man on Earth

The Final Terror: see: The Campsite Massacre

A Fistful of Dollars: see: Per un pugno di dollari

Fist of Fury: US: The Big Boss; Br: Fists of Fury

Fists of Fury: see: Fist of Fury

Il Fiume del grande caimano: alt: Alligators

Five Million Years to Earth: see: Quatermass and the Pit

Flesh for Frankenstein: alt: Andy Warhol's Frankenstein; Italian title: Il Mostro e in tavola... Baron Frankenstein

Flick: see: Dr Frankenstein on Campus

The Folks at Red Wolf Inn: alt: Terror at Red Wolf Inn; alt: Terror House; vid: Terror on the Menu

Forbidden World: alt: Mutant

The Forbin Project: alt: Colossus — The Forbin Project

Forest of Fear: see: Bloodeaters

The Forest Primevil: see: The Campsite Massacre

Frankenstein on Campus: see: Dr Frankenstein on Campus

Frankenstein's Bloody Terror: see: La Marca del Hombre Lobo

Freakmaker: see: The Mutations

Freaky Fairy Tales: see: Dead Time Stories

Friday the 13th, Part VI — Jason Lives!: Br: Jason Lives! — Friday the 13th, Part VI

Frightmare: see: The Horror Star

Frog Dreaming: US: The Quest

Frozen Terror: see: Macabro

La Frusta e il corpo: Eng: The Whip and the Flesh; US: What?

Full Circle: US: The Haunting of Julia

Full Moon: see: Moonchild

Future Cop: see: Trancers

Future Kill: pre-r: Splatter; Br: Night of the Alien

G

Galaxy of Terror: alt: Mindwarp; alt: An Infinity of Horrors; alt: Planet of Horrors

The Gallery Murders: see: L'uccello dalle piume di cristallo

Ganja and Hess: alt: Double Possession: alt: Blood Couple

Gates of Hell: see: La Paura nella citta dei morti viventi

Ghost Warrior: see: SwordKill

Girls' Night Out: see: The Scaremaker

Girls School Screamers: pre-r: The Portrait

The Godfather of Harlem: see: Black Caesar

God Told Me To: alt: Demon

The Golem: see: Der Golem: Wie in der Welt Kam

Der Golem: Wie in der Welt Kam: Eng: The Golem

El Gran Amor del Conde Dracula: Br: Dracula's Great Love; US: Dracula's Virgin Lovers; alt: Cemetery Girls

Great White: see: L'Ultimo squalo

The Grim Reaper: see: Antropophagus

Guardian of Hell: see: Il Altro inferno

Guyana — Cult of the Damned: see: Guyana — el Crimen del Siglo

Guyana — el Crimen del Siglo: US: Guyana — Cult of the Damned

H

Halloween Party: Br: Night of the Demons

Handgun: alt: Deep in the Heart

Hangar 18: alt: Invasion Force

The Hatchet Murders: see: Profondo rosso

The Haunted House of Horror: US: Horror House

The Haunting of Julia: see: Full Circle

Held Hostage: see: Fight for Your Life

Hercules at the Centre of the Earth: see: Ercole al centro della terra

Hidden Thoughts: see: Natural Enemies

High Rise: see: Someone is Watching Me

The Hollywood Meatcleaver Massacre: alt: Revenge of the Dead; alt: Meatcleaver Massacre

The Hollywood Strangler: see: Don't Answer the Phone

Holocaust 2000: US: The Chosen

The Holy Terror: see: Communion

Homecoming Night: see: Night of the Creeps

The Horrible Dr Hitchcock: see: L'Orrible segretto del Dr Hichcock

Horror Creatures of the Prehistoric Planet: see: Horror of the Blood Monsters

Horror Hospital: US: The Computer Killers

Horror Hotel: see: Death Trap

Horror House: see: The Haunted House of Horror

Horror of the Blood Monsters: alt: Creatures of the Prehistoric Planet: alt: Horror Creatures of the Prehistoric Planet ; alt: Vampire Men of the Lost Planet

Horror on Snape Island: see: Tower of Evil

Horror Planet: see: Inseminoid

The Horror Star: alt: Frightmare; vid: Body Snatchers

Hospital Massacre: see: X-Ray

The Hounds of Zaroff: see: The Most Dangerous Game

Hour of the Wolf: see: Vargtimmen

House in Nightmare Park: alt: Night of the Laughing Dead: alt: Crazy House

House of Crazies: see: Asylum

House of Doom: see: Los Ojos azules de la muneca rota

House of Evil: see: The Evil

House of Evil: see: The House on Sorority Row

House of Mortal Sin: pre-r/US: Confessional

House of Psychotic Women: see: Los Ojos azules de la muneca rota

The House of Usher: Br: The Fall of the House of Usher

The House on Sorority Row: Br: House of Evil

The House on Straw Mountain: see: Exposé

The House That Vanished: see: Scream . . . and Die!

Human Experiments: alt: Beyond the Gate

Humanoids From the Deep: Br: Monster

Hungry Wives: see: Jack's Wife

I

Idaho Transfer: vid: Deranged

I Dismember Mama: alt: Poor Albert and Little Annie

I Don't Want to Be Born: vid: It's Growing Inside Her; US: Devil Within Her; alt: The Monster

I Hate Your Guts: see: Fight for Your Life

The Imp: see: Sorority Babes in the Slime Ball Bowl-a-Rama

Im Zeichen des Kreuzes: Eng: Due to an Act of God

Incense for the Damned: US: Bloodsuckers: pre-r: Doctors Wear Scarlet

The Incredible Torture Show: alt: Bloodsucking Freaks

The Incredibly Strange Creatures Who Stopped Living and Became Mixed-Up Zombies!!?: alt: Teenage Psycho Meets Bloody Mary

Incubo sulla citta: US: City of the Walking Dead

Incubus: Br: The Incubus

The Incubus: see: Incubus

Inferno in diretta: Eng: Cut and Run

An Infinity of Horrors: see: Galaxy of Terror

Insect: see: Blue Monkey

Invasion Force: see: Hangar 18

Invasion of the Flesh Hunters: see: Apocalisse domani

Island of the Burning Damned: see: Night of the Big Heat

Island of the Burning Doomed: see: Night of the Big Heat

Island of the Damned: see: Quien puede matar un niño?

Island of the Fishmen: see: L'Isola. degli uomini pesce

Island of the Mutations: see: L'Isola degli uomini pesce

L'Isola degli uomini pesce: Br: Island of the Mutations: US: Screamers: alt: Island of the Fishmen

I Spit On Your Grave: pre-r: Day of the Woman

Is This Trip Really Necessary?: alt: Blood of the Iron Maiden

It Came . . . Without Warning: see: Without Warning

It Fell from the Sky: see: The Alien Dead

It Happened at Lakewood Manor: see: Panic at Lakewood Manor

It's Growing Inside Her: see: I Don't Want to Be Born

I Was a Teenage Frankenstein: Br: Teenage Frankenstein

J

Jack's Wife: alt: Hungry Wives; vid: Season of the Witch

Jason Lives! — Friday the 13th, Part VI: see: Friday the 13th, Part VI — Jason Lives!

Jungfrukallen: Eng: The Virgin Spring

Jungle Holocaust: see: L'Ultimo mondo cannibale

K

Das Kabinett des Dr Caligari: Eng: The Cabinet of Dr Caligari

Kill and Go Hide: see: The Child

Kill Baby, Kill: see: Operazione paura

Killbots: see: Chopping Mall

The Killer Behind the Mask: see: Savage Weekend

Killer's Curse: see: Nurse Sherri

The Killing Touch: see: Fatal Games

A Kiss From Eddie: see: Sweet Kill

Kiss of Evil: see: Kiss of the Vampire

Kiss of the Tarantula: alt: Shudder

Kiss of the Vampire: US: Kiss of Evil

Knuckle Men: see: Terminal Island

Krug and Company: see: Last House on the Left

L

Land of the Minotaur: see: The Devil's Men

The Last Days of Man on Earth: see: The Final Program

Last House on the Left: pre-r: Sex Crime of the Century; pre-r: Night of Vengeance; pre-r: Krug and Company

Last House on the Left 2: see: Antefatto

The Last Survivor: see: L'Ultimo mondo cannibale

The Legacy: TV: The Legacy of Maggie Walsh

The Legacy of Maggie Walsh: see: The Legacy

The Legendary Curse of Lemora: see: Lemora — A Child's Tale of the Supernatural

Legend of Doom House: see: Malpertuis

Legend of Hillbilly John: pre-r: Who Fears the Devil?; alt: The Ballad of Hillbilly John

Legend of Spider Forest: see: Venom

Legend of the Bayou: see: Death Trap

Legend of the Seven Golden Vampires: US: The Seven Brothers Meet Dracula

Lemora — A Child's Tale of the Supernatural: alt: The Legendary Curse of Lemora: alt: Lemora — The Lady Dracula

Lemora — The Lady Dracula: see: Lemora — A Child's Tale of the Supernatural

Lesbian Vampires: see: Vampyros Lesbos — Die Erbin des Dracula

Look What's Happened to Rosemary's Baby: alt: Rosemary's Baby II

Love at First Gulp: see: *Dracula Exotica*
Love — Vampire Style: see: *Beiss Mich, Liebling*
Una Lucertola con la pelle di donna: US: *Schizoid*
Lust at First Bite: see: *Dracula Sucks*

M
Macabro: US: *Frozen Terror*
Madhouse: pre-r: *The Revenge of Dr Death*
Mad Max 2: US: *The Road Warrior*
The Majorettes: alt: *One by One*
Make Them Die Slowly: see: *Cannibal ferox*
Malpertuis: Br: *Legend of Doom House*
Man From Deep River: see: *Il Paese del sesso selveggio*
Mangiati vivi dai cannibali: US: *Doomed to Die*
Manhattan Baby: alt: *L'Occhio del male;* Br: *Possessed;* US: *Eye of the Evil Dead*
The Manitou: Br: *Manitou — Spirit of Evil*
Manitou — Spirit of Evil: see: *The Manitou*
The Man With the Synthetic Brain: see: *Blood of Ghastly Horror*
La Marca del Hombre Lobo: US: *Frankenstein's Bloody Terror*
Mark of the Beast: see: *Fear No Evil*
La Maschera del demonio: Br: *Revenge of the Vampire;* US: *Black Sunday*
Massacre Time: see: *Tempo di massacro*
Matthew Hopkins — Witchfinder General: US: *The Conqueror Worm;* alt: *Witchfinder General*
Meatcleaver Massacre: see: *The Hollywood Meatcleaver Massacre*
Il Medaglione insanguinato: alt: *The Cursed Medallion*
Messiah of Evil: pre-r: *The Second Coming;* alt: *Revenge of the Screaming Dead;* alt: *Return of the Living Dead;* alt: *Dead People*
1990: I Guerrieri del Bronx: US: *1990: The Bronx Warrior*
Mindwarp: see: *Galaxy of Terror*
Mondo cannibale: Eng: *Cannibals*
Monster: see: *Humanoids From the Deep*
The Monster: see: *I Don't Want to Be Born*
Monster of Terror: US: *Die, Monster, Die!*
Monster Shark: see: *Shark — rosso nell' oceano*
La Montagna del dio cannibale: US: *Slave of the Cannibal God*
Moonchild: alt: *Full Moon*
The Most Dangerous Game: Br: *The Hounds of Zaroff*
Il Mostro e in tavola... Baron Frankenstein: see: *Flesh for Frankenstein*
Ms .45: alt: *Angel of Vengeance*
Murder By Telephone: see: *Schizoid*
Mutant: see: *Forbidden World*
Mutant: alt: *Dark Shadows:* alt: *Night Shadows*
Mutant 2: see: *The Falling*
The Mutations: vid: *The Freakmaker*
The Mutilator: see: *Fall Break*
The Mysterious Monsters: alt: *Bigfoot — The Mysterious Monster*

N
The Naked Thrill: see: *La Comtesse aux seins nus*
Natural Enemies: vid: *Hidden Thoughts*
Necromancy: alt: *The Witching*
The Nesting: pre-r: *Phobia*
The New Last House on the Left: see: *L'Ultimo Treno Della Notte*
The Night Andy Came Home: see: *Dead of Night*
The Night God Screamed: Br: *Scream*
Night is the Phantom: see: *La Frusta e il corpo*

Nightmare: Br: *Nightmares in a Damaged Brain*
Nightmare Never Ends: see: *Cataclysm*
Nightmares: US: *Stage Fright*
Nightmares in a Damaged Brain: see: *Nightmare*
Night of Anubis: see: *Night of the Living Dead*
Night of the Alien: see: *Future Kill*
Night of the Big Heat: alt: *Island of the Burning Doomed;* US: *Island of the Burning Damned*
Night of the Creeps: vid: *Homecoming Night*
Night of the Death Cult: see: *La Noche de las Gaviotas*
Night of the Demon (1958): US: *Curse of the Demon*
Night of the Demons: see: *Halloween Party*
Night of the Flesh Eaters: see: *Night of the Living Dead*
Night of the Laughing Dead: see: *House in Nightmare Park*
Night of the Living Dead: pre-r: *Night of Anubis;* pre-r: *Night of the Flesh Eaters*
Night of the Zombies: see: *Virus — inferno dei morti viventi*
Night of Vengeance: see: *Last House on the Left*
Night School: Br: *Terror Eyes*
Night Train Murders: see: *L'Ultimo Treno Della Notte*
Night Warning: see: *Butcher, Baker, Nightmare Maker*
1990: The Bronx Warrior: see: *1990: I Guerrieri del Bronx*
The Ninth Configuration: alt: *Twinkle, Twinkle, Killer Kane*
Nosferatu, A Symphony of Terror: see: *Nosferatu — eine Symphonie des Grauens*
Nosferatu — eine Symphonie des Grauens: Eng: *Nosferatu, A Symphony of Terror*
Nosferatu — Phantom der Nacht: Eng: *Nosferatu the Vampyre*
Nosferatu the Vampyre: see: *Nosferatu — Phantom der Nacht*
Le Notti del terrore: alt: *Zombi 3;* alt: *Zombie Horror;* US: *Burial Ground*

O
Obsessed: see: *L'Ossessa*
L'Occhio del male: see: *Manhattan Baby*
Off Limits: Br: *Saigon*
The Offspring: see: *From a Whisper to a Scream*
Los Ojos azules de la muneca rota: US: *House of Psychotic Women;* alt: *House of Doom*
Old Dracula: see: *Vampira*
Olivia: Br: *Double Jeopardy;* alt: *A Taste of Sin;* alt: *Beyond the Bridge;* pre-r: *Faces of Fear*
One by One: see: *The Majorettes*
One Dark Night: pre-r: *Rest in Peace;* vid: *Entity Force*
Operazione paura: US: *Kill Baby, Kill;* Br: *Curse of the Dead*
Order of Death: US: *Corrupt;* alt: *Cop Killer*
La Orgia de los Muertos: US: *Beyond the Living Dead*
Orgy of the Blood Parasites: see: *Shivers*
L'Orrible segretto del Dr Hichcock: US: *The Horrible Dr Hitchcock;* Br: *Terror of Dr Hitchcock;* alt: *Raptus*
L'Ossessa: alt: *Obsessed;* US: *The Eerie Midnight Horror Show;* alt: *The Devil's Obsession;* alt: *The Tormented*
L'Ossessione che uccide: Br: *Satan's Altar;* US: *Unconscious;* alt: *The Wailing*
El Otro Inferno: see: *Il Altro inferno*

P
Il Paese del sesso selvaggio: Br: *Deep River Savages;* US: *Sacrifice!;* alt: *Man From Deep River*
Pandemonium: pre-r: *Thursday the 12th*

Panic at Lakewood Manor: alt: It Happened at Lakewood Manor; pre-r: Ants

The Parasite Murders: see: Shivers

La Paura nella citta dei morti viventi: US: Gates of Hell; alt: Twilight of the Dead

Perfect Strangers: pre-r/Br: Blind Alley

Per un pugno di dollari: Eng: A Fistful of Dollars

Phantom of Terror: see: L'Uccello dalle piume di cristallo

Phenomena: Eng: Creepers

Phobia: see: The Nesting

Pigs: alt: The Strange Exorcism of Lynn Hart; alt: Love Exorcist; alt: Daddy's Deadly Darling

Piranha 2: The Spawning: see: Piranha II: Flying Killers

Piranha II: Flying Killers: US: Piranha 2: The Spawning

Plague: alt: Plague — M3: The Gemini Strain

Plague — M3: The Gemini Strain: see: Plague

Planet of Horrors: see: Galaxy of Terror

Poor Albert and Little Annie: see: I Dismember Mama

Possessed: see: Manhattan Baby

Premonition: Br: The Impure

The Presence: see: Il Altro inferno

El Proceso de las brujas: Br: The Bloody Judge

Profondo rosso: alt: Dripping Deep Red; alt: The Sabre Tooth Tiger; alt: The Hatchet Murders

The Prowler: Br: Rosemary's Killer; pre-r: The Graduation

Psycho a-Go-Go: see: Blood of Ghastly Horror

Psycho From Texas: vid: Evil + Hate = Killer; alt: The Butcher

Psycho Killer: see: The Psycho Lover

The Psycho Lover: Br: Psycho Killer

Q

Q: alt: The Winged Serpent

Quatermass and the Pit: US: Five Million Years to Earth

The Quatermass Experiment: US: The Creeping Unknown

Quatermass 2: US: Enemy From Space

R

RageWar: pre-r: Digital Dreams; alt: The Dungeonmaster

Raptus: see: L'Orrible segretto del Dr Hichcock

The Rats: see: Deadly Eyes

Raw Meat: see: Death Line

Redneck County: alt: Redneck County Rape

Redneck County Rape: see: Redneck County

La Regina dei Cannibale: see: Zombi holocaust

The Reincarnate: vid: The Dark Side

La Reine des Vampires: see: Le Viol du Vampire

Requiem pour un Vampire: see: Vierges et Vampires

Rest in Peace: see: One Dark Night

Return From the Past: see: Dr Terror's Gallery of Horrors

The Returning: Br: The Witch Doctor

Return of the Aliens: see: The Deadly Spawn

Return of the Exorcist: see: Un Urlo dalle tenebre

Return of the Living Dead: see: Messiah of Evil

The Revenge of Dr Death: see: Madhouse

Revenge of the Bogeyman: see: Boogeyman 2

Revenge of the Dead: see: The Hollywood Meatcleaver Massacre

Revenge of the Screaming Dead: see: Messiah of Evil

Revenge of the Vampire: see: La Maschera del demonio

Rituals: alt: The Creeper

The Road Warrior: see: Mad Max 2

Roma 2033: I Centurioni del futuro: Br: 2033: The Fighter Centurions; US: Rome 2072 AD: The New Gladiators

Rome 2072 AD: The New Gladiators: see: Roma 2033: I Centurioni del futuro

Rosemary's Baby II: see: Look What's Happened to Rosemary's Baby

Rosemary's Killer: see: The Prowler

Rosso Sangue: alt: Antropophagus 2

Il Rosso segno della follia: Br: Blood Brides

Rottweiler: vid: Dogs of Hell

S

The Sabre Tooth Tiger: see: Profondo rosso

Sacrifice!: see: Il Paese del sesso selvaggio

Saigon: see: Off Limits

The Satanic Rites of Dracula: US: Count Dracula and His Vampire Brides

Satan's Altar: see: L'Ossessione che uccide

Satan's Skin: see: Blood on Satan's Claw

Savage Apocalypse: see: Apocalisse domani

Savage Weekend: alt: The Killer Behind the Mask; pre-r: The Upstate Murders

The Scaremaker: alt: Girls' Night Out

Schizo: alt: Amuck!; alt: Blood of the Undead

Schizoid: see: Una Lucertola con la pelle di donna

Schizoid: alt: Murder By Telephone

Schlock: alt: The Banana Monster

Scream: see: The Night God Screamed

Screamers: see: L'Isola degli uomini pesce

Season of the Witch: see: Jack's Wife

The Second Coming: see: Messiah of Evil

The Second Coming of Suzanne: vid: Suzanne

Serum: see: Dr Black and Mr Hyde

The Seven Brothers Meet Dracula: see: Legend of the Seven Golden Vampires

Seven Doors of Death: see: E tu vivrai nel terrore . . . L'Aldila

Sex Crime of the Century: see: Last House on the Left

The Sex Demons: see: Os Demonios

Sex on the Groove Tube: see: The Case of the Full Moon Murders

Shadow of Chikara: alt: Wishbone Cutter

Shark: see: L'Ultimo squalo

Shark — rosso nell' oceano: Eng: Devouring Waves; alt: Monster Shark

Shivers: alt: The Parasite Murders; US: They Came From Within; pre-r: Orgy of the Blood Parasites

Shock transfert — suspence — hypnos: US: Beyond the Door II

Shock Waves: pre-r: Death Corps; Br: Almost Human

Shudder: see: Kiss of the Tarantula

Sicarius — The Midnight Party: see: La Comtesse aux seins nus

El Signo del Vampiro: see: Vampyros Lesbos — Die Erbin des Dracula

Silent Night, Evil Night: see: Black Christmas

Sisters: Br: Blood Sisters

Slaughter High: see: April Fools' Day

The Slaughterers: see: Apocalisse domani

Slave of the Cannibal God: see: La Montagna del dio cannibale

Slaves: alt: Sweet Suzy; alt: Blacksnake!

Sleepaway Camp: Br: Nightmare Vacation

Sleepless Nights: see: The Slumber Party Massacre

Slithis: see: Spawn of the Slithis

The Slumber Party Massacre: pre-r: Sleepless Nights; vid: The Slumber Party Murders

The Slumber Party Murders: see: The Slumber Party Massacre

Small Town Massacre: see: Strange Behavior

Snapshot: alt: *The Day Before Halloween*
Someone is Watching Me: pre-r: *High Rise*
Son of Blob: see: *Beware! The Blob*
Spaceship: see: *The Creature Wasn't Nice*
Spasms: pre-r: *Death Bite*
Spawn of the Slithis: alt: *Slithis*
Spider Baby; or, The Maddest Story Ever Told: alt: *The Liver Eaters*; pre-r: *Cannibal Orgy*
Splatter: see: *Future Kill*
Spookies: pre: *Twisted Souls*
Sssssssss: Br: *Sssnake*
Sssnake: see: *Sssssssss*
Stage Fright: see: *Nightmares*
StageFright: see: *Deliria*
Starlight Slaughter: see: *Death Trap*
Strange Behavior: alt: *Dead Kids*; vid: *Small Town Massacre*
The Strange Exorcism of Lynn Hart: see: *Pigs*
A Stranger in Our House: alt: *Summer of Fear*
A Stranger in the House: see: *Black Christmas*
The Studio Murders: see: *Fantasies*
Suburbia: alt: *The Wild Side*
Sugar Hill: Br: *Voodoo Girl*; TV: *The Zombies of Sugar Hill*
Summer of Fear: see: *A Stranger in Our House*
Superstition: Br: *The Witch*
Survival Run: see: *Damnation Alley*
Suzanne: see: *The Second Coming of Suzanne*
Sweet Suzy: see: *Slaves*
Sword of the Barbarians: see: *Sangraal, la spada di fuoco*
SwordKill: alt: *Ghost Warrior*
Symptoms: alt: *The Blood Virgin*

T

A Taste of Sin: see: *Olivia*
Teenage Frankenstein: see: *I Was a Teenage Frankenstein*
Teenage Psycho Meets Bloody Mary: see: *The Incredibly Strange Creatures Who Stopped Living and Became Mixed-Up Zombies!!?*
Tempo di massacro: US: *The Brute and the Beast*; alt: *Massacre Time*; vid: *Colt Concert*
The Tempter: see: *Antechristo*
Tender Flesh: see: *Welcome to Arrow Beach*
Tenebrae: US: *Unsane*
Terminal Choice: alt: *Death Bed*; alt: *Death List*; alt: *Critical List*; alt: *Trauma*
Terminal Island: Br: *Knuckle Men*
Terror at London Bridge: see: *Bridge Across Time*
Terror at Red Wolf Inn: see: *The Folks at Red Wolf Inn*
Terror Circus: alt: *Barn of the Naked Dead*
Terror Eyes: see: *Night School*
Terror House: see: *The Folks at Red Wolf Inn*
Terror of Dr Hitchcock: see: *L'Orrible segretto del Dr Hichcock*
Terror on the Menu: see: *The Folks at Red Wolf Inn*
There's Always Vanilla: alt: *The Affair*; alt: *At Play With the Angels*
They Came From Within: see: *Shivers*
Thin Air: see: *The Body Stealers*
Thursday the 12th: see: *Pandemonium*
Time Warp Terror: see: *Bloody New Year*
The Titan Find: alt: *Creature*
Tomb of the Undead: see: *Garden of the Dead*
The Tormented: see: *L'Ossessa*
Tower of Evil: US: *Horror on Snape Island*; vid: *Beyond the Fog*

Toxic Zombies: see: *Bloodeaters*
Trancers: alt: *Future Cop*
Transformations: see: *Underworld*
Trap Them and Kill Them: see: *Emanuelle e gli ultimi cannibali*
Trauma: see: *Terminal Choice*
Turkey Shoot: US: *Escape 2000*
2019: After the Fall of New York: see: *2019, dopo la caduta di New York*
2033: The Fighter Centurions: see: *Roma 2033: I Centurioni del futuro*
Twilight of the Dead: see: *La Paura nella citta dei morti viventi*
Twinkle, Twinkle, Killer Kane: see: *The Ninth Configuration*
Twisted Souls: see: *Spookies*
Twitch of the Death Nerve: see: *Antefatto*

U

L'Uccello dalle piume di cristallo: Br: *The Gallery Murders*; alt: *Phantom of Terror*
L'Ultimo mondo cannibale: US: *The Last Survivor*; alt: *Jungle Holocaust*; Br: *Cannibal*; alt: *Carnivorous*
L'Ultimo squalo: Br: *Great White*; US: *Shark*
Unconscious: see: *L'Ossessione che uccide*
Underworld: alt: *Transformations*
Unsane: see: *Tenebrae*
The Upstate Murders: see: *Savage Weekend*
Un Urlo dalle tenebre; Br: *Naked Exorcism*; vid: *Return of the Exorcist*: alt: *L'Esorcista n.2*; vid: *Exorcist III*

V

Vampira: US: *Old Dracula*
The Vampire Beast Craves Blood: see: *The Blood Beast Terror*
Vampire Men of the Lost Planet: see: *Horror of the Blood Monsters*
Vampire Women: see: *Le Viol du Vampire*
I Vampiri: Br: *Lust of the Vampire*; US: *The Devil's Commandment*
Vampyres: alt: *Vampyres — Daughters of Dracula*
Vampyres — Daughters of Dracula: see: *Vampyres*
Vampyros Lesbos — Die Erbin des Dracula: Eng: *Lesbian Vampires*; Spanish title: *El Signo del Vampiro*
Vargtimmen: Eng: *Hour of the Wolf*
The Velvet House: see: *The Corpse*
The Velvet Vampire: vid: *The Waking Hour*
Venom (1971): alt: *Legend of Spider Forest*
The Veteran: see: *Dead of Night (1974)*
Vierges et vampires: alt: *Requiem pour un vampire*; US: *Caged Virgins*; US: *Crazed Vampire*
Le Viol du vampire: alt: *La Reine des vampires*; alt: *Vampire Women*
The Virgin Spring: see: *Jungfrukallen*
Virus — inferno dei morti viventi: US: *Night of the Zombies*
Visions...: alt: *Visions of Death*
Visions of Death: see: *Visions...*
Voodoo Girl: see: *Sugar Hill*

W

The Wailing: see: *L'Ossessione che uccide*
The Waking Hour: see: *The Velvet Vampire*
Ward 13: see: *X-Ray*
Warlock Moon: vid: *Bloody Spa*
Warlords of the 21st Century: see: *Battletruck*
The Warning: see: *Without Warning*

The Watts Monster: see: Dr Black and Mr Hyde
Welcome to Arrow Beach: alt: Tender Flesh
What?: see: La Frusta e il corpo
The Whip and the Flesh: see: La Frusta e il corpo
Who Fears the Devil?: see: Legend of Hillbilly John
The Wild Side: see: Suburbia
The Winged Serpent: see: Q
Wired to Kill: see: Booby Trap
Wishbone Cutter: see: Shadow of Chikara
The Witch: see: Superstition
The Witch Doctor: see: The Returning
Witchfinder General: see: Matthew Hopkins — Witchfinder General
The Witching: see: Necromancy
Without Warning: alt: The Warning; alt: It Came ... Without Warning; alt: Alien Warning
Woman From Deep River: see: Cannibal ferox

X
X-Ray: alt: Hospital Massacre; alt: Ward 13

The XYZ Murders: see: Crimewave

Y
You Better Watch Out: alt: Christmas Evil
Young Sherlock Holmes: Br: Young Sherlock Holmes and the Pyramid of Fear
Young Sherlock Holmes and the Pyramid of Fear: see: Young Sherlock Holmes

Z
Zoltan — Hound of Dracula: see: Dracula's Dog
Zombie Child: see: The Child
Zombie Horror: see: Le Notti del terrore
Zombi holocaust: alt: La Regina dei Cannibale; US: Dr Butcher, MD
Zombies: see: Dawn of the Dead
The Zombies of Sugar Hill: see: Sugar Hill
Zombi 3: see: Le Notti del terrore

index

Bold type refers to illustrations.

index

index

index

index

index

index

index

index

index

index

index

index